Celtic Fairy Tales

Celtic Fairy Tales

Collected by Joseph Jacobs

Celtic Fairy Tales and
More Celtic Fairy Tales
combined to produce one large volume

LOMOND BOOKS

This edition published for Lomond Books 2000 by Parragon

Parragon
Queen Street House
4 Queen Street
Bath, BA1 1HE, UK

ISBN 1 84204 015 2

A copy of the British Library Cataloguing-in-Publication Data
is available from the British Library.

Printed and bound in the EC

Contents

Celtic Fairy Tales

Collected by
JOSEPH JACOBS

Illustrated by
JOHN D. BATTEN

Preface

AST year, in giving the young ones a volume of English Fairy Tales, my difficulty was one of collection. This time, in offering them specimens of the rich folk-fancy of the Celts of these islands, my trouble has rather been one of selection. Ireland began to collect her folk-tales almost as early as any country in Europe, and Croker has found a whole school of successors in Carleton, Griffin, Kennedy, Curtin, and Douglas Hyde. Scotland had the great name of Campbell, and has still efficient followers in MacDougall, MacInnes, Carmichael, Macleod, and Campbell of Tiree. Gallant little Wales has no name to rank alongside these; in this department the Cymru have shown less vigour than the Gaedhel. Perhaps the Eisteddfod, by offering prizes for the collection of Welsh folk-tales, may remove this inferiority. Meanwhile Wales must be content to be somewhat scantily represented among the Fairy Tales of the Celts, while the extinct Cornish tongue has only contributed one tale.

Preface

In making my selection I have chiefly tried to make the stories characteristic. It would have been easy, especially from Kennedy, to have made up a volume entirely filled with " Grimm's Goblins " *à la Celtique*. But one can have too much even of that very good thing, and I have therefore avoided as far as possible the more familiar " formulæ " of folk-tale literature. To do this I had to withdraw from the English-speaking Pale both in Scotland and Ireland, and I laid down the rule to include only tales that have been taken down from Celtic peasants ignorant of English.

Having laid down the rule, I immediately proceeded to break it. The success of a fairy book, I am convinced, depends on the due admixture of the comic and the romantic: Grimm and Asbjörnsen knew this secret, and they alone. But the Celtic peasant who speaks Gaelic takes the pleasure of telling tales somewhat sadly: so far as he has been printed and translated, I found him, to my surprise, conspicuously lacking in humour. For the comic relief of this volume I have therefore had to turn mainly to the Irish peasant of the Pale ; and what richer source could I draw from ?

For the more romantic tales I have depended on the Gaelic, and, as I know about as much of Gaelic as an Irish Nationalist M.P., I have had to depend on translators. But I have felt myself more at liberty than the translators themselves, who have generally been over-literal, in changing, excising, or modifying the original. I have even gone further. In order that the tales should be characteristically

Preface

Celtic, I have paid more particular attention to tales that are to be found on both sides of the North Channel. In re-telling them I have had no scruple in interpolating now and then a Scotch incident into an Irish variant of the same story, or *vice versâ*. Where the translators appealed to English folk-lorists and scholars, I am trying to attract English children. They translated ; I endeavoured to transfer. In short, I have tried to put myself into the position of an *ollamh* or *sheenachie* familiar with both forms of Gaelic, and anxious to put his stories in the best way to attract English children. I trust I shall be forgiven by Celtic scholars for the changes I have had to make to effect this end.

The stories collected in this volume are longer and more detailed than the English ones I brought together last Christmas. The romantic ones are certainly more romantic, and the comic ones perhaps more comic, though there may be room for a difference of opinion on this latter point. This superiority of the Celtic folk-tales is due as much to the conditions under which they have been collected, as to any innate superiority of the folk-imagination. The folk-tale in England is in the last stages of exhaustion. The Celtic folk-tales have been collected while the practice of story-telling is still in full vigour, though there are every signs that its term of life is already numbered. The more the reason why they should be collected and put on record while there is yet time. On the whole, the industry of the collectors of Celtic folk-lore is to be

Preface

commended, as may be seen from the survey of it I have prefixed to the Notes and References at the end of the volume. Among these, I would call attention to the study of the legend of Beth Gellert, the origin of which, I believe, I have settled.

While I have endeavoured to render the language of the tales simple and free from bookish artifice, I have not felt at liberty to retell the tales in the English way. I have not scrupled to retain a Celtic turn of speech, and here and there a Celtic word, which I have *not* explained within brackets—a practice to be abhorred of all good men. A few words unknown to the reader only add effectiveness and local colour to a narrative, as Mr. Kipling well knows.

One characteristic of the Celtic folk-lore I have endeavoured to represent in my selection, because it is nearly unique at the present day in Europe. Nowhere else is there so large and consistent a body of oral tradition about the national and mythical heroes as amongst the Gaels. Only the *byline*, or hero-songs of Russia, equal in extent the amount of knowledge about the heroes of the past that still exists among the Gaelic-speaking peasantry of Scotland and Ireland. And the Irish tales and ballads have this peculiarity, that some of them have been extant, and can be traced for well nigh a thousand years. I have selected as a specimen of this class the Story of Deirdre, collected among the Scotch peasantry a few years ago, into which I have been able to insert a passage taken from an

Preface

Irish vellum of the twelfth century. I could have more than filled this volume with similar oral traditions about Finn (the Fingal of Macpherson's " Ossian "). But the story of Finn, as told by the Gaelic peasantry of to-day, deserves a volume by itself, while the adventures of the Ultonian hero, Cuchulain, could easily fill another.

I have endeavoured to include in this volume the best and most typical stories told by the chief masters of the Celtic folk-tale, Campbell, Kennedy, Hyde, and Curtin, and to these I have added the best tales scattered elsewhere. By this means I hope I have put together a volume, containing both the best, and the best known folk-tales of the Celts. I have only been enabled to do this by the courtesy of those who owned the copyright of these stories. Lady Wilde has kindly granted me the use of her effective version of " The Horned Women ;" and I have specially to thank Messrs. Macmillan for right to use Kennedy's " Legendary Fictions," and Messrs. Sampson Low & Co., for the use of Mr. Curtin's Tales.

In making my selection, and in all doubtful points of treatment, I have had resource to the wide knowledge of my friend Mr. Alfred Nutt in all branches of Celtic folk-lore. If this volume does anything to represent to English children the vision and colour, the magic and charm, of the Celtic folk-imagination, this is due in large measure to the care with which Mr. Nutt has watched its inception and progress. With him by my side I could venture into regions where the non-Celt wanders at his own risk.

Preface

Lastly, I have again to rejoice in the co-operation of my friend, Mr. J. D. Batten, in giving form to the creations of the folk-fancy. He has endeavoured in his illustrations to retain as much as possible of Celtic ornamentation ; for all details of Celtic archæology he has authority. Yet both he and I have striven to give Celtic things as they appear to, and attract, the English mind, rather than attempt the hopeless task of representing them as they are to Celts. The fate of the Celt in the British Empire bids fair to resemble that of the Greeks among the Romans. "They went forth to battle, but they always fell," yet the captive Celt has enslaved his captor in the realm of imagination. The present volume attempts to begin the pleasant captivity from the earliest years. If it could succeed in giving a common fund of imaginative wealth to the Celtic and the Saxon children of these isles, it might do more for a true union of hearts than all your politics.

1892   JOSEPH JACOBS.

Contents

Contents

[For Nos. XXVII–XLVI, see Book Two in
the second part of this volume.]

Connla and the Fairy Maiden

ONNLA of the Fiery Hair was son of Conn of the Hundred Fights. One day as he stood by the side of his father on the height of Usna, he saw a maiden clad in strange attire coming towards him.

" Whence comest thou, maiden ? " said Connla.

" I come from the Plains of the Ever Living," she said, " there where there is neither death nor sin. There we keep holiday alway, nor need we help from any in our joy. And in all our pleasure we have no strife. And because we have our homes in the round green hills, men call us the Hill Folk."

The king and all with him wondered much to hear a voice when they saw no one. For save Connla alone, none saw the Fairy Maiden.

" To whom art thou talking, my son ? " said Conn the king.

Then the maiden answered, " Connla speaks to a young, fair maid, whom neither death nor old age awaits. I love Connla, and now I call him away to the Plain of Pleasure,

Moy Mell, where Boadag is king for aye, nor has there been complaint or sorrow in that land since he has held the kingship. Oh, come with me, Connla of the Fiery Hair, ruddy as the dawn with thy tawny skin. A fairy crown awaits thee to grace thy comely face and royal form. Come, and never shall thy comeliness fade, nor thy youth, till the last awful day of judgment."

The king in fear at what the maiden said, which he heard though he could not see her, called aloud to his Druid, Coran by name.

"Oh, Coran of the many spells," he said, "and of the cunning magic, I call upon thy aid. A task is upon me too great for all my skill and wit, greater than any laid upon me since I seized the kingship. A maiden unseen has met us, and by her power would take from me my dear, my comely son. If thou help not, he will be taken from thy king by woman's wiles and witchery."

Then Coran the Druid stood forth and chanted his spells towards the spot where the maiden's voice had been heard. And none heard her voice again, nor could Connla see her longer. Only as she vanished before the Druid's mighty spell, she threw an apple to Connla.

For a whole month from that day Connla would take nothing, either to eat or to drink, save only from that apple. But as he ate it grew again and always kept whole. And all the while there grew within him a mighty yearning and longing after the maiden he had seen.

But when the last day of the month of waiting came, Connla stood by the side of the king his father on the Plain of Arcomin, and again he saw the maiden come towards him, and again she spoke to him.

" 'Tis a glorious place, forsooth, that Connla holds among shortlived mortals awaiting the day of death. But now the folk of life, the ever-living ones, beg and bid thee come to Moy Mell, the Plain of Pleasure, for they have learnt to know thee, seeing thee in thy home among thy dear ones."

When Conn the king heard the maiden's voice he called to his men aloud and said :

" Summon swift my Druid Coran, for I see she has again this day the power of speech."

Then the maiden said : " Oh, mighty Conn, fighter of a hundred fights, the Druid's power is little loved ; it has little honour in the mighty land, peopled with so many of the upright. When the Law will come, it will do away with the Druid's magic spells that come from the lips of the false black demon."

Then Conn the king observed that since the maiden came Connla his son spoke to none that spake to him. So Conn of the hundred fights said to him, " Is it to thy mind what the woman says, my son ? "

" 'Tis hard upon me," then said Connla ; " I love my own folk above all things ; but yet, but yet a longing seizes me for the maiden."

When the maiden heard this, she answered and said : " The ocean is not so strong as the waves of thy longing. Come with me in my curragh, the gleaming, straight-gliding crystal canoe. Soon we can reach Boadag's realm. I see the bright sun sink, yet far as it is, we can reach it before dark. There is, too, another land worthy of thy journey, a land joyous to all that seek it. Only wives and maidens dwell there. If thou wilt, we can seek it and live there alone together in joy."

When the maiden ceased to speak, Connla of the Fiery Hair rushed away from them and sprang into the curragh, the gleaming, straight-gliding crystal canoe. And then they all, king and court, saw it glide away over the bright sea towards the setting sun. Away and away, till eye could see it no longer, and Connla and the Fairy Maiden went their way on the sea, and were no more seen, nor did any know where they came.

Guleesh

HERE was once a boy in the County Mayo; Guleesh was his name. There was the finest rath a little way off from the gable of the house, and he was often in the habit of seating himself on the fine grass bank that was running round it. One night he stood, half leaning against the gable of the house, and looking up into the sky, and watching the beautiful white moon over his head. After he had been standing that way for a couple of hours, he said to himself : " My bitter grief that I am not gone away out of this place altogether. I'd sooner be any place in the world than here. Och, it's well for you, white moon," says he, "that's turning round, turning round, as you please yourself, and no man can put you back. I wish I was the same as you."

Hardly was the word out of his mouth when he heard a great noise coming like the sound of many people running together, and talking, and laughing, and making sport, and the sound went by him like a whirl of wind, and he was listening to it going into the rath. " Musha, by my soul," says he, " but ye're merry enough, and I'll follow ye."

What was in it but the fairy host, though he did not know at first that it was they who were in it, but he followed them into the rath. It's there he heard the *fulparnee*, and the *folpornee*, the *rap-lay-hoota*, and the *roolya-boolya*, that they had there, and every man of them crying out as loud as he could : " My horse, and bridle, and saddle ! My horse, and bridle, and saddle ! "

" By my hand," said Guleesh, " my boy, that's not bad. I'll imitate ye," and he cried out as well as they : " My horse, and bridle, and saddle ! My horse, and bridle, and saddle ! " And on the moment there was a fine horse with a bridle of gold, and a saddle of silver, standing before him. He leaped up on it, and the moment he was on its back he saw clearly that the rath was full of horses, and of little people going riding on them.

Said a man of them to him : " Are you coming with us to-night, Guleesh ? "

" I am surely," said Guleesh.

" If you are, come along," said the little man, and out they went all together, riding like the wind, faster than the fastest horse ever you saw a-hunting, and faster than the fox and the hounds at his tail.

The cold winter's wind that was before them, they overtook her, and the cold winter's wind that was behind them, she did not overtake them. And stop nor stay of that full race, did they make none, until they came to the brink of the sea.

Then every one of them said : " Hie over cap ! Hie over cap ! " and that moment they were up in the air, and before Guleesh had time to remember where he was, they were down on dry land again, and were going like the wind.

At last they stood still, and a man of them said to Guleesh :
" Guleesh, do you know where you are now ? "

" Not a know," says Guleesh.

" You're in France, Guleesh," said he. " The daughter
of the king of France is to be married to-night, the handsomest woman that the sun ever saw, and we must do our
best to bring her with us, if we're only able to carry her
off; and you must come with us that we may be able to
put the young girl up behind you on the horse, when we'll
be bringing her away, for it's not lawful for us to put her
sitting behind ourselves. But you're flesh and blood, and
she can take a good grip of you, so that she won't fall off
the horse. Are you satisfied, Guleesh, and will you do
what we're telling you ? "

" Why shouldn't I be satisfied ? " said Guleesh. " I'm
satisfied, surely, and anything that ye will tell me to do I'll
do it without doubt."

They got off their horses there, and a man of them said
a word that Guleesh did not understand, and on the
moment they were lifted up, and Guleesh found himself and
his companions in the palace. There was a great feast
going on there, and there was not a nobleman or a gentleman in the kingdom but was gathered there, dressed in silk
and satin, and gold and silver, and the night was as bright
as the day with all the lamps and candles that were lit, and
Guleesh had to shut his two eyes at the brightness. When
he opened them again and looked from him, he thought he
never saw anything as fine as all he saw there. There
were a hundred tables spread out, and their full of meat and
drink on each table of them, flesh-meat, and cakes and
sweetmeats, and wine and ale, and every drink that ever a

man saw. The musicians were at the two ends of the hall, and they were playing the sweetest music that ever a man's ear heard, and there were young women and fine youths in the middle of the hall, dancing and turning, and going round so quickly and so lightly, that it put a *soorawn* in Guleesh's head to be looking at them. There were more there playing tricks, and more making fun and laughing, for such a feast as there was that day had not been in France for twenty years, because the old king had no children alive but only the one daughter, and she was to be married to the son of another king that night. Three days the feast was going on, and the third night she was to be married, and that was the night that Guleesh and the sheehogues came, hoping, if they could, to carry off with them the king's young daughter.

Guleesh and his companions were standing together at the head of the hall, where there was a fine altar dressed up, and two bishops behind it waiting to marry the girl, as soon as the right time should come. Now nobody could see the sheehogues, for they said a word as they came in, that made them all invisible, as if they had not been in it at all.

" Tell me which of them is the king's daughter," said Guleesh, when he was becoming a little used to the noise and the light.

" Don't you see her there away from you?" said the little man that he was talking to.

Guleesh looked where the little man was pointing with his finger, and there he saw the loveliest woman that was, he thought, upon the ridge of the world. The rose and the lily were fighting together in her face, and one could not tell which of them got the victory. Her arms and hands were like the lime, her mouth as red as a strawberry when it is ripe, her foot was as small and as light as another one's hand, her form was smooth and slender, and her hair was falling down from her head in buckles of gold. Her garments and dress were woven with gold and silver, and the bright stone that was in the ring on her hand was as shining as the sun.

Guleesh was nearly blinded with all the loveliness and beauty that was in her ; but when he looked again, he saw that she was crying, and that there was the trace of tears in her eyes. "It can't be," said Guleesh, "that there's grief on her, when everybody round her is so full of sport and merriment."

"Musha, then, she is grieved," said the little man ; "for it's against her own will she's marrying, and she has no love for the husband she is to marry. The king was going to give her to him three years ago, when she was only fifteen, but she said she was too young, and requested him to leave her as she was yet. The king gave her a year's grace, and when that year was up he gave her another year's grace, and then another ; but a week or a day he would not give her longer, and she is eighteen years old to-night, and it's time for her to marry ; but, indeed," says he, and he crooked his mouth in an ugly way—"indeed, it's no king's son she'll marry, if I can help it."

Guleesh pitied the handsome young lady greatly when he heard that, and he was heart-broken to think that it would be necessary for her to marry a man she did not like, or, what was worse, to take a nasty sheehogue for a husband. However, he did not say a word, though he could not help giving many a curse to the ill-luck that was laid out for himself, to be helping the people that were to snatch her away from her home and from her father.

He began thinking, then, what it was he ought to do to save her, but he could think of nothing. " Oh ! if I could only give her some help and relief," said he, " I wouldn't care whether I were alive or dead ; but I see nothing that I can do for her."

He was looking on when the king's son came up to her and asked her for a kiss, but she turned her head away from him. Guleesh had double pity for her then, when he saw the lad taking her by the soft white hand, and drawing her out to dance. They went round in the dance near where Guleesh was, and he could plainly see that there were tears in her eyes.

When the dancing was over, the old king, her father, and her mother the queen, came up and said that this was the right time to marry her, that the bishop was ready, and it was time to put the wedding-ring on her and give her to her husband.

The king took the youth by the hand, and the queen took her daughter, and they went up together to the altar, with the lords and great people following them.

When they came near the altar, and were no more than about four yards from it, the little sheehogue stretched out his foot before the girl, and she fell. Before she was able to rise again he threw something that was in his hand upon her, said a couple of words, and upon the moment the maiden was gone from amongst them. Nobody could see her, for that word made her invisible. The little man*een* seized her and raised her up behind Guleesh, and the king nor no one else saw them, but out with them through the hall till they came to the door.

Oro! dear Mary! it's there the pity was, and the trouble, and the crying, and the wonder, and the searching, and the *rookawn*, when that lady disappeared from their eyes, and without their seeing what did it. Out of the

door of the palace they went, without being stopped or hindered, for nobody saw them, and, "My horse, my bridle, and saddle!" says every man of them. "My horse, my bridle, and saddle!" says Guleesh; and on the moment the horse was standing ready caparisoned before him. "Now, jump up, Guleesh," said the little man, "and put the lady behind you, and we will be going; the morning is not far off from us now."

Guleesh raised her up on the horse's back, and leaped up

himself before her, and, " Rise, horse," said he ; and his horse, and the other horses with him, went in a full race until they came to the sea.

" Hie over cap !" said every man of them.

" Hie over cap !" said Guleesh ; and on the moment the horse rose under him, and cut a leap in the clouds, and came down in Erin.

They did not stop there, but went of a race to the place where was Guleesh's house and the rath. And when they came as far as that, Guleesh turned and caught the young girl in his two arms, and leaped off the horse.

" I call and cross you to myself, in the name of God !" said he ; and on the spot, before the word was out of his mouth, the horse fell down, and what was in it but the beam of a plough, of which they had made a horse ; and every other horse they had, it was that way they made it. Some of them were riding on an old besom, and some on a broken stick, and more on a bohalawn or a hemlock-stalk.

The good people called out together when they heard what Guleesh said :

" Oh ! Guleesh, you clown, you thief, that no good may happen you, why did you play that trick on us ? "

But they had no power at all to carry off the girl, after Guleesh had consecrated her to himself.

" Oh ! Guleesh, isn't that a nice turn you did us, and we so kind to you ? What good have we now out of our journey to France. Never mind yet, you clown, but you'll pay us another time for this. Believe us, you'll repent it."

" He'll have no good to get out of the young girl," said the little man that was talking to him in the palace before that, and as he said the word he moved over to her and struck her a slap on the side of the head. "Now," says he, "she'll be without talk any more; now, Guleesh, what good will she be to you when she'll be dumb? It's time for us to go—but you'll remember us, Guleesh!"

When he said that he stretched out his two hands, and before Guleesh was able to give an answer, he and the rest of them were gone into the rath out of his sight, and he saw them no more.

He turned to the young woman and said to her: "Thanks be to God, they're gone. Would you not sooner stay with me than with them?" She gave him no answer. "There's trouble and grief on her yet," said Guleesh in his own mind, and he spoke to her again: "I am afraid that you must spend this night in my father's house, lady, and if there is anything that I can do for you, tell me, and I'll be your servant."

The beautiful girl remained silent, but there were tears in her eyes, and her face was white and red after each other.

"Lady," said Guleesh, "tell me what you would like me to do now. I never belonged at all to that lot of shee-hogues who carried you away with them. I am the son of an honest farmer, and I went with them without knowing it. If I'll be able to send you back to your father I'll do it, and I pray you make any use of me now that you may wish."

He looked into her face, and he saw the mouth moving as if she was going to speak, but there came no word from it.

"It cannot be," said Guleesh, "that you are dumb.

Did I not hear you speaking to the king's son in the palace to-night ?   Or has that devil made you really dumb, when he struck his nasty hand on your jaw ?"

The girl raised her white smooth hand, and laid her finger on her tongue, to show him that she had lost her voice and power of speech, and the tears ran out of her two eyes like streams, and Guleesh's own eyes were not dry, for as rough as he was on the outside he had a soft heart, and could not stand the sight of the young girl, and she in that unhappy plight.

He began thinking with himself what he ought to do, and he did not like to bring her home with himself to his father's house, for he knew well that they would not believe him, that he had been in France and brought back with him the king of France's daughter, and he was afraid they might make a mock of the young lady or insult her.

As he was doubting what he ought to do, and hesitating, he chanced to remember the priest.   "Glory be to God," said he, "I know now what I'll do ; I'll bring her to the priest's house, and he won't refuse me to keep the lady and care her." He turned to the lady again and told her that he was loth to take her to his father's house, but that there was an excellent priest very friendly to himself, who would take good care of her, if she wished to remain in his house ; but that if there was any other place she would rather go, he said he would bring her to it.

She bent her head, to show him she was obliged, and gave him to understand that she was ready to follow him any place he was going.   "We will go to the priest's house, then," said he ; "he is under an obligation to me, and will do anything I ask him."

They went together accordingly to the priest's house, and the sun was just rising when they came to the door. Guleesh beat it hard, and as early as it was the priest was up, and opened the door himself. He wondered when he saw Guleesh and the girl, for he was certain that it was coming wanting to be married they were.

" Guleesh, Guleesh, isn't it the nice boy you are that you can't wait till ten o'clock or till twelve, but that you must be coming to me at this hour, looking for marriage, you and your sweetheart ? You ought to know that I can't marry you at such a time, or, at all events, can't marry you lawfully. But ubbubboo ! " said he, suddenly, as he looked again at the young girl, " in the name of God, who have you here ? Who is she, or how did you get her ? "

" Father," said Guleesh, " you can marry me, or anybody else, if you wish ; but it's not looking for marriage I came to you now, but to ask you, if you please, to give a lodging in your house to this young lady."

The priest looked at him as though he had ten heads on him ; but without putting any other question to him, he desired him to come in, himself and the maiden, and when they came in, he shut the door, brought them into the parlour, and put them sitting.

" Now, Guleesh," said he, " tell me truly who is this young lady, and whether you're out of your senses really, or are only making a joke of me."

" I'm not telling a word of lie, nor making a joke of you," said Guleesh ; " but it was from the palace of the king of France I carried off this lady, and she is the daughter of the king of France."

He began his story then, and told the whole to the priest, and the priest was so much surprised that he could not help calling out at times, or clapping his hands together.

When Guleesh said from what he saw he thought the girl was not satisfied with the marriage that was going to take place in the palace before he and the sheehogues broke it up, there came a red blush into the girl's cheek, and he was more certain than ever that she had sooner be as she was——badly as she was——than be the married wife of the man she hated.   When Guleesh said that he would be very thankful to the priest if he would keep her in his own house, the kind man said he would do that as long as Guleesh pleased, but that he did not know what they ought to do with her, because they had no means of sending her back to her father again.

Guleesh answered that he was uneasy about the same thing, and that he saw nothing to do but to keep quiet until they should find some opportunity of doing something better.   They made it up then between themselves that the priest should let on that it was his brother's daughter he had, who was come on a visit to him from another county, and that he should tell everybody that she was dumb, and do his best to keep every one away from her.   They told the young girl what it was they intended to do, and she showed by her eyes that she was obliged to them.

Guleesh went home then, and when his people asked him where he had been, he said that he had been asleep at the foot of the ditch, and had passed the night there.

There was great wonderment on the priest's neighbours at the girl who came so suddenly to his house without any one knowing where she was from, or what business she had there. Some of the people said that everything was not as it ought to be, and others, that Guleesh was not like the same man that was in it before, and that it was a great story, how he was drawing every day to the priest's house, and that the priest had a wish and a respect for him, a thing they could not clear up at all.

That was true for them, indeed, for it was seldom the day went by but Guleesh would go to the priest's house, and have a talk with him, and as often as he would come he used to hope to find the young lady well again, and with leave to speak ; but, alas ! she remained dumb and silent, without relief or cure. Since she had no other means of talking, she carried on a sort of conversation between herself and himself, by moving her hand and fingers, winking her eyes, opening and shutting her mouth, laughing or smiling, and a thousand other signs, so that it was not long until they understood each other very well. Guleesh was always thinking how he should send her back to her father ; but there was no one to go with her, and he himself did not know what road to go, for he had never been out of his own country before the night he brought her away with him. Nor had the priest any better knowledge than he ; but when Guleesh asked him, he wrote three or four letters to the king of France, and gave them to buyers and sellers of wares, who used to be going from place to place across the sea ; but they all went astray, and never a one came to the king's hand.

This was the way they were for many months, and Guleesh was falling deeper and deeper in love with her every day, and it was plain to himself and the priest that

she liked him.   The boy feared greatly at last, lest the
king should really hear where his daughter was, and take
her back from himself, and he besought the priest to write
no more, but to leave the matter to God.

So they passed the time for a year, until there came a
day when Guleesh was lying by himself on the grass, on
the last day of the last month in autumn, and he was thinking
over again in his own mind of everything that happened to
him from the day that he went with the sheehogues across
the sea.   He remembered then, suddenly, that it was one
November night that he was standing at the gable of the
house, when the whirlwind came, and the sheehogues in it,
and he said to himself: "We have November night again
to-day, and I'll stand in the same place I was last year,
until I see if the good people come again.   Perhaps I
might see or hear something that would be useful to me,
and might bring back her talk again to Mary"—that was
the name himself and the priest called the king's daughter,
for neither of them knew her right name.   He told his
intention to the priest, and the priest gave him his
blessing.

Guleesh accordingly went to the old rath when the night
was darkening, and he stood with his bent elbow leaning on
a grey old flag, waiting till the middle of the night should
come.   The moon rose slowly, and it was like a knob of
fire behind him ; and there was a white fog which was
raised up over the fields of grass and all damp places,
through the coolness of the night after a great heat in the
day.   The night was calm as is a lake when there is not a
breath of wind to move a wave on it, and there was no
sound to be heard but the *cronawn* of the insects that would

go by from time to time, or the hoarse sudden scream of the wild-geese, as they passed from lake to lake, half a mile up in the air over his head ; or the sharp whistle of the golden and green plover, rising and lying, lying and rising, as they do on a calm night. There were a thousand thousand bright stars shining over his head, and there was a little frost out, which left the grass under his foot white and crisp.

He stood there for an hour, for two hours, for three hours, and the frost increased greatly, so that he heard the breaking of the *traneens* under his foot as often as he moved. He was thinking, in his own mind, at last, that the sheehogues would not come that night, and that it was as good for him to return back again, when he heard a sound far away from him, coming towards him, and he recognised what it was at the first moment. The sound increased, and at first it was like the beating of waves on a stony shore, and then it was like the falling of a great waterfall, and at last it was like a loud storm in the tops of the trees, and then the whirlwind burst into the rath of one rout, and the sheehogues were in it.

It all went by him so suddenly that he lost his breath with it, but he came to himself on the spot, and put an ear on himself, listening to what they would say.

Scarcely had they gathered into the rath till they all began shouting, and screaming, and talking amongst themselves ; and then each one of them cried out : " My horse, and bridle, and saddle ! My horse, and bridle, and saddle ! " and Guleesh took courage, and called out as loudly as any of them : " My horse, and bridle, and saddle ! My horse, and bridle, and saddle ! " But before the word was well out of his mouth, another man cried out : " Ora ! Guleesh, my boy, are you here with us again ? How are you getting on with your woman ? There's no use in your calling for your horse to-night. I'll go bail you won't play such a trick on us again. It was a good trick you played on us last year ? "

" It was," said another man ; " he won't do it again."

" Isn't he a prime lad, the same lad ! to take a woman with him that never said as much to him as, ' How do you do ? ' since this time last year ! " says the third man.

" Perhaps he likes to be looking at her," said another voice.

" And if the *omadawn* only knew that there's an herb growing up by his own door, and if he were to boil it and give it to her, she'd be well," said another voice.

" That's true for you."

" He is an omadawn."

" Don't bother your head with him ; we'll be going."

" We'll leave the *bodach* as he is."

And with that they rose up into the air, and out with them with one *roolya-boolya* the way they came ; and they left poor Guleesh standing where they found him, and the two eyes going out of his head, looking after them and wondering.

He did not stand long till he returned back, and he thinking in his own mind on all he saw and heard, and wondering whether there was really an herb at his own door that would bring back the talk to the king's daughter. " It can't be," says he to himself, " that they would tell it to me, if there was any virtue in it ; but perhaps the sheehogue didn't observe himself when he let the word slip out of his mouth. I'll search well as soon as the sun rises, whether there's any plant growing beside the house except thistles and dockings."

He went home, and as tired as he was he did not sleep a wink until the sun rose on the morrow. He got up then, and it was the first thing he did to go out and search

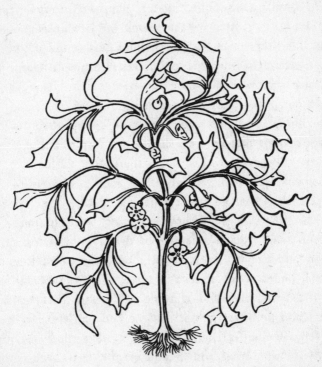

well through the grass round about the house, trying could he get any herb that he did not recognise. And, indeed, he was not long searching till he observed a large strange herb that was growing up just by the gable of the house.

He went over to it, and observed it closely, and saw

that there were seven little branches coming out of the stalk, and seven leaves growing on every branch*een* of them ; and that there was a white sap in the leaves. " It's very wonderful," said he to himself, " that I never noticed this herb before. If there's any virtue in an herb at all, it ought to be in such a strange one as this."

He drew out his knife, cut the plant, and carried it into his own house ; stripped the leaves off it and cut up the stalk ; and there came a thick, white juice out of it, as there comes out of the sow-thistle when it is bruised, except that the juice was more like oil.

He put it in a little pot and a little water in it, and laid it on the fire until the water was boiling, and then he took a cup, filled it half up with the juice, and put it to his own mouth. It came into his head then that perhaps it was poison that was in it, and that the good people were only tempting him that he might kill himself with that trick, or put the girl to death without meaning it. He put down the cup again, raised a couple of drops on the top of his finger, and put it to his mouth. It was not bitter, and, indeed, had a sweet, agreeable taste. He grew bolder then, and drank the full of a thimble of it, and then as much again, and he never stopped till he had half the cup drunk. He fell asleep after that, and did not wake till it was night, and there was great hunger and great thirst on him.

He had to wait, then, till the day rose ; but he determined, as soon as he should wake in the morning, that he would go to the king's daughter and give her a drink of the juice of the herb.

As soon as he got up in the morning, he went over to the priest's house with the drink in his hand, and he never

felt himself so bold and valiant, and spirited and light, as he
was that day, and he was quite certain that it was the
drink he drank which made him so hearty.

When he came to the house, he found the priest and the
young lady within, and they were wondering greatly why
he had not visited them for two days.

He told them all his news, and said that he was certain
that there was great power in that herb, and that it would
do the lady no hurt, for he tried it himself and got good
from it, and then he made her taste it, for he vowed and
swore that there was no harm in it.

Guleesh handed her the cup, and she drank half of it,
and then fell back on her bed and a heavy sleep came on

her, and she never woke out of that sleep till the day on the morrow.

Guleesh and the priest sat up the entire night with her, waiting till she should awake, and they between hope and unhope, between expectation of saving her and fear of hurting her.

She awoke at last when the sun had gone half its way through the heavens. She rubbed her eyes and looked like a person who did not know where she was. She was like one astonished when she saw Guleesh and the priest in the same room with her, and she sat up doing her best to collect her thoughts.

The two men were in great anxiety waiting to see would she speak, or would she not speak, and when they remained silent for a couple of minutes, the priest said to her: " Did you sleep well, Mary ? "

And she answered him : " I slept, thank you."

No sooner did Guleesh hear her talking than he put a shout of joy out of him, and ran over to her and fell on his two knees, and said: " A thousand thanks to God, who has given you back the talk ; lady of my heart, speak again to me."

The lady answered him that she understood it was he who boiled that drink for her, and gave it to her ; that she was obliged to him from her heart for all the kindness he showed her since the day she first came to Ireland, and that he might be certain that she never would forget it.

Guleesh was ready to die with satisfaction and delight. Then they brought her food, and she ate with a good appetite, and was merry and joyous, and never left off talking with the priest while she was eating.

After that Guleesh went home to his house, and stretched

himself on the bed and fell asleep again, for the force of the herb was not all spent, and he passed another day and a night sleeping. When he woke up he went back to the priest's house, and found that the young lady was in the same state, and that she was asleep almost since the time that he left the house.

He went into her chamber with the priest, and they remained watching beside her till she awoke the second time, and she had her talk as well as ever, and Guleesh was greatly rejoiced. The priest put food on the table again, and they ate together, and Guleesh used after that to come to the house from day to day, and the friendship that was between him and the king's daughter increased, because she had no one to speak to except Guleesh and the priest, and she liked Guleesh best.

So they married one another, and that was the fine wedding they had, and if I were to be there then, I would not be here now; but I heard it from a birdeen that there was neither cark nor care, sickness nor sorrow, mishap nor misfortune on them till the hour of their death, and may the same be with me, and with us all!

The Field of Boliauns

NE fine day in harvest—it was indeed Lady-
day in harvest, that everybody knows to be
one of the greatest holidays in the year—
Tom Fitzpatrick was taking a ramble through
the ground, and went along the sunny side
of a hedge; when all of a sudden he heard a clacking sort
of noise a little before him in the hedge. "Dear me," said
Tom, "but isn't it surprising to hear the stonechatters
singing so late in the season?" So Tom stole on, going on
the tops of his toes to try if he could get a sight of what
was making the noise, to see if he was right in his guess.
The noise stopped; but as Tom looked sharply through the
bushes, what should he see in a nook of the hedge but a
brown pitcher, that might hold about a gallon and a half of
liquor; and by-and-by a little wee teeny tiny bit of an old
man, with a little *motty* of a cocked hat stuck upon the top

of his head, a deeshy daushy leather apron hanging before him, pulled out a little wooden stool, and stood up upon it, and dipped a little piggin into the pitcher, and took out the full of it, and put it beside the stool, and then sat down under the pitcher, and began to work at putting a heel-piece on a bit of a brogue just fit for himself. "Well, by the powers," said Tom to himself, "I often heard tell of the Lepracauns, and, to tell God's truth, I never rightly believed in them—but here's one of them in real earnest. If I go knowingly to work, I'm a made man. They say a body must never take their eyes off them, or they'll escape."

Tom now stole on a little further, with his eye fixed on the little man just as a cat does with a mouse. So when he got up quite close to him, "God bless your work, neighbour," said Tom.

The little man raised up his head, and "Thank you kindly," said he.

"I wonder you'd be working on the holiday!" said Tom.

"That's my own business, not yours," was the reply.

"Well, may be you'd be civil enough to tell *us* what you've got in the pitcher there?" said Tom.

"That I will, with pleasure," said he; "it's good beer."

"Beer!" said Tom. "Thunder and fire! where did you get it?"

"Where did I get it, is it? Why, I made it. And what do you think I made it of?"

"Devil a one of me knows," said Tom; "but of malt, I suppose, what else?"

"There you're out. I made it of heath."

"Of heath!" said Tom, bursting out laughing; "sure you don't think me to be such a fool as to believe that?"

"Do as you please," said he, "but what I tell you is the truth. Did you never hear tell of the Danes."

"Well, what about *them?*" said Tom.

"Why, all the about them there is, is that when they were here they taught us to make beer out of the heath, and the secret's in my family ever since."

"Will you give a body a taste of your beer?" said Tom.

"I'll tell you what it is, young man, it would be fitter for you to be looking after your father's property than to be bothering decent quiet people with your foolish questions. There now, while you're idling away your time here, there's the cows have broke into the oats, and are knocking the corn all about."

Tom was taken so by surprise with this that he was just on the very point of turning round when he recollected himself; so, afraid that the like might happen again, he made a grab at the Lepracaun, and caught him up in his hand; but in his hurry he overset the pitcher, and spilt all the beer, so that he could not get a taste of it to tell what sort it was. He then swore that he would kill him if he did not show him where his money was. Tom looked so wicked and so bloody-minded that the little man was quite frightened; so says he, "Come along with me a couple of fields off, and I'll show you a crock of gold."

So they went, and Tom held the Lepracaun fast in his hand, and never took his eyes from off him, though they had to cross hedges and ditches, and a crooked bit of bog, till at last they came to a great field all full of boliauns, and the Lepracaun pointed to a big boliaun, and says he, "Dig under that boliaun, and you'll get the great crock all full of guineas."

Tom in his hurry had never thought of bringing a spade with him, so he made up his mind to run home and fetch one ; and that he might know the place again he took off one of his red garters, and tied it round the boliaun.

Then he said to the Lepracaun, " Swear ye'll not take that garter away from that boliaun."   And the Lepracaun swore right away not to touch it.

" I suppose," said the Lepracaun, very civilly, " you have no further occasion for me ? "

" No," says Tom ; " you may go away now, if you please, and God speed you, and may good luck attend you wherever you go."

" Well, good-bye to you, Tom Fitzpatrick," said the Lepracaun ; " and much good may it do you when you get it."

So Tom ran for dear life, till he came home and got a spade, and then away with him, as hard as he could go, back to the field of boliauns ; but when he got there, lo and behold ! not a boliaun in the field but had a red garter, the very model of his own, tied about it ; and as to digging up the whole field, that was all nonsense, for there were more than forty good Irish acres in it. So Tom came home again with his spade on his shoulder, a little cooler than he went, and many's the hearty curse he gave the Lepracaun every time he thought of the neat turn he had served him.

The Horned Women

RICH woman sat up late one night carding
and preparing wool, while all the family
and servants were asleep. Suddenly a
knock was given at the door, and a voice
called, "Open! open!"

"Who is there?" said the woman of the house.

"I am the Witch of one Horn," was answered.

The mistress, supposing that one of her neighbours had
called and required assistance, opened the door, and a
woman entered, having in her hand a pair of wool-carders,
and bearing a horn on her forehead, as if growing there.
She sat down by the fire in silence, and began to card

the wool with violent haste. Suddenly she paused, and said aloud: "Where are the women? they delay too long."

Then a second knock came to the door, and a voice called as before, "Open! open!"

The mistress felt herself obliged to rise and open to the call, and immediately a second witch entered, having two horns on her forehead, and in her hand a wheel for spinning wool.

"Give me place," she said; "I am the Witch of the two Horns," and she began to spin as quick as lightning.

And so the knocks went on, and the call was heard, and the witches entered, until at last twelve women sat round the fire—the first with one horn, the last with twelve horns.

And they carded the thread, and turned their spinning-wheels, and wound and wove, all singing together an ancient rhyme, but no word did they speak to the mistress of the house. Strange to hear, and frightful to look upon, were these twelve women, with their horns and their wheels; and the mistress felt near to death, and she tried to rise that she might call for help, but she could not move, nor could she utter a word or a cry, for the spell of the witches was upon her.

Then one of them called to her in Irish, and said, "Rise, woman, and make us a cake."

Then the mistress searched for a vessel to bring water from the well that she might mix the meal and make the cake, but she could find none.

And they said to her, "Take a sieve and bring water in it."

And she took the sieve and went to the well; but the water poured from it, and she could fetch none for the cake, and she sat down by the well and wept.

Then a voice came by her and said, " Take yellow clay and moss, and bind them together, and plaster the sieve so that it will hold."

This she did, and the sieve held the water for the cake ; and the voice said again :

" Return, and when thou comest to the north angle of the house, cry aloud three times and say, ' The mountain of the Fenian women and the sky over it is all on fire.' "

And she did so.

When the witches inside heard the call, a great and terrible cry broke from their lips, and they rushed forth with wild lamentations and shrieks, and fled away to Slievenamon, where was their chief abode. But the Spirit of the Well bade the mistress of the house to enter and prepare her home against the enchantments of the witches if they returned again.

And first, to break their spells, she sprinkled the water in which she had washed her child's feet, the feet-water, outside the door on the threshold ; secondly, she took the cake which in her absence the witches had made of meal mixed with the blood drawn from the sleeping family, and she broke the cake in bits, and placed a bit in the mouth of each sleeper, and they were restored ; and she took the cloth they had woven, and placed it half in and half out of the chest with the padlock ; and lastly, she secured the door with a great crossbeam fastened in the jambs, so that the witches could not enter, and having done these things she waited.

Not long were the witches in coming back, and they raged and called for vengeance.

" Open ! open !" they screamed ; " open, feet-water !"

" I cannot," said the feet-water ; " I am scattered on the ground, and my path is down to the Lough."

" Open, open, wood and trees and beam !" they cried to the door.

" I cannot," said the door, " for the beam is fixed in the jambs and I have no power to move."

" Open, open, cake that we have made and mingled with blood !" they cried again.

" I cannot," said the cake, " for I am broken and bruised, and my blood is on the lips of the sleeping children."

Then the witches rushed through the air with great cries, and fled back to Slievenamon, uttering strange curses on the Spirit of the Well, who had wished their ruin ; but the woman and the house were left in peace, and a mantle dropped by one of the witches in her flight was kept hung up by the mistress in memory of that night ; and this mantle was kept by the same family from generation to generation for five hundred years after.

Conall Yellowclaw

ONALL YELLOWCLAW was a sturdy tenant in Erin : he had three sons. There was at that time a king over every fifth of Erin. It fell out for the children of the king that was near Conall, that they themselves and the children of Conall came to blows. The children of Conall got the upper hand, and they killed the king's big son. The king sent a message for Conall, and he said to him—" Oh, Conall ! what made your sons go to spring on my sons till my big son was killed by your children? but I see that though I follow you revengefully, I shall not be much better for it, and I will now set a thing before you, and if you will do it, I will not follow you with revenge. If you and your sons will get me the brown horse of the king of Lochlann, you shall get the souls of your sons."

"Why," said Conall, " should not I do the pleasure of the king, though there should be no souls of my sons in dread at all. Hard is the matter you require of me, but I will lose my own life, and the life of my sons, or else I will do the pleasure of the king."

After these words Conall left the king, and he went home : when he got home he was under much trouble and perplexity. When he went to lie down he told his wife the thing the king had set before him. His wife took much sorrow that he was obliged to part from herself, while she knew not if she should see him more.

"Oh, Conall," said she, "why didst not thou let the king do his own pleasure to thy sons, rather than be going now, while I know not if ever I shall see thee more?"

When he rose on the morrow, he set himself and his three sons in order, and they took their journey towards Lochlann, and they made no stop but tore through ocean till they reached it. When they reached Lochlann they did not know what they should do. Said the old man to his sons, "Stop ye, and we will seek out the house of the king's miller."

When they went into the house of the king's miller, the man asked them to stop there for the night. Conall told the miller that his own children and the children of his king had fallen out, and that his children had killed the king's son, and there was nothing that would please the king but that he should get the brown horse of the king of Lochlann.

"If you will do me a kindness, and will put me in a way to get him, for certain I will pay ye for it."

"The thing is silly that you are come to seek," said the miller; "for the king has laid his mind on him so greatly that you will not get him in any way unless you steal him; but if you can make out a way, I will keep it secret."

"This is what I am thinking," said Conall, "since you

are working every day for the king, you and your gillies could put myself and my sons into five sacks of bran."

"The plan that has come into your head is not bad," said the miller.

The miller spoke to his gillies, and he said to them to do this, and they put them in five sacks. The king's gillies came to seek the bran, and they took the five sacks with them, and they emptied them before the horses. The servants locked the door, and they went away.

When they rose to lay hand on the brown horse, said Conall, "You shall not do that. It is hard to get out of this ; let us make for ourselves five hiding holes, so that if they hear us we may go and hide." They made the holes, then they laid hands on the horse. The horse was pretty well unbroken, and he set to making a terrible noise through the stable. The king heard the noise. "It must be my brown horse," said he to his gillies ; "find out what is wrong with him."

The servants went out, and when Conall and his sons saw them coming they went into the hiding holes. The servants looked amongst the horses, and they did not find anything wrong ; and they returned and they told this to the king, and the king said to them that if nothing was wrong they should go to their places of rest. When the gillies had time to be gone, Conall and his sons laid their hands again on the horse. If the noise was great that he made before, the noise he made now was seven times greater. The king sent a message for his gillies again, and said for certain there was something troubling the brown horse. "Go and look well about him." The servants went out, and they went to their hiding holes. The servants rum-

maged well, and did not find a thing. They returned and
they told this.

" That is marvellous for me," said the king : " go you to
lie down again, and if I notice it again I will go out myself."

When Conall and his sons perceived that the gillies were
gone, they laid hands again on the horse, and one of them
caught him, and if the noise that the horse made on the
two former times was great, he made more this time.

" Be this from me," said the king ; " it must be that
some one is troubling my brown horse." He sounded the
bell hastily, and when his waiting-man came to him, he
said to him to let the stable gillies know that something
was wrong with the horse. The gillies came, and the king
went with them. When Conall and his sons perceived the
company coming they went to the hiding holes.

The king was a wary man, and he saw where the horses
were making a noise.

" Be wary," said the king, " there are men within the
stable, let us get at them somehow."

The king followed the tracks of the men, and he found
them. Every one knew Conall, for he was a valued tenant
of the king of Erin, and when the king brought them up out
of the holes he said, " Oh, Conall, is it you that are here ? "

" I am, O king, without question, and necessity made me
come. I am under thy pardon, and under thine honour,
and under thy grace." He told how it happened to him,
and that he had to get the brown horse for the king of
Erin, or that his sons were to be put to death. " I knew
that I should not get him by asking, and I was going to
steal him."

"Yes, Conall, it is well enough, but come in," said the king. He desired his look-out men to set a watch on the sons of Conall, and to give them meat. And a double watch was set that night on the sons of Conall.

"Now, O Conall," said the king, "were you ever in a harder place than to be seeing your lot of sons hanged to-morrow? But you set it to my goodness and to my grace, and say that it was necessity brought it on you, so I must not hang you. Tell me any case in which you were as hard as this, and if you tell that, you shall get the soul of your youngest son."

"I will tell a case as hard in which I was," said Conall. "I was once a young lad, and my father had much land, and he had parks of year-old cows, and one of them had just calved, and my father told me to bring her home. I found the cow, and took her with us. There fell a shower of snow. We went into the herd's bothy, and we took the cow and the calf in with us, and we were letting the shower pass from us. Who should come in but one cat and ten, and one great one-eyed fox-coloured cat as head bard over them. When they came in, in very deed I myself had no liking for their company. 'Strike up with you,' said the head bard, 'why should we be still? and sing a cronan to Conall Yellowclaw.' I was amazed that my name was known to the cats themselves. When they had sung the cronan, said the head bard, 'Now, O Conall, pay the reward of the cronan that the cats have sung to thee.' 'Well then,' said I myself, 'I have no reward whatsoever for you, unless you should go down and take that calf.' No sooner said I the word than the two cats and ten went down to attack the calf, and in very deed, he did not last

them long. ' Play up with you, why should you be silent ?
Make a cronan to Conall Yellow,' said the head bard. Certainly I had no liking at all for the cronan, but up came the
one cat and ten, and if they did not sing me a cronan then
and there! ' Pay them now their reward,' said the great
fox-coloured cat. ' I am tired myself of yourselves and
your rewards,' said I. ' I have no reward for you unless
you take that cow down there." They betook themselves
to the cow, and indeed she did not last them long.

" ' Why will you be silent ? Go up and sing a cronan
to Conall Yellowclaw,' said the head bard. And surely, oh,
king, I had no care for them or for their cronan, for I began
to see that they were not good comrades. When they had
sung me the cronan they betook themselves down where the
head bard was. ' Pay now their reward, said the head
bard ; and for sure, oh king, I had no reward for them ;
and I said to them, ' I have no reward for you.' And
surely, oh king, there was catterwauling between them.
So I leapt out at a turf window that was at the back of the
house. I took myself off as hard as I might into the wood.
I was swift enough and strong at that time ; and when I
felt the rustling toirm of the cats after me I climbed into
as high a tree as I saw in the place, and one that was close
in the top ; and I hid myself as well as I might. The
cats began to search for me through the wood, and they
could not find me ; and when they were tired, each one said
to the other that they would turn back. ' But,' said the
one-eyed fox-coloured cat that was commander-in-chief over
them, ' you saw him not with your two eyes, and though
I have but one eye, there's the rascal up in the tree.' When
he had said that, one of them went up in the tree, and as

he was coming where I was, I drew a weapon that I had and I killed him. 'Be this from me!' said the one-eyed one—'I must not be losing my company thus; gather round the root of the tree and dig about it, and let down that villain to earth.' On this they gathered about the tree, and they dug about the root, and the first branching root that they cut, she gave a shiver to fall, and I myself gave a shout, and it was not to be wondered at. There was in the neighbourhood

of the wood a priest, and he had ten men with him delving, and he said, 'There is a shout of a man in extremity and I must not be without replying to it.' And the wisest of the men said, 'Let it alone till we hear it again.' The cats began again digging wildly, and they broke the next root; and I myself gave the next shout, and in very deed it was not a weak one. 'Certainly,' said the priest, 'it is a man in extremity—let us move.' They set themselves in order for moving. And the cats arose on the tree, and they broke the third root, and the tree fell on her elbow. Then I gave the third shout. The stalwart men hastened, and when they saw how the cats served the tree, they began at them with the spades; and they themselves and the cats began at each other, till the cats ran away. And surely, oh king, I did not move till I saw the last one of them off. And then I came home. And there's the hardest case in which I ever was; and it seems to me that tearing by the cats were harder than hanging to-morrow by the king of Lochlann."

"Och! Conall," said the king, "you are full of words. You have freed the soul of your son with your tale; and if you tell me a harder case than that you will get your second youngest son, and then you will have two sons."

"Well then," said Conall, "on condition that thou dost that, I will tell thee how I was once in a harder case than to be in thy power in prison to-night."

"Let's hear," said the king.

"I was then," said Conall, "quite a young lad, and I went out hunting, and my father's land was beside the sea, and it was rough with rocks, caves, and rifts. When I was going on the top of the shore, I saw as if there were a smoke coming up between two rocks, and I began to look what might be the meaning of the smoke coming up there. When I was looking, what should I do but fall; and the place was so full of heather, that neither bone nor skin was broken. I knew not how I should get out of this. I was not looking before me, but I kept looking overhead the way I came—and thinking that the day would never come that I could get up there. It was terrible for me to be there till I should die. I heard a great clattering coming, and what was there but a great giant and two dozen of goats with him, and a buck at their head. And when the giant had tied the goats, he came up and he said to me, 'Hao O! Conall, it's long since my knife has been rusting in my pouch waiting for thy tender flesh.' 'Och!' said I, 'it's not much you will be bettered by me, though you should tear me asunder; I will make but one meal for you. But I see that you are one-eyed. I am a good leech, and I will give you the sight of the other eye.' The giant went and he drew the great cal-dron on the site of the fire. I myself was telling him how

he should heat the water, so that I should give its sight to
the other eye. I got heather and I made a rubber of it, and
I set him upright in the caldron. I began at the eye that
was well, pretending to him that I would give its sight to
the other one, till I left them as bad as each other ; and
surely it was easier to spoil the one that was well than to
give sight to the other.

"When he saw that he could not see a glimpse, and when
I myself said to him that I would get out in spite of him,
he gave a spring out of the water, and he stood in the
mouth of the cave, and he said that he would have revenge
for the sight of his eye. I had but to stay there crouched
the length of the night, holding in my breath in such a way
that he might not find out where I was.

"When he felt the birds calling in the morning, and
knew that the day was, he said—'Art thou sleeping ?
Awake and let out my lot of goats.' I killed the buck.
He cried, 'I do believe that thou art killing my buck.'

"'I am not,' said I, 'but the ropes are so tight that I take
long to loose them.' I let out one of the goats, and there he
was caressing her, and he said to her, 'There thou art thou
shaggy, hairy white goat, and thou seest me, but I see thee
not.' I kept letting them out by the way of one and one,
as I flayed the buck, and before the last one was out I had
him flayed bag-wise. Then I went and I put my legs in
place of his legs, and my hands in place of his forelegs, and
my head in place of his head, and the horns on top of my
head, so that the brute might think that it was the buck. I
went out. When I was going out the giant laid his hand
on me, and he said, 'There thou art, thou pretty buck ;
thou seest me, but I see thee not.' When I myself got out,

and I saw the world about me, surely, oh, king! joy was on me. When I was out and had shaken the skin off me, I said to the brute, ' I am out now in spite of you.'

" ' Aha ! ' said he, ' hast thou done this to me. Since thou wert so stalwart that thou hast got out, I will give thee a ring that I have here ; keep the ring, and it will do thee good.'

" ' I will not take the ring from you,' said I, ' but throw it, and I will take it with me.' He threw the ring on the flat ground, I went myself and I lifted the ring, and I put it on my finger. When he said me then, ' Is the ring fitting thee ?' I said to him, 'It is.' Then he said, 'Where art thou, ring ?' And the ring said, ' I am here.' The brute went and went towards where the ring was speaking, and now I saw that I was in a harder case than ever I was. I drew a dirk. I cut the finger from off me, and I threw it from me as far as I could out on the loch, and there was a great depth in the place. He shouted, ' Where art thou, ring ?' And the ring said, ' I am here,' though it was on the bed of ocean. He gave a spring after the ring, and out he went in the sea. And I was as pleased then when I saw him drowning, as though you should grant my own life and the life of my two sons with me, and not lay any more trouble on me.

" When the giant was drowned I went in, and I took with me all he had of gold and silver, and I went home, and surely great joy was on my people when I arrived. And as a sign now look, the finger is off me."

" Yes, indeed, Conall, you are wordy and wise," said the king. " I see the finger is off you. You have freed your two sons, but tell me a case in which you ever were that is harder than to be looking on your son being hanged to-morrow, and you shall get the soul of your eldest son."

"Then went my father," said Conall, "and he got me a wife, and I was married. I went to hunt. I was going beside the sea, and I saw an island over in the midst of the loch, and I came there where a boat was with a rope before her, and a rope behind her, and many precious things within her. I looked myself on the boat to see how I might get part of them. I put in the one foot, and the other foot was on the ground, and when I raised my head what was it but the boat over in the middle of the loch, and she never stopped till she reached the island. When I went out of the boat the boat returned where she was before. I did not know now what I should do. The place was without meat or clothing, without the appearance of a house on it. I came out on the top of a hill. Then I came to a glen ; I saw in it, at the bottom of a hollow, a woman with a child, and the child was naked on her knee, and she had a knife in her hand. She tried to put the knife to the throat of the babe, and the babe began to laugh in her face, and she began to cry, and she threw the knife behind her. I thought to myself that I was near my foe and far from my friends, and I called to the woman, 'What are you doing here ?' And she said to me, 'What brought you here ?' I told her myself word upon word how I came. 'Well then,' said she, 'it was so I came also.' She showed me to the place where I should come in where she was. I went in, and I said to her, 'What was the matter that you were putting the knife on the neck of the child ?' 'It is that he must be cooked for the giant who is here, or else no more of my world will be before me.' Just then we could be hearing the footsteps of the giant, 'What shall I do? what shall I do?' cried the woman. I went to the caldron, and by luck it was not hot, so in it I got just as the brute came in. 'Hast thou boiled that youngster for me?' he cried. 'He's not done yet,' said she, and I cried out from the caldron, 'Mammy, mammy, it's boiling I am.' Then the giant laughed out HAI, HAW, HOGARAICH, and heaped on wood under the caldron.

"And now I was sure I would scald before I could get out of that. As fortune favoured me, the brute slept beside the caldron. There I was scalded by the bottom of the caldron. When she perceived that he was asleep, she set her mouth quietly to the hole that was in the lid, and she said to me 'was I alive?' I said I was. I put up my head, and the hole in the lid was so large, that my head went through easily. Everything was coming easily with me till I began to bring up my hips. I left the skin of my hips behind me, but I came out. When I got out of the caldron I knew not what to do; and she said to me that there was no weapon that would kill him but his own weapon. I began to draw his spear and every breath that he drew I thought I would be down his throat, and when his breath came out I was back again just as far. But with every ill that befell me I got the spear loosed from him. Then I was as one under a bundle of straw in a great wind for I could not manage the spear. And it was fearful to look on the brute, who had but one eye in the midst of his face; and it was not agreeable for the like of me to attack him. I drew the dart as best I could, and I set it in his eye. When he felt this he gave his head a lift, and he struck the other end of the dart on the top of the cave, and it went through to the back of his head. And he fell cold dead where he was ; and you may be sure, oh king, that joy was on me. I myself and the woman went out on clear ground, and we passed the night there. I went and got the boat with which I came, and she was no way lightened, and took the woman and the child over on dry land ; and I returned home."

The king of Lochlann's mother was putting on a fire at this time, and listening to Conall telling the tale about the child.

"Is it you," said she, "that were there ? "

"Well then," said he, "'twas I."

"Och! och!" said she, "'twas I that was there, and the king is the child whose life you saved ; and it is to you that life thanks should be given." Then they took great joy.

The king said, "Oh, Conall, you came through great hardships. And now the brown horse is yours, and his sack full of the most precious things that are in my treasury."

They lay down that night, and if it was early that Conall rose, it was earlier than that that the queen was on foot making ready. He got the brown horse and his sack full of gold and silver and stones of great price, and then Conall and his three sons went away, and they returned home to the Erin realm of gladness. He left the gold and silver in his house, and he went with the horse to the king. They were good friends evermore. He returned home to his wife, and they set in order a feast ; and that was a feast if ever there was one, oh son and brother.

Hudden and Dudden and
Donald O'Neary

THERE was once upon a time two farmers, and
their names were Hudden and Dudden.
They had poultry in their yards, sheep on
the uplands, and scores of cattle in the
meadow-land alongside the river.   But for
all that they weren't happy.   For just between their two
farms there lived a poor man by the name of Donald
O'Neary.   He had a hovel over his head and a strip of
grass that was barely enough to keep his one cow, Daisy,
from starving, and, though she did her best, it was but
seldom that Donald got a drink of milk or a roll of butter
from Daisy.   You would think there was little here to make

Hudden and Dudden jealous, but so it is, the more one has the more one wants, and Donald's neighbours lay awake of nights scheming how they might get hold of his little strip of grass-land. Daisy, poor thing, they never thought of; she was just a bag of bones.

One day Hudden met Dudden, and they were soon grumbling as usual, and all to the tune of " If only we could get that vagabond Donald O'Neary out of the country."

" Let's kill Daisy," said Hudden at last ; " if that doesn't make him clear out, nothing will."

No sooner said than agreed, and it wasn't dark before Hudden and Dudden crept up to the little shed where lay poor Daisy trying her best to chew the cud, though she hadn't had as much grass in the day as would cover your hand. And when Donald came to see if Daisy was all snug for the night, the poor beast had only time to lick his hand once before she died.

Well, Donald was a shrewd fellow, and downhearted though he was, began to think if he could get any good out of Daisy's death. He thought and he thought, and the next day you could have seen him trudging off early to the fair, Daisy's hide over his shoulder, every penny he had jingling in his pockets. Just before he got to the fair, he made several slits in the hide, put a penny in each slit, walked into the best inn of the town as bold as if it belonged to him, and, hanging the hide up to a nail in the wall, sat down.

" Some of your best whisky," says he to the landlord. But the landlord didn't like his looks. " Is it fearing I won't pay you, you are?" says Donald ; " why I have a hide here that gives me all the money I want." And with

that he hit it a whack with his stick and out hopped a
penny. The landlord opened his eyes, as you may fancy.

" What'll you take for that hide ? "

" It's not for sale, my good man."

" Will you take a gold piece ?"

" It's not for sale, I tell you. Hasn't it kept me and
mine for years ? " and with that Donald hit the hide
another whack and out jumped a second penny.

Well, the long and the short of it was that Donald let the
hide go, and, that very evening, who but he should walk
up to Hudden's door ?

" Good-evening, Hudden. Will you lend me your best
pair of scales ? "

Hudden stared and Hudden scratched his head, but he
lent the scales.

When Donald was safe at home, he pulled out his
pocketful of bright gold and began to weigh each piece in
the scales. But Hudden had put a lump of butter at the
bottom, and so the last piece of gold stuck fast to the
scales when he took them back to Hudden.

If Hudden had stared before, he stared ten times more
now, and no sooner was Donald's back turned, than he
was off as hard as he could pelt to Dudden's.

" Good-evening, Dudden. That vagabond, bad luck to
him ——"

" You mean Donald O'Neary ?"

" And who else should I mean ? He's back here weighing
out sackfuls of gold."

" How do you know that ?"

" Here are my scales that he borrowed, and here's a gold
piece still sticking to them."

Off they went together, and they came to Donald's door. Donald had finished making the last pile of ten gold pieces. And he couldn't finish because a piece had stuck to the scales.

In they walked without an " If you please " or " By your leave."

" Well, *I* never !" that was all *they* could say.

" Good-evening, Hudden ; good-evening, Dudden. Ah ! you thought you had played me a fine trick, but you never did me a better turn in all your lives. When I found poor Daisy dead, I thought to myself, ' Well, her hide may fetch something ; ' and it did. Hides are worth their weight in gold in the market just now."

Hudden nudged Dudden, and Dudden winked at Hudden.

" Good-evening, Donald O'Neary."

" Good-evening, kind friends."

The next day there wasn't a cow or a calf that belonged to Hudden or Dudden but her hide was going to the fair in Hudden's biggest cart drawn by Dudden's strongest pair of horses.

When they came to the fair, each one took a hide over his arm, and there they were walking through the fair, bawling out at the top of their voices : ' Hides to sell! hides to sell!'"

Out came the tanner :

" How much for your hides, my good men ?"

" Their weight in gold."

" It's early in the day to come out of the tavern." That was all the tanner said, and back he went to his yard.

" Hides to sell !   Fine fresh hides to sell!"

Out came the cobbler.

" How much for your hides, my men ? "

" Their weight in gold."

" Is it making game of me you are !   Take that for your pains," and the cobbler dealt Hudden a blow that made him stagger.

Up the people came running from one end of the fair to the other.   " What's the matter ?   What's the matter?" cried they.

" Here are a couple of vagabonds selling hides at their weight in gold," said the cobbler.

" Hold 'em fast ; hold 'em fast!" bawled the innkeeper, who was the last to come up, he was so fat.   " I'll wager it's one of the rogues who tricked me out of thirty gold pieces yesterday for a wretched hide."

It was more kicks than halfpence that Hudden and
Dudden got before they were well on their way home again,
and they didn't run the slower because all the dogs of the
town were at their heels.

Well, as you may fancy, if they loved Donald little
before, they loved him less now.

"What's the matter, friends?" said he, as he saw them
tearing along, their hats knocked in, and their coats torn
off, and their faces black and blue. "Is it fighting you've
been? or mayhap you met the police, ill luck to them?"

"We'll police you, you vagabond. It's mighty smart
you thought yourself, deluding us with your lying tales."

"Who deluded you? Didn't you see the gold with
your own two eyes?"

But it was no use talking. Pay for it he must, and
should. There was a meal-sack handy, and into it Hudden
and Dudden popped Donald O'Neary, tied him up tight,
ran a pole through the knot, and off they started for the
Brown Lake of the Bog, each with a pole-end on his
shoulder, and Donald O'Neary between.

But the Brown Lake was far, the road was dusty,
Hudden and Dudden were sore and weary, and parched
with thirst. There was an inn by the roadside.

"Let's go in," said Hudden; "I'm dead beat. It's
heavy he is for the little he had to eat."

If Hudden was willing, so was Dudden. As for Donald,
you may be sure his leave wasn't asked, but he was lumped
down at the inn door for all the world as if he had been
a sack of potatoes.

"Sit still, you vagabond," said Dudden; "if we don't
mind waiting, you needn't."

Donald held his peace, but after a while he heard the glasses clink, and Hudden singing away at the top of his voice.

" I won't have her, I tell you ; I won't have her !" said Donald. But nobody heeded what he said.

" I won't have her, I tell you ; I won't have her !" said Donald, and this time he said it louder ; but nobody heeded what he said.

" I won't have her, I tell you ; I won't have her !" said Donald ; and this time he said it as loud as he could.

" And who won't you have, may I be so bold as to ask ?" said a farmer, who had just come up with a drove of cattle, and was turning in for a glass.

" It's the king's daughter. They are bothering the life out of me to marry her."

" You're the lucky fellow. I'd give something to be in your shoes."

" Do you see that now ! Wouldn't it be a fine thing for a farmer to be marrying a princess, all dressed in gold and jewels ?"

" Jewels, do you say ? Ah, now, couldn't you take me with you ?"

" Well, you're an honest fellow, and as I don't care for the king's daughter, though she's as beautiful as the day, and is covered with jewels from top to toe, you shall have her. Just undo the cord, and let me out ; they tied me up tight, as they knew I'd run away from her."

Out crawled Donald ; in crept the farmer.

" Now lie still, and don't mind the shaking ; it's only rumbling over the palace steps you'll be. And maybe they'll abuse you for a vagabond, who won't have the

king's daughter; but you needn't mind that. Ah! it's a
deal I'm giving up for you, sure as it is that I don't care
for the princess."

"Take my cattle in exchange," said the farmer; and you
may guess it wasn't long before Donald was at their tails
driving them homewards.

Out came Hudden and Dudden, and the one took one
end of the pole, and the other the other.

"I'm thinking he's heavier," said Hudden.

"Ah, never mind," said Dudden; "it's only a step now
to the Brown Lake."

"I'll have her now! I'll have her now!" bawled the
farmer, from inside the sack.

"By my faith, and you shall though," said Hudden, and
he laid his stick across the sack.

"I'll have her! I'll have her!" bawled the farmer, louder
than ever.

"Well, here you are," said Dudden, for they were now
come to the Brown Lake, and, unslinging the sack, they
pitched it plump into the lake.

"You'll not be playing your tricks on us any longer,"
said Hudden.

"True for you," said Dudden. "Ah, Donald, my boy,
it was an ill day when you borrowed my scales."

Off they went, with a light step and an easy heart, but
when they were near home, who should they see but
Donald O'Neary, and all around him the cows were
grazing, and the calves were kicking up their heels and
butting their heads together.

"Is it you, Donald?" said Dudden. "Faith, you've
been quicker than we have."

"True for you, Dudden, and let me thank you kindly; the turn was good, if the will was ill. You'll have heard, like me, that the Brown Lake leads to the Land of Promise. I always put it down as lies, but it is just as true as my word. Look at the cattle."

Hudden stared, and Dudden gaped; but they couldn't get over the cattle; fine fat cattle they were too.

"It's only the worst I could bring up with me," said Donald O'Neary; "the others were so fat, there was no driving them. Faith, too, it's little wonder they didn't care to leave, with grass as far as you could see, and as sweet and juicy as fresh butter."

"Ah, now, Donald, we haven't always been friends," said Dudden, "but, as I was just saying, you were ever a decent lad, and you'll show us the way, won't you?"

"I don't see that I'm called upon to do that; there is a power more cattle down there. Why shouldn't I have them all to myself?"

"Faith, they may well say, the richer you get, the harder the heart. You always were a neighbourly lad, Donald. You wouldn't wish to keep the luck all to yourself?"

"True for you, Hudden, though 'tis a bad example you set me. But I'll not be thinking of old times. There is plenty for all there, so come along with me."

Off they trudged, with a light heart and an eager step. When they came to the Brown Lake, the sky was full of little white clouds, and, if the sky was full, the lake was as full.

"Ah! now, look, there they are," cried Donald, as he pointed to the clouds in the lake.

"Where? where?" cried Hudden, and "Don't be greedy!"

cried Dudden, as he jumped his hardest to be up first with the fat cattle. But if he jumped first, Hudden wasn't long behind.

They never came back. Maybe they got too fat, like the cattle. As for Donald O'Neary, he had cattle and sheep all his days to his heart's content.

The Shepherd of Myddvai

U P in the Black Mountains in Caermarthenshire lies the lake known as Lyn y Van Vach. To the margin of this lake the shepherd of Myddvai once led his lambs, and lay there whilst they sought pasture. Suddenly, from the dark waters of the lake, he saw three maidens rise. Shaking the bright drops from their hair and gliding to the shore, they wandered about amongst his flock. They had more than mortal beauty, and he was filled with love for her that came nearest to him. He offered her the

bread he had with him, and she took it and tried it, but
then sang to him :

> Hard-baked is thy bread,
> 'Tis not easy to catch me,

and then ran off laughing to the lake.

Next day he took with him bread not so well done, and
watched for the maidens. When they came ashore he
offered his bread as before, and the maiden tasted it and
sang :

> Unbaked is thy bread,
> I will not have thee,

and again disappeared in the waves.

A third time did the shepherd of Myddvai try to attract
the maiden, and this time he offered her bread that he had
found floating about near the shore. This pleased her,
and she promised to become his wife if he were able
to pick her out from among her sisters on the following day.
When the time came the shepherd knew his love by the
strap of her sandal. Then she told him she would be as
good a wife to him as any earthly maiden could be unless
he should strike her three times without cause. Of course
he deemed that this could never be ; and she, summoning from the lake three cows, two oxen, and a bull, as
her marriage portion, was led homeward by him as his
bride.

The years passed happily, and three children were born
to the shepherd and the lake-maiden. But one day
here were going to a christening, and she said to her
husband it was far to walk, so he told her to go for the
horses.

" I will," said she, " if you bring me my gloves which I've left in the house."

But when he came back with the gloves, he found she had not gone for the horses ; so he tapped her lightly on the shoulder with the gloves, and said, "Go, go."

" That's one," said she.

Another time they were at a wedding, when suddenly the lake-maiden fell a-sobbing and a-weeping, amid the joy and mirth of all around her.

Her husband tapped her on the shoulder, and asked her, " Why do you weep ? "

" Because they are entering into trouble ; and trouble is upon you ; for that is the second causeless blow you have given me. Be careful ; the third is the last."

The husband was careful never to strike her again. But one day at a funeral she suddenly burst out into fits of laughter. Her husband forgot, and touched her rather roughly on the shoulder, saying, " Is this a time for laughter ? "

" I laugh," she said, " because those that die go out of trouble, but your trouble has come. The last blow has been struck ; our marriage is at an end, and so farewell." And with that she rose up and left the house and went to their home.

Then she, looking round upon her home, called to the cattle she had brought with her :

> Brindle cow, white speckled,
> Spotted cow, bold freckled,
> Old white face, and gray Geringer,
> And the white bull from the king's coast,
> Grey ox, and black calf,
> All, all, follow me home,

Now the black calf had just been slaughtered, and was hanging on the hook ; but it got off the hook alive and well and followed her ; and the oxen, though they were ploughing, trailed the plough with them and did her bidding. So she fled to the lake again, they following her, and with them plunged into the dark waters. And to this day is the furrow seen which the plough left as it was dragged across the mountains to the tarn.

Only once did she come again, when her sons were grown to manhood, and then she gave them gifts of healing by which they won the name of Meddygon Myddvai, the physicians of Myddvai.

The Sprightly Tailor

SPRIGHTLY tailor was employed by the great Macdonald, in his castle at Saddell, in order to make the laird a pair of trews, used in olden time.   And trews being the vest and breeches united in one piece, and ornamented with fringes, were very comfortable, and suitable to be worn in walkin or dancing.   And Macdonald had said to the tailor, that if he would make the trews by night in the church, he would get a handsome reward. For it was thought that the old ruined church was haunted, and that fearsome things were to be seen there at night.

The tailor was well aware of this ; but he was a sprightly man, and when the laird dared him to make the trews by night in the church, the tailor was not to be daunted, but took it in hand to gain the prize. So, when night came, away he went up the glen, about half a mile distance from the castle, till he came to the old church. Then he chose him a nice gravestone for a seat and he lighted his candle, and put on his thimble, and set to work at the trews ; plying his needle nimbly, and thinking about the hire that the laird would have to give him.

For some time he got on pretty well, until he felt the floor all of a tremble under his feet ; and looking about him, but keeping his fingers at work, he saw the appearance of a great human head rising up through the stone pavement of the church. And when the head had risen above the surface, there came from it a great, great voice. And the voice said : " Do you see this great head of mine ? "

" I see that, but I'll sew this ! " replied the sprightly tailor ; and he stitched away at the trews.

Then the head rose higher up through the pavement, until its neck appeared. And when its neck was shown, the thundering voice came again and said : " Do you see this great neck of mine ? "

" I see that, but I'll sew this ! " said the sprightly tailor ; and he stitched away at his trews.

Then the head and neck rose higher still, until the great shoulders and chest were shown above the ground. And again the mighty voice thundered : " Do you see this great chest of mine ? "

And again the sprightly tailor replied : " I see that, but I'll sew this ! " and stitched away at his trews.

And still it kept rising through the pavement, until it

shook a great pair of arms in the tailor's face, and said :
" Do you see these great arms of mine ? "

" I see those, but I'll sew this ! " answered the tailor ;
and he stitched hard at his trews, for he knew that he had
no time to lose.

The sprightly tailor was taking the long stitches, when he
saw it gradually rising and rising through the floor, until it
lifted out a great leg, and stamping with it upon the pavement, said in a roaring voice : " Do you see this great leg
of mine ? "

" Aye, aye : I see that, but I'll sew this ! " cried the
tailor ; and his fingers flew with the needle, and he took
such long stitches, that he was just come to the end of the
trews, when it was taking up its other leg. But before it
could pull it out of the pavement, the sprightly tailor had
finished his task ; and, blowing out his candle, and springing
from off his gravestone, he buckled up, and ran out of the
church with the trews under his arm. Then the fearsome
thing gave a loud roar, and stamped with both his feet upon
the pavement, and out of the church he went after the
sprightly tailor.

Down the glen they ran, faster than the stream when the
flood rides it ; but the tailor had got the start and a nimble
pair of legs, and he did not choose to lose the laird's reward.
And though the thing roared to him to stop, yet the
sprightly tailor was not the man to be beholden to a
monster. So he held his trews tight, and let no darkness
grow under his feet, until he had reached Saddell Castle.
He had no sooner got inside the gate, and shut it, than the
apparition came up to it ; and, enraged at losing his prize,
struck the wall above the gate, and left there the mark of

his five great fingers. Ye may see them plainly to this day, if ye'll only peer close enough.

But the sprightly tailor gained his reward : for Macdonald paid him handsomely for the trews, and never discovered that a few of the stitches were somewhat long.

The Story of Deirdre

THERE was a man in Ireland once who was called Malcolm Harper. The man was a right good man, and he had a goodly share of this world's goods. He had a wife, but no family. What did Malcolm hear but that a soothsayer had come home to the place, and as the man was a right good man, he wished that the soothsayer might come near them. Whether it was that he was invited or that he came of himself, the soothsayer came to the house of Malcolm.

" Are you doing any soothsaying ? " says Malcolm.

" Yes, I am doing a little. Are you in need of soothsaying ? "

" Well, I do not mind taking soothsaying from you, if you had soothsaying for me, and you would be willing to do it."

" Well, I will do soothsaying for you. What kind of soothsaying do you want ? "

" Well, the soothsaying I wanted was that you would tell me my lot or what will happen to me, if you can give me knowledge of it ."

" Well, I am going out, and when I return, I will tell you."

And the soothsayer went forth out of the house and he was not long outside when he returned.

" Well," said the soothsayer, " I saw in my second sight that it is on account of a daughter of yours that the greatest amount of blood shall be shed that has ever been shed in Erin since time and race began. And the three most famous heroes that ever were found will lose their heads on her account."

After a time a daughter was born to Malcolm, he did not allow a living being to come to his house, only himself and the nurse. He asked this woman, " Will you yourself bring up the child to keep her in hiding far away where eye will not see a sight of her nor ear hear a word about her?"

The woman said she would, so Malcolm got three men, and he took them away to a large mountain, distant and far from reach, without the knowledge or notice of any one. He caused there a hillock, round and green, to be dug out of the middle, and the hole thus made to be covered care-

fully over so that a little company could dwell there together.
This was done.

Deirdre and her foster-mother dwelt in the bothy mid
the hills without the knowledge or the suspicion of any living
person about them and without anything occurring, until
Deirdre was sixteen years of age. Deirdre grew like the
white sapling, straight and trim as the rash on the moss.
She was the creature of fairest form, of loveliest aspect, and
of gentlest nature that existed between earth and heaven in
all Ireland——whatever colour of hue she had before, there
was nobody that looked into her face but she would blush
fiery red over it.

The woman that had charge of her, gave Deirdre every
information and skill of which she herself had knowledge
and skill. There was not a blade of grass growing from
root, nor a bird singing in the wood, nor a star shining from
heaven but Deirdre had a name for it. But one thing, she
did not wish her to have either part or parley with any
single living man of the rest of the world. But on a gloomy
winter night, with black, scowling clouds, a hunter of game
was wearily travelling the hills, and what happened but
that he missed the trail of the hunt, and lost his course and
companions. A drowsiness came upon the man as he
wearily wandered over the hills, and he lay down by the
side of the beautiful green knoll in which Deirdre lived, and
he slept. The man was faint from hunger and wandering,
and benumbed with cold, and a deep sleep fell upon him.
When he lay down beside the green hill where Deirdre was,
a troubled dream came to the man, and he thought that he
enjoyed the warmth of a fairy broch, the fairies being inside
playing music. The hunter shouted out in his dream, if there

was any one in the broch, to let him in for the Holy One's sake. Deirdre heard the voice and said to her foster-mother: "O foster-mother, what cry is that?" "It is nothing at all, Deirdre—merely the birds of the air astray and seeking each other. But let them go past to the bosky glade. There is no shelter or house for them here." "Oh, foster-mother, the bird asked to get inside for the sake of the God of the Elements, and you yourself tell me that anything that is asked in His name we ought to do. If you will not allow the bird that is being benumbed with cold, and done to death with hunger, to be let in, I do not think much of your language or your faith. But since I give credence to your language and to your faith, which you taught me, I will myself let in the bird." And Deirdre arose and drew the bolt from the leaf of the door, and she let in the hunter. She placed a seat in the place for sitting, food in the place for eating, and drink in the place for drinking for the man who came to the house. "Oh, for this life and raiment, you man that came in, keep restraint on your tongue!" said the old woman. "It is not a great thing for you to keep your mouth shut and your tongue quiet when you get a home and shelter of a hearth on a gloomy winter's night." "Well," said the hunter, "I may do that—keep my mouth shut and my tongue quiet, since I came to the house and received hospitality from you; but by the hand of thy father and grandfather, and by your own two hands, if some other of the people of the world saw this beauteous creature you have here hid away, they would not long leave her with you, I swear."

"What men are these you refer to?" said Deirdre.

"Well, I will tell you, young woman," said the hunter.

"They are Naois, son of Uisnech, and Allen and Arden his two brothers."

"What like are these men when seen, if we were to see them?" said Deirdre.

"Why, the aspect and form of the men when seen are these," said the hunter: "they have the colour of the raven on their hair, their skin like swan on the wave in whiteness, and their cheeks as the blood of the brindled red calf, and their speed and their leap are those of the salmon of the torrent and the deer of the grey mountain side. And Naois is head and shoulders over the rest of the people of Erin."

"However they are," said the nurse, "be you off from here and take another road. And, King of Light and Sun! in good sooth and certainty, little are my thanks for yourself or for her that let you in!"

The hunter went away, and went straight to the palace of King Connachar. He sent word in to the king that he wished to speak to him if he pleased. The king answered the message and came out to speak to the man. "What is the reason of your journey?" said the king to the hunter.

"I have only to tell you, O king," said the hunter, "that I saw the fairest creature that ever was born in Erin, and I came to tell you of it."

"Who is this beauty and where is she to be seen, when she was not seen before till you saw her, if you did see her?"

"Well, I did see her," said the hunter. "But, if I did, no man else can see her unless he get directions from me as to where she is dwelling."

"And will you direct me to where she dwells? and the

reward of your directing me will be as good as the reward of your message," said the king.

"Well, I will direct you, O king, although it is likely that this will not be what they want," said the hunter.

Connachar, King of Ulster, sent for his nearest kinsmen, and he told them of his intent. Though early rose the song of the birds mid the rocky caves and the music of the birds in the grove, earlier than that did Connachar, King of Ulster, arise, with his little troop of dear friends, in the delightful twilight of the fresh and gentle May; the dew was heavy on each bush and flower and stem, as they went to bring Deirdre forth from the green knoll where she stayed. Many a youth was there who had a lithe leaping and lissom step when they started whose step was faint, failing, and faltering when they reached the bothy on account of the length of the way and roughness of the road. "Yonder, now, down in the bottom of the glen is the bothy where the woman dwells, but I will not go nearer than this to the old woman," said the hunter.

Connachar with his band of kinsfolk went down to the green knoll where Deirdre dwelt and he knocked at the door of the bothy. The nurse replied, "No less than a king's command and a king's army could put me out of my bothy to-night. And I should be obliged to you, were you to tell who it is that wants me to open my bothy door." "It is I, Connachar, King of Ulster." When the poor woman heard who was at the door, she rose with haste and let in the king and all that could get in of his retinue.

When the king saw the woman that was before him that he had been in quest of, he thought he never saw in the course of the day nor in the dream of night a creature so fair as Deirdre and he gave his full heart's weight of love to her. Deirdre was raised on the topmost of the heroes' shoulders and she and her foster-mother were brought to the Court of King Connachar of Ulster.

With the love that Connachar had for her, he wanted to marry Deirdre right off there and then, will she nill she marry him. But she said to him, " I would be obliged to you if you will give me the respite of a year and a day." He said " I will grant you that, hard though it is, if you will give me your unfailing promise that you will marry me at the year's end." And she gave the promise. Connachar got for her a woman-teacher and merry modest maidens fair that would lie down and rise with her, that would play and speak with her. Deirdre was clever in maidenly duties and wifely understanding, and Connachar thought he never saw with bodily eye a creature that pleased him more.

Deirdre and her women companions were one day out on the hillock behind the house enjoying the scene, and drinking in the sun's heat. What did they see coming but three men a-journeying. Deirdre was looking at the men that were coming, and wondering at them. When the men neared them, Deirdre remembered the language of the huntsman, and she said to herself that these were the three sons of Uisnech, and that this was Naois, he having what was above the bend of the two shoulders above the men of Erin all. The three brothers went past without taking any notice of them, without even glancing at the young girls on the hillock. What happened but that love for Naois struck the heart of Deirdre, so that she could not but follow after him. She girded up her raiment and went after the men that went past the base of the knoll, leaving her women attendants there. Allen and Arden had heard of the woman that Connachar, King of Ulster, had with him, and they thought that, if Naois, their brother, saw her, he would have her himself, more especially as she was not married to the King. They perceived the woman coming, and called on one another to hasten their step as they had a long distance to travel, and the dusk of night was coming on. They did so. She cried: " Naois, son of Uisnech, will you leave me ? " " What piercing, shrill cry is that—the most melodious my ear ever heard, and the shrillest that ever struck my heart of all the cries I ever heard ? " " It is anything else but the wail of the wave-swans of Connachar," said his brothers. " No! yonder is a woman's cry of distress," said Naois, and he swore he would not go further until he saw from whom the cry came, and Naois turned back. Naois and Deirdre met, and Deirdre kissed Naois three times, and a kiss each to his brothers. With the confusion that she was in, Deirdre went into a crimson blaze of fire, and her colour came and went as rapidly as the movement of the aspen by the stream side. Naois thought he never saw a fairer creature, and Naois gave Deirdre the love that he never gave to thing, to vision, or to creature but to herself.

Then Naois placed Deirdre on the topmost height of his shoulder, and told his brothers to keep up their pace, and they kept up their pace. Naois thought that it would not be well for him to remain in Erin on account of the way in which Connachar, King of Ulster, his uncle's son, had gone against him because of the woman, though he had not married her ; and he turned back to Alba, that is, Scotland. He reached the side of Loch-Ness and made

his habitation there. He could kill the salmon of the
torrent from out his own door, and the deer of the grey
gorge from out his window. Naois and Deirdre and Allen
and Arden dwelt in a tower, and they were happy so long
a time as they were there.

By this time the end of the period came at which Deirdre
had to marry Connachar, King of Ulster. Connachar made
up his mind to take Deirdre away by the sword whether
she was married to Naois or not. So he prepared a great
and gleeful feast. He sent word far and wide through
Erin all to his kinspeople to come to the feast. Connachar
thought to himself that Naois would not come though he
should bid him; and the scheme that arose in his mind
was to send for his father's brother, Ferchar Mac Ro, and
to send him on an embassy to Naois. He did so; and
Connachar said to Ferchar, " Tell Naois, son of Uisnech,
that I am setting forth a great and gleeful feast to my
friends and kinspeople throughout the wide extent of Erin
all, and that I shall not have rest by day nor sleep by night
if he and Allen and Arden be not partakers of the feast."

Ferchar Mac Ro and his three sons went on their journey,
and reached the tower where Naois was dwelling by the
side of Loch Etive. The sons of Uisnech gave a cordial
kindly welcome to Ferchar Mac Ro and his three sons, and
asked of him the news of Erin. " The best news that I
have for you," said the hardy hero, " is that Connachar,
King of Ulster, is setting forth a great sumptuous feast to
his friends and kinspeople throughout the wide extent of
Erin all, and he has vowed by the earth beneath him, by
the high heaven above him, and by the sun that wends to
the west, that he will have no rest by day nor sleep by

night if the sons of Uisnech, the sons of his own father's brother, will not come back to the land of their home and the soil of their nativity, and to the feast likewise, and he has sent us on embassy to invite you."

" We will go with you," said Naois.

" We will," said his brothers.

But Deirdre did not wish to go with Ferchar Mac Ro, and she tried every prayer to turn Naois from going with him—she said :

" I saw a vision, Naois, and do you interpret it to me," said Deirdre—then she sang :

> O Naois, son of Uisnech, hear
> What was shown in a dream to me.
>
> There came three white doves out of the South
> Flying over the sea,
> And drops of honey were in their mouth
> From the hive of the honey-bee.
>
> O Naois, son of Uisnech, hear,
> What was shown in a dream to me.
>
> I saw three grey hawks out of the south
> Come flying over the sea,
> And the red red drops they bare in their mouth
> They were dearer than life to me.

Said Naois :—

> It is nought but the fear of woman's heart,
> And a dream of the night, Deirdre.

" The day that Connachar sent the invitation to his feast will be unlucky for us if we don't go, O Deirdre."

" You will go there," said Ferchar Mac Ro ; " and if Connachar show kindness to you, show ye kindness to him ; and if he will display wrath towards you display ye wrath towards him, and I and my three sons will be with you."

"We will," said Daring Drop. "We will," said Hardy Holly. "We will," said Fiallan the Fair.

"I have three sons, and they are three heroes, and in any harm or danger that may befall you, they will be with you, and I myself will be along with them." And Ferchar Mac Ro gave his vow and his word in presence of his arms that, in any harm or danger that came in the way of the sons of Uisnech, he and his three sons would not leave head on live body in Erin, despite sword or helmet, spear or shield, blade or mail, be they ever so good.

Deirdre was unwilling to leave Alba, but she went with Naois. Deirdre wept tears in showers and she sang :

> Dear is the land, the land over there,
>> Alba full of woods and lakes ;
> Bitter to my heart is leaving thee,
> But I go away with Naois.

Ferchar Mac Ro did not stop till he got the sons of Uisnech away with him, despite the suspicion of Deirdre.

> The coracle was put to sea,
>> The sail was hoisted to it ;
> And the second morrow they arrived
> On the white shores of Erin.

As soon as the sons of Uisnech landed in Erin, Ferchar Mac Ro sent word to Connachar, king of Ulster, that the men whom he wanted were come, and let him now show kindness to them. "Well," said Connachar, "I did not expect that the sons of Uisnech would come, though I sent for them, and I am not quite ready to receive them. But there is a house down yonder where I keep strangers, and let them go down to it to-day, and my house will be ready before them to-morrow."

But he that was up in the palace felt it long that he was not getting word as to how matters were going on for those down in the house of the strangers. " Go you, Gelban Grednach, son of Lochlin's King, go you down and bring me information as to whether her former hue and complexion are on Deirdre. If they be, I will take her out with edge of blade and point of sword, and if not, let Naois, son of Uisnech, have her for himself," said Connachar.

Gelban, the cheering and charming son of Lochlin's King, went down to the place of the strangers, where the sons of Uisnech and Deirdre were staying. He looked in through the bicker-hole on the door-leaf. Now she that he gazed upon used to go into a crimson blaze of blushes when any one looked at her. Naois looked at Deirdre and knew that some one was looking at her from the back of the door-leaf. He seized one of the dice on the table before him and fired it through the bicker-hole, and knocked the eye out of Gelban Grednach the Cheerful and Charming, right through the back of his head. Gelban returned back to the palace of King Connachar.

" You were cheerful, charming, going away, but you are cheerless, charmless, returning. What has happened to you, Gelban ? But have you seen her, and are Deirdre's hue and complexion as before ? " said Connachar.

" Well, I have seen Deirdre, and I saw her also truly, and while I was looking at her through the bicker-hole on the door, Naois, son of Uisnech, knocked out my eye with one of the dice in his hand. But of a truth and verity, although he put out even my eye, it were my desire still to remain looking at her with the other eye, were it not for the hurry you told me to be in," said Gelban.

"That is true," said Connachar; "let three hundred brave heroes go down to the abode of the strangers, and let them bring hither to me Deirdre, and kill the rest."

Connachar ordered three hundred active heroes to go down to the abode of the strangers and to take Deirdre up with them and kill the rest. "The pursuit is coming," said Deirdre.

"Yes, but I will myself go out and stop the pursuit," said Naois.

"It is not you, but we that will go," said Daring Drop, and Hardy Holly, and Fiallan the Fair; "it is to us that our father entrusted your defence from harm and danger when he himself left for home." And the gallant youths, full noble, full manly, full handsome, with beauteous brown locks, went forth girt with battle arms fit for fierce fight and clothed with combat dress for fierce contest fit, which was burnished, bright, brilliant, bladed, blazing, on which were many pictures of beasts and birds and creeping things, lions and lithe-limbed tigers, brown eagle and harrying hawk and adder fierce; and the young heroes laid low three-thirds of the company.

Connachar came out in haste and cried with wrath: "Who is there on the floor of fight, slaughtering my men?"

"We, the three sons of Ferchar Mac Ro."

"Well," said the king, "I will give a free bridge to your grandfather, a free bridge to your father, and a free bridge each to you three brothers, if you come over to my side to-night."

" Well, Connachar, we will not accept that offer from you nor thank you for it. Greater by far do we prefer to go home to our father and tell the deeds of heroism we have done, than accept anything on these terms from you. Naois, son of Uisnech, and Allen and Arden are as nearly related to yourself as they are to us, though you are so keen to shed their blood, and you would shed our blood also, Connachar." And the noble, manly, handsome youths with beauteous, brown locks returned inside. " We are now," said they, " going home to tell our father that you are now safe from the hands of the king." And the youths all fresh and tall and lithe and beautiful, went home to their father to tell that the sons of Uisnech were safe. This happened at the parting of the day and night in the morning twilight time, and Naois said they must go away, leave that house, and return to Alba.

Naois and Deirdre, Allan and Arden started to return to Alba. Word came to the king that the company he was in pursuit of were gone. The king then sent for Duanan Gacha Druid, the best magician he had, and he spoke to him as follows :—" Much wealth have I expended on you, Duanan Gacha Druid, to give schooling and learning and magic mystery to you, if these people get away from me to-day without care, without consideration or regard for me, without chance of overtaking them, and without power to stop them."

" Well, I will stop them," said the magician, " until the company you send in pursuit return." And the magician placed a wood before them through which no man could go, but the sons of Uisnech marched through the wood without halt or hesitation, and Deirdre held on to Naois's hand.

"What is the good of that? that will not do yet," said Connachar. "They are off without bending of their feet or stopping of their step, without heed or respect to me, and I am without power to keep up to them or opportunity to turn them back this night."

"I will try another plan on them," said the druid; and he placed before them a grey sea instead of a green plain. The three heroes stripped and tied their clothes behind their heads, and Naois placed Deirdre on the top of his shoulder.

> They stretched their sides to the stream,
> And sea and land were to them the same,
> The rough grey ocean was the same
> As meadow-land green and plain.

"Though that be good, O Duanan, it will not make the heroes return," said Connachar; "they are gone without regard for me, and without honour to me, and without power on my part to pursue them or to force them to return this night."

"We shall try another method on them, since yon one did not stop them," said the druid. And the druid froze the grey ridged sea into hard rocky knobs, the sharpness of sword being on the one edge and the poison power of adders on the other. Then Arden cried that he was getting tired, and nearly giving over. "Come you, Arden, and sit on my right shoulder," said Naois. Arden came and sat on Naois's shoulder. Arden was long in this posture when he died; but though he was dead Naois would not let him go. Allen then cried out that he was getting faint and nigh-well giving up. When Naois heard his prayer, he gave forth the piercing sigh of death, and asked Allen to lay hold of him and he would bring him to land.

Allen was not long when the weakness of death came on him and his hold failed. Naois looked around, and when he saw his two well-beloved brothers dead, he cared not

whether he lived or died, and he gave forth the bitter sigh of death, and his heart burst.

"They are gone," said Duanan Gacha Druid to the king,

" and I have done what you desired me. The sons of Uisnech are dead and they will trouble you no more ; and you have your wife hale and whole to yourself."

" Blessings for that upon you and may the good results accrue to me, Duanan. I count it no loss what I spent in the schooling and teaching of you. Now dry up the flood, and let me see if I can behold Deirdre," said Connachar. And Duanan Gacha Druid dried up the flood from the plain and the three sons of Uisnech were lying together dead, without breath of life, side by side on the green meadow plain and Deirdre bending above showering down her tears.

Then Deirdre said this lament : " Fair one, loved one, flower of beauty ; beloved upright and strong ; beloved noble and modest warrior. Fair one, blue-eyed, beloved of thy wife ; lovely to me at the trysting-place came thy clear voice through the woods of Ireland. I cannot eat or smile henceforth. Break not to-day, my heart : soon enough shall I lie within my grave. Strong are the waves of sorrow, but stronger is sorrow's self, Connachar."

The people then gathered round the heroes' bodies and asked Connachar what was to be done with the bodies. The order that he gave was that they should dig a pit and put the three brothers in it side by side.

Deirdre kept sitting on the brink of the grave, constantly asking the gravediggers to dig the pit wide and free. When the bodies of the brothers were put in the grave, Deirdre said :—

> Come over hither, Naois, my love,
> Let Arden close to Allen lie ;
> If the dead had any sense to feel,
> Ye would have made a place for Deirdre.

The men did as she told them. She jumped into the grave and lay down by Naois, and she was dead by his side.

The king ordered the body to be raised from out the grave and to be buried on the other side of the loch. It was done as the king bade, and the pit closed. Thereupon a fir shoot grew out of the grave of Deirdre and a fir shoot from the grave of Naois, and the two shoots united in a knot above the loch. The king ordered the shoots to be cut down, and this was done twice, until, at the third time, the wife whom the king had married caused him to stop this work of evil and his vengeance on the remains of the dead.

Munachar and Manachar

HERE once lived a Munachar and a Manachar, a long time ago, and it is a long time since it was, and if they were alive now they would not be alive then. They went out together to pick raspberries, and as many as Munachar used to pick Manachar used to eat. Munachar said he must go look for a rod to make a gad to hang Manachar, who ate his raspberries every one ; and he came to the rod. "What news the day ? " said the rod. " It is my own news that I'm seeking. Going looking for a rod, a rod to make a gad, a gad to hang Manachar, who ate my raspberries every one."

"You will not get me," said the rod, " until you get an axe to cut me." He came to the axe. "What news to-day ? " said the axe. " It's my own news I'm seeking. Going looking for an axe, an axe to cut a rod, a rod to make a gad, a gad to hang Manachar, who ate my raspberries every one."

"You will not get me," said the axe, " until you get a

flag to edge me." He came to the flag. "What news to-day?" says the flag. "It's my own news I'm seeking. Going looking for a flag, flag to edge axe, axe to cut a rod, a rod to make a gad, a gad to hang Manachar, who ate my raspberries every one."

"You will not get me," says the flag, "till you get water to wet me." He came to the water. "What news to-day?" says the water. "It's my own news that I'm seeking. Going looking for water, water to wet flag to edge axe, axe to cut a rod, a rod to make a gad, a gad to hang Manachar, who ate my raspberries every one."

"You will not get me," said the water, "until you get a deer who will swim me." He came to the deer. "What news to-day?" says the deer. "It's my own news I'm seeking. Going looking for a deer, deer to swim water, water to wet flag, flag to edge axe, axe to cut a rod, a rod to make a gad, a gad to hang Manachar, who ate my raspberries every one."

"You will not get me," said the deer, "until you get a hound who will hunt me." He came to the hound. "What news to-day?" says the hound. "It's my own news I'm seeking. Going looking for a hound, hound to hunt deer, deer to swim water, water to wet flag, flag to edge axe, axe to cut a rod, a rod to make a gad, a gad to hang Manachar, who ate my raspberries every one."

"You will not get me," said the hound, "until you get a bit of butter to put in my claw." He came to the butter. "What news to-day?" says the butter. "It's my own news I'm seeking. Going looking for butter, butter to go in claw of hound, hound to hunt deer, deer to swim water, water to wet flag, flag to edge axe, axe to cut a rod, a rod to make a gad, a gad to hang Manachar, who ate my raspberries every one."

" You will not get me," said the butter, " until you get a cat who shall scrape me." He came to the cat. " What news to-day ? " said the cat. " It's my own news I'm seeking. Going looking for a cat, cat to scrape butter, butter to go in claw of hound, hound to hunt deer, deer to swim water, water to wet flag, flag to edge axe, axe to cut a rod, a rod to make a gad, gad to hang Manachar, who ate my raspberries every one."

" You will not get me," said the cat, " until you will get milk which you will give me." He came to the cow. " What news to-day ? " said the cow. " It's my own news I'm seeking. Going looking for a cow, cow to give me milk, milk I will give to the cat, cat to scrape butter, butter to go in claw of hound, hound to hunt deer, deer to swim water, water to wet flag, flag to edge axe, axe to cut a rod, a rod to make a gad, a gad to hang Manachar, who ate my raspberries every one."

" You will not get any milk from me," said the cow, " until you bring me a whisp of straw from those threshers yonder." He came to the threshers. " What news to-day ? " said the threshers. " It's my own news I'm seeking. Going looking for a whisp of straw from ye to give to the cow, the cow to give me milk, milk I will give to the cat, cat to scrape butter, butter to go in claw of hound, hound to hunt deer, deer to swim water, water to wet flag, flag to edge axe, axe to cut a rod, a rod to make a gad, a gad to hang Manachar, who ate my raspberries every one."

" You will not get any whisp of straw from us," said the

threshers, " until you bring us the makings of a cake from the miller over yonder." He came to the miller. " What news to-day ? " said the miller. " It's my own news I'm seeking. Going looking for the makings of a cake which I will give to the threshers, the threshers to give me a whisp of straw, the whisp of straw I will give to the cow, the cow to give me milk, milk I will give to the cat, cat to scrape butter, butter to go in claw of hound, hound to hunt deer, deer to swim water, water to wet flag, flag to edge axe, axe to cut a rod, a rod to make a gad, a gad to hang Manachar, who ate my raspberries every one."

" You will not get any makings of a cake from me," said the miller, " till you bring me the full of that sieve of water from the river over there."

He took the sieve in his hand and went over to the river, but as often as ever he would stoop and fill it with water, the moment he raised it the water would run out of it again, and sure, if he had been there from that day till this, he never could have filled it. A crow went flying by him, over his head. " Daub ! daub ! " said the crow. " My blessings on ye, then," said Munachar, " but it's the good advice you have," and he took the red clay and the daub that was by the brink, and he rubbed it to the bottom of the sieve, until all the holes were filled, and then the sieve held the water, and he brought the water to the miller, and the miller gave him the makings of a cake, and he gave the makings of the cake to the threshers, and the threshers gave him a whisp of straw, and he gave the whisp of straw to the cow, and the cow gave him milk, the milk he gave to the cat, the cat scraped the butter, the butter went into the claw of the hound, the hound hunted the deer, the deer

swam the water, the water wet the flag, the flag sharpened
the axe, the axe cut the rod, and the rod made a gad, and
when he had it ready to hang Manachar he found that
Manachar had BURST.

Gold-Tree and Silver-Tree

ONCE upon a time there was a king who had a wife, whose name was Silver-tree, and a daughter, whose name was Gold-tree. On a certain day of the days, Gold-tree and Silver-tree went to a glen, where there was a well, and in it there was a trout.

Said Silver-tree, "Troutie, bonny little fellow, am not I the most beautiful queen in the world?"

"Oh! indeed you are not."

"Who then?"

"Why, Gold-tree, your daughter."

Silver-tree went home, blind with rage. She lay down on the bed, and vowed she would never be well until she could get the heart and the liver of Gold-tree, her daughter, to eat.

At nightfall the king came home, and it was told him

that Silver-tree, his wife, was very ill. He went where she was, and asked her what was wrong with her.

" Oh! only a thing which you may heal if you like."

" Oh! indeed there is nothing at all which I could do for you that I would not do."

" If I get the heart and the liver of Gold-tree, my daughter, to eat, I shall be well."

Now it happened about this time that the son of a great king had come from abroad to ask Gold-tree for marrying. The king now agreed to this, and they went abroad.

The king then went and sent his lads to the hunting-hill for a he-goat, and he gave its heart and its liver to his wife to eat ; and she rose well and healthy.

A year after this Silver-tree went to the glen, where there was the well in which there was the trout.

" Troutie, bonny little fellow," said she, " am not I the most beautiful queen in the world ?"

" Oh! indeed you are not."

" Who then ?"

" Why, Gold-tree, your daughter."

" Oh! well, it is long since she was living. It is a year since I ate her heart and liver."

" Oh! indeed she is not dead. She is married to a great prince abroad."

Silver-tree went home, and begged the king to put the long-ship in order, and said, " I am going to see my dear Gold-tree, for it is so long since I saw her." The long-ship was put in order, and they went away.

It was Silver-tree herself that was at the helm, and she steered the ship so well that they were not long at all before they arrived.

The prince was out hunting on the hills. Gold-tree knew the long-ship of her father coming.

"Oh!" said she to the servants, "my mother is coming, and she will kill me."

"She shall not kill you at all; we will lock you in a room where she cannot get near you."

This is how it was done; and when Silver-tree came ashore, she began to cry out:

"Come to meet your own mother, when she comes to see you," Gold-tree said that she could not, that she was locked in the room, and that she could not get out of it.

"Will you not put out," said Silver-tree, "your little  finger through the key-hole, so that your own mother may give a kiss to it?"

She put out her little finger, and Silver-tree went and put a poisoned stab in it, and Gold-tree fell dead.

When the prince came home, and found Gold-tree dead, he was in great sorrow, and when he saw how beautiful she was, he did not bury her at all, but he locked her in a room where nobody would get near her.

In the course of time he married again, and the whole house was under the hand of this wife but one room, and he himself always kept the key of that room. On a certain day of the days he forgot to take the key with him, and the second wife got into the room. What did she see there but the most beautiful woman that she ever saw.

She began to turn and try to wake her, and she noticed the poisoned stab in her finger. She took the stab out, and Gold-tree rose alive, as beautiful as she was ever.

At the fall of night the prince came home from the hunting-hill, looking very downcast.

"What gift," said his wife, "would you give me that I could make you laugh?"

"Oh! indeed, nothing could make me laugh, except Gold-tree were to come alive again."

"Well, you'll find her alive down there in the room."

When the prince saw Gold-tree alive he made great rejoicings, and he began to kiss her, and kiss her, and kiss her. Said the second wife, "Since she is the first one you had it is better for you to stick to her, and I will go away."

"Oh! indeed you shall not go away, but I shall have both of you."

At the end of the year, Silver-tree went to the glen, where there was the well, in which there was the trout.

"Troutie, bonny little fellow," said she, "am not I the most beautiful queen in the world?"

"Oh! indeed you are not."

"Who then?"

"Why, Gold-tree, your daughter."

"Oh! well, she is not alive. It is a year since I put the poisoned stab into her finger."

" Oh ! indeed she is not dead at all, at all."

Silver-tree went home, and begged the king to put the long-ship in order, for that she was going to see her dear Gold-tree, as it was so long since she saw her. The long-ship was put in order, and they went away. It was Silver-tree herself that was at the helm, and she steered the ship so well that they were not long at all before they arrived.

The prince was out hunting on the hills. Gold-tree knew her father's ship coming.

" Oh !" said she, " my mother is coming, and she will kill me."

" Not at all," said the second wife ; " we will go down to meet her."

Silver-tree came ashore. "Come down, Gold-tree, love," said she, " for your own mother has come to you with a precious drink."

" It is a custom in this country," said the second wife, " that the person who offers a drink takes a draught out of it first."

Silver-tree put her mouth to it, and the second wife went and struck it so that some of it went down her throat, and she fell dead. They had only to carry her home a dead corpse and bury her.

The prince and his two wives were long alive after this, pleased and peaceful.

I left them there.

King O'Toole and His Goose

CH, I thought all the world, far and near, had heerd o' King O'Toole—well, well, but the darkness of mankind is untellible! Well, sir, you must know, as you didn't hear it afore, that there was a king, called King O'Toole, who was a fine old king in the old ancient times, long ago ; and it was he that owned the churches in the early days. The king, you see, was the right sort ; he was the real boy, and loved sport as he loved his life, and hunting in particular ; and from the rising o' the sun, up he got, and away he went over the mountains after the deer ; and fine times they were.

Well, it was all mighty good, as long as the king had his health ; but, you see, in course of time the king grew old, by raison he was stiff in his limbs, and when he got stricken in years, his heart failed him, and he was lost entirely for want o' diversion, because he couldn't go a-hunting no longer ; and, by dad, the poor king was obliged at last to get a goose to divert him. Oh, you may laugh, if you like, but it's truth I'm telling you ; and the way the goose diverted him was this-a-way: You see, the goose used to swim across the lake, and go diving for trout, and catch fish on a Friday for the king, and flew every other day round about the lake, diverting the poor king. All went on mighty well until, by dad, the goose got stricken in years like her master, and couldn't divert him no longer, and then it was that the poor king was lost entirely. The king was walkin' one mornin' by the edge of the lake, lamentin' his

cruel fate, and thinking of drowning himself, that could get no diversion in life, when all of a sudden, turning round the corner, who should he meet but a mighty decent young man coming up to him.

"God save you," says the king to the young man.

"God save you kindly, King O'Toole," says the young man.

"True for you," says the king. "I am King O'Toole," says he, "prince and plennypennytinchery of these parts," says he; "but how came ye to know that?" says he.

"Oh, never mind," says St. Kavin.

You see it was Saint Kavin, sure enough—the saint himself in disguise, and nobody else. "Oh, never mind," says he, "I know more than that. May I make bold to ask how is your goose, King O'Toole?" says he.

"Blur-an-agers, how came ye to know about my goose?" says the king.

"Oh, no matter; I was given to understand it," says Saint Kavin.

After some more talk the king says, "What are you?"

"I'm an honest man," says Saint Kavin.

"Well, honest man," says the king, "and how is it you make your money so aisy?"

"By makin' old things as good as new," says Saint Kavin.

"Is it a tinker you are?" says the king.

"No," says the saint; "I'm no tinker by trade, King O'Toole; I've a better trade than a tinker," says he— "what would you say," says he, "if I made your old goose as good as new?"

My dear, at the word of making his goose as good as new, you'd think the poor old king's eyes were ready to jump out of his head. With that the king whistled, and down came the poor goose, just like a hound, waddling up to the poor cripple, her master, and as like him as two peas. The minute the saint clapt his eyes on the goose, "I'll do the job for you," says he, "King O'Toole."

"By *Jaminee!*" says King O'Toole, "if you do, I'll say you're the cleverest fellow in the seven parishes."

"Oh, by dad," says St. Kavin, "you must say more nor that—my horn's not so soft all out," says he, "as to repair your old goose for nothing ; what'll you gi' me if I do the job for you ?——that's the chat," says St. Kavin.

" I'll give you whatever you ask," says the king ; " isn't that fair ? "

" Divil a fairer," says the saint ; " that's the way to do business. Now," says he, " this is the bargain I'll make with you, King O'Toole : will you gi' me all the ground the goose flies over, the first offer, after I make her as good as new ? "

" I will," says the king.

" You won't go back o' your word ? " says St. Kavin.

" Honour bright ! " says King O'Toole, holding out his fist.

" Honour bright ! " says St. Kavin, back agin, " it's a bargain. Come here ! " says he to the poor old goose— " come here, you unfortunate ould cripple, and it's I that'll make you the sporting bird." With that, my dear, he took up the goose by the two wings—" Criss o' my cross an you," says he, markin' her to grace with the blessed sign at the same minute—and throwing her up in the air, " whew," says he, jist givin' her a blast to help her ; and with that, my jewel, she took to her heels, flyin' like one o' the eagles themselves, and cutting as many capers as a swallow before a shower of rain.

Well, my dear, it was a beautiful sight to see the king standing with his mouth open, looking at his poor old goose flying as light as a lark, and better than ever she was : and when she lit at his feet, patted her on the head, and " *Ma vourneen*," says he, " but you are the *darlint* o' the world."

" And what do you say to me," says Saint Kavin, " for making her the like ? "

" By Jabers," says the king, " I say nothing beats the art o' man, barring the bees."

" And do you say no more nor that ? " says Saint Kavin.

" And that I'm beholden to you," says the king.

" But will you gi'e me all the ground the goose flew over ? " says Saint Kavin.

" I will," says King O'Toole, " and you're welcome to it," says he, " though it's the last acre I have to give."

" But you'll keep your word true ? " says the saint.

" As true as the sun," says the king.

" It's well for you, King O'Toole, that you said that

word," says he ; " for if you didn't say that word, the devil the bit o' your goose would ever fly agin."

When the king was as good as his word, Saint Kavin was pleased with him, and then it was that he made himself known to the king. "And," says he, "King O'Toole, you're a decent man, for I only came here to try you. You don't know me," says he, "because I'm disguised."

"Musha! then," says the king, "who are you?"

"I'm Saint Kavin," said the saint, blessing himself.

"Oh, queen of heaven!" says the king, making the sign of the cross between his eyes, and falling down on his knees before the saint ; " is it the great Saint Kavin," says he, "that I've been discoursing all this time without knowing it," says he, "all as one as if he was a lump of a *gossoon?*—and so you're a saint?" says the king.

"I am," says Saint Kavin.

"By Jabers, I thought I was only talking to a dacent boy," says the king.

"Well, you know the difference now," says the saint. "I'm Saint Kavin," says he, "the greatest of all the saints."

And so the king had his goose as good as new, to divert him as long as he lived : and the saint supported him after he came into his property, as I told you, until the day of his death—and that was soon after ; for the poor goose thought he was catching a trout one Friday ; but, my jewel, it was a mistake he made—and instead of a trout, it was a thieving horse-eel ; and instead of the goose killing a trout for the king's supper—by dad, the eel killed the king's goose—and small blame to him ; but he didn't ate her, because he darn't ate what Saint Kavin had laid his blessed hands on.

The Wooing of Olwen

HORTLY after the birth of Kilhuch, the son of King Kilyth, his mother died. Before her death she charged the king that he should not take a wife again until he saw a briar with two blossoms upon her grave, and the king sent every morning to see if anything were growing thereon. After many years the briar appeared, and he took to wife the widow of King Doged. She foretold to her stepson, Kilhuch, that it was his destiny to marry a maiden named Olwen, or none other, and he, at his father's bidding, went to the court of his cousin, King Arthur, to ask as a boon the hand of the maiden. He rode upon a grey steed with shell-formed hoofs, having a bridle of linked gold, and a saddle also of gold. In his hand were two spears of silver, well-tempered, headed with steel, of an edge to wound the wind and cause blood to flow, and swifter than the fall of the dew-drop from the blade of reed grass upon the earth when the dew of June is at its heaviest. A gold-hilted sword was on his thigh, and the blade was of gold, having inlaid upon it a cross of the hue of the lightning of heaven. Two brindled, white-breasted greyhounds, with strong collars of rubies, sported round him, and his courser cast up four sods with its four hoofs like four swallows about his head. Upon the steed was a four-cornered cloth of purple, and an apple of gold was at each corner. Precious gold was upon the stirrups and shoes, and the blade of grass bent not beneath them, so light was the courser's tread as he went towards the gate of King Arthur's palace.

Arthur received him with great ceremony, and asked him to remain at the palace ; but the youth replied that he came not to consume meat and drink, but to ask a boon of the king.

Then said Arthur, "Since thou wilt not remain here, chieftain, thou shalt receive the boon, whatsoever thy tongue may name, as far as the wind dries and the rain moistens, and the sun revolves, and the sea encircles, and the earth extends, save only my ships and my mantle, my sword, my lance, my shield, my dagger, and Guinevere my wife."

So Kilhuch craved of him the hand of Olwen, the daughter of Yspathaden Penkawr, and also asked the favour and aid of all Arthur's court.

Then said Arthur, " O chieftain, I have never heard of the maiden of whom thou speakest, nor of her kindred, but I will gladly send messengers in search of her."

And the youth said, " I will willingly grant from this night to that at the end of the year to do so."

Then Arthur sent messengers to every land within his dominions to seek for the maiden ; and at the end of the year Arthur's messengers returned without having gained any knowledge or information concerning Olwen more than on the first day.

Then said Kilhuch, "Every one has received his boon, and I yet lack mine. I will depart and bear away thy honour with me."

Then said Kay, "Rash chieftain! dost thou reproach Arthur? Go with us, and we will not part until thou dost either confess that the maiden exists not in the world, or until we obtain her."

Thereupon Kay rose up.

Kay had this peculiarity, that his breath lasted nine nights and nine days under water, and he could exist nine nights and nine days without sleep. A wound from Kay's sword no physician could heal. Very subtle was Kay. When it pleased him he could render himself as tall as the highest tree in the forest. And he had another peculiarity— so great was the heat of his nature, that, when it rained hardest, whatever he carried remained dry for a handbreadth above and a handbreath below his hand; and when his companions were coldest, it was to them as fuel with which to light their fire.

And Arthur called Bedwyr, who never shrank from any enterprise upon which Kay was bound. None was equal to him in swiftness throughout this island except Arthur and Drych Ail Kibthar. And although he was one-handed, three warriors could not shed blood faster than he on the field of battle. Another property he had; his lance would produce a wound equal to those of nine opposing lances.

And Arthur called to Kynthelig the guide. "Go thou upon this expedition with the Chieftain." For as good a guide was he in a land which he had never seen as he was in his own.

He called Gwrhyr Gwalstawt Ieithoedd, because he knew all tongues.

He called Gwalchmai, the son of Gwyar, because he never returned home without achieving the adventure of which he went in quest. He was the best of footmen and the best of knights. He was nephew to Arthur, the son of his sister, and his cousin.

And Arthur called Menw, the son of Teirgwaeth, in order that if they went into a savage country, he might cast a charm and an illusion over them, so that none might see them whilst they could see every one.

They journeyed on till they came to a vast open plain, wherein they saw a great castle, which was the fairest in the world. But so far away was it that at night it seemed no nearer, and they scarcely reached it on the third day. When they came before the castle they beheld a vast flock of sheep, boundless and without end. They told their errand to the herdsman, who endeavoured to dissuade them, since none who had come thither on that quest had returned alive. They gave to him a gold ring, which he conveyed to his wife, telling her who the visitors were.

On the approach of the latter, she ran out with joy to greet them, and sought to throw her arms about their necks. But Kay, snatching a billet out of the pile, placed the log between her two hands, and she squeezed it so that it became a twisted coil.

" O woman," said Kay, " if thou hadst squeezed me thus, none could ever again have set their affections on me. Evil love were this."

They entered the house, and after meat she told them that the maiden Olwen came there every Saturday to wash.

They pledged their faith that they would not harm her, and a message was sent to her. So Olwen came, clothed in a robe of flame-coloured silk, and with a collar of ruddy gold, in which were emeralds and rubies, about her neck. More golden was her hair than the flower of the broom, and her skin was whiter than the foam of the wave, and fairer were her hands and her fingers than the blossoms of the wood anemone amidst the spray of the meadow fountain. Brighter were her glances than those of a falcon ; her bosom was more snowy than the breast of the white swan, her cheek redder than the reddest roses. Whoso beheld was filled with her love. Four white trefoils sprang up wherever she trod, and therefore was she called Olwen.

Then Kilhuch, sitting beside her on a bench, told her his love, and she said that he would win her as his bride if he granted whatever her father asked.

Accordingly they went up to the castle and laid their request before him.

" Raise up the forks beneath my two eyebrows which have fallen over my eyes," said Yspathaden Penkawr, " that I may see the fashion of my son-in-law."

They did so, and he promised them an answer on the morrow. But as they were going forth, Yspathaden seized one of the three poisoned darts that lay beside him and threw it back after them.

And Bedwyr caught it and flung it back, wounding Yspathaden in the knee.

Then said he, " A cursed ungentle son-in-law, truly. I shall ever walk the worse for his rudeness. This poisoned iron pains me like the bite of a gad-fly. Cursed be the smith who forged it, and the anvil whereon it was wrought."

The knights rested in the house of Custennin the herds-man, but the next day at dawn they returned to the castle and renewed their request.

Yspathaden said it was necessary that he should consult

Olwen's four great-grandmothers and her four great-grand-sires.

The knights again withdrew, and as they were going he took the second dart and cast it after them.

But Menw caught it and flung it back, piercing Yspa-thaden's breast with it, so that it came out at the small of his back.

"A cursed ungentle son-in-law, truly," says he, "the hard iron pains me like the bite of a horse-leech. Cursed be the hearth whereon it was heated! Henceforth whenever

I go up a hill, I shall have a scant in my breath and a pain in my chest."

On the third day the knights returned once more to the palace, and Yspathaden took the third dart and cast it at them.

But Kilhuch caught it and threw it vigorously, and wounded him through the eyeball, so that the dart came out at the back of his head.

" A cursed ungentle son-in-law, truly. As long as I remain alive my eyesight will be the worse. Whenever I go against the wind my eyes will water, and peradventure my head will burn, and I shall have a giddiness every new moon. Cursed be the fire in which it was forged. Like the bite of a mad dog is the stroke of this poisoned iron."

And they went to meat.

Said Yspathaden Penkawr, " Is it thou that seekest my daughter ? "

" It is I," answered Kilhuch.

" I must have thy pledge that thou wilt not do towards me otherwise than is just, and when I have gotten that which I shall name, my daughter thou shalt have."

" I promise thee that willingly," said Kilhuch, "name what thou wilt."

" I will do so," said he.

" Throughout the world there is not a comb or scissors with which I can arrange my hair, on account of its rankness, except the comb and scissors that are between the two ears of Turch Truith, the son of Prince Tared. He will not give them of his own free will, and thou wilt not be able to compel him."

" It will be easy for me to compass this, although thou mayest think that it will not be easy."

" Though thou get this, there is yet that which thou wilt not get. It will not be possible to hunt Turch Truith without Drudwyn the whelp of Greid, the son of Eri, and know that throughout the world there is not a huntsman who can hunt with this dog, except Mabon the son of Modron. He was taken from his mother when three nights old, and it is not known where he now is, nor whether he is living or dead."

" It will be easy for me to compass this, although thou mayest think that it will not be easy."

" Though thou get this, there is yet that which thou wilt not get. Thou wilt not get Mabon, for it is not known where he is, unless thou find Eidoel, his kinsman in blood, the son of Aer. For it would be useless to seek for him. He is his cousin."

" It will be easy for me to compass this, although thou mayest think that it will not be easy. Horses shall I have, and chivalry ; and my lord and kinsman Arthur will obtain for me all these things. And I shall gain thy daughter, and thou shalt lose thy life."

" Go forward. And thou shalt not be chargeable for food or raiment for my daughter while thou art seeking these things ; and when thou hast compassed all these marvels, thou shalt have my daughter for wife."

Now, when they told Arthur how they had sped, Arthur said, " Which of these marvels will it be best for us to seek first ? "

" It will be best," said they, " to seek Mabon the son of Modron ; and he will not be found unless we first find Eidoel, the son of Aer, his kinsman."

Then Arthur rose up, and the warriors of the Islands of Britain with him, to seek for Eidoel ; and they proceeded until they came before the castle of Glivi, where Eidoel was imprisoned.

Glivi stood on the summit of his castle, and said, " Arthur, what requirest thou of me, since nothing remains to me in this fortress, and I have neither joy nor pleasure in it ; neither wheat nor oats ? "

Said Arthur, " Not to injure thee came I hither, but to seek for the prisoner that is with thee."

" I will give thee my prisoner, though I had not thought to give him up to any one ; and therewith shalt thou have my support and my aid."

His followers then said unto Arthur, " Lord, go thou home, thou canst not proceed with thy host in quest of such small adventures as these."

Then said Arthur, " It were well for thee, Gwrhyr Gwalstawt Ieithoedd, to go upon this quest, for thou knowest all languages, and art familiar with those of the birds and the beasts.   Go, Eidoel, likewise with my men in search of thy cousin.   And as for you, Kay and Bedwyr, I have hope of whatever adventure ye are in quest of, that ye will achieve it.   Achieve ye this adventure for me."

These went forward until they came to the Ousel of Cilgwri, and Gwrhyr adjured her for the sake of Heaven, saying, " Tell me if thou knowest aught of Mabon, the son of Modron, who was taken when three nights old from between his mother and the wall.

And the Ousel answered, "When I first came here there was a smith's anvil in this place, and I was then a young bird, and from that time no work has been done upon it, save the pecking of my beak every evening, and now there is not so much as the size of a nut remaining thereof ; yet the vengeance of Heaven be upon me if during all that time I have ever heard of the man for whom you inquire. Nevertheless, there is a race of animals who were formed before me, and I will be your guide to them."

So they proceeded to the place where was the Stag of Redynvre.

" Stag of Redynvre, behold we are come to thee, an embassy from Arthur, for we have not heard of any animal older than thou. Say, knowest thou aught of Mabon ? "

The stag said, " When first I came hither, there was a plain all around me, without any trees save one oak sapling, which grew up to be an oak with an hundred branches. And that oak has since perished, so that now nothing remains of it but the withered stump ; and from that day to this I have been here, yet have I never heard of the man for whom you inquire. Nevertheless, I will be your guide to the place where there is an animal which was formed before I was."

So they proceeded to the place where was the Owl of Cwm Cawlwyd, to inquire of him concerning Mabon.

And the owl said, " If I knew I would tell you. When first I came hither, the wide valley you see was a wooded glen. And a race of men came and rooted it up. And there grew there a second wood, and this wood is the third. My wings, are they not withered stumps ? Yet all this time, even until to-day, I have never heard of the man for whom you inquire. Nevertheless, I will be the guide of Arthur's embassy until you come to the place where is the oldest animal in this world, and the one who has travelled most, the eagle of Gwern Abwy."

When they came to the eagle, Gwrhyr asked it the same question ; but it replied, " I have been here for a great space of time, and when I first came hither there was a rock here, from the top of which I pecked at the stars every evening, and now it is not so much as a span high. From that day to this I have been here, and I have never heard of the man for whom you inquire, except once when I went in search of food as far as Llyn Llyw. And when I came there, I struck my talons into a salmon, thinking he would serve me as food for a long time. But he drew me into the deep, and I was scarcely able to escape from him. After that I went with my whole kindred to attack him and to try to destroy him, but he sent messengers and made peace with me, and came and besought me to take fifty fish-spears out of his back. Unless he know something of him whom you seek, I cannot tell you who may. However, I will guide you to the place where he is."

So they went thither, and the eagle said, " Salmon of Llyn Llyw, I have come to thee with an embassy from Arthur to ask thee if thou knowest aught concerning Mabon, the son of Modron, who was taken away at three nights old from between his mother and the wall."

And the salmon answered, " As much as I know I will tell thee. With every tide I go along the river upwards, until I come near to the walls of Gloucester, and there have I found such wrong as I never found elsewhere ; and to the end that ye may give credence thereto, let one of you go thither upon each of my two shoulders."

So Kay and Gwrhyr went upon his shoulders, and they

proceeded till they came to the wall of the prison, and they heard a great wailing and lamenting from the dungeon.

Said Gwrhyr, " Who is it that laments in this house of stone ? "

And the voice replied, " Alas, it is Mabon, the son of Modron, who is here imprisoned ! "

Then they returned and told Arthur, who, summoning his warriors, attacked the castle.

And whilst the fight was going on, Kay and Bedwyr, mounting on the shoulders of the fish, broke into the dungeon, and brought away with them Mabon, the son of Modron.

Then Arthur summoned unto him all the warriors that were in the three islands of Britain and in the three islands adjacent ; and he went as far as Esgeir Oervel in Ireland where the Boar Truith was with his seven young pigs. And the dogs were let loose upon him from all sides. But he wasted the fifth part of Ireland, and then set forth through the sea to Wales. Arthur and his hosts, and his horses, and his dogs followed hard after him. But ever and awhile the boar made a stand, and many a champion of Arthur's did he slay. Throughout all Wales did Arthur follow him, and one by one the young pigs were killed. At length, when he would fain have crossed the Severn and escaped into Cornwall, Mabon the son of Modron came up with him, and Arthur fell upon him together with the champions of Britain. On the one side Mabon the son of Modron spurred his steed and snatched his razor from him, whilst Kay came up with him on the other side and took from him the scissors. But before they could obtain the comb he had regained the ground with his feet, and from the moment that he reached the shore, neither dog nor man nor horse could overtake him until he came to Cornwall. There Arthur and his hosts followed in his track until they overtook him in Cornwall. Hard had been their trouble before, but it was child's play to what they met in seeking the comb. Win it they did, and the Boar Truith they hunted into the deep sea, and it was never known whither he went.

Then Kilhuch set forward, and as many as wished ill to Yspathaden Penkawr. And they took the marvels with them to his court. And Kaw of North Britain came and shaved his beard, skin and flesh clean off to the very bone from ear to ear.

" Art thou shaved, man ? " said Kilhuch.

" I am shaved," answered he.

" Is thy daughter mine now ? "

" She is thine, but therefore needst thou not thank me, but Arthur who hath accomplished this for thee. By my free will thou shouldst never have had her, for with her I lose my life."

Then Goreu the son of Custennin seized him by the hair of his head and dragged him after him to the keep, and cut off his head and placed it on a stake on the citadel.

Thereafter the hosts of Arthur dispersed themselves each man to his own country.

Thus did Kilhuch son of Kelython win to wife Olwen, the daughter of Yspathaden Penkawr.

Jack and His Comrades

ONCE there was a poor widow, as often there has been, and she had one son. A very scarce summer came, and they didn't know how they'd live till the new potatoes would be fit for eating. So Jack said to his mother one evening, " Mother, bake my cake, and kill my hen, till I go seek my fortune ; and if I meet it, never fear but I'll soon be back to share it with you."

So she did as he asked her, and he set out at break of day on his journey. His mother came along with him to the yard gate, and says she, " Jack, which would you rather have, half the cake and half the hen with my blessing, or the whole of 'em with my curse ? "

" O musha, mother," says Jack, " why do you ax me that question ? sure you know I wouldn't have your curse and Damer's estate along with it."

" Well, then, Jack," says she, " here's the whole lot of 'em, with my thousand blessings along with them." So she stood on the yard fence and blessed him as far as her eyes could see him.

Well, he went along and along till he was tired, and

ne'er a farmer's house he went into wanted a boy. At last his road led by the side of a bog, and there was a poor ass up to his shoulders near a big bunch of grass he was striving to come at.

"Ah, then, Jack asthore," says he, "help me out or I'll be drowned."

"Never say't twice," says Jack, and he pitched in big stones and sods into the slob, till the ass got good ground under him.

"Thank you, Jack," says he, when he was out on the hard road ; "I'll do as much for you another time. Where are you going ? "

"Faith, I'm going to seek my fortune till harvest comes in, God bless it ! "

"And if you like," says the ass, "I'll go along with you ; who knows what luck we may have ! "

"With all my heart, it's getting late, let us be jogging."

Well, they were going through a village, and a whole army of gossoons were hunting a poor dog with a kettle tied to his tail. He ran up to Jack for protection, and the ass let such a roar out of him, that the little thieves took to their heels as if the ould boy was after them.

"More power to you, Jack," says the dog.

"I'm much obleeged to you : where is the baste and yourself going ? "

"We're going to seek our fortune till harvest comes in."

"And wouldn't I be proud to go with you ! " says the dog, "and get rid of them ill conducted boys ; purshuin' to 'em."

"Well, well, throw your tail over your arm, and come along."

They got outside the town, and sat down under an old wall, and Jack pulled out his bread and meat, and shared with the dog; and the ass made his dinner on a bunch of thistles. While they were eating and chatting, what should come by but a poor half-starved cat, and the moll-row he gave out of him would make your heart ache.

"You look as if you saw the tops of nine houses since breakfast," says Jack; "here's a bone and something on it."

"May your child never know a hungry belly!" says Tom; "it's myself that's in need of your kindness. May I be so bold as to ask where yez are all going?"

"We're going to seek our fortune till the harvest comes in, and you may join us if you like."

"And that I'll do with a heart and a half," says the cat, "and thank'ee for asking me.'"

Off they set again, and just as the shadows of the trees were three times as long as themselves, they heard a great cackling in a field inside the road, and out over the ditch jumped a fox with a fine black cock in his mouth.

"Oh, you anointed villain!" says the ass, roaring like thunder.

"At him, good dog!" says Jack, and the word wasn't out of his mouth when Coley was in full sweep after the Red Dog. Reynard dropped his prize like a hot potato, and was off like shot, and the poor cock came back fluttering and trembling to Jack and his comrades.

"O musha, naybours!" says he, "wasn't it the heigth o' luck that threw you in my way! Maybe I won't remember your kindness if ever I find you in hardship; and where in the world are you all going?"

"We're going to seek our fortune till the harvest comes in ; you may join our party if you like, and sit on Neddy's crupper when your legs and wings are tired."

Well, the march began again, and just as the sun was gone down they looked around, and there was neither cabin nor farm house in sight.

"Well, well," says Jack, "the worse luck now the better another time, and it's only a summer night after all. We'll go into the wood, and make our bed on the long grass."

No sooner said than done. Jack stretched himself on a bunch of dry grass, the ass lay near him, the dog and cat lay in the ass's warm lap, and the cock went to roost in the next tree.

Well, the soundness of deep sleep was over them all, when the cock took a notion of crowing.

"Bother you, Black Cock !" says the ass : "you disturbed me from as nice a wisp of hay as ever I tasted. What's the matter ? "

"It's daybreak that's the matter : don't you see light yonder ? "

"I see a light indeed," says Jack, "but it's from a candle it's coming, and not from the sun. As you've roused us we may as well go over, and ask for lodging."

So they all shook themselves, and went on through grass, and rocks, and briars, till they got down into a hollow, and there was the light coming through the shadow, and along with it came singing, and laughing, and cursing.

"Easy, boys !" says Jack : "walk on your tippy toes till we see what sort of people we have to deal with."

So they crept near the window, and there they saw six robbers inside, with pistols, and blunderbushes, and cutlashes, sitting at a table, eating roast beef and pork, and drinking mulled beer, and wine, and whisky punch.

"Wasn't that a fine haul we made at the Lord of Dunlavin's!" says one ugly-looking thief with his mouth full, "and it's little we'd get only for the honest porter! here's his purty health!"

"The porter's purty health!" cried out every one of them, and Jack bent his finger at his comrades.

"Close your ranks, my men," says he in a whisper, "and let every one mind the word of command."

So the ass put his fore-hoofs on the sill of the window, the dog got on the ass's head, the cat on the dog's head, and the cock on the cat's head. Then Jack made a sign, and they all sung out like mad.

"Hee-haw, hee-haw!" roared the ass; "bow-wow!" barked the dog; "meaw-meaw!" cried the cat; "cock-a-doodle-doo!' crowed the cock.

"Level your pistols!" cried Jack, "and make smithereens of 'em. Don't leave a mother's son of 'em alive; present, fire!"

With that they gave another halloo, and smashed every pane in the window. The robbers were frightened out of their lives.   They blew out the candles, threw down the table, and skelped out at the back door as if they were in earnest, and never drew rein till they were in the very heart of the wood.

Jack and his party got into the room, closed the shutters, lighted the candles, and ate and drank till hunger and thirst were gone.   Then they lay down to rest ;—Jack in the bed, the ass in the stable, the dog on the door-mat, the cat by the fire, and the cock on the perch.

At first the robbers were very glad to find themselves safe in the thick wood, but they soon began to get vexed.

" This   damp grass is very different from our warm room," says one.

" I was obliged to drop a fine pig's foot," says another.

" I didn't get a tayspoonful of my last tumbler," says another.

" And all the Lord of Dunlavin's gold and silver that we left behind ! " says the last.

" I think I'll venture back," says the captain, " and see if we can recover anything."

" That's a good boy ! " said they all, and away he went.

The lights were all out, and so he groped his way to the fire, and there the cat flew in his face, and tore him with teeth and claws.   He let a roar out of him, and made for the room door, to look for a candle inside.   He trod on the dog's tail, and if he did, he got the marks of his teeth in his arms, and legs, and thighs.

" Thousand murders ! " cried he ; " I wish I was out of this unlucky house."

When he got to the street door, the cock dropped down

upon him with his claws and bill, and what the cat and dog done to him was only a flay-bite to what he got from the cock.

" Oh, tattheration to you all, you unfeeling vagabones ! " says he, when he recovered his breath ; and he staggered and spun round and round till he reeled into the stable, back foremost, but the ass received him with a kick on the broadest part of his small clothes, and laid him comfortably on the dunghill.

When he came to himself, he scratched his head, and began to think what happened him ; and as soon as he found that his legs were able to carry him, he crawled away, dragging one foot after another, till he reached the wood.

" Well, well," cried them all, when he came within hearing, " any chance of our property ? "

" You may say chance," says he, " and it's itself is the poor chance all out.   Ah, will any of you pull a bed of dry grass for me ?   All the sticking-plaster in Enniscorthy will be too little for the cuts and bruises I have on me.   Ah, if you only knew what I have gone through for you !   When I got to the kitchen fire, looking for a sod of lighted turf, what should be there but an old woman carding flax, and you may see the marks she left on my face with the cards.   I made to the room door as fast as I could, and who should I stumble over but a cobbler and his seat, and if he did not work at me with his awls and his pinchers you may call me a rogue.   Well, I got away from him somehow, but when I was passing through the door, it must be the divel himself that pounced down on me with his claws, and his teeth, that were equal to sixpenny nails, and his wings—ill luck be in his road !   Well, at last I reached the stable, and there, by way of salute, I got a pelt from a sledge-hammer that sent me half a mile off. If you don't believe me, I'll give you leave to go and judge for yourselves."

" Oh, my poor captain," says they, " we believe you to the nines. Catch us, indeed, going within a hen's race of that unlucky cabin ! "

Well, before the sun shook his doublet next morning, Jack and his comrades were up and about. They made a hearty breakfast on what was left the night before, and then they all agreed to set off to the castle of the Lord of Dunlavin, and give him back all his gold and silver. Jack put it all in the two ends of a sack and laid it across Neddy's back, and all took the road in their hands. Away they went, through bogs, up hills, down dales, and sometimes along the yellow high road, till they came to the hall-door of the Lord of Dunlavin, and who should be there, airing his powdered head, his white stockings, and his red breeches, but the thief of a porter.

He gave a cross look to the visitors, and says he to Jack, " What do you want here, my fine fellow ? there isn't room for you all."

" We want," says Jack, " what I'm sure you haven't to give us—and that is, common civility."

" Come, be off, you lazy strollers ! " says he, " while a cat 'ud be licking her ear, or I'll let the dogs at you."

" Would you tell a body," says the cock that was perched on the ass's head, " who was it that opened the door for the robbers the other night ? "

Ah ! maybe the porter's red face didn't turn the colour of his frill, and the Lord of Dunlavin and his pretty daughter, that were standing at the parlour window unknownst to the porter, put out their heads.

"I'd be glad, Barney," says the master, "to hear your answer to the gentleman with the red comb on him."

"Ah, my lord, don't believe the rascal; sure I didn't open the door to the six robbers."

"And how did you know there were six, you poor innocent?" said the lord.

"Never mind, sir," says Jack, "all your gold and silver is there in that sack, and I don't think you will begrudge us our supper and bed after our long march from the wood of Athsalach."

"Begrudge, indeed! Not one of you will ever see a poor day if I can help it."

So all were welcomed to their heart's content, and the ass and the dog and the cock got the best posts in the farmyard, and the cat took possession of the kitchen. The lord took Jack in hands, dressed him from top to toe in broadcloth, and frills as white as snow, and turnpumps, and put a watch in his fob. When they sat down to dinner, the lady of the house said Jack had the air of a born gentleman about him, and the lord said he'd make him his steward. Jack brought his mother, and settled her comfortably near the castle, and all were as happy as you please.

The Shee an Gannon and the
Gruagach Gaire

THE Shee an Gannon was born in the morning, named at noon, and went in the evening to ask his daughter of the king of Erin.

"I will give you my daughter in marriage," said the king of Erin; "you won't get her, though, unless you go and bring me back the tidings that I want, and tell me what it is that put a stop to the laughing of the Gruagach Gaire, who before this laughed always, and laughed so loud that the whole world heard him. There are twelve iron spikes out here in the garden behind my castle. On eleven of the spikes are the heads of kings' sons who came seeking my daughter in marriage, and all of them went away to get the knowledge I wanted. Not one was able to get it and tell me what stopped the Gruagach Gaire from laughing. I took the heads off them all when they came back without the tidings for which they went, and I'm greatly in dread that your head'll be on the twelfth spike, for I'll do the same to you that I did to the eleven kings' sons unless you tell what put a stop to the laughing of the Gruagach."

The Shee an Gannon made no answer, but left the king and pushed away to know could he find why the Gruagach was silent.

He took a glen at a step, a hill at a leap, and travelled all day till evening. Then he came to a house. The master of the house asked him what sort was he, and he said : " A young man looking for hire."

" Well," said the master of the house, " I was going to-morrow to look for a man to mind my cows. If you'll work for me, you'll have a good place, the best food a man could have to eat in this world, and a soft bed to lie on."

The Shee an Gannon took service, and ate his supper. Then the master of the house said : " I am the Gruagach Gaire ; now that you are my man and have eaten your supper, you'll have a bed of silk to sleep on."

Next morning after breakfast the Gruagach said to the Shee an Gannon : " Go out now and loosen my five golden cows and my bull without horns, and drive them to pasture ; but when you have them out on the grass, be careful you don't let them go near the land of the giant."

The new cowboy drove the cattle to pasture, and when near the land of the giant, he saw it was covered with woods and surrounded by a high wall. He went up, put his back against the wall, and threw in a great stretch of it ; then he went inside and threw out another great stretch of the wall, and put the five golden cows and the bull without horns on the land of the giant.

Then he climbed a tree, ate the sweet apples himself,

and threw the sour ones down to the cattle of the Gruagach Gaire.

Soon a great crashing was heard in the woods,—the noise of young trees bending, and old trees breaking. The cowboy looked around, and saw a five-headed giant pushing through the trees ; and soon he was before him.

" Poor miserable creature ! " said the giant ; " but weren't you impudent to come to my land and trouble me in this way ? You're too big for one bite, and too small for two. I don't know what to do but tear you to pieces."

" You nasty brute," said the cowboy, coming down to him from the tree, " 'tis little I care for you ;" and then they went at each other. So great was the noise between them that there was nothing in the world but what was looking on and listening to the combat.

They fought till late in the afternoon, when the giant was getting the upper hand ; and then the cowboy thought that if the giant should kill him, his father and mother would never find him or set eyes on him again, and he would never get the daughter of the king of Erin. The heart in his body grew strong at this thought. He sprang on the giant, and with the first squeeze and thrust he put him to his knees in the hard ground, with the second thrust to his waist, and with the third to his shoulders.

" I have you at last ; you're done for now ! " said the cowboy. Then he took out his knife, cut the five heads off the giant, and when he had them off he cut out the tongues and threw the heads over the wall.

Then he put the tongues in his pocket and drove home the cattle. That evening the Gruagach couldn't find vessels enough in all his place to hold the milk of the five golden cows.

But when the cowboy was on the way home with the cattle, the son of the king of Tisean came and took the giant's heads and claimed the princess in marriage when the Gruagach Gaire should laugh.

After supper the cowboy would give no talk to his master, but kept his mind to himself, and went to the bed of silk to sleep.

On the morning the cowboy rose before his master, and the first words he said to the Gruagach were:

"What keeps you from laughing, you who used to laugh so loud that the whole world heard you?"

"I'm sorry," said the Gruagach, "that the daughter of the king of Erin sent you here."

"If you don't tell me of your own will, I'll make you tell me," said the cowboy; and he put a face on himself that was terrible to look at, and running through the house like a madman, could find nothing that would give pain enough to the Gruagach but some ropes made of untanned sheepskin hanging on the wall.

He took these down, caught the Gruagach, fastened him by the three smalls, and tied him so that his little toes were whispering to his ears. When he was in this state the Gruagach said: "I'll tell you what stopped my laughing if you set me free."

So the cowboy unbound him, the two sat down together, and the Gruagach said:—

"I lived in this castle here with my twelve sons. We ate, drank, played cards, and enjoyed ourselves, till one day when my sons and I were playing, a slender brown hare came rushing in, jumped on to the hearth, tossed up the ashes to the rafters and ran away.

"On another day he came again; but if he did, we were ready for him, my twelve sons and myself. As soon as he tossed up the ashes and ran off, we made after him, and followed him till nightfall, when he went into a glen. We saw a light before us. I ran on, and came to a house with a great apartment, where there was a man named Yellow Face with twelve daughters, and the hare was tied to the side of the room near the women.

"There was a large pot over the fire in the room, and a great stork boiling in the pot. The man of the house said to me: 'There are bundles of rushes at the end of the room, go there and sit down with your men!'

"He went into the next room and brought out two pikes, one of wood, the other of iron, and asked me which of the pikes would I take. I said, 'I'll take the iron one;' for I thought in my heart that if an attack should come on me, I could defend myself better with the iron than the wooden pike.

"Yellow Face gave me the iron pike, and the first chance of taking what I could out of the pot on the point of the pike. I got but a small piece of the stork, and the man of the house took all the rest on his wooden pike. We had to fast that night; and when the man and his twelve daughters ate the flesh of the stork, they hurled the bare bones in the faces of my sons and myself.

"We had to stop all night that way, beaten on the faces by the bones of the stork.

"Next morning, when we were going away, the man of the house asked me to stay a while; and going into the next room, he brought out twelve loops of iron and one of wood, and said to me : ' Put the heads of your twelve sons into the iron loops, or your own head into the wooden one ; ' and I said : ' I'll put the twelve heads of my sons in the iron loops, and keep my own out of the wooden one.'

" He put the iron loops on the necks of my twelve sons, and put the wooden one on his own neck. Then he snapped the loops one after another, till he took the heads off my twelve sons and threw the heads and bodies out of the house ; but he did nothing to hurt his own neck.

" When he had killed my sons he took hold of me and stripped the skin and flesh from the small of my back down, and when he had done that he took the skin of a black sheep that had been hanging on the wall for seven years and clapped it on my body in place of my own flesh and skin ; and the sheepskin grew on me, and every year since then I shear myself, and every bit of wool I use for the stockings that I wear I clip off my own back."

When he had said this, the Gruagach showed the cowboy his back covered with thick black wool.

After what he had seen and heard, the cowboy said : " I know now why you don't laugh, and small blame to you. But does that hare come here still ? "

" He does indeed," said the Gruagach.

Both went to the table to play, and they were not long playing cards when the hare ran in ; and before they could stop him he was out again.

But the cowboy made after the hare, and the Gruagach after the cowboy, and they ran as fast as ever their legs could carry them till nightfall ; and when the hare was entering the castle where the twelve sons of the Gruagach were killed, the cowboy caught him by the two hind legs and dashed out his brains against the wall; and the skull of the hare was knocked into the chief room of the castle, and fell at the feet of the master of the place.

"Who has dared to interfere with my fighting pet?" screamed Yellow Face.

"I," said the cowboy; "and if your pet had had manners, he might be alive now."

The cowboy and the Gruagach stood by the fire. A stork was boiling in the pot, as when the Gruagach came the first time. The master of the house went into the next room and brought out an iron and a wooden pike, and asked the cowboy which would he choose.

"I'll take the wooden one," said the cowboy; "and you may keep the iron one for yourself."

So he took the wooden one; and going to the pot, brought out on the pike all the stork except a small bite, and he and the Gruagach fell to eating, and they were eating the flesh of the stork all night. The cowboy and the Gruagach were at home in the place that time.

In the morning the master of the house went into the next room, took down the twelve iron loops with a wooden one, brought them out, and asked the cowboy which would he take, the twelve iron or the one wooden loop.

"What could I do with the twelve iron ones for myself or my master? I'll take the wooden one."

He put it on, and taking the twelve iron loops, put them on the necks of the twelve daughters of the house, then snapped the twelve heads off them, and turning to their father, said: "I'll do the same thing to you unless you bring the twelve sons of my master to life, and make them as well and strong as when you took their heads."

The master of the house went out and brought the twelve to life again ; and when the Gruagach saw all his

sons alive and as well as ever, he let a laugh out of himself, and all the Eastern world heard the laugh.

Then the cowboy said to the Gruagach : " It's a bad thing you have done to me, for the daughter of the king of Erin will be married the day after your laugh is heard."

" Oh ! then we must be there in time," said the Gruagach ; and they all made away from the place as fast as ever they could, the cowboy, the Gruagach, and his twelve sons.

They hurried on ; and when within three miles of the king's castle there was such a throng of people that no one could go a step ahead. " We must clear a road through this," said the cowboy.

" We must indeed," said the Gruagach ; and at it they went, threw the people some on one side and some on the other, and soon they had an opening for themselves to the king's castle.

As they went in, the daughter of the king of Erin and the son of the king of Tisean were on their knees just going to be married. The cowboy drew his hand on the bridegroom, and gave a blow that sent him spinning till he stopped under a table at the other side of the room.

" What scoundrel struck that blow ? " asked the king of Erin.

" It was I," said the cowboy.

" What reason had you to strike the man who won my daughter ? "

" It was I who won your daughter, not he ; and if you don't believe me, the Gruagach Gaire is here himself. He'll tell you the whole story from beginning to end, and show you the tongues of the giant."

So the Gruagach came up and told the king the whole story, how the Shee an Gannon had become his cowboy, had guarded the five golden cows and the bull without horns, cut off the heads of the five-headed giant, killed the wizard hare, and brought his own twelve sons to life. " And then," said the Gruagach, " he is the only man in the whole world I have ever told why I stopped laughing, and the only one who has ever seen my fleece of wool."

When the king of Erin heard what the Gruagach said,

and saw the tongues of the giant fitted in the head, he made the Shee an Gannon kneel down by his daughter, and they were married on the spot.

Then the son of the king of Tisean was thrown into prison, and the next day they put down a great fire, and the deceiver was burned to ashes.

The wedding lasted nine days, and the last day was better than the first.

The Story-Teller at Fault

A T the time when the Tuatha De Dannan held the sovereignty of Ireland, there reigned in Leinster a king, who was remarkably fond of hearing stories. Like the other princes and chieftains of the island, he had a favourite story-teller, who held a large estate from his Majesty, on condition of telling him a new story every night of his life, before he went to sleep. Many indeed were the stories he knew, so that he had already reached a good old age without failing even for a single night in his task ; and such was the skill he displayed that whatever cares of state or other annoyances might prey upon the monarch's mind, his story-teller was sure to send him to sleep.

One morning the story-teller arose early, and as his custom was, strolled out into his garden turning over in his mind incidents which he might weave into a story for the king at night. But this morning he found himself quite at fault ; after pacing his whole demesne, he returned to his house without being able to think of anything new or strange. He found no difficulty in " there was once a king

who had three sons " or " one day the king of all Ireland,"
but further than that he could not get. At length he went
in to breakfast, and found his wife much perplexed at his
delay.

" Why don't you come to breakfast, my dear?" said she.

" I have no mind to eat anything," replied the story-
teller ; " long as I have been in the service of the king of
Leinster, I never sat down to breakfast without having a new
story ready for the evening, but this morning my mind is
quite shut up, and I don't know what to do. I might as
well lie down and die at once. I'll be disgraced for ever
this evening, when the king calls for his story-teller."

Just at this moment the lady looked out of the window.

" Do you see that black thing at the end of the field ? "
said she.

" I do," replied her husband.

They drew nigh, and saw a miserable looking old man
lying on the ground with a wooden leg placed beside him.

" Who are you, my good man ? " asked the story-teller.

" Oh, then, 'tis little matter who I am. I'm a poor, old,
lame, decrepit, miserable creature, sitting down here to rest
awhile."

" An' what are you doing with that box and dice I see in
your hand ? "

" I am waiting here to see if any one will play a game
with me," replied the beggar man.

" Play with you ! Why what has a poor old man like
you to play for ? "

" I have one hundred pieces of gold in this leathern
purse," replied the old man.

" You may as well play with him," said the story-teller's

wife ; "and perhaps you'll have something to tell the king in the evening."

A smooth stone was placed between them, and upon it they cast their throws.

It was but a little while and the story-teller lost every penny of his money.

" Much good may it do you, friend," said he. " What better hap could I look for, fool that I am ! "

" Will you play again ? " asked the old man.

" Don't be talking, man : you have all my money."

" Haven't you chariot and horses and hounds ? "

" Well, what of them ! "

" I'll stake all the money I have against thine."

" Nonsense, man ! Do you think for all the money in Ireland, I'd run the risk of seeing my lady tramp home on foot ? "

" Maybe you'd win," said the bocough.

" Maybe I wouldn't," said the story-teller.

" Play with him, husband," said his wife. " I don't mind walking, if you do, love."

" I never refused you before," said the story-teller, " and I won't do so now."

Down he sat again, and in one throw lost houses, hounds, and chariot.

" Will you play again ? " asked the beggar.

" Are you making game of me, man ; what else have I to stake ? "

" I'll stake all my winnings against your wife," said the old man.

The story-teller turned away in silence, but his wife stopped him.

"Accept his offer," said she. "This is the third time, and who knows what luck you may have? You'll surely win now."

They played again, and the story-teller lost. No sooner had he done so, than to his sorrow and surprise, his wife went and sat down near the ugly old beggar.

"Is that the way you're leaving me?" said the story-teller.

"Sure I was won," said she. "You would not cheat the poor man, would you?"

"Have you any more to stake?" asked the old man.

"You know very well I have not," replied the story-teller.

"I'll stake the whole now, wife and all, against your own self," said the old man.

Again they played, and again the story-teller lost.

"Well! here I am, and what do you want with me?"

"I'll soon let you know," said the old man, and he took from his pocket a long cord and a wand.

"Now," said he to the story-teller, "what kind of animal would you rather be, a deer, a fox, or a hare? You have your choice now, but you may not have it later."

To make a long story short, the story-teller made his choice of a hare; the old man threw the cord round him, struck him with the wand, and lo! a long-eared, frisking hare was skipping and jumping on the green.

But it wasn't for long; who but his wife called the hounds, and set them on him. The hare fled, the dogs followed. Round the field ran a high wall, so that run as he might, he couldn't get out, and mightily diverted were beggar and lady to see him twist and double.

In vain did he take refuge with his wife, she kicked him back again to the hounds, until at length the beggar stopped the hounds, and with a stroke of the wand, panting and breathless, the story-teller stood before them again.

" And how did you like the sport ? " said the beggar.

" It might be sport to others," replied the story-teller looking at his wife, " for my part I could well put up with the loss of it."

" Would it be asking too much," he went on to the beggar, " to know who you are at all, or where you come from, or why you take a pleasure in plaguing a poor old man like me ? "

" Oh ! " replied the stranger, " I'm an odd kind of good-for-little fellow, one day poor, another day rich, but if you wish to know more about me or my habits, come with me and perhaps I may show you more than you would make out if you went alone."

" I'm not my own master to go or stay," said the story-teller, with a sigh.

The stranger put one hand into his wallet and drew out of it before their eyes a well-looking middle-aged man, to whom he spoke as follows :

" By all you heard and saw since I put you into my wallet, take charge of this lady and of the carriage and horses, and have them ready for me whenever I want them."

Scarcely had he said these words when all vanished, and the story-teller found himself at the Foxes' Ford, near the castle of Red Hugh O'Donnell. He could see all but none could see him.

O'Donnell was in his hall, and heaviness of flesh and weariness of spirit were upon him.

" Go out," said he to his doorkeeper, " and see who or what may be coming."

The doorkeeper went, and what he saw was a lank, grey beggarman ; half his sword bared behind his haunch, his two

shoes full of cold road-a-wayish water sousing about him, the tips of his two ears out through his old hat, his two shoulders out through his scant tattered cloak, and in his hand a green wand of holly.

" Save you, O Donnell," said the lank grey beggarman.

"And you likewise," said O'Donnell. "Whence come you, and what is your craft?"

> "I come from the outmost stream of earth,
> From the glens where the white swans glide,
> A night in Islay, a night in Man,
> A night on the cold hillside."

"It's the great traveller you are," said O'Donnell. "Maybe you've learnt something on the road."

"I am a juggler," said the lank grey beggarman, "and for five pieces of silver you shall see a trick of mine."

"You shall have them," said O'Donnell; and the lank grey beggarman took three small straws and placed them in his hand.

"The middle one," said he, "I'll blow away; the other two I'll leave."

"Thou canst not do it," said one and all.

But the lank grey beggarman put a finger on either outside straw and, whiff, away he blew the middle one.

"'Tis a good trick," said O'Donnell; and he paid him his five pieces of silver.

"For half the money," said one of the chief's lads, "I'll do the same trick."

"Take him at his word, O'Donnell."

The lad put the three straws on his hand, and a finger on either outside straw and he blew; and what happened but that the fist was blown away with the straw.

"Thou art sore, and thou wilt be sorer," said O'Donnell.

"Six more pieces, O'Donnell, and I'll do another trick for thee," said the lank grey beggarman.

"Six shalt thou have."

"Seest thou my two ears! One I'll move but not t'other."

"'Tis easy to see them, they're big enough, but thou canst never move one ear and not the two together."

The lank grey beggarman put his hand to his ear, and he gave it a pull.

O'Donnell laughed and paid him the six pieces.

"Call that a trick," said the fistless lad, "any one can do that," and so saying, he put up his hand, pulled his ear, and what happened was that he pulled away ear and head.

"Sore thou art, and sorer thou'lt be," said O'Donnell.

"Well, O'Donnell," said the lank grey beggarman, "strange are the tricks I've shown thee, but I'll show thee a stranger one yet for the same money."

"Thou hast my word for it," said O'Donnell.

With that the lank grey beggarman took a bag from under his armpit, and from out the bag a ball of silk, and he unwound the ball and he flung it slantwise up into the clear blue heavens, and it became a ladder; then he took a hare and placed it upon the thread, and up it ran; again he took out a red-eared hound, and it swiftly ran up after the hare.

"Now," said the lank grey beggarman; "has any one a mind to run after the dog and on the course?"

"I will," said a lad of O'Donnell's.

"Up with you then," said the juggler; "but I warn you if you let my hare be killed I'll cut off your head when you come down."

The lad ran up the thread and all three soon disappeared. After looking up for a long time, the lank grey beggarman said: "I'm afraid the hound is eating the hare, and that our friend has fallen asleep."

Saying this he began to wind the thread, and down came the lad fast asleep; and down came the red-eared hound and in his mouth the last morsel of the hare.

He struck the lad a stroke with the edge of his sword, and so cast his head off. As for the hound, if he used it no worse, he used it no better.

" It's little I'm pleased, and sore I'm angered," said O'Donnell, " that a hound and a lad should be killed at my court."

" Five pieces of silver twice over for each of them," said the juggler, " and their heads shall be on them as before."

" Thou shalt get that," said O'Donnell.

Five pieces, and again five were paid him, and lo! the lad had his head and the hound his. And though they lived to the uttermost end of time, the hound would never touch a hare again, and the lad took good care to keep his eyes open.

Scarcely had the lank grey beggarman done this when he vanished from out their sight, and no one present could say if he had flown through the air or if the earth had swallowed him up.

> He moved as wave tumbling o'er wave
> As whirlwind following whirlwind,
> As a furious wintry blast,
> So swiftly, sprucely, cheerily,
> Right proudly,
> And no stop made
> Until he came
> To the court of Leinster's King,
> He gave a cheery light leap
> O'er top of turret,
> Of court and city
> Of Leinster's King.

Heavy was the flesh and weary the spirit of Leinster's

king. 'Twas the hour he was wont to hear a story, but send he might right and left, not a jot of tidings about the story-teller could he get.

"Go to the door," said he to his doorkeeper, "and see if a soul is in sight who may tell me something about my story-teller."

The doorkeeper went, and what he saw was a lank grey beggarman, half his sword bared behind his haunch, his two old shoes full of cold road-a-wayish water sousing about him, the tips of his two ears out through his old hat, his two shoulders out through his scant tattered cloak, and in his hand a three-stringed harp.

"What canst thou do?" said the doorkeeper.

"I can play," said the lank grey beggarman.

"Never fear," added he to the story-teller, "thou shalt see all, and not a man shall see thee."

When the king heard a harper was outside, he bade him in.

"It is I that have the best harpers in the five-fifths of Ireland," said he, and he signed them to play. They did so, and if they played, the lank grey beggarman listened.

"Heardst thou ever the like?" said the king.

"Did you ever, O king, hear a cat purring over a bowl of broth, or the buzzing of beetles in the twilight, or a shrill tongued old woman scolding your head off?"

"That I have often," said the king.

"More melodious to me," said the lank grey beggarman, "were the worst of these sounds than the sweetest harping of thy harpers."

When the harpers heard this, they drew their swords and rushed at him, but instead of striking him, their blows fell on each other, and soon not a man but was cracking his neighbour's skull and getting his own cracked in turn.

When the king saw this, he thought it hard the harpers weren't content with murdering their music, but must needs murder each other.

" Hang the fellow who began it all," said he ; " and if I can't have a story, let me have peace."

Up came the guards, seized the lank grey beggarman, marched him to the gallows and hanged him high and dry. Back they marched to the hall, and who should they see but the lank grey beggarman seated on a bench with his mouth to a flagon of ale.

" Never welcome you in," cried the captain of the guard, " didn't we hang you this minute, and what brings you here ? "

" Is it me myself, you mean ? "

" Who else ? " said the captain.

" May your hand turn into a pig's foot with you when you think of tying the rope ; why should you speak of hanging me ? "

Back they scurried to the gallows, and there hung the king's favourite brother.

Back they hurried to the king who had fallen fast asleep.

" Please your Majesty," said the captain, " we hanged that strolling vagabond, but here he is back again as well as ever."

" Hang him again," said the king, and off he went to sleep once more.

They did as they were told, but what happened was that

they found the king's chief harper hanging where the lank grey beggarman should have been.

The captain of the guard was sorely puzzled.

" Are you wishful to hang me a third time ? " said the lank grey beggarman.

" Go where you will," said the captain, " and as fast as you please if you'll only go far enough.   It's trouble enough you've given us already."

" Now you're reasonable," said the beggarman ; " and since you've given up trying to hang a stranger because he finds fault with your music, I don't mind telling you that if you go back to the gallows you'll find your friends sitting on the sward none the worse for what has happened."

As he said these words he vanished ; and the story-teller found himself on the spot where they first met, and where his wife still was with the carriage and horses.

" Now," said the lank grey beggarman, " I'll torment you no longer.   There's your carriage and your horses, and your money and your wife ; do what you please with them."

" For my carriage and my horses and my hounds," said the story-teller, " I thank you ; but my wife and my money you may keep."

" No," said the other.   " I want neither, and as for your wife, don't think ill of her for what she did, she couldn't help it."

" Not help it !   Not help kicking me into the mouth of my own hounds !   Not help casting me off for the sake of a beggarly old ———"

" I'm not as beggarly or as old as ye think.   I am Angus of the Bruff ; many a good turn you've done me with the

King of Leinster. This morning my magic told me the difficulty you were in, and I made up my mind to get you out of it. As for your wife there, the power that changed your body changed her mind. Forget and forgive as man and wife should do, and now you have a story for the King of Leinster when he calls for one ; " and with that he disap-appeared.

It's true enough he now had a story fit for a king. From first to last he told all that had befallen him ; so long and loud laughed the king that he couldn't go to sleep at all. And he told the story-teller never to trouble for fresh stories, but every night as long as he lived he listened again and he laughed afresh at the tale of the lank grey beggarman.

The Sea-Maiden

THERE was once a poor old fisherman, and one year he was not getting much fish. On a day of days, while he was fishing, there rose a sea-maiden at the side of his boat, and she asked him, "Are you getting much fish?" The old man answered and said, "Not I." "What reward would you give me for sending plenty of fish to you?" "Ach!" said the old man, "I have not much to spare." "Will you give me the first son you have?" said she. "I would give ye that, were I to have a son," said he. "Then go home, and remember me when your son is twenty years of age, and you yourself will get plenty of fish after this." Everything happened as the sea-maiden said, and he himself got plenty of fish; but when the end of the twenty years was nearing, the old man was growing more and more sorrowful and heavy hearted, while he counted each day as it came.

He had rest neither day nor night. The son asked his father one day, "Is any one troubling you?" The old

man said, " Some one is, but that's nought to do with you
nor any one else." The lad said, " I *must* know what it is."
His father told him at last how the matter was with him and
the sea-maiden. " Let not that put you in any trouble," said
the son ; " I will not oppose you." " You shall not ; you
shall not go, my son, though I never get fish any more."
" If you will not let me go with you, go to the smithy, and
let the smith make me a great strong sword, and I will
go seek my fortune."

His father went to the smithy, and the smith made a
doughty sword for him. His father came home with the
sword. The lad grasped it and gave it a shake or two,
and it flew into a hundred splinters. He asked his father
to go to the smithy and get him another sword in which
there should be twice as much weight ; and so his father
did, and so likewise it happened to the next sword—it
broke in two halves. Back went the old man to the
smithy ; and the smith made a great sword, its like he
never made before. " There's thy sword for thee," said
the smith, " and the fist must be good that plays this
blade." The old man gave the sword to his son ; he gave
it a shake or two. " This will do," said he ; " it's high
time now to travel on my way."

On the next morning he put a saddle on a black horse
that his father had, and he took the world for his pillow.
When he went on a bit, he fell in with the carcass of a
sheep beside the road. And there were a great black dog,
a falcon, and an otter, and they were quarrelling over the
spoil. So they asked him to divide it for them. He came
down off the horse, and he divided the carcass amongst the
three. Three shares to the dog, two shares to the otter,

and a share to the falcon. "For this," said the dog, "if swiftness of foot or sharpness of tooth will give thee aid, mind me, and I will be at thy side." Said the otter, "If the swimming of foot on the ground of a pool will loose thee, mind me, and I will be at thy side." Said the falcon, "If hardship comes on thee, where swiftness of wing or crook of a claw will do good, mind me, and I will be at thy side."

On this he went onward till he reached a king's house, and he took service to be a herd, and his wages were to be according to the milk of the cattle. He went away with the cattle, and the grazing was but bare. In the evening when he took them home they had not much milk, the place was so bare, and his meat and drink was but spare that night.

On the next day he went on further with them; and at last he came to a place exceedingly grassy, in a green glen, of which he never saw the like.

But about the time when he should drive the cattle homewards, who should he see coming but a great giant with his sword in his hand? "Hɪ! Ho!! Hogarach!!!" says the giant. "Those cattle are mine; they are on my land, and a dead man art thou." "I say not that," says the herd; "there is no knowing, but that may be easier to say than to do."

He drew the great clean-sweeping sword, and he neared the giant. The herd drew back his sword, and the head was off the giant in a twinkling. He leaped on the black horse, and he went to look for the giant's house. In went the herd, and that's the place where there was money in plenty, and dresses of each kind in the wardrobe with gold and

silver, and each thing finer than the other. At the mouth
of night he took himself to the king's house, but he took
not a thing from the giant's house. And when the cattle
were milked this night there *was* milk. He got good
feeding this night, meat and drink without stint, and the
king was hugely pleased that he had caught such a herd.
He went on for a time in this way, but at last the glen
grew bare of grass, and the grazing was not so good.

So he thought he would go a little further forward in
on the giant's land ; and he sees a great park of grass.
He returned for the cattle, and he put them into the
park.

They were but a short time grazing in the park when a
great wild giant came full of rage and madness. " Hi !
Haw !! Hogaraich !!! " said the giant. " It is a drink of
thy blood that will quench my thirst this night." " There
is no knowing," said the herd, " but that's easier to say
than to do." And at each other went the men. *There*
was shaking of blades ! At length and at last it seemed
as if the giant would get the victory over the herd. Then
he called on the dog, and with one spring the black dog
caught the giant by the neck, and swiftly the herd struck off
his head.

He went home very tired this night, but it's a wonder if
the king's cattle had not milk. The whole family was
delighted that they had got such a herd.

Next day he betakes himself to the castle. When he
reached the door, a little flattering carlin met him standing
in the door. " All hail and good luck to thee, fisher's son ;
'tis I myself am pleased to see thee ; great is the honour
for this kingdom, for thy like to be come into it—thy coming

in is fame for this little bothy; go in first; honour to the
gentles; go on, and take breath."

"In before me, thou crone; I like not flattery out of
doors; go in and let's hear thy speech." In went the
crone, and when her back was to him he drew his sword
and whips her head off; but the sword flew out of his
hand. And swift the crone gripped her head with both
hands, and puts it on her neck as it was before. The dog
sprung on the crone, and she struck the generous dog with
the club of magic; and there he lay. But the herd
struggled for a hold of the club of magic, and with one
blow on the top of the head she was on earth in the
twinkling of an eye. He went forward, up a little, and
there was spoil! Gold and silver, and each thing
more precious than another, in the crone's castle. He
went back to the king's house, and then there was rejoicing.

He followed herding in this way for a time; but one
night after he came home, instead of getting "All hail"
and "Good luck" from the dairymaid, all were at crying
and woe.

He asked what cause of woe there was that night. The
dairymaid said "There is a great beast with three heads in
the loch, and it must get some one every year, and the lot
had come this year on the king's daughter, and at midday
to-morrow she is to meet the Laidly Beast at the upper
end of the loch, but there is a great suitor yonder who is
going to rescue her."

"What suitor is that?" said the herd. "Oh, he is a
great General of arms," said the dairymaid, "and when he
kills the beast, he will marry the king's daughter, for the

king has said that he who could save his daughter should get her to marry."

But on the morrow, when the time grew near, the king's daughter and this hero of arms went to give a meeting to the beast, and they reached the black rock, at the upper end of the loch. They were but a short time there when the beast stirred in the midst of the loch;

but when the General saw this terror of a beast with three heads, he took fright, and he slunk away, and he hid himself. And the king's daughter was under fear and under trembling, with no one at all to save her. Suddenly she sees a doughty handsome youth, riding a black horse, and coming where she was. He was marvellously arrayed and full armed, and his black dog moved after him. "There is gloom on your face, girl," said the youth; "what do you here?"

"Oh! that's no matter," said the king's daughter. "It's not long I'll be here, at all events."

"I say not that," said he.

"A champion fled as likely as you, and not long since," said she.

"He is a champion who stands the war," said the youth. And to meet the beast he went with his sword and his dog. But there was a spluttering and a splashing between himself and the beast! The dog kept doing all he might, and the king's daughter was palsied by fear of the noise of the beast! One of them would now be under, and now above. But at last he cut one of the heads off it. It gave one roar, and the son of earth, echo of the rocks, called to its screech, and it drove the loch in spindrift from end to end, and in a twinkling it went out of sight.

"Good luck and victory follow you, lad!" said the king's daughter. "I am safe for one night, but the beast will come again and again, until the other two heads come off it." He caught the beast's head, and he drew a knot through it, and he told her to bring it with her there to-morrow. She gave him a gold ring, and went home with the head on her shoulder, and the herd betook himself to the cows. But she had not gone far when this great General saw her, and he said to her, "I will kill you if you do not say that 'twas I took the head off the beast." "Oh!" says she, "'tis I will say it; who else took the head off the beast but you!" They reached the king's house, and the head was on the General's shoulder. But here was rejoicing, that she should come home alive and whole, and this great captain with the beast's head full of blood in his hand. On the morrow they went away, and

there was no question at all but that this hero would save
the king's daughter.

They reached the same place, and they were not long
there when the fearful Laidly Beast stirred in the midst of the
loch, and the hero slunk away as he did on yesterday, but
it was not long after this when the man of the black horse
came, with another dress on. No matter; she knew that
it was the very same lad. "It is I am pleased to see
you," said she. "I am in hopes you will handle your great
sword to-day as you did yesterday. Come up and take
breath." But they were not long there when they saw the
beast steaming in the midst of the loch.

At once he went to meet the beast, but *there* was
Cloopersteich and Claperstich, spluttering, splashing, raving,
and roaring on the beast! They kept at it thus for a long
time, and about the mouth of night he cut another head
off the beast. He put it on the knot and gave it to her.
She gave him one of her earrings, and he leaped on the
black horse, and he betook himself to the herding. The
king's daughter went home with the heads. The General
met her, and took the heads from her, and he said to her,
that she must tell that it was he who took the head off
the beast this time also. "Who else took the head off
the beast but you?" said she. They reached the king's
house with the heads. Then there was joy and. gladness.

About the same time on the morrow, the two went away.
The officer hid himself as he usually did. The king's
daughter betook herself to the bank of the loch. The hero
of the black horse came, and if roaring and raving were on
the beast on the days that were passed, this day it was

horrible. But no matter, he took the third head off the
beast, and drew it through the knot, and gave it to her.
She gave him her other earring, and then she went home
with the heads. When they reached the king's house, all
were full of smiles, and the General was to marry the
king's daughter the next day. The wedding was going on,

and every one about the castle longing till the priest should
come. But when the priest came, she would marry only the
one who could take the heads off the knot without cutting
it. "Who should take the heads off the knot but the man
that put the heads on?" said the king.

The General tried them, but he could not loose them and
at last there was no one about the house but had tried to
take the heads off the knot, but they could not. The king
asked if there were any one else about the house that

would try to take the heads off the knot. They said that
the herd had not tried them yet. Word went for the herd ;
and he was not long throwing them hither and thither.
" But stop a bit, my lad," said the king's daughter ; "the
man that took the heads off the beast, he has my ring and
my two earrings." The herd put his hand in his pocket,
and he threw them on the board. " Thou art my man,"
said the king's daughter. The king was not so pleased
when he saw that it was a herd who was to marry his
daughter, but he ordered that he should be put in a better
dress ; but his daughter spoke, and she said that he had a
dress as fine as any that ever was in his castle ; and thus
it happened. The herd put on the giant's golden dress,
and they married that same day.

They were now married, and everything went on well.
But one day, and it was the namesake of the day when his
father had promised him to the sea-maiden, they were
sauntering by the side of the loch, and lo and behold ! she
came and took him away to the loch without leave or asking. The king's daughter was now mournful, tearful, blind-
sorrowful for her married man ; she was always with her
eye on the loch. An old soothsayer met her, and she told
how it had befallen her married mate. Then he told her
the thing to do to save her mate, and that she did.

She took her harp to the sea-shore, and sat and played ;
and the sea-maiden came up to listen, for sea-maidens are
fonder of music than all other creatures. But when the
wife saw the sea-maiden she stopped. The sea-maiden
said, " Play on ! " but the princess said, " No, not till I see
my man again." So the sea-maiden put up his head out of
the loch. Then the princess played again, and stopped till

the sea-maiden put him up to the waist. Then the princess played and stopped again, and this time the sea-maiden put him all out of the loch, and he called on the falcon and became one and flew on shore. But the sea-maiden took the princess, his wife.

Sorrowful was each one that was in the town on this night. Her man was mournful, tearful, wandering down and up about the banks of the loch, by day and night. The old soothsayer met him. The soothsayer told him that there was no way of killing the sea-maiden but the one way, and this is it—" In the island that is in the midst of the loch is the white-footed hind of the slenderest legs and the swiftest step, and though she be caught, there will spring a hoodie out of her, and though the hoodie should be caught, there will spring a trout out of her, but there is an egg in the mouth of the trout, and the soul of the sea-maiden is in the egg, and if the egg breaks, she is dead."

Now, there was no way of getting to this island, for the sea-maiden would sink each boat and raft that would go on the loch. He thought he would try to leap the strait with the black horse, and even so he did. The black horse leaped the strait. He saw the hind, and he let the black dog after her, but when he was on one side of the island, the hind would be on the other side. "Oh! would the black dog of the carcass of flesh were here!" No sooner spoke he the word than the grateful dog was at his side; and after the hind he went, and they were not long in bringing her to earth. But he no sooner caught her than a hoodie sprang out of her. "Would that the falcon grey, of sharpest eye and swiftest wing, were here!" No sooner said he this than the falcon was after the hoodie, and she was not long putting her to earth; and as the hoodie fell on the bank of the loch, out of her jumps the trout. "Oh! that thou wert by me now, oh otter!" No sooner said than the otter was at his side, and out on the loch she leaped, and brings the trout from the midst of the loch; but no sooner was the otter on shore with the trout than the egg came from his mouth. He sprang and he put his foot on it. 'Twas then the sea-maiden appeared, and she said, "Break not the egg, and you shall get all you ask." "Deliver to me my wife!" In the wink of an eye she was by his side. When he got hold of her hand in both his hands, he let his foot down on the egg, and the sea-maiden died.

A Legend of Knockmany

HAT Irish man, woman, or child has not heard of our renowned Hibernian Hercules, the great and glorious Fin M'Coul? Not one, from Cape Clear to the Giant's Causeway, nor from that back again to Cape Clear. And, by-the-way, speaking of the Giant's Causeway brings me at once to the beginning of my story. Well, it so happened that Fin and his men were all working at the Causeway, in order to make a bridge across to Scotland; when Fin, who was very fond of his wife Oonagh, took it into his head that he would go home and see how the poor woman got on in his absence. So, accordingly, he pulled up a fir-tree, and, after lopping off the roots and branches, made a walking-stick of it, and set out on his way to Oonagh.

Oonagh, or rather Fin, lived at this time on the very tip-top of Knockmany Hill, which faces a cousin of its own called Cullamore, that rises up, half-hill, half-mountain, on the opposite side.

There was at that time another giant, named Cucullin—some say he was Irish, and some say he was Scotch—but whether Scotch or Irish, sorrow doubt of it but he was a targer. No other giant of the day could stand before him; and such was his strength, that, when well vexed, he could give a stamp that shook the country about him. The fame and name of him went far and near; and nothing in the shape of a man, it was said, had any chance with him in a fight. By one blow of his fists he flattened a thunderbolt and kept it in his pocket, in the shape of a pancake, to show to all his enemies, when they were about to fight him. Undoubtedly he had given every giant in Ireland a considerable beating, barring Fin M'Coul himself; and he swore that he would never rest, night or day, winter or summer, till he would serve Fin with the same sauce, if he could catch him. However, the short and long of it was, with reverence be it spoken, that Fin heard Cucullin was coming to the Causeway to have a trial of strength with him; and he was seized with a very warm and sudden fit of affection for his wife, poor woman, leading a very lonely, uncomfortable life of it in his absence. He accordingly pulled up the fir-tree, as I said before, and having snedded it into a walking-stick, set out on his travels to see his darling Oonagh on the top of Knockmany, by the way.

In truth, the people wondered very much why it was that Fin selected such a windy spot for his dwelling-house, and they even went so far as to tell him as much.

"What can you mane, Mr. M'Coul," said they, "by pitching your tent upon the top of Knockmany, where you never are without a breeze, day or night, winter or summer, and where you're often forced to take your nightcap without either going to bed or turning up your little finger; ay, an' where, besides this, there's the sorrow's own want of water?"

"Why," said Fin, "ever since I was the height of a round tower, I was known to be fond of having a good prospect of my own; and where the dickens, neighbours, could I find a better spot for a good prospect than the top of Knockmany? As for water, I am sinking a pump, and, plase goodness, as soon as the Causeway's made, I intend to finish it."

Now, this was more of Fin's philosophy; for the real state of the case was, that he pitched upon the top of Knockmany in order that he might be able to see Cucullin coming towards the house. All we have to say is, that if he wanted a spot from which to keep a sharp look-out— and, between ourselves, he did want it grievously—barring Slieve Croob, or Slieve Donard, or its own cousin, Cullamore, he could not find a neater or more convenient situation for it in the sweet and sagacious province of Ulster.

"God save all here!" said Fin, good-humouredly, on putting his honest face into his own door.

"Musha, Fin, avick, an' you're welcome home to your own Oonagh, you darlin' bully." Here followed a smack that is said to have made the waters of the lake at the bottom of the hill curl, as it were, with kindness and sympathy.

Fin spent two or three happy days with Oonagh, and felt himself very comfortable, considering the dread he had of Cucullin. This, however, grew upon him so much that his wife could not but perceive something lay on his mind which he kept altogether to himself. Let a woman alone, in the meantime, for ferreting or wheedling a secret out of her good man, when she wishes.   Fin was a proof of this.

"It's this Cucullin," said he, "that's troubling me. When the fellow gets angry, and begins to stamp, he'll shake you a whole townland; and it's well known that he can stop a thunderbolt, for he always carries one about him in the shape of a pancake, to show to any one that might misdoubt it."

As he spoke, he clapped his thumb in his mouth, which he always did when he wanted to prophesy, or to know anything that happened in his absence; and the wife asked him what he did it for.

"He's coming," said Fin; "I see him below Dungannon."

"Thank goodness, dear! an' who is it, avick? Glory be to God!"

"That baste, Cucullin," replied Fin; "and how to manage I don't know.   If I run away, I am disgraced; and I know that sooner or later I must meet him, for my thumb tells me so."

"When will he be here?" said she.

"To-morrow, about two o'clock," replied Fin, with a groan.

"Well, my bully, don't be cast down," said Oonagh; "depend on me, and maybe I'll bring you better out of this scrape than ever you could bring yourself, by your rule o' thumb."

She then made a high smoke on the top of the hill, after which she put her finger in her mouth, and gave three whistles, and by that Cucullin knew he was invited to Culla-more—for this was the way that the Irish long ago gave a sign to all strangers and travellers, to let them know they were welcome to come and take share of whatever was going.

In the meantime, Fin was very melancholy, and did not know what to do, or how to act at all. Cucullin was an ugly customer to meet with ; and, the idea of the " cake " aforesaid flattened the very heart within him. What chance could he have, strong and brave though he was, with a man who could, when put in a passion, walk the country into earthquakes and knock thunderbolts into pancakes ? Fin knew not on what hand to turn him. Right or left— backward or forward—where to go he could form no guess whatsoever.

"Oonagh," said he, "can you do nothing for me ? Where's all your invention ? Am I to be skivered like a rabbit before your eyes, and to have my name disgraced for ever in the sight of all my tribe, and me the best man among them ? How am I to fight this man-mountain— this huge cross between an earthquake and a thunderbolt ? —with a pancake in his pocket that was once ———"

" Be easy, Fin," replied Oonagh ; "troth, I'm ashamed of you. Keep your toe in your pump, will you ? Talking of pancakes, maybe, we'll give him as good as any he brings with him—thunderbolt or otherwise. If I don't treat him to as smart feeding as he's got this many a day, never trust Oonagh again. Leave him to me, and do just as I bid you."

This relieved Fin very much ; for, after all, he had great confidence in his wife, knowing, as he did, that she had got him out of many a quandary before. Oonagh then drew the nine woollen threads of different colours, which she always did to find out the best way of succeeding in anything of importance she went about. She then platted them into three plats with three colours in each, putting one on her right arm, one round her heart, and the third round her right ankle, for then she knew that nothing could fail with her that she undertook.

Having everything now prepared, she sent round to the neighbours and borrowed one-and-twenty iron griddles, which she took and kneaded into the hearts of one-and-twenty cakes of bread, and these she baked on the fire in the usual way, setting them aside in the cupboard according as they were done. She then put down a large pot of new milk, which she made into curds and whey. Having done all this, she sat down quite contented, waiting for his arrival on the next day about two o'clock, that being the hour at which he was expected—for Fin knew as much by the sucking of his thumb. Now this was a curious property that Fin's thumb had. In this very thing, moreover, he was very much resembled by his great foe, Cucullin ; for it was well known that the huge strength he possessed all lay in the middle finger of his right hand, and that, if he happened by any mischance to lose it, he was no more, for all his bulk, than a common man.

At length, the next day, Cucullin was seen coming across the valley, and Oonagh knew that it was time to commence operations. She immediately brought the cradle, and made Fin to lie down in it, and cover himself up with the clothes.

"You must pass for your own child," said she ; "so just lie there snug, and say nothing, but be guided by me."

About two o'clock, as he had been expected, Cucullin came in. "God save all here!" said he; "is this where the great Fin M'Coul lives?"

"Indeed it is, honest man," replied Oonagh; "God save you kindly—won't you be sitting?"

"Thank you, ma'am," says he, sitting down; "you're Mrs. M'Coul, I suppose?"

"I am," said she; "and I have no reason, I hope, to be ashamed of my husband."

"No," said the other, "he has the name of being the strongest and bravest man in Ireland; but for all that, there's a man not far from you that's very desirous of taking a shake with him. Is he at home?"

"Why, then, no," she replied; "and if ever a man left his house in a fury, he did. It appears that some one told him of a big basthoon of a giant called Cucullin being down at the Causeway to look for him, and so he set out there to try if he could catch him. Troth, I hope, for the poor giant's sake, he won't meet with him, for if he does, Fin will make paste of him at once."

"Well," said the other, "I am Cucullin, and I have been seeking him these twelve months, but he always kept clear of me; and I will never rest night or day till I lay my hands on him."

At this Oonagh set up a loud laugh, of great contempt, by-the-way, and looked at him as if he was only a mere handful of a man.

"Did you ever see Fin?" said she, changing her manner all at once.

"How could I?" said he; "he always took care to keep his distance."

" I thought so," she replied ; " I judged as much ; and if you take my advice, you poor-looking creature, you'll pray night and day that you may never see him, for I tell you it will be a black day for you when you do. But, in the meantime, you perceive that the wind's on the door, and as Fin himself is from home, maybe you'd be civil enough to turn the house, for it's always what Fin does when he's here."

This was a startler even to Cucullin ; but he got up, however, and after pulling the middle finger of his right hand until it cracked three times, he went outside, and getting his arms about the house, turned it as she had wished. When Fin saw this, he felt the sweat of fear oozing out through every pore of his skin ; but Oonagh, depending upon her woman's wit, felt not a whit daunted.

" Arrah, then," said she, " as you are so civil, maybe you'd do another obliging turn for us, as Fin's not here to do it himself. You see, after this long stretch of dry weather we've had, we feel very badly off for want of water. Now, Fin says there's a fine spring-well somewhere under the rocks behind the hill here below, and it was his intention to pull them asunder ; but having heard of you, he left the place in such a fury, that he never thought of it. Now, if you try to find it, troth I'd feel it a kindness."

She then brought Cucullin down to see the place, which was then all one solid rock ; and, after looking at it for some time, he cracked his right middle finger nine times, and, stooping down, tore a cleft about four hundred feet deep, and a quarter of a mile in length, which has since been christened by the name of Lumford's Glen.

" You'll now come in," said she, " and eat a bit of such

humble fare as we can give you. Fin, even although he and you are enemies, would scorn not to treat you kindly in his own house ; and, indeed, if I didn't do it even in his absence, he would not be pleased with me."

She accordingly brought him in, and placing half-a-dozen of the cakes we spoke of before him, together with a can or two of butter, a side of boiled bacon, and a stack of cabbage, she desired him to help himself——for this, be it known, was long before the invention of potatoes. Cucullin put one of the cakes in his mouth to take a huge whack out of it, when he made a thundering noise, something between a growl and a yell. "Blood and fury!" he shouted ; "how is this ? Here are two of my teeth out ! What kind of bread this is you gave me."

"What's the matter ?" said Oonagh coolly.

"Matter !" shouted the other again ; "why, here are the two best teeth in my head gone."

"Why," said she, "that's Fin's bread——the only bread he ever eats when at home ; but, indeed, I forgot to tell you that nobody can eat it but himself, and that child in the cradle there. I thought, however, that, as you were reported to be rather a stout little fellow of your size, you might be able to manage it, and I did not wish to affront a man that thinks himself able to fight Fin. Here's another cake——maybe it's not so hard as that."

Cucullin at the moment was not only hungry, but ravenous, so he accordingly made a fresh set at the second cake, and immediately another yell was heard twice as loud as the first. "Thunder and gibbets!" he roared, "take your bread out of this, or I will not have a tooth in my head ; there's another pair of them gone!"

" Well, honest man," replied Oonagh, " if you're not able to eat the bread, say so quietly, and don't be wakening the child in the cradle there. There, now, he's awake upon me."

Fin now gave a skirl that startled the giant, as coming from such a youngster as he was supposed to be.

" Mother " said he, " I'm hungry—get me something to eat." Oonagh went over, and putting into his hand a cake that had no griddle in it, Fin, whose appetite in the meantime had been sharpened by seeing eating going forward, soon swallowed it. Cucullin was thunderstruck, and secretly thanked his stars that he had the good fortune to miss meeting Fin, for, as he said to himself, " I'd have no chance with a man who could eat such bread as that, which even his son that's but in his cradle can munch before my eyes."

"I'd like to take a glimpse at the lad in the cradle," said he to Oonagh ; "for I can tell you that the infant who can manage that nutriment is no joke to look at, or to feed of a scarce summer."

"With all the veins of my heart," replied Oonagh; "get up, acushla, and show this decent little man something that won't be unworthy of your father, Fin M'Coul."

Fin, who was dressed for the occasion as much like a boy as possible, got up, and bringing Cucullin out, "Are you strong ?" said he.

"Thunder an' ounds !" exclaimed the other, "what a voice in so small a chap !"

"Are you strong ?" said Fin again ; "are you able to squeeze water out of that white stone ?" he asked, putting one into Cucullin's hand. The latter squeezed and squeezed the stone, but in vain.

"Ah, you're a poor creature !" said Fin. "You a giant ! Give me the stone here, and when I'll show what Fin's little son can do, you may then judge of what my daddy himself is."

Fin then took the stone, and exchanging it for the curds, he squeezed the latter until the whey, as clear as water, oozed out in a little shower from his hand.

"I'll now go in," said he, "to my cradle; for I scorn to lose my time with any one that's not able to eat my daddy's bread, or squeeze water out of a stone. Bedad, you had better be off out of this before he comes back ; for if he catches you, it's in flummery he'd have you in two minutes."

Cucullin, seeing what he had seen, was of the same opinion himself; his knees knocked together with the terror of Fin's return, and he accordingly hastened to bid Oonagh farewell, and to assure her, that from that day out, he never wished to hear of, much less to see, her husband. " I admit fairly that I'm not a match for him," said he, " strong as I am; tell him I will avoid him as I would the plague, and that I will make myself scarce in this part of the country while I live."

Fin, in the meantime, had gone into the cradle, where he lay very quietly, his heart at his mouth with delight that Cucullin was about to take his departure, without discovering the tricks that had been played off on him.

" It's well for you," said Oonagh, " that he doesn't happen to be here, for it's nothing but hawk's meat he'd make of you."

" I know that," says Cucullin; " divil a thing else he'd make of me; but before I go, will you let me feel what kind of teeth Fin's lad has got that can eat griddle-bread like that ? "

" With all pleasure in life," said she; " only, as they're far back in his head, you must put your finger a good way in."

Cucullin was surprised to find such a powerful set of grinders in one so young; but he was still much more so on finding, when he took his hand from Fin's mouth, that he had left the very finger upon which his whole strength depended, behind him. He gave one loud groan, and fell down at once with terror and weakness. This was all Fin wanted, who now knew that his most powerful and bitterest enemy was at his mercy. He started out of the cradle, and in a few minutes the great Cucullin, that was for such a length of time the terror of him and all his followers, lay a corpse before him. Thus did Fin, through the wit and invention of Oonagh, his wife, succeed in overcoming his enemy by cunning, which he never could have done by force.

Fair, Brown, and Trembling

KING HUGH CÚRUCHA lived in Tir Conal, and he had three daughters, whose names were Fair, Brown, and Trembling.

Fair and Brown had new dresses, and went to church every Sunday. Trembling was kept at home to do the cooking and work. They would not let her go out of the house at all ; for she was more beautiful than the other two, and they were in dread she might marry before themselves.

They carried on in this way for seven years. At the end of seven years the son of the king of Emania fell in love with the eldest sister.

One Sunday morning, after the other two had gone to church, the old henwife came into the kitchen to Trembling, and said : " It's at church you ought to be this day, instead of working here at home."

" How could I go ? " said Trembling. " I have no clothes good enough to wear at church ; and if my sisters were to see me there, they'd kill me for going out of the house."

" I'll give you," said the henwife, " a finer dress than

either of them has ever seen. And now tell me what dress will you have ? "

" I'll have," said Trembling, " a dress as white as snow, and green shoes for my feet."

Then the henwife put on the cloak of darkness, clipped a piece from the old clothes the young woman had on, and asked for the whitest robes in the world and the most beautiful that could be found, and a pair of green shoes.

That moment she had the robe and the shoes, and she brought them to Trembling, who put them on. When Trembling was dressed and ready, the henwife said : " I have a honey-bird here to sit on your right shoulder, and a honey-finger to put on your left. At the door stands a milk-white mare, with a golden saddle for you to sit on, and a golden bridle to hold in your hand."

Trembling sat on the golden saddle ; and when she was ready to start, the henwife said : " You must not go inside the door of the church, and the minute the people rise up at the end of Mass, do you make off, and ride home as fast as the mare will carry you."

When Trembling came to the door of the church there was no one inside who could get a glimpse of her but was striving to know who she was ; and when they saw her hurrying away at the end of Mass, they ran out to overtake her. But no use in their running ; she was away before any man could come near her. From the minute she left the church till she got home, she overtook the wind before her, and outstripped the wind behind.

She came down at the door, went in, and found the henwife had dinner ready. She put off the white robes, and had on her old dress in a twinkling.

When the two sisters came home the henwife asked :
" Have you any news to-day from the church ? "

" We have great news," said they. " We saw a
wonderful grand lady at the church-door. The like of the
robes she had we have never seen on woman before. It's
little that was thought of our dresses beside what she had
on ; and there wasn't a man at the church, from the king
to the beggar, but was trying to look at her and know who
she was."

The sisters would give no peace till they had two dresses
like the robes of the strange lady ; but honey-birds and
honey-fingers were not to be found.

Next Sunday the two sisters went to church again, and
left the youngest at home to cook the dinner.

After they had gone, the henwife came in and asked :
" Will you go to church to-day ? "

" I would go," said Trembling, " if I could get the
going."

" What robe will you wear ? " asked the henwife.

" The finest black satin that can be found, and red shoes
for my feet."

" What colour do you want the mare to be ? "

" I want her to be so black and so glossy that I can see
myself in her body."

The henwife put on the cloak of darkness, and asked for
the robes and the mare. That moment she had them.
When Trembling was dressed, the henwife put the honey-
bird on her right shoulder and the honey-finger on her left.
The saddle on the mare was silver, and so was the bridle.

When Trembling sat in the saddle and was going away,
the henwife ordered her strictly not to go inside the door of

the church, but to rush away as soon as the people rose at the end of Mass, and hurry home on the mare before any man could stop her.

That Sunday the people were more astonished than ever, and gazed at her more than the first time; and all they were thinking of was to know who she was. But they had no chance; for the moment the people rose at the end of Mass she slipped from the church, was in the silver saddle, and home before a man could stop her or talk to her.

The henwife had the dinner ready. Trembling took off her satin robe, and had on her old clothes before her sisters got home.

" What news have you to-day ? " asked the henwife of the sisters when they came from the church.

" Oh, we saw the grand strange lady again ! And it's little that any man could think of our dresses after looking at the robes of satin that she had on ! And all at church, from high to low, had their mouths open, gazing at her, and no man was looking at us."

The two sisters gave neither rest nor peace till they got dresses as nearly like the strange lady's robes as they could find. Of course they were not so good ; for the like of those robes could not be found in Erin.

When the third Sunday came, Fair and Brown went to church dressed in black satin. They left Trembling at home to work in the kitchen, and told her to be sure and have dinner ready when they came back.

After they had gone and were out of sight, the henwife came to the kitchen and said : " Well, my dear, are you for church to-day ? "

" I would go if I had a new dress to wear."

" I'll get you any dress you ask for.   What dress would you like ? " asked the henwife.

" A dress red as a rose from the waist down, and white as snow from the waist up ; a cape of green on my shoulders ; and a hat on my head with a red, a white, and a green feather in it ; and shoes for my feet with the toes red, the middle white, and the backs and heels green."

The henwife put on the cloak of darkness, wished for all these things, and had them.   When Trembling was dressed, the henwife put the honey-bird on her right shoulder and the honey-finger on her left, and, placing the hat on her head, clipped a few hairs from one lock and a few from another with her scissors, and that moment the most beautiful golden hair was flowing down over the girl's shoulders.   Then the henwife asked what kind of a mare she would ride.   She said white, with blue and gold-coloured diamond-shaped spots all over her body, on her back a saddle of gold, and on her head a golden bridle.

The mare stood there before the door, and a bird sitting between her ears, which began to sing as soon as Trembling was in the saddle, and never stopped till she came home from the church.

The fame of the beautiful strange lady had gone out through the world, and all the princes and great men that were in it came to church that Sunday, each one hoping that it was himself would have her home with him after Mass.

The son of the king of Emania forgot all about the eldest sister, and remained outside the church, so as to catch the strange lady before she could hurry away.

The church was more crowded than ever before, and

there were three times as many outside. There was such a throng before the church that Trembling could only come inside the gate.

As soon as the people were rising at the end of Mass, the lady slipped out through the gate, was in the golden saddle in an instant, and sweeping away ahead of the wind. But if she was, the prince of Emania was at her side, and, seizing her by the foot, he ran with the mare for thirty perches, and never let go of the beautiful lady till the shoe was pulled from her foot, and he was left behind with it in his hand. She came home as fast as the mare could carry her, and was thinking all the time that the henwife would kill her for losing the shoe.

Seeing her so vexed and so changed in the face, the old woman asked : " What's the trouble that's on you now ? "

" Oh ! I've lost one of the shoes off my feet," said Trembling.

" Don't mind that ; don't be vexed," said the henwife ; " maybe it's the best thing that ever happened to you."

Then Trembling gave up all the things she had to the henwife, put on her old clothes, and went to work in the kitchen. When the sisters came home, the henwife asked : " Have you any news from the church ? "

" We have indeed," said they, " for we saw the grandest sight to-day. The strange lady came again, in grander array than before. On herself and the horse she rode were the finest colours of the world, and between the ears of the horse was a bird which never stopped singing from the time she came till she went away. The lady herself is the most beautiful woman ever seen by man in Erin."

After Trembling had disappeared from the church, the

son of the king of Emania said to the other kings' sons :
" I will have that lady for my own."

They all said : " You didn't win her just by taking the
shoe off her foot ; you'll have to win her by the point of the
sword ; you'll have to fight for her with us before you can
call her your own."

" Well," said the son of the king of Emania, " when I
find the lady that shoe will fit, I'll fight for her, never fear,
before I leave her to any of you."

Then all the kings' sons were uneasy, and anxious to
know who was she that lost the shoe ; and they began to
travel all over Erin to know could they find her. The
prince of Emania and all the others went in a great company
together, and made the round of Erin ; they went everywhere,—north, south, east, and west. They visited every
place where a woman was to be found, and left not a house
in the kingdom they did not search, to know could they find
the woman the shoe would fit, not caring whether she was
rich or poor, of high or low degree.

The prince of Emania always kept the shoe ; and when
the young women saw it, they had great hopes, for it was
of proper size, neither large nor small, and it would beat
any man to know of what material it was made. One
thought it would fit her if she cut a little from her great
toe ; and another, with too short a foot, put something
in the tip of her stocking. But no use ; they only
spoiled their feet, and were curing them for months
afterwards.

The two sisters, Fair and Brown, heard that the princes
of the world were looking all over Erin for the woman that
could wear the shoe, and every day they were talking of

trying it on; and one day Trembling spoke up and said:
" Maybe it's my foot that the shoe will fit."

" Oh, the breaking of the dog's foot on you! Why say
so when you were at home every Sunday ? "

They were that way waiting, and scolding the younger
sister, till the princes were near the place. The day they
were to come, the sisters put Trembling in a closet, and
locked the door on her. When the company came to the
house, the prince of Emania gave the shoe to the sisters.
But though they tried and tried, it would fit neither of
them.

" Is there any other young woman in the house ? " asked
the prince.

" There is," said Trembling, speaking up in the closet ;
" I'm here."

" Oh! we have her for nothing but to put out the ashes,"
said the sisters.

But the prince and the others wouldn't leave the house
till they had seen her ; so the two sisters had to open the
door. When Trembling came out, the shoe was given to
her, and it fitted exactly.

The prince of Emania looked at her and said: " You
are the woman the shoe fits, and you are the woman I took
the shoe from."

Then Trembling spoke up, and said : " Do you stay here
till I return."

Then she went to the henwife's house. The old woman
put on the cloak of darkness, got everything for her she
had the first Sunday at church, and put her on the white
mare in the same fashion. Then Trembling rode along
the highway to the front of the house. All who saw

her the first time said : " This is the lady we saw at church."

Then she went away a second time, and a second time came back on the black mare in the second dress which the henwife gave her. All who saw her the second Sunday said : " That is the lady we saw at church."

A third time she asked for a short absence, and soon came back on the third mare and in the third dress. All who saw her the third time said : " That is the lady we saw at church." Every man was satisfied, and knew that she was the woman.

Then all the princes and great men spoke up, and said to the son of the king of Emania : " You'll have to fight now for her before we let her go with you."

" I'm here before you, ready for combat," answered the prince.

Then the son of the king of Lochlin stepped forth. The struggle began, and a terrible struggle it was. They fought for nine hours ; and then the son of the king of Lochlin stopped, gave up his claim, and left the field. Next day the son of the king of Spain fought six hours, and yielded his claim. On the third day the son of the king of Nyerfói fought eight hours, and stopped. The fourth day the son of the king of Greece fought six hours, and stopped. On the fifth day no more strange princes wanted to fight ; and all the sons of kings in Erin said they would not fight with a man of their own land, that the strangers had had their chance, and, as no others came to claim the woman, she belonged of right to the son of the king of Emania.

The marriage-day was fixed, and the invitations were sent out. The wedding lasted for a year and a day. When the wedding was over, the king's son brought home the bride, and when the time came a son was born. The young woman sent for her eldest sister, Fair, to be with her and care for her. One day, when Trembling was well, and when her husband was away hunting, the two sisters went out to walk; and when they came to the seaside, the eldest pushed the youngest sister in. A great whale came and swallowed her.

The eldest sister came home alone, and the husband asked, " Where is your sister ? "

" She has gone home to her father in Ballyshannon; now that I am well, I don't need her."

" Well," said the husband, looking at her, " I'm in dread it's my wife that has gone."

" Oh! no," said she; " it's my sister Fair that's gone."

Since the sisters were very much alike, the prince was in doubt. That night he put his sword between them, and said : " If you are my wife, this sword will get warm ; if not, it will stay cold."

In the morning when he rose up, the sword was as cold as when he put it there.

It happened, when the two sisters were walking by the seashore, that a little cowboy was down by the water minding cattle, and saw Fair push Trembling into the sea ; and next day, when the tide came in, he saw the whale swim up and throw her out on the sand. When she was on the sand she said to the cowboy : " When you go home in the evening with the cows, tell the master that my sister Fair pushed me into the sea yesterday ; that a whale swallowed me, and then threw me out, but will come again and swallow me with the coming of the next tide ; then he'll go out with the tide, and come again with to-morrow's tide, and throw me again on the strand. The whale will cast me out three times. I'm under the enchantment of this whale, and cannot leave the beach or escape myself. Unless my husband saves me before I'm swallowed the fourth time, I shall be lost. He must come and shoot the whale with a silver bullet when he turns on the broad of his back. Under the breast-fin of the whale is a reddish-brown spot. My husband must hit him in that spot, for it is the only place in which he can be killed."

When the cowboy got home, the eldest sister gave him a draught of oblivion, and he did not tell.

Next day he went again to the sea. The whale came and cast Trembling on shore again. She asked the boy : " Did you tell the master what I told you to tell him ? "

" I did not," said he ; " I forgot."

" How did you forget ? " asked she.

" The woman of the house gave me a drink that made me forget."

" Well, don't forget telling him this night ; and if she gives you a drink, don't take it from her."

As soon as the cowboy came home, the eldest sister offered him a drink. He refused to take it till he had delivered his message and told all to the master. The third day the prince went down with his gun and a silver bullet in it. He was not long down when the whale came and threw Trembling upon the beach as the two days before. She had no power to speak to her husband till he had killed the whale. Then the whale went out, turned over once on the broad of his back, and showed the spot for a moment only. That moment the prince fired. He had but the one chance, and a short one at that ; but he took it, and hit the spot, and the whale, mad with pain, made the sea all around red with blood, and died.

That minute Trembling was able to speak, and went home with her husband, who sent word to her father what the eldest sister had done. The father came, and told him any death he chose to give her to give it. The prince told the father he would leave her life and death with himself. The father had her put out then on the sea in a barrel, with provisions in it for seven years.

In time Trembling had a second child, a daughter. The prince and she sent the cowboy to school, and trained him up as one of their own children, and said : " If the little girl that is born to us now lives, no other man in the world will get her but him."

The cowboy and the prince's daughter lived on till

they were married. The mother said to her husband:
" You could not have saved me from the whale but for the
little cowboy; on that account I don't grudge him my
daughter."

The son of the king of Emania and Trembling had
fourteen children, and they lived happily till the two died of
old age.

Jack and His Master

A POOR woman had three sons. The eldest and second eldest were cunning clever fellows, but they called the youngest Jack the Fool, because they thought he was no better than a simpleton. The eldest got tired of staying at home, and said he'd go look for service. He stayed away a whole year, and then came back one day, dragging one foot after the other, and a poor wizened face on him, and he as cross as two sticks. When he was rested and got something to eat, he told them how he got service with the Gray Churl of the Townland of Mischance, and that the agreement was, whoever would first say he was sorry for his bargain, should get an inch wide of the skin of his back, from shoulder to hips, taken off. If it was the master, he should also pay double wages; if it was the servant, he should get no wages at all. "But the thief," says he, "gave me so little to eat, and kept me so hard at work, that flesh and blood couldn't stand it; and when he asked me once, when I was in a passion, if I was sorry for my bargain, I was mad enough to say I was, and here I am disabled for life."

Vexed enough were the poor mother and brothers ; and the second eldest said on the spot he'd go and take service with the Gray Churl, and punish him by all the annoyance he'd give him till he'd make him say he was sorry for his agreement. " Oh, won't I be glad to see the skin coming off the old villain's back ! " said he. All they could say had no effect : he started off for the Townland of Mischance, and in a twelvemonth he was back just as miserable and helpless as his brother.

All the poor mother could say didn't prevent Jack the Fool from starting to see if he was able to regulate the Gray Churl. He agreed with him for a year for twenty pounds, and the terms were the same.

" Now, Jack," said the Gray Churl, " if you refuse to do anything you are able to do, you must lose a month's wages."

" I'm satisfied," said Jack ; " and if you stop me from doing a thing after telling me to do it, you are to give me an additional month's wages."

" I am satisfied," says the master.

" Or if you blame me for obeying your orders, you must give the same."

" I am satisfied," said the master again.

The first day that Jack served he was fed very poorly, and was worked to the saddleskirts. Next day he came in just before the dinner was sent up to the parlour. They were taking the goose off the spit, but well becomes Jack he whips a knife off the dresser, and cuts off one side of the breast, one leg and thigh, and one wing, and fell to. In came the master, and began to abuse him for his assurance. " Oh, you know, master, you're to feed me, and wherever the goose goes won't have to be filled again till supper. Are you sorry for our agreement ? "

The master was going to cry out he was, but he bethought himself in time. " Oh no, not at all," said he.

" That's well," said Jack.

Next day Jack was to go clamp turf on the bog. They weren't sorry to have him away from the kitchen at dinner time. He didn't find his breakfast very heavy on his stomach ; so he said to the mistress, " I think, ma'am, it will be better for me to get my dinner now, and not lose time coming home from the bog."

" That's true, Jack," said she. So she brought out a good cake, and a print of butter, and a bottle of milk, thinking he'd take them away to the bog. But Jack kept his seat, and never drew rein till bread, butter, and milk went down the red lane.

" Now, mistress," said he, " I'll be earlier at my work to-morrow if I sleep comfortably on the sheltery side of a pile of dry peat on dry grass, and not be coming here and going back. So you may as well give me my supper, and be done with the day's trouble." She gave him that, thinking he'd take it to the bog ; but he fell to on the spot, and did not leave a scrap to tell tales on him ; and the mistress was a little astonished.

He called to speak to the master in the haggard, and said he, " What are servants asked to do in this country after aten their supper ? "

" Nothing at all, but to go to bed."

" Oh, very well, sir." He went up on the stable-loft, stripped, and lay down, and some one that saw him told the master. He came up.

"Jack, you anointed scoundrel, what do you mean?"

"To go to sleep, master. The mistress, God bless her, is after giving me my breakfast, dinner, and supper, and yourself told me that bed was the next thing. Do you blame me, sir?"

"Yes, you rascal, I do."

"Hand me out one pound thirteen and fourpence, if you please, sir."

"One divel and thirteen imps, you tinker! what for?"

"Oh, I see, you've forgot your bargain. Are you sorry for it?"

"Oh, ya—no, I mean. I'll give you the money after your nap."

Next morning early, Jack asked how he'd be employed that day. "You are to be holding the plough in that fallow, outside the paddock." The master went over about nine o'clock to see what kind of a ploughman was Jack, and what did he see but the little boy driving the bastes, and the sock and coulter of the plough skimming along the sod, and Jack pulling ding-dong again' the horses.

"What are you doing, you contrary thief?" said the master.

"An' ain't I strivin' to hold this divel of a plough, as you told me; but that ounkrawn of a boy keeps whipping on the bastes in spite of all I say; will you speak to him?"

"No, but I'll speak to you. Didn't you know, you bosthoon, that when I said 'holding the plough,' I meant reddening the ground."

"Faith, an' if you did, I wish you had said so. Do you blame me for what I have done?"

The master caught himself in time, but he was so stomached, he said nothing.

" Go on and redden the ground now, you knave, as other ploughmen do."

" An' are you sorry for our agreement ? "

" Oh, not at all, not at all ! "

Jack ploughed away like a good workman all the rest of the day.

In a day or two the master bade him go and mind the cows in a field that had half of it under young corn. " Be sure, particularly," said he, " to keep Browney from the wheat ; while she's out of mischief there's no fear of the rest."

About noon, he went to see how Jack was doing his duty, and what did he find but Jack asleep with his face to the sod, Browney grazing near a thorn-tree, one end of a long rope round her horns, and the other end round the tree, and the rest of the beasts all trampling and eating the green wheat. Down came the switch on Jack.

" Jack, you vagabone, do you see what the cows are at ? "

" And do you blame, master ? "

" To be sure, you lazy sluggard, I do ? "

" Hand me out one pound thirteen and fourpence, master. You said if I only kept Browney out of mischief, the rest would do no harm. There she is as harmless as a lamb. Are you sorry for hiring me, master ? "

" To be—that is, not at all. I'll give you your money when you go to dinner. Now, understand me ; don't let a cow go out of the field nor into the wheat the rest of the day."

" Never fear, master ! " and neither did he. But the

churl would rather than a great deal he had not hired him.

The next day three heifers were missing, and the master bade Jack go in search of them.

" Where will I look for them?" said Jack.

" Oh, every place likely and unlikely for them all to be in."

The churl was getting very exact in his words. When he was coming into the bawn at dinner-time, what work did he find Jack at but pulling armfuls of the thatch off the roof, and peeping into the holes he was making?

" What are you doing there, you rascal?"

" Sure, I'm looking for the heifers, poor things!"

" What would bring them there?"

" I don't think anything could bring them in it; but I looked first into the likely places, that is, the cow-houses, and the pastures, and the fields next 'em, and now I'm looking in the unlikeliest place I can think of. Maybe it's not pleasing to you it is."

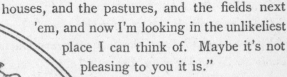

" And to be sure it isn't pleasing to me, you aggravating goose-cap!"

" Please, sir, hand me one pound thirteen and four pence before you sit down to your dinner. I'm afraid it's sorrow that's on you for hiring me at all."

" May the div—oh no ; I'm not sorry. Will you begin, if you please, and put in the thatch again, just as if you were doing it for your mother's cabin ? "

" Oh, faith I will, sir, with a heart and a half ;" and by the time the farmer came out from his dinner, Jack had the roof better than it was before, for he made the boy give him new straw.

Says the master when he came out, " Go, Jack, and look for the heifers, and bring them home."

" And where will I look for 'em ? "

" Go and search for them as if they were your own." The heifers were all in the paddock before sunset.

Next morning, says the master, " Jack, the path across the bog to the pasture is very bad ; the sheep does be sinking in it every step ; go and make the sheep's feet a good path." About an hour after he came to the edge of the bog, and what did he find Jack at but sharpening a carving knife, and the sheep standing or grazing round.

" Is this the way you are mending the path, Jack ? " said he.

" Everything must have a beginning, master," said Jack, " and a thing well begun is half done. I am sharpening the knife, and I'll have the feet off every sheep in the flock while you'd be blessing yourself."

" Feet off my sheep, you anointed rogue ! and what would you be taking their feet off for ? "

" An' sure to mend the path as you told me. Says you, ' Jack, make a path with the foot of the sheep.' "

" Oh, you fool, I meant make good the path for the sheep's feet."

" It's a pity you didn't say so, master. Hand me out

one pound thirteen and fourpence if you don't like me to finish my job."

" Divel do you good with your one pound thirteen and fourpence ! "

" It's better pray than curse, master. Maybe you're sorry for your bargain ? "

" And to be sure I am——not yet, any way."

The next night the master was going to a wedding ; and says he to Jack, before he set out : " I'll leave at midnight, and I wish you to come and be with me home, for fear I might be overtaken with the drink. If you're there before, you may throw a sheep's eye at me, and I'll be sure to see that they'll give you something for yourself."

About eleven o'clock, while the master was in great spirits, he felt something clammy hit him on the cheek. It fell beside his tumbler, and when he looked at it what was it but the eye of a sheep. Well, he couldn't imagine who threw it at him, or why it was thrown at him. After a little he got a blow on the other cheek, and still it was by another sheep's eye. Well, he was very vexed, but he thought better to say nothing. In two minutes more, when he was opening his mouth to take a sup, another sheep's eye was slapped into it. He sputtered it out, and cried, " Man o' the house, isn't it a great shame for you to have any one in the room that would do such a nasty thing ? "

" Master," says Jack, " don't blame the honest man. Sure it's only myself that was throwin' them sheep's eyes at you, to remind you I was here, and that I wanted to drink the bride and bridegroom's health. You know yourself bade me."

" I know that you are a great rascal ; and where did you get the eyes ? "

" An' where would I get em' but in the heads of your own sheep ? Would you have me meddle with the bastes of any neighbour, who might put me in the Stone Jug for it ? "

" Sorrow on me that ever I had the bad luck to meet with you."

" You're all witness," said Jack, " that my master says he is sorry for having met with me. My time is up. Master, hand me over double wages, and come into the next room, and lay yourself out like a man that has some decency in him, till I take a strip of skin an inch broad from your shoulder to your hip."

Every one shouted out against that ; but, says Jack, " You didn't hinder him when he took the same strips from the backs of my two brothers, and sent them home in that state, and penniless, to their poor mother."

When the company heard the rights of the business, they were only too eager to see the job done. The master bawled and roared, but there was no help at hand. He was stripped to his hips, and laid on the floor in the next room, and Jack had the carving knife in his hand ready to begin..

" Now you cruel old villain," said he, giving the knife a couple of scrapes along the floor, " I'll make you an offer. Give me, along with my double wages, two hundred guineas to support my poor brothers, and I'll do without the strap."

" No ! " said he, " I'd let you skin me from head to foot first."

" Here goes then," said Jack with a grin, but the first little scar he gave, Churl roared out, " Stop your hand ; I'll give the money."

" Now, neighbours," said Jack, " you mustn't think worse of me than I deserve. I wouldn't have the heart to take an eye out of a rat itself ; I got half a dozen of them from the butcher, and only used three of them."

So all came again into the other room, and Jack was made sit down, and everybody drank his health, and he drank everybody's health at one offer. And six stout fellows saw himself and the master home, and waited in the parlour while he went up and brought down the two hundred guineas, and double wages for Jack himself. When he got home, he brought the summer along with him to the poor mother and the disabled brothers ; and he was no more Jack the Fool in the people's mouths, but " Skin Churl Jack."

Beth Gellert

PRINCE LLEWELYN had a favourite grey-hound named Gellert that had been given to him by his father-in-law, King John. He was as gentle as a lamb at home but a lion in the chase. One day Llewelyn went to the chase and blew his horn in front of his castle. All his other dogs came to the call but Gellert never answered it. So he blew a louder blast on his horn and called Gellert by name, but still the greyhound did not come. At last Prince Llewelyn could wait no longer and went off to the hunt without Gellert. He had little sport that day because Gellert was not there, the swiftest and boldest of his hounds.

He turned back in a rage to his castle, and as he came to the gate, who should he see but Gellert come bounding out to meet him. But when the hound came near him, the Prince was startled to see that his lips and fangs were dripping with blood. Llewelyn started back and the grey-hound crouched down at his feet as if surprised or afraid at the way his master greeted him.

Now Prince Llewelyn had a little son a year old with whom Gellert used to play, and a terrible thought crossed the Prince's mind that made him rush towards the child's nursery. And the nearer he came the more blood and disorder he found about the rooms. He rushed into it and found the child's cradle overturned and daubed with blood.

Prince Llewelyn grew more and more terrified, and sought for his little son everywhere. He could find him nowhere but only signs of some terrible conflict in which much blood had been shed. At last he felt sure the dog had destroyed his child, and shouting to Gellert, " Monster, thou hast devoured my child," he drew out his sword and plunged it in the greyhound's side, who fell with a deep yell and still gazing in his master's eyes.

As Gellert raised his dying yell, a little child's cry answered it from beneath the cradle, and there Llewelyn found his child unharmed and just awakened from sleep. But just beside him lay the body of a great gaunt wolf all torn to pieces and covered with blood. Too late, Llewelyn learned what had happened while he was away. Gellert had stayed behind to guard the child and had fought and slain the wolf that had tried to destroy Llewelyn's heir.

In vain was all Llewelyn's grief; he could not bring his faithful dog to life again. So he buried him outside the castle walls within sight of the great mountain of Snowdon, where every passer-by might see his grave, and raised over it a great cairn of stones. And to this day the place is called Beth Gellert, or the Grave of Gellert.

The Tale of Ivan

THERE were formerly a man and a woman living in the parish of Llanlavan, in the place which is called Hwrdh. And work became scarce, so the man said to his wife, " I will go search for work, and you may live here." So he took fair leave, and travelled far toward the East, and at last came to the house of a farmer and asked for work.

" What work can ye do ? " said the farmer.

" I can do all kinds of work," said Ivan.

Then they agreed upon three pounds for the year's wages.

When the end of the year came his master showed him the three pounds. " See, Ivan," said he, " here's your wage ; but if you will give it me back I'll give you a piece of advice instead."

" Give me my wage," said Ivan.

"No, I'll not," said the master; "I'll explain my advice."

"Tell it me, then," said Ivan.

Then said the master, "Never leave the old road for the sake of a new one."

After that they agreed for another year at the old wages, and at the end of it Ivan took instead a piece of advice, and this was it: "Never lodge where an old man is married to a young woman."

The same thing happened at the end of the third year, when the piece of advice was: "Honesty is the best policy."

But Ivan would not stay longer, but wanted to go back to his wife.

"Don't go to-day," said his master; "my wife bakes to-morrow, and she shall make thee a cake to take home to thy good woman."

And when Ivan was going to leave, "Here," said his master, "here is a cake for thee to take home to thy wife, and, when ye are most joyous together, then break the cake, and not sooner."

So he took fair leave of them and travelled towards home, and at last he came to Wayn Her, and there he met three merchants from Tre Rhyn, of his own parish, coming home from Exeter Fair. "Oho! Ivan," said they, "come with us; glad are we to see you. Where have you been so long?"

"I have been in service," said Ivan, "and now I'm going home to my wife."

"Oh, come with us! you'll be right welcome."

But when they took the new road Ivan kept to the old

one. And robbers fell upon them before they had gone far from Ivan as they were going by the fields of the houses in the meadow. They began to cry out, "Thieves!" and Ivan shouted out "Thieves!" too. And when the robbers heard Ivan's shout they ran away, and the merchants went by the new road and Ivan by the old one till they met again at Market-Jew.

"Oh, Ivan," said the merchants, "we are beholding to you; but for you we would have been lost men. Come lodge with us at our cost, and welcome."

When they came to the place where they used to lodge, Ivan said, "I must see the host."

"The host," they cried; "what do you want with the host? Here is the hostess, and she's young and pretty. If you want to see the host you'll find him in the kitchen."

So he went into the kitchen to see the host; he found him a weak old man turning the spit.

"Oh! oh!" quoth Ivan, "I'll not lodge here, but will go next door."

"Not yet," said the merchants, "sup with us, and welcome."

Now it happened that the hostess had plotted with a certain monk in Market-Jew to murder the old man in his bed that night while the rest were asleep, and they agreed to lay it on the lodgers.

So while Ivan was in bed next door, there was a hole in the pine-end of the house, and he saw a light through it. So he got up and looked, and heard the monk speaking. "I had better cover this hole," said he, "or people in the next house may see our deeds." So he stood with his back against it while the hostess killed the old man.

But meanwhile Ivan out with his knife, and putting it through the hole, cut a round piece off the monk's robe.

The very next morning the hostess raised the cry that her husband was murdered, and as there was neither man nor child in the house but the merchants, she declared they ought to be hanged for it.

So they were taken and carried to prison, till at last Ivan came to them. "Alas! alas! Ivan," cried they, "bad luck sticks to us; our host was killed last night, and we shall be hanged for it."

"Ah, tell the justices," said Ivan, "to summon the real murderers."

"Who knows," they replied, "who committed the crime?"

"Who committed the crime!" said Ivan. "If I cannot prove who committed the crime, hang me in your stead."

So he told all he knew, and brought out the piece of cloth from the monk's robe, and with that the merchants were set at liberty, and the hostess and the monk were seized and hanged.

Then they came all together out of Market-Jew, and they said to him: "Come as far as Coed Carrn y Wylfa, the Wood of the Heap of Stones of Watching, in the parish of Burman. Then their two roads separated, and though the merchants wished Ivan to go with them, he would not go with them, but went straight home to his wife.

And when his wife saw him she said: "Home in the nick of time. Here's a purse of gold that I've found; it has no name, but sure it belongs to the great lord yonder. I was just thinking what to do when you came."

Then Ivan thought of the third counsel, and he said: " Let us go and give it to the great lord."

So they went up to the castle, but the great lord was not in it, so they left the purse with the servant that minded the gate, and then they went home again and lived in quiet for a time.

But one day the great lord stopped at their house for a drink of water, and Ivan's wife said to him: " I hope your lordship found your lordship's purse quite safe with all its money in it."

" What purse is that you are talking about ? " said the lord.

" Sure, it's your lordship's purse that I left at the castle," said Ivan.

" Come with me and we will see into the matter," said the lord.

So Ivan and his wife went up to the castle, and there they pointed out the man to whom they had given the purse, and he had to give it up and was sent away from the castle. And the lord was so pleased with Ivan that he made him his servant in the stead of the thief.

" Honesty's the best policy ! " quoth Ivan, as he skipped about in his new quarters. " How joyful I am ! "

Then he thought of his old master's cake that he was to eat when he was most joyful, and when he broke it, lo and behold, inside it was his wages for the three years he had been with him.

Andrew Coffey

Y grandfather, Andrew Coffey, was known to the whole barony as a quiet, decent man. And if the whole barony knew him, he knew the whole barony, every inch, hill and dale, bog and pasture, field and covert. Fancy his surprise one evening, when he found himself in a part of the demesne he couldn't recognise a bit. He and his good horse were always stumbling up against some tree or stumbling down into some bog-hole that by rights didn't ought to be there. On the top of all this the rain came pelting down wherever there was a clearing, and the cold March wind tore through the trees. Glad he was then when he saw a light in the distance, and drawing near found a cabin, though for the life of him he couldn't think how it came there. However, in he walked, after tying up his horse, and right welcome was the brushwood fire blazing on the hearth. And there stood a chair right and tight, that seemed to say, "Come, sit down in me." There wasn't a soul else in the room. Well, he did sit, and got a little warm and cheered

after his drenching. But all the while he was wondering and wondering.

" Andrew Coffey! Andrew Coffey!"

Good heavens! who was calling him, and not a soul in sight? Look around as he might, indoors and out, he could find no creature with two legs or four, for his horse was gone.

" ANDREW COFFEY! ANDREW COFFEY! tell me a story."

It was louder this time, and it was nearer. And then what a thing to ask for! It was bad enough not to be let sit by the fire and dry oneself, without being bothered for a story.

" **Andrew Coffey! Andrew Coffey!** Tell me a story, or it'll be the worse for you."

My poor grandfather was so dumbfounded that he could only stand and stare.

" ANDREW COFFEY! ANDREW COFFEY! I told you it'd be the worse for you."

And with that, out there bounced, from a cupboard that Andrew Coffey had never noticed before, *a man*. And the man was in a towering rage. But it wasn't that. And he carried as fine a blackthorn as you'd wish to crack a man's head with. But it wasn't that either. But when my grandfather clapped eyes on him, he knew him for Patrick Rooney, and all the world knew *he'd* gone overboard, fishing one night long years before.

Andrew Coffey would neither stop nor stay, but he took to his heels and was out of the house as hard as he could. He ran and he ran taking little thought of what was before till at last he ran up against a big tree. And then he sat down to rest.

He hadn't sat for a moment when he heard voices. "It's heavy he is, the vagabond." "Steady now, we'll rest when we get under the big tree yonder." Now that happened to be the tree under which Andrew Coffey was sitting. At least he thought so, for seeing a branch handy he swung himself up by it and was soon snugly hidden away. Better see than be seen, thought he.

The rain had stopped and the wind fallen. The night was blacker than ever, but Andrew Coffey could see four men, and they were carrying between them a long box. Under the tree they came, set the box down, opened it, and who should they bring out but—Patrick Rooney. Never a word did he say, and he looked as pale as old snow.

Well, one gathered brushwood, and another took out tinder and flint, and soon they had a big fire roaring, and my grandfather could see Patrick plainly enough. If he had kept still before, he kept stiller now. Soon they had four poles up and a pole across, right over the fire, for all the world like a spit, and on to the pole they slung Patrick Rooney.

"He'll do well enough," said one; "but who's to mind him whilst we're away, who'll turn the fire, who'll see that he doesn't burn?"

With that Patrick opened his lips: "Andrew Coffey," said he.

"Andrew Coffey! Andrew Coffey! Andrew Coffey! Andrew Coffey!"

"I'm much obliged to you, gentlemen," said Andrew Coffey, "but indeed I know nothing about the business."

"You'd better come down, Andrew Coffey," said Patrick.

It was the second time he spoke, and Andrew Coffey decided he would come down. The four men went off and he was left all alone with Patrick.

Then he sat and he kept the fire even, and he kept the spit turning, and all the while Patrick looked at him.

Poor Andrew Coffey couldn't make it all out at all, at all, and he stared at Patrick and at the fire, and he thought of the little house in the wood, till he felt quite dazed.

"Ah, but it's burning me ye are!" says Patrick, very short and sharp.

"I'm sure I beg your pardon," said my grandfather "but might I ask you a question?"

"If you want a crooked answer," said Patrick; "turn away or it'll be the worse for you."

But my grandfather couldn't get it out of his head; hadn't everybody, far and near, said Patrick had fallen overboard. There was enough to think about, and my grandfather did think.

"Andrew Coffey! Andrew Coffey! it's burning me ye are."

Sorry enough my grandfather was, and he vowed he wouldn't do so again.

"You'd better not," said Patrick, and he gave him a cock of his eye, and a grin of his teeth, that just sent a shiver down Andrew Coffey's back. Well it was odd, that here he should be in a thick wood he had never set eyes upon, turning Patrick Rooney upon a spit. You can't wonder at my grandfather thinking and thinking and not minding the fire.

"ANDREW COFFEY, ANDREW COFFEY, IT'S THE DEATH OF YOU I'LL BE."

And with that what did my grandfather see, but Patrick unslinging himself from the spit and his eyes glared and his teeth glistened.

It was neither stop nor stay my grandfather made, but out he ran into the night of the wood. It seemed to him

there wasn't a stone but was for his stumbling, not a branch but beat his face, not a bramble but tore his skin. And wherever it was clear the rain pelted down and the cold March wind howled along.

Glad he was to see a light, and a minute after he was kneeling, dazed, drenched, and bedraggled by the hearth side. The brushwood flamed, and the brushwood crackled, and soon my grandfather began to feel a little warm and dry and easy in his mind.

"**Andrew Coffey ! Andrew Coffey !**"

It's hard for a man to jump when he has been through all my grandfather had, but jump he did. And when he looked around, where should he find himself but in the very cabin he had first met Patrick in.

" Andrew Coffey, Andrew Coffey, tell me a story."

" Is it a story you want ?" said my grandfather as bold as may be, for he was just tired of being frightened. " Well if you can tell me the rights of this one, I'll be thankful."

And he told the tale of what had befallen him from first to last that night. The tale was long, and may be Andrew Coffey was weary. It's asleep he must have fallen, for when he awoke he lay on the hill-side under the open heavens, and his horse grazed at his side.

The Battle of the Birds

 WILL tell you a story about the wren. There was once a farmer who was seeking a servant, and the wren met him and said: "What are you seeking?"

"I am seeking a servant," said the farmer to the wren.

"Will you take me?" said the wren.

"You, you poor creature, what good would you do?"

"Try me," said the wren.

So he engaged him, and the first work he set him to do was threshing in the barn. The wren threshed (what did he thresh with? Why a flail to be sure), and he knocked off one grain. A mouse came out and she eats that.

"I'll trouble you not to do that again," said the wren.

He struck again, and he struck off two grains. Out came the mouse and she eats them. So they arranged a contest to see who was strongest, and the wren brings his twelve birds, and the mouse her tribe.

" You have your tribe with you," said the wren.

" As well as yourself," said the mouse, and she struck out her leg proudly. But the wren broke it with his flail, and there was a pitched battle on a set day.

When every creature and bird was gathering to battle, the son of the king of Tethertown said that he would go to see the battle, and that he would bring sure word home to his father the king, who would be king of the creatures this year. The battle was over before he arrived all but one fight, between a great black raven and a snake. The snake was twined about the raven's neck, and the raven held the snake's throat in his beak, and it seemed as if the snake would get the victory over the raven. When the king's son saw this he helped the raven, and with one blow takes the head off the snake. When the raven had taken breath, and saw that the snake was dead, he said, " For thy kindness to me this day, I will give thee a sight. Come up now on the root of my two wings." The king's son put his hands about the raven before his wings, and, before he stopped, he took him over nine Bens, and nine Glens, and nine Mountain Moors.

" Now," said the raven, " see you that house yonder ? Go now to it. It is a sister of mine that makes her dwelling in it ; and I will go bail that you are welcome. And if she asks you, Were you at the battle of the birds ? say you were. And if she asks, ' Did you see any one like me,' say you did, but be sure that you meet me to-morrow morning here, in this place." The king's son got good and right good treatment that night. Meat of each meat, drink of each drink, warm water to his feet, and a soft bed for his limbs.

On the next day the raven gave him the same sight over six Bens, and six Glens, and six Mountain Moors. They saw a bothy far off, but, though far off, they were soon there. He got good treatment this night, as before—plenty of meat and drink, and warm water to his feet, and a soft bed to his limbs—and on the next day it was the same thing, over three Bens and three Glens, and three Mountain Moors.

On the third morning, instead of seeing the raven as at the other times, who should meet him but the handsomest lad he ever saw, with gold rings in his hair, with a bundle in his hand. The king's son asked this lad if he had seen a big black raven.

Said the lad to him, "You will never see the raven again, for I am that raven. I was put under spells by a bad druid; it was meeting you that loosed me, and for that you shall get this bundle. Now," said the lad, "you must turn back on the self-same steps, and lie a night in each house as before; but you must not loose the bundle which I gave ye, till in the place where you would most wish to dwell."

The king's son turned his back to the lad, and his face to his father's house; and he got lodging from the raven's sisters, just as he got it when going forward. When he was nearing his father's house he was going through a close wood. It seemed to him that the bundle was growing heavy, and he thought he would look what was in it.

When he loosed the bundle he was astonished. In a twinkling he sees the very grandest place he ever saw. A great castle, and an orchard about the castle, in which was every kind of fruit and herb. He stood full of wonder and regret for having loosed the bundle—for it was not in his power to put it back again——and he would have wished this pretty place to be in the pretty little green hollow that was opposite his father's house ; but he looked up and saw a great giant coming towards him.

" Bad's the place where you have built the house, king's son," says the giant.

" Yes, but it is not here I would wish it to be, though it happens to be here by mishap," says the king's son.

" What's the reward for putting it back in the bundle as it was before ? "

" What's the reward you would ask ? " says the king's son.

" That you will give me the first son you have when he is seven years of age," says the giant.

" If I have a son you shall have him," said the king's son.

In a twinkling the giant put each garden, and orchard, and castle in the bundle as they were before.

" Now," says the giant, " take your own road, and I will take mine ; but mind your promise, and if you forget I will remember."

The king's son took to the road, and at the end of a few days he reached the place he was fondest of. He loosed the bundle, and the castle was just as it was before. And when he opened the castle door he sees the handsomest maiden he ever cast eye upon.

" Advance, king's son," said the pretty maid ; " everything is in order for you, if you will marry me this very day."

" It's I that am willing," said the king's son. And on the same day they married.

But at the end of a day and seven years, who should be seen coming to the castle but the giant. The king's son was reminded of his promise to the giant, and till now he had not told his promise to the queen.

"Leave the matter between me and the giant," says the queen.

"Turn out your son," says the giant; "mind your promise."

"You shall have him," says the king, "when his mother puts him in order for his journey."

The queen dressed up the cook's son, and she gave him to the giant by the hand. The giant went away with him; but he had not gone far when he put a rod in the hand of the little laddie. The giant asked him—

"If thy father had that rod what would he do with it?"

"If my father had that rod he would beat the dogs and the cats, so that they shouldn't be going near the king's meat," said the little laddie.

"Thou'rt the cook's son," said the giant. He catches him by the two small ankles and knocks him against the stone that was beside him. The giant turned back to the castle in rage and madness, and he said that if they did not send out the king's son to him, the highest stone of the castle would be the lowest.

Said the queen to the king, "We'll try it yet; the butler's son is of the same age as our son."

She dressed up the butler's son, and she gives him to the giant by the hand. The giant had not gone far when he put the rod in his hand.

"If thy father had that rod," says the giant, "what would he do with it?"

" He would beat the dogs and the cats when they would be coming near the king's bottles and glasses."

" Thou art the son of the butler," says the giant and dashed his brains out too. The giant returned in a very great rage and anger. The earth shook under the sole of his feet, and the castle shook and all that was in it.

" OUT HERE WITH THY SON," says the giant, " or in a twinkling the stone that is highest in the dwelling will be the lowest." So they had to give the king's son to the giant.

When they were gone a little bit from the earth, the giant showed him the rod that was in his hand and said: " What would thy father do with this rod if he had it ? "

The king's son said : " My father has a braver rod than that."

And the giant asked him, " Where is thy father when he has that brave rod ? "

And the king's son said: " He will be sitting in his kingly chair."

Then the giant understood that he had the right one.

The giant took him to his own house, and he reared him as his own son. On a day of days when the giant was from home, the lad heard the sweetest music he ever heard in a room at the top of the giant's house. At a glance he saw the finest face he had ever seen. She beckoned to him to come a bit nearer to her, and she said her name was Auburn Mary but she told him to go this time, but to be sure to be at the same place about that dead midnight.

And as he promised he did. The giant's daughter was at his side in a twinkling, and she said, " To-morrow you will get the choice of my two sisters to marry ; but say that you will not take either, but me. My father wants me to marry the son of the king of the Green City, but I don't like him." On the morrow the giant took out his three daughters, and he said :

" Now, son of the king of Tethertown, thou hast not lost by living with me so long. Thou wilt get to wife one of the two eldest of my daughters, and with her leave to go home with her the day after the wedding."

" If you will give me this pretty little one," says the king's son, " I will take you at your word."

The giant's wrath kindled, and he said : " Before thou gett'st her thou must do the three things that I ask thee to do."

" Say on," says the king's son.

The giant took him to the byre.

" Now," says the giant, " a hundred cattle are stabled here, and it has not been cleansed for seven years. I am going from home to-day, and if this byre is not cleaned before night comes, so clean that a golden apple will run from end to end of it, not only thou shalt not get my daughter, but 'tis only a drink of thy fresh, goodly, beautiful blood that will quench my thirst this night."

He begins cleaning the byre, but he might just as well to keep baling the great ocean. After midday when sweat was blinding him, the giant's youngest daughter came where he was, and she said to him :

" You are being punished, king's son."

" I am that," says the king's son.

" Come over," says Auburn Mary, " and lay down your weariness."

" I will do that," says he, " there is but death awaiting

me, at any rate." He sat down near her. He was so
tired that he fell asleep beside her. When he awoke, the
giant's daughter was not to be seen, but the byre was so
well cleaned that a golden apple would run from end to end
of it and raise no stain. In comes the giant, and he said :

" Hast thou cleaned the byre, king's son ? "

" I have cleaned it," says he.

" Somebody cleaned it," says the giant.

" You did not clean it, at all events," said the king's
son.

" Well, well !" says the giant, " since thou wert so
active to-day, thou wilt get to this time to-morrow to thatch
this byre with birds' down, from birds with no two feathers
of one colour."

The king's son was on foot before the sun ; he caught
up his bow and his quiver of arrows to kill the birds. He
took to the moors, but if he did, the birds were not so easy
to take. He was running after them till the sweat was
blinding him. About mid-day who should come but
Auburn Mary.

" You are exhausting yourself, king's son," says she.

" I am," said he.

" There fell but these two blackbirds, and both of one
colour."

" Come over and lay down your weariness on this pretty
hillock," says the giant's daughter.

" It's I am willing," said he.

He thought she would aid him this time, too, and he sat
down near her, and he was not long there till he fell
asleep.

When he awoke, Auburn Mary was gone. He thought

he would go back to the house, and he sees the byre
thatched with feathers. When the giant came home, he
said :

"Hast thou thatched the byre, king's son ?"

"I thatched it," says he.

"Somebody thatched it," says the giant.

"You did not thatch it," says the king's son.

"Yes, yes!" says the giant. "Now," says the giant,
"there is a fir tree beside that loch down there, and there
is a magpie's nest in its top. The eggs thou wilt find in
the nest. I must have them for my first meal. Not one
must be burst or broken, and there are five in the nest."

Early in the morning the king's son went where the tree
was, and that tree was not hard to hit upon. Its match
was not in the whole wood. From the foot to the first
branch was five hundred feet. The king's son was going
all round the tree. She came who was always bringing
help to him.

"You are losing the skin of your hands and feet."

"Ach! I am," says he. "I am no sooner up than
down."

"This is no time for stopping," says the giant's daughter.
"Now you must kill me, strip the flesh from my bones,
take all those bones apart, and use them as steps for
climbing the tree. When you are climbing the tree, they
will stick to the glass as if they had grown out of it ; but
when you are coming down, and have put your foot on
each one, they will drop into your hand when you touch
them. Be sure and stand on each bone, leave none
untouched ; if you do, it will stay behind. Put all my
flesh into this clean cloth by the side of the spring at the

roots of the tree.   When you come to the earth, arrange
my bones together, put the flesh over them, sprinkle it with
water from the spring, and I shall be alive before you.
But don't forget a bone of me on the tree."

"How could I kill you," asked the king's son, "after
what you have done for me?"

"If you won't obey, you and I are done for," said
Auburn Mary.   "You must climb the tree, or we are lost;
and to climb the tree you must do as I say."

The king's son obeyed.   He killed Auburn Mary, cut
the flesh from her body, and unjointed the bones, as she
had told him.

As he went up, the king's son put the bones of Auburn
Mary's body against the side of the tree, using them as
steps, till he came under the nest and stood on the last
bone.

Then he took the eggs, and coming down, put his
foot on every bone, then took it with him, till he came to
the last bone, which was so near the ground that he failed
to touch it with his foot.

He now placed all the bones of Auburn Mary in order
again at the side of the spring, put the flesh on them,
sprinkled it with water from the spring.   She rose up
before him, and said: "Didn't I tell you not to leave a
bone of my body without stepping on it?   Now I am lame
for life!   You left my little finger on the tree without
touching it, and I have but nine fingers."

"Now," says she, "go home with the eggs quickly, and
you will get me to marry to-night if you can know me.   I
and my two sisters will be arrayed in the same garments,
and made like each other, but look at me when my father

says, 'Go to thy wife, king's son;' and you will see a hand without a little finger."

He gave the eggs to the giant.

"Yes, yes!" says the giant, "be making ready for your marriage."

Then, indeed, there was a wedding, and it *was* a wedding! Giants and gentlemen, and the son of the king of the Green City was in the midst of them. They were married, and the dancing began, that was a dance! The giant's house was shaking from top to bottom.

But bed time came, and the giant said, "It is time for thee to go to rest, son of the king of Tethertown; choose thy bride to take with thee from amidst those."

She put out the hand off which the little finger was, and he caught her by the hand.

"Thou hast aimed well this time too; but there is no knowing but we may meet thee another way," said the giant.

But to rest they went. "Now," says she, "sleep not, or else you are a dead man. We must fly quick, quick, or for certain my father will kill you."

Out they went, and on the blue grey filly in the stable they mounted. "Stop a while," says she, "and I will play a trick to the old hero." She jumped in, and cut an apple into nine shares, and she put two shares at the head of the bed, and two shares at the foot of the bed, and two shares at the door of the kitchen, and two shares at the big door, and one outside the house.

The giant awoke and called, "Are you asleep?"

"Not yet," said the apple that was at the head of the bed.

At the end of a while he called again.

"Not yet," said the apple that was at the foot of the bed.

A while after this he called again: "Are your asleep?"

"Not yet," said the apple at the kitchen door.

The giant called again.

The apple that was at the big door answered.

"You are now going far from me," says the giant.

"Not yet," says the apple that was outside the house.

"You are flying," says the giant. The giant jumped on his feet, and to the bed he went, but it was cold—empty.

"My own daughter's tricks are trying me," said the giant. "Here's after them," says he.

At the mouth of day, the giant's daughter said that her father's breath was burning her back.

"Put your hand, quick," said she, "in the ear of the grey filly, and whatever you find in it, throw it behind us."

"There is a twig of sloe tree," said he.

"Throw it behind us," said she.

No sooner did he that, than there were twenty miles of blackthorn wood, so thick that scarce a weasel could go through it.

The giant came headlong, and there he is fleecing his head and neck in the thorns.

"My own daughter's tricks are here as before," said the giant; "but if I had my own big axe and wood knife here, I would not be long making a way through this."

He went home for the big axe and the wood knife, and sure he was not long on his journey, and he was the boy behind the big axe. He was not long making a way through the blackthorn.

"I will leave the axe and the wood knife here till I return," says he.

"If you leave 'em, leave 'em," said a hoodie that was in a tree, "we'll steal 'em, steal 'em."

"If you will do that," says the giant, "I must take them home." He returned home and left them at the house.

At the heat of day the giant's daughter felt her father's breath burning her back.

"Put your finger in the filly's ear, and throw behind whatever you find in it."

He got a splinter of grey stone, and in a twinkling there were twenty miles, by breadth and height, of great grey rock behind them.

The giant came full pelt, but past the rock he could not go.

"The tricks of my own daughter are the hardest things that ever met me," says the giant; "but if I had my lever and my mighty mattock, I would not be long in making my way through this rock also."

There was no help for it, but to turn the chase for them; and he was the boy to split the stones. He was not long in making a road through the rock.

"I will leave the tools here, and I will return no more."

"If you leave 'em, leave 'em," says the hoodie, "we will steal 'em, steal 'em."

"Do that if you will; there is no time to go back."

At the time of breaking the watch, the giant's daughter said that she felt her father's breath burning her back.

"Look in the filly's ear, king's son, or else we are lost."

He did so, and it was a bladder of water that was in her

ear this time. He threw it behind him and there was a fresh-water loch, twenty miles in length and breadth, behind them.

The giant came on, but with the speed he had on him, he was in the middle of the loch, and he went under, and he rose no more.

On the next day the young companions were come in sight of his father's house. " Now," says she, " my father is drowned, and he won't trouble us any more ; but before we go further," says she, " go you to your father's house, and tell that you have the likes of me ; but let neither man nor creature kiss you, for if you do, you will not remember that you have ever seen me."

Every one he met gave him welcome and luck, and he charged his father and mother not to kiss him ; but as mishap was to be, an old greyhound was indoors, and she knew him, and jumped up to his mouth, and after that he did not remember the giant's daughter.

She was sitting at the well's side as he left her, but the king's son was not coming. In the mouth of night she climbed up into a tree of oak that was beside the well, and she lay in the fork of that tree all night. A shoemaker had a house near the well, and about mid-day on the morrow, the shoemaker asked his wife to go for a drink for him out of the well. When the shoemaker's wife reached the well, and when she saw the shadow of her that was in the tree, thinking it was her own shadow—and she never thought till now that she was so handsome—she gave a cast to the dish that was in her hand, and it was broken on the ground, and she took herself to the house without vessel or water.

" Where is the water, wife ? " said the shoemaker.

" You shambling, contemptible old carle, without grace, I have stayed too long your water and wood thrall."

" I think, wife, that you have turned crazy. Go you, daughter, quickly, and fetch a drink for your father."

His daughter went, and in the same way so it happened to her. She never thought till now that she was so lovable, and she took herself home.

" Up with the drink," said her father.

" You home-spun shoe carle, do you think I am fit to be your thrall ? "

The poor shoemaker thought that they had taken a turn in their understandings, and he went himself to the well. He saw the shadow of the maiden in the well, and he looked up to the tree, and he sees the finest woman he ever saw.

" Your seat is wavering, but your face is fair," said the shoemaker. " Come down, for there is need of you for a short while at my house."

The shoemaker understood that this was the shadow that had driven his people mad. The shoemaker took her to his house, and he said that he had but a poor bothy, but that she should get a share of all that was in it.

One day, the shoemaker had shoes ready, for on that very day the king's son was to be married. The shoemaker was going to the castle with the shoes of the young people, and the girl said to the shoemaker, " I would like to get a sight of the king's son before he marries."

" Come with me," says the shoemaker, " I am well acquainted with the servants at the castle, and you shall get a sight of the king's son and all the company."

And when the gentles saw the pretty woman that was here they took her to the wedding-room, and they filled for her a glass of wine. When she was going to drink what is in it, a flame went up out of the glass, and a golden pigeon and a silver pigeon sprang out of it. They were flying about when three grains of barley fell on the floor. The silver pigeon sprung, and ate that up.

Said the golden pigeon to him, "If you remembered when I cleared the byre, you would not eat that without giving me a share."

Again there fell three other grains of barley, and the silver pigeon sprung, and ate that up as before.

"If you remembered when I thatched the byre, you would not eat that without giving me my share," says the golden pigeon.

Three other grains fall, and the silver pigeon sprung, and ate that up.

"If you remembered when I harried the magpie's nest, you would not eat that without giving me my share," says the golden pigeon; "I lost my little finger bringing it down, and I want it still."

The king's son minded, and he knew who it was that was before him.

"Well," said the king's son to the guests at the feast, "when I was a little younger than I am now, I lost the key of a casket that I had. I had a new key made, but after it was brought to me I found the old one. Now, I'll leave it to any one here to tell me what I am to do. Which of the keys should I keep?"

"My advice to you," said one of the guests, "is to keep

the old key, for it fits the lock better and you're more used to it."

Then the king's son stood up and said: " I thank you for a wise advice and an honest word. This is my bride the daughter of the giant who saved my life at the risk of her own. I'll have her and no other woman."

So the king's son married Auburn Mary and the wedding lasted long and all were happy. But all I got was butter on a live coal, porridge in a basket, and they sent me for water to the stream, and the paper shoes came to an end.

Brewery of Eggshells

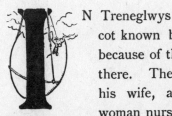N Treneglwys there is a certain shepherd's cot known by the name of Twt y Cymrws because of the strange strife that occurred there. There once lived there a man and his wife, and they had twins whom the woman nursed tenderly. One day she was called away to the house of a neighbour at some distance. She did not much like going and leaving her little ones

all alone in a solitary house, especially as she had heard tell of the good folk haunting the neighbourhood.

Well, she went and came back as soon as she could, but on her way back she was frightened to see some old elves of the blue petticoat crossing her path though it was midday. She rushed home, but found her two little ones in the cradle and everything seemed as it was before.

But after a time the good people began to suspect that something was wrong, for the twins didn't grow at all.

The man said : " They're not ours."

The woman said : " Whose else should they be ? "

And so arose the great strife so that the neighbours named the cottage after it. It made the woman very sad, so one evening she made up her mind to go and see the Wise Man of Llanidloes, for he knew everything and would advise her what to do.

So she went to Llanidloes and told the case to the Wise Man. Now there was soon to be a harvest of rye and oats, so the Wise Man said to her, " When you are getting dinner for the reapers, clear out the shell of a hen's egg and boil some potage in it, and then take it to the door as if you meant it as a dinner for the reapers. Then listen if the twins say anything. If you hear them speaking of things beyond the understanding of children, go back and take them up and throw them into the waters of Lake Elvyn. But if you don't hear anything remarkable, do them no injury."

So when the day of the reap came the woman did all that the Wise Man ordered, and put the eggshell on the fire and took it off and carried it to the door, and there she stood

and listened. Then she heard one of the children say to
the other :

> Acorn before oak I knew,
>   An egg before a hen,
> But I never heard of an eggshell brew
>   A dinner for harvest men.

So she went back into the house, seized the children and
threw them into the Llyn, and the goblins in their blue
trousers came and saved their dwarfs and the mother
had her own children back and so the great strife
ended.

The Lad with the Goat-skin

ONG ago, a poor widow woman lived down near the iron forge, by Enniscorth, and she was so poor she had no clothes to put on her son ; so she used to fix him in the ash-hole, near the fire, and pile the warm ashes about him ; and according as he grew up, she sunk the pit deeper. At last, by hook or by crook, she got a goat-skin, and fastened it round his waist, and he felt quite grand, and took a walk down the street. So says she to him next morning, "Tom, you thief, you never done any good yet, and you six foot high, and past nineteen ;—take that rope and bring me a faggot from the wood."

" Never say't twice, mother," says Tom—" here goes."

When he had it gathered and tied, what should come up but a big giant, nine foot high, and made a lick of a club at him. Well become Tom, he jumped a-one side, and picked up a ram-pike ; and the first crack he gave the big fellow, he made him kiss the clod.

" If you have e'er a prayer," says Tom, " now's the time to say it, before I make fragments of you."

" I have no prayers," says the giant ; "but if you spare

my life I'll give you that club ; and as long as you keep from sin, you'll win every battle you ever fight with it."

Tom made no bones about letting him off ; and as soon as he got the club in his hands, he sat down on the bresna, and gave it a tap with the kippeen, and says, " Faggot, I had great trouble gathering you, and run the risk of my life for you, the least you can do is to carry me home." And sure enough, the wind o' the word was all it wanted. It went off through the wood, groaning and crackling, till it came to the widow's door.

Well, when the sticks were all burned, Tom was sent off again to pick more ; and this time he had to fight with a giant that had two heads on him. Tom had a little more trouble with him—that's all ; and the prayers he said, was to give Tom a fife, that nobody could help dancing when he was playing it. Begonies, he made the big faggot dance home, with himself sitting on it. The next giant was a beautiful boy with three heads on him. He had neither prayers nor catechism no more nor the others ; and so he gave Tom a bottle of green ointment, that wouldn't let you be burned, nor scalded, nor wounded. " And now," says he, " there's no more of us. You may come and gather sticks here till little Lunacy Day in Harvest, without giant or fairy-man to disturb you."

Well, now, Tom was prouder nor ten paycocks, and used to take a walk down street in the heel of the evening ; but some o' the little boys had no more manners than if they were Dublin jackeens, and put out their tongues at Tom's club and Tom's goat-skin. He didn't like that at all, and it would be mean to give one of them a clout. At last, what should come through the town but a kind of a bellman, only it's a big bugle he had, and a huntsman's cap on his head, and a kind of a painted shirt. So this—he wasn't a bellman, and I don't know what to call him—bugle-man, maybe, proclaimed that the King of Dublin's daughter was so melancholy that she didn't give a laugh for seven years, and that her father would grant her in marriage to whoever could make her laugh three times.

"That's the very thing for me to try," says Tom; and so, without burning any more daylight, he kissed his mother, curled his club at the little boys, and off he set along the yalla highroad to the town of Dublin.

At last Tom came to one of the city gates, and the guards laughed and cursed at him instead of letting him in. Tom stood it all for a little time, but at last one of them—out of fun, as he said—drove his bayonet half an inch or so into his side. Tom done nothing but take the fellow by the scruff o' the neck and the waistband of his corduroys, and fling him into the canal. Some run to pull the fellow out, and others to let manners into the vulgarian with their swords and daggers; but a tap from his club sent them headlong into the moat or down on the stones, and they were soon begging him to stay his hands.

So at last one of them was glad enough to show Tom the way to the palace-yard; and there was the king, and the queen, and the princess, in a gallery, looking at all sorts of wrestling, and sword-playing, and long-dances, and mumming, all to please the princess; but not a smile came over her handsome face.

Well, they all stopped when they seen the young giant, with his boy's face, and long black hair, and his short curly beard—for his poor mother couldn't afford to buy razors—

and his great strong arms, and bare legs, and no covering but the goat-skin that reached from his waist to his knees. But an envious wizened bit of a fellow, with a red head, that wished to be married to the princess, and didn't like how she opened her eyes at Tom, came forward, and asked his business very snappishly.

" My business," says Tom, says he, " is to make the beautiful princess, God bless her, laugh three times."

" Do you see all them merry fellows and skilful swordsmen," says the other, " that could eat you up with a grain of salt, and not a mother's soul of 'em ever got a laugh from her these seven years ? "

So the fellows gathered round Tom, and the bad man aggravated him till he told them he didn't care a pinch o' snuff for the whole bilin' of 'em ; let 'em come on, six at a time, and try what they could do.

The king, who was too far off to hear what they were saying, asked what did the stranger want.

" He wants," says the red-headed fellow, " to make hares of your best men."

" Oh ! " says the king, " if that's the way, let one of 'em turn out and try his mettle."

So one stood forward, with sword and pot-lid, and made a cut at Tom. He struck the fellow's elbow with the club, and up over their heads flew the sword, and down went the owner of it on the gravel from a thump he got on the helmet. Another took his place, and another, and another, and then half a dozen at once, and Tom sent swords, helmets, shields, and bodies, rolling over and over, and themselves bawling out that they were kilt, and disabled, and damaged, and rubbing their poor elbows and hips, and limping away. Tom contrived not to kill any one ; and the princess was so amused, that she let a great sweet laugh out of her that was heard over all the yard.

" King of Dublin," says Tom," " I've quarter your daughter."

And the king didn't know whether he was glad or sorry, and all the blood in the princess's heart run into her cheeks.

So there was no more fighting that day, and Tom was invited to dine with the royal family. Next day, Redhead told Tom of a wolf, the size of a yearling heifer, that used to be serenading about the walls, and eating people and cattle ; and said what a pleasure it would give the king to have it killed.

" With all my heart," says Tom ; " send a jackeen to show me where he lives, and we'll see how he behaves to a stranger."

The princess was not well pleased, for Tom looked a different person with fine clothes and a nice green birredh over his long curly hair ; and besides, he'd got one laugh out of her. However, the king gave his consent ; and in an hour and a half the horrible wolf was walking into the palace-yard, and Tom a step or two behind, with his club on his shoulder, just as a shepherd would be walking after a pet lamb.

The king and queen and princess were safe up in their gallery, but the officers and people of the court that wor padrowling about the great bawn, when they saw the big baste coming in, gave themselves up, and began to make for doors and gates ; and the wolf licked his chops, as if he was saying, "Wouldn't I enjoy a breakfast off a couple of yez !"

The king shouted out, "O Tom with the Goat-skin, take away that terrible wolf, and you must have all my daughter."

But Tom didn't mind him a bit. He pulled out his flute and began to play like vengeance ; and dickens a man or

boy in the yard but began shovelling away heel and toe, and the wolf himself was obliged to get on his hind legs and dance "Tatther Jack Walsh," along with the rest. A good deal of the people got inside, and shut the doors, the way the hairy fellow wouldn't pin them ; but Tom kept playing, and the outsiders kept dancing and shouting, and the wolf kept dancing and roaring with the pain his legs were giving him ; and all the time he had his eyes on Red-head, who was shut out along with the rest. Wherever Redhead went, the wolf followed, and kept one eye on him and the other on Tom, to see if he would give him leave to eat him. But Tom shook his head, and never stopped the tune, and Redhead never stopped dancing and bawling, and the wolf dancing and roaring, one leg up and the other down, and he ready to drop out of his standing from fair tiresomeness.

When the princess seen that there was no fear of any one being kilt, she was so diverted by the stew that Red-head was in, that she gave another great laugh ; and well become Tom, out he cried, "King of Dublin, I have two halves of your daughter."

"Oh, halves or alls," says the king, "put away that divel of a wolf, and we'll see about it."

So Tom put his flute in his pocket, and says he to the baste that was sittin' on his currabingo ready to faint, "Walk off to your mountain, my fine fellow, and live like a respectable baste ; and if ever I find you come within seven miles of any town, I'll ———"

He said no more, but spit in his fist, and gave a flourish of his club. It was all the poor divel of a wolf wanted : he put his tail between his legs, and took to his pumps without looking at man or mortal, and neither sun, moon, or stars ever saw him in sight of Dublin again.

At dinner every one laughed but the foxy fellow ; and sure enough he was laying out how he'd settle poor Tom next day.

"Well, to be sure !" says he, "King of Dublin, you are in luck. There's the Danes moidhering us to no end.

Deuce run to Lusk wid 'em! and if any one can save us from 'em, it is this gentleman with the goat-skin. There is a flail hangin' on the collar-beam in hell, and neither Dane nor devil can stand before it."

" So," says Tom to the king, "will you let me have the other half of the princess if I bring you the flail?"

" No, no," says the princess; " I'd rather never be your wife than see you in that danger."

But Redhead whispered and nudged Tom about how shabby it would look to reneague the adventure. So he asked which way he was to go, and Redhead directed him.

Well, he travelled and travelled, till he came in sight of the walls of hell; and, bedad, before he knocked at the gates, he rubbed himself over with the greenish ointment. When he knocked, a hundred little imps popped their heads out through the bars, and axed him what he wanted.

" I want to speak to the big divel of all," says Tom: " open the gate."

It wasn't long till the gate was thrune open, and the Ould Boy received Tom with bows and scrapes, and axed his business.

" My business isn't much," says Tom. " I only came for the loan of that flail that I see hanging on the collar-beam, for the King of Dublin to give a thrashing to the Danes."

" Well," says the other, " the Danes is much better

customers to me ; but since you walked so far I won't refuse. Hand that flail," says he to a young imp ; and he winked the far-off eye at the same time. So, while some were barring the gates, the young devil climbed up, and took down the flail that had the handstaff and booltheen both made out of red-hot iron. The little vagabond was grinning to think how it would burn the hands o' Tom, but the dickens a burn it made on him, no more nor if it was a good oak sapling.

" Thankee," says Tom. " Now would you open the gate for a body, and I'll give you no more trouble."

" Oh, tramp ! " says Ould Nick ; " is that the way ? It is easier getting inside them gates than getting out again. Take that tool from him, and give him a dose of the oil of stirrup."

So one fellow put out his claws to seize on the flail, but Tom gave him such a welt of it on the side of the head that he broke off one of his horns, and made him roar like a devil as he was. Well, they rushed at Tom, but he gave them, little and big, such a thrashing as they didn't forget for a while. At last says the ould thief of all, rubbing his elbow, " Let the fool out ; and woe to whoever lets him in again, great or small."

So out marched Tom, and away with him, without minding the shouting and cursing they kept up at him from the tops of the walls ; and when he got home to the big bawn of the palace, there never was such running and racing as to see himself and the flail. When he had his story told, he laid down the flail on the stone steps, and bid no one for their lives to touch it. If the king, and queen, and princess, made much of him before, they made

ten times more of him now ; but Redhead, the mean scruff-
hound, stole over, and thought to catch hold of the flail to
make an end of him.   His fingers hardly touched it, when
he let a roar out of him as if heaven and earth were coming
together, and kept flinging his arms about and dancing, that
it was pitiful to look at him.   Tom run at him as soon as
he could rise, caught his hands in his own two, and rubbed
them this way and that, and the burning pain left them
before you could reckon one.   Well the poor fellow,
between the pain that was only just gone, and the comfort
he was in, had the comicalest face that you ever see, it was
such a mixtherum-gatherum of laughing and crying.
Everybody burst out a laughing—the princess could not
stop no more than the rest ; and then says Tom, " Now,
ma'am, if there were fifty halves of you, I hope you'll give
me them all."

Well, the princess looked at her father, and by my word,
she came over to Tom, and put her two delicate hands into
his two rough ones, and I wish it was myself was in his
shoes that day !

Tom would not bring the flail into the palace.   You may
be sure no other body went near it ; and when the early
risers were passing next morning, they found two long
clefts in the stone, where it was after burning itself an
opening downwards, nobody could tell how far.   But a
messenger came in at noon, and said that the Danes were
so frightened when they heard of the flail coming into
Dublin, that they got into their ships, and sailed away.

Well, I suppose, before they were married, Tom got
some man, like Pat Mara of Tomenine, to learn him the
" principles of politeness," fluxions, gunnery and fortifi-

cation, decimal fractions, practice, and the rule of three direct, the way he'd be able to keep up a conversation with the royal family. Whether he ever lost his time learning them sciences, I'm not sure, but it's as sure as fate that his mother never more saw any want till the end of her days.

Notes and References

IT may be as well to give the reader some account of the enormous extent of the Celtic folk-tales in existence. I reckon these to extend to 2000, though only about 250 are in print The former number exceeds that known in France, Italy, Germany, and Russia, where collection has been most active, and is only exceeded by the MS. collection of Finnish folk-tales at Helsingfors, said to exceed 12,000. As will be seen. this superiority of the Celts is due to the phenomenal and patriotic activity of one man, the late J. F. Campbell, of Islay, whose *Popular Tales* and MS. collections (partly described by Mr. Alfred Nutt in *Folk-Lore*, i. 369–83) contain references to no less than 1281 tales (many of them, of course, variants and scraps). Celtic folk-tales, while more numerous, are also the oldest of the tales of modern European races ; some of them—*e g.*, "Connla." in the present selection, occurring in the oldest Irish vellums. They include (1) fairy tales properly so-called—*i.e.*, tales or anecdotes *about* fairies, hobgoblins, &c., told as natural occurrences ; (2) hero-tales, stories of adventure told of national or mythical heroes ; (3) folk-tales proper, describing marvellous adventures of otherwise unknown heroes, in which there is a defined plot and supernatural characters (speaking animals, giants, dwarfs, &c.) ; and finally (4) drolls, comic anecdotes of feats of stupidity or cunning.

The collection of Celtic folk-tales began in IRELAND as early as 1825, with T. Crofton Croker's *Fairy Legends and Traditions of the South of Ireland.* This contained some 38 anecdotes of the first class mentioned above, anecdotes showing the belief of the Irish peasantry in the existence of fairies, gnomes, goblins, and the like. The Grimms did Croker the honour of translating part of his book, under the title of *Irische Elfenmärchen*. Among the novelists and tale-writers of the schools of Miss Edgeworth and Lever folk-tales were occasionally utilised, as by Carleton in his *Traits and Stories*, by S. Lover in his *Legends and Stories*, and by G. Griffin in his *Tales of a Jury-Room*. These all tell their tales in the manner of the stage Irishman. Chapbooks, *Royal Fairy Tales* and *Hibernian Tales*, also contained genuine folk-tales, and attracted Thackeray's attention in his *Irish Sketch-Book*. The Irish Grimm, however, was Patrick Kennedy, a Dublin bookseller, who believed in fairies, and in five years (1866–71) printed about 100 folk- and hero-tales and drolls (classes 2, 3, and 4 above) in his *Legendary Fictions of the Irish Celts*, 1866, *Fireside Stories of Ireland*, 1870, and *Bardic Stories of Ireland*, 1871 ; all three are now unfortunately out of print. He tells his stories neatly and with spirit, and retains much that is *volkstümlich* in his diction. He derived his materials from the English-speaking peasantry of county Wexford, who changed from Gaelic to English while story-telling was in full vigour, and therefore carried over the stories with the change of language. Lady Wylde has told many folk-tales very effectively in her *Ancient Legends of Ireland*, 1887. More recently two collectors have published stories gathered from peasants of the West and North who can only speak Gaelic. These are by an American gentleman named Curtin, *Myths and Folk-Tales of Ireland*, 1890 ; while Dr. Douglas Hyde has published in *Beside the Fireside*, 1891, spirited English versions of some of the stories he had published in the original Irish in his *Leabhar Sgeulaighteachta*, Dublin, 1889. Miss Maclintoch has a large MS. collection, part of which has appeared in various periodicals ; and Messrs. Larminie and D. Fitzgerald are known to have much story material in their possession.

But beside these more modern collections there exist in old and middle Irish a large number of hero-tales (class 2) which formed the staple of the old *ollahms* or bards. Of these tales of " cattle-liftings, elopements, battles, voyages, courtships, caves, lakes, feasts, sieges, and eruptions," a bard of even the fourth class had to know seven fifties, presumably one for each day of the year. Sir William Temple knew of a north-country gentleman of Ireland who was sent to sleep every evening with a fresh tale from his bard. The *Book of Leinster*, an Irish vellum of the twelfth century, contains a list of 189 of these hero-tales, many of which are extant to this day ; E. O'Curry gives the list in the Appendix to his *MS. Materials of Irish History*.

Another list of about 70 is given in the preface to the third volume of the Ossianic Society's publications. Dr. Joyce published a few of the more celebrated of these in *Old Celtic Romances;* others appeared in *Atlantis* (see notes on "Deirdre"), others in Kennedy's *Bardic Stories*, mentioned above.

Turning to SCOTLAND, we must put aside Chambers' *Popular Rhymes of Scotland*, 1842, which contains for the most part folk-tales common with those of England rather than those peculiar to the Gaelic-speaking Scots. The first name here in time as in importance is that of J. F. Campbell, of Islay. His four volumes, *Popular Tales of the West Highlands* (Edinburgh, 1860-2, recently republished by the Islay Association), contain some 120 folk- and hero-tales, told with strict adherence to the language of the narrators, which is given with a literal, a rather too literal, English version. This careful accuracy has given an un-English air to his versions, and has prevented them attaining their due popularity. What Campbell has published represents only a tithe of what he collected. At the end of the fourth volume he gives a list of 791 tales, &c., collected by him or his assistants in the two years 1859–61 ; and in his MS. collections at Edinburgh are two other lists containing 400 more tales. Only a portion of these are in the Advocates' Library ; the rest, if extant, must be in private hands, though they are distinctly of national importance and interest.

Campbell's influence has been effective of recent years in Scotland. The *Celtic Magazine* (vols. xii. and xiii.), while under the editorship of Mr. MacBain, contained several folk- and hero-tales in Gaelic, and and so did the *Scotch Celtic Review*. These were from the collections of Messrs. Campbell of Tiree, Carmichael, and K. Mackenzie. Recently Lord Archibald Campbell has shown laudable interest in the preservation of Gaelic folk- and hero-tales. Under his auspices a whole series of handsome volumes, under the general title of *Waifs and Strays of Celtic Tradition*, has been recently published, four volumes having already appeared, each accompanied by notes by Mr. Alfred Nutt, which form the most important aid to the study of Celtic Folk-Tales since Campbell himself. Those to the second volume in particular (Tales collected by Rev. D. MacInnes) fill 100 pages, with condensed information on all aspects of the subject dealt with in the light of the most recent research in the European folk-tales as well as on Celtic literature. Thanks to Mr. Nutt, Scotland is just now to the fore in the collection and study of the British Folk-Tale.

WALES makes a poor show beside Ireland and Scotland. Sikes' *British Goblins*, and the tales collected by Prof. Rhys in *Y Cymrodor*, vols. ii.–vi., are mainly of our first-class fairy anecdotes. Borrow, in his *Wild Wales*, refers to a collection of fables in a journal called *The Greal*, while the *Cambrian Quarterly Magazine* for 1830 and 1831 contained a few fairy anecdotes, including a curious version of the " Brewery of Eggshells " from the Welsh. In the older literature, the *Iolo MS.*, published by the Welsh MS. Society, has a few fables and apologues, and the charming *Mabinogion*, translated by Lady Guest, has tales that can trace back to the twelfth century and are on the border-line between folk-tales and hero-tales.

CORNWALL and MAN are even worse than Wales. Hunt's *Drolls from the West of England* has nothing distinctively Celtic, and it is only by a chance Lhuyd chose a folk-tal as his specimen of Cornish in his *Archæologia Britannica*, 1709 (see *Tale of Ivan*). The Manx folk-tales published, including the most recent by Mr. Moore, in his *Folk-Lore of the Isle of Man*, 1891, are mainly fairy anecdotes and legends.

From this survey of the field of Celtic folk-tales it is clear that Ireland and Scotland provide the lion's share. The interesting thing to notice is the remarkable similarity of Scotch and Irish folk-tales. The continuity of language and culture between these two divisions of Gaeldom has clearly brought about this identity of their folk-tales. As will be seen from the following notes, the tales found in Scotland can almost invariably be paralleled by those found in Ireland, and *vice versâ*. This result is a striking confirmation of the general truth that the folk-lores of different countries resemble one another in proportion to their contiguity and to the continuity of language and culture between them.

Another point of interest in these Celtic folk-tales is the light they throw upon the relation of hero-tales and folk-tales (classes 2 and 3 above). Tales told of Finn or Cuchulain, and therefore coming under the definition of hero-tales, are found elsewhere told of anonymous or unknown heroes. The question is, were the folk-tales the earliest, and were they localised and applied to the heroes, or were the heroic sagas generalised and applied to an unknown τὶς? All the evidence, in my opinion, inclines to the former view, which, as applied to Celtic folk-tales, is of very great literary importance ; for it is becoming more and more recognised, thanks chiefly to the admirable work of Mr. Alfred Nutt, in his *Studies on the Holy Grail*, that the outburst of

European Romance in the twelfth century was due, in large measure, to an infusion of Celtic hero-tales into the literature of the Romance-speaking nations. Now the remarkable thing is, how these hero-tales have lingered on in oral tradition even to the present day. (See a marked case in " Deirdre.") We may, therefore, hope to see considerable light thrown on the most characteristic spiritual product of the Middle Ages, the literature of Romance and the spirit of chivalry, from the Celtic folk-tales of the present day. Mr. Alfred Nutt has already shown this to be true of a special section of Romance literature, that connected with the Holy Grail, and it seems probable that further study will extend the field of application of this new method of research.

The Celtic folk-tale again has interest in retaining many traits of primitive conditions among the early inhabitants of these isles which are preserved by no other record. Take, for instance, the calm assumption of polygamy in " Gold Tree and Silver Tree." That represents a state of feeling that is decidedly pre-Christian. The belief in an external soul "Life Index," recently monographed by Mr. Frazer in his " Golden Bough," also finds expression in a couple of the Tales (see notes on "Sea-Maiden" and "Fair, Brown, and Trembling "), and so with many other primitive ideas.

Care, however, has to be taken in using folk-tales as evidence for primitive practice among the nations where they are found. For the tales may have come from another race—that is, for example, probably the case with "Gold Tree and Silver Tree" (see Notes). Celtic tales are of peculiar interest in this connection, as they afford one of the best fields for studying the problem of diffusion, the most pressing of the problems of the folk-tales just at present, at least in my opinion. The Celts are at the furthermost end of Europe. Tales that travelled to them could go no further and must therefore be the last links in the chain.

For all these reasons, then, Celtic folk-tales are of high scientific interest to the folk-lorist, while they yield to none in imaginative and literary qualities. In any other country of Europe some national means of recording them would have long ago been adopted. M. Luzel, e.g., was commissioned by the French Minister of Public Instruction to collect and report on the Breton folk-tales. England, here as elsewhere without any organised means of scientific research in the historical and philological sciences, has to depend on the enthusiasm of a few private individuals for work of national importance. Every Celt of these islands or in the Gaeldom beyond the sea, and every Celt-lover among the English-speaking nations, should regard it as one of the duties of the race to put its traditions on record in the few years that now remain before they will cease for ever to be living in the hearts and memories of the humbler members of the race.

In the following Notes I have done as in my *English Fairy Tales*, and given first, the *sources* whence I drew the tales, then *parallels* at length for the British Isles, with bibliographical references for parallels abroad, and finally, *remarks* where the tales seemed to need them. In these I have not wearied or worried the reader with conventional tall talk about the Celtic genius and its manifestations in the folk-tale ; on that topic one can only repeat Matthew Arnold when at his best, in his *Celtic Literature*. Nor have I attempted to deal with the more general aspects of the study of the Celtic folk-tale. For these I must refer to Mr. Nutt's series of papers in *The Celtic Magazine*, vol. xii., or, still better, to the masterly introductions he is contributing to the series of *Waifs and Strays of Celtic Tradition*, and to Dr. Hyde's *Beside the Fireside*. In my remarks I have mainly confined myself to discussing the origin and diffusion of the various tales, so far as anything definite could be learnt or conjectured on that subject.

Before proceeding to the Notes, I may " put in," as the lawyers say, a few summaries of the results reached in them. Of the twenty-six tales, twelve (i., ii., v., viii., ix., x., xi., xv., xvi., xvii., xix., xxiv.) have Gaelic originals ; three (vii., xiii., xxv.) are from the Welsh; one (xxii.) from the now extinct Cornish ; one an adaptation of an English poem founded on a Welsh tradition (xxi., " Gellert ") ; and the remaining nine are what may be termed Anglo-Irish. Regarding their diffusion among the Celts, twelve are both Irish and Scotch (iv., v., vi., ix., x., xiv.–xvii., xix., xx., xxiv) ; one (xxv.) is common to Irish and Welsh ; and one (xxii.) to Irish and Cornish ; seven are found only among the Celts in Ireland (i.–iii., xii., xviii., xxii., xxvi) ; two (viii., xi.) among the Scotch ; and three (vii., xiii., xxi.) among the Welsh. Finally, so far as we can ascertain their origin, four (v., xvi., xxi., xxii.) are from the East ; five (vi., x., xiv., xx., xxv.) are European drolls ; three of the romantic tales seem to have been imported (vii., ix., xix.) ; while three others are possibly Celtic exportations to the Continent (xv., xvii., xxiv.) though the last may have previously come thence ; the remaining eleven are, as far as known, original to Celtic lands. Somewhat the same result would come out, I believe, as the analysis of any representative collection of folk-tales of any European district.

I. CONNLA AND THE FAIRY MAIDEN.

Source.—From the old Irish "Echtra Condla chaim maic Cuind Chetchathaig" of the *Leabhar na h-Uidhre* ("Book of the Dun Cow"), which must have been written before 1106, when its scribe Maelmori ("Servant of Mary") was murdered. The original is given by Windisch in his *Irish Grammar*, p. 120, also in the *Trans. Kilkenny Archæol. Soc.* for 1874. A fragment occurs in a Rawlinson MS., described by Dr. W. Stokes, *Tripartite Life*, p. xxxvi. I have used the translation of Prof. Zimmer in his *Keltische Beitrage*, ii. (*Zeits. f. deutsches Altertum*, Bd. xxxiii. 262–4). Dr. Joyce has a somewhat florid version in his *Old Celtic Romances*, from which I have borrowed a touch or two. I have neither extenuated nor added aught but the last sentence of the Fairy Maiden's last speech. Part of the original is in metrical form, so that the whole is of the *cante-fable* species which I believe to be the original form of the folk-tale (*Cf. Eng. Fairy Tales*, notes, p. 240, and *infra*, p. 257).

Parallels.—Prof. Zimmer's paper contains three other accounts of the *terra repromissionis* in the Irish sagas, one of them being the similar adventure of Cormac the nephew of Connla, or Condla Ruad as he should be called. The fairy apple of gold occurs in Cormac Mac Art's visit to the Brug of Manannan (Nutt's *Holy Grail*, 193).

Remarks.—Conn the hundred-fighter had the head-kingship of Ireland 123–157 A.D., according to the *Annals of the Four Masters*, i. 105. On the day of his birth the five great roads from Tara to all parts of Ireland were completed : one of them from Dublin is still used. Connaught is said to have been named after him, but this is scarcely consonant with Joyce's identification with Ptolemy's *Nagnatai* (*Irish Local Names*, i. 75). But there can be little doubt of Conn's existence as a powerful ruler in Ireland in the second century. The historic existence of Connla seems also to be authenticated by the reference to him as Conly, the eldest son of Conn, in the Annals of Clonmacnoise. As Conn was succeeded by his third son, Art Enear, Connla was either slain or disappeared during his father's lifetime. Under these circumstances it is not unlikely that our legend grew up within the century after Conn—*i.e.*, during the latter half of the second century.

As regards the present form of it, Prof. Zimmer (*l.c.* 261–2) places it in the seventh century. It has clearly been touched up by a Christian hand who introduced the reference to the day of judgment and to the waning power of the Druids. But nothing turns upon this interpolation, so that it is likely that even the present form of the legend is pre-Christian—*i.e.* for Ireland, prePatrician, before the fifth century.

The tale of Connla is thus the earliest fairy tale of modern Europe. Besides this interest it contains an early account of one of the most characteristic Celtic conceptions, that of the earthly Paradise, the Isle of Youth, *Tir-na n-Og*. This has impressed itself on the European imagination ; in the Arthuriad it is represented by the Vale of Avalon, and as represented in the various Celtic visions of the future life, it forms one of the main sources of Dante's *Divina Commedia*. It is possible too, I think, that the Homeric Hesperides and the Fortunate Isles of the ancients had a Celtic origin (as is well known, the early place-names of Europe are predominantly Celtic). I have found, I believe, a reference to the conception in one of the earliest passages in the classics dealing with the Druids. Lucan, in his *Pharsalia* (i. 450–8), addresses them in these high terms of reverence :

> Et vos barbaricos ritus, moremque sinistrum,
> Sacrorum, Druidæ, positis repetistis ab armis,
> Solis nôsse Deos et cœli numera vobis
> Aut solis nescire datum ; nemora alta remotis
> Incolitis lucis.   Vobis auctoribus umbræ,
> Non tacitas Erebi sedes, Ditisque profundi,
> Pallida regna p. tunt : *regit idem spiritus artus*
> *Orbe alio :* longæ, canitis si cognita, vitæ
> Mors media est.

The passage certainly seems to me to imply a different conception from the ordinary classical views of the life after death, the dark and dismal plains of Erebus peopled with ghosts ; and the passage I have italicised would chime in well with the conception of a continuance of youth (*idem spiritus*) in Tir-na n-Og (*orbe alio*).

One of the most pathetic, beautiful, and typical scenes in Irish legend is the return of Ossian from Tir-na n-Og, and his interview with St. Patrick. The old faith and the new, the old order of things and that which replaced it, meet in two of the most characteristic products of the Irish imagination (for the Patrick of legend is as much a legendary figure as Oisin himself). Ossian had gone away to Tir-na n-Og with the fairy Niamh under very much the same circumstances as Condla Ruad ; time flies in the land of eternal youth, and when Ossian returns, after a year as he thinks, more than three centuries had passed, and St. Patrick had just succeeded in introducing the new faith. The contrast of Past and Present has never been more vividly or beautifully represented.

II. GULEESH.

Source.—From Dr. Douglas Hyde's *Beside the Fire*, 104–28, where it is a translation from the same author's *Leabhar Sgeulaighteachta*. Dr Hyde got it from one Shamus O'Hart, a gamekeeper of French-park. One is curious to know how far the very beautiful landscapes in the story are due to Dr. Hyde, who confesses to have only taken notes. I have omitted a journey to Rome, paralleled, as Mr. Nutt has pointed out, by the similar one of Michael Scott (*Waifs and Strays*, i. 46), and not bearing on the main lines of the story. I have also dropped a part of Guleesh's name: in the original he is "Guleesh na guss dhu," Guleesh of the black feet, because he never washed them; nothing turns on this in the present form of the story, but one cannot but suspect it was of importance in the original form.

Parallels.—Dr. Hyde refers to two short stories, "Midnight Ride" (to Rome) and "Stolen Bride," in Lady Wilde's *Ancient Legends*. But the closest parallel is given by Miss Maclintock's Donegal tale of "Jamie Freel and the Young Lady," reprinted in Mr. Yeats' *Irish Folk and Fairy Tales*, 52–9. In the *Hibernian Tales*, "Mann o' Malaghan and the Fairies," as reported by Thackeray in the *Irish Sketch-Book*, c. xvi., begins like "Guleesh."

III. FIELD OF BOLIAUNS.

Source.—T. Crofton Croker's *Fairy Legends of the South of Ireland*, ed. Wright, pp. 135–9. In the original the gnome is a Cluricaune, but as a friend of Mr. Batten's has recently heard the tale told of a Lepracaun, I have adopted the better known title.

Remarks.—*Lepracaun* is from the Irish *leith bhrogan*, the one-shoemaker (*cf.* brogue), according to Dr. Hyde. He is generally seen (and to this day, too) working at a single shoe, *cf.* Croker's story "Little Shoe," *l.c.* pp. 142–4. According to a writer in the *Revue Celtique*, i. 256, the true etymology is *luchor pan*, "little man" Dr. Joyce also gives the same etymology in *Irish Names and Places*, i. 183, where he mentions several places named after them.

IV. HORNED WOMEN.

Source.—Lady Wilde's *Ancient Legends*, the first story.

Parallels.—A similar version was given by Mr. D. Fitzgerald in the *Revue Celtique*, iv. 181, but without the significant and impressive horns. He refers to *Cornhill* for February 1877, and to Campbell's "Sauntraigh" No. xxii. *Pop. Tales*, ii. 52–4, in which a "woman of peace" (a fairy) borrows a woman's kettle and returns it with flesh in it, but at last the woman refuses, and is persecuted by the fairy. I fail to see much analogy. A much closer one is in Campbell, ii. p. 63, where fairies are got rid of by shouting "Dunveilg is on fire." The familiar "lady-bird, lady-bird, fly away home, your house is on fire and your children at home," will occur to English minds. Another version in Kennedy's *Legendary Fictions*, p. 164, "Black Stairs on Fire."

Remarks.—Slievenamon is a famous fairy palace in Tipperary according to Dr. Joyce, *l.c.* i. 178. It was the hill on which Finn stood when he gave himself as the prize to the Irish maiden who should run up it quickest. Grainne won him with dire consequences, as all the world knows or ought to know (Kennedy, *Legend Fict.*, 222, "How Fion selected a Wife").

V. CONAL YELLOWCLAW.

Source.—Campbell, *Pop. Tales of West Highlands*, No. v. pp. 105–8, "Conall Cra Bhuidhe." I have softened the third episode, which is somewhat too ghastly in the original. I have translated "Cra Bhuide" Yellowclaw on the strength of Campbell's etymology, *l.c.* p. 158.

Parallels.—Campbell's vi. and vii. are two variants showing how widespread the story is in Gaelic Scotland. It occurs in Ireland where it has been printed in the chapbook, *Hibernian Tales*, as the "Black Thief and the Knight of the Glen," the Black Thief being Conall, and the knight corresponding to the King of Lochlan (it is given in Mr. Lang's *Red Fairy Book*). Here it attracted the notice of Thackeray, who gives a good abstract of it in his *Irish Sketch-Book*, ch. xvi. He thinks it "worthy of the Arabian Nights, as wild and odd as an Eastern tale." "That fantastical way of bearing testimony to the previous tale by producing an old woman who says the tale is not only true, but who was the very old woman who lived in the giant's castle is almost" (why "almost," Mr. Thackeray?) "a stroke of genius." The incident of the giant's breath occurs in the story of Koisha Kayn, MacInnes' *Tales*,

i. 241, as well as the Polyphemus one, *ibid.* 265. One-eyed giants are frequent in Celtic folk-tales (*e.g.*, in *The Pursuit of Diarmaid* and in the *Mabinogi* of Owen).

Remarks.—Thackeray's reference to the "Arabian Nights" is especially apt, as the tale of Conall is a framework story like *The* 1001 *Nights*, the three stories told by Conall being framed, as it were, in a fourth which is nominally the real story. This method employed by the Indian story-tellers and from them adopted by Boccaccio and thence into all European literatures (Chaucer, Queen Margaret, &c.), is generally thought to be peculiar to the East, and to be ultimately derived from the Jatakas or Birth Stories of the Buddha who tells his adventures in former incarnations. Here we find it in Celtdom, and it occurs also in "The Story-teller at Fault" in this collection, and the story of *Koisha Kayn* in MacInnes' *Argyllshire Tales*, a variant of which collected but not published by Campbell has no less than nineteen tales enclosed in a framework. The question is whether the method was adopted independently in Ireland, or was due to foreign influences. Confining ourselves to "Conal Yellowclaw," it seems not unlikely that the whole story is an importation. For the second episode is clearly the story of Polyphemus from the Odyssey which was known in Ireland perhaps as early as the tenth century (see Prof. K. Meyer's edition of *Merugud Uilix maic Leirtis*, Pref. p. xii). It also crept into the voyages of Sindbad in the *Arabian Nights*. And as told in the Highlands it bears comparison even with the Homeric version. As Mr. Nutt remarks (*Celt. Mag.* xii.) the address of the giant to the buck is as effective as that of Polyphemus to his ram. The narrator, James Wilson, was a blind man who would naturally feel the pathos of the address; "it comes from the heart of the narrator;" says Campbell (*l.c.*, 148), "it is the ornament which his mind hangs on the frame of the story."

VI. HUDDEN AND DUDDEN.

Source.—From oral tradition, by the late D. W. Logie, taken down by Mr. Alfred Nutt.

Parallels.—Lover has a tale, "Little Fairly," obviously derived from this folk-tale; and there is another very similar, "Darby Darly." Another version of our tale is given under the title "Donald and his Neighbours," in the chapbook *Hibernian Tales*, whence it was reprinted by Thackeray in his *Irish Sketch-Book*, c. xvi. This has the incident of the "accidental matricide," on which see Prof. R. Köhler on Gonzenbach *Sicil. Mährchen*, ii. 224. No less than four tales of Campbell are of this type (*Pop. Tales*, ii. 218-31). M. Cosquin, in his "Contes populaires de Lorraine," the storehouse of "storiology," has elaborate excursuses in this class of tales attached to his Nos. x. and xx. Mr. Clouston discusses it also in his *Pop. Tales*, ii. 229-88. Both these writers are inclined to trace the chief incidents to India. It is to be observed that one of the earliest popular drolls in Europe, *Unibos*, a Latin poem of the eleventh, and perhaps the tenth, century, has the main outlines of the story, the fraudulent sale of worthless objects and the escape from the sack trick. The same story occurs in Straparola, the European earliest collection of folk-tales in the sixteenth century. On the other hand, the gold sticking to the scales is familiar to us in *Ali Baba*. (*Cf.* Cosquin, *l.c.*, i. 225-6, 229).

Remarks.—It is indeed curious to find, as M. Cosquin points out a cunning fellow tied in a sack getting out by crying, " I won't marry the princess," in countries so far apart as Ireland, Sicily (Gonzenbach, No. 71), Afghanistan (Thorburn, *Bannu*, p. 184), and Jamaica (*Folk-Lore Record*, iii. 53). It is indeed impossible to think these are disconnected, and for drolls of this kind a good case has been made out for the borrowing hypotheses by M. Cosquin and Mr. Clouston. Who borrowed from whom is another and more difficult question which has to be judged on its merits in each individual case.

This is a type of Ce-tic folk-tales which are European in spread, have analogies with the East, and can only be said to be Celtic by adoption and by colouring. They form a distinct section of the tales told by the Celts, and must be represented in any characteristic selection. Other examples are xi., xv., xx., and perhaps xxii.

VII. SHEPHERD OF MYDDVAI.

Source.—Preface to the edition of "The Physicians of Myddvai"; their prescription-book, from the Red Book of Hergest, published by the Welsh MS. Society in 1861. The legend is not given in the Red Book, but from oral tradition by Mr. W. Rees, p. xxi. As this is the first of the Welsh tales in this book it may be as well to give the reader such guidance as I can afford him on the intricacies of Welsh pronunciation, especially with regard to the mysterious *w*'s and *y*'s of Welsh orthography. For *w* substitute double *o*, as in "*fool*," and for *y*, the short *u* in b*u*t, and as near approach to Cymric speech will be reached as is possible for the outlander. It may be added that double *d* equals *th*, and double *l* is something like *Fl*, as Shakespeare knew in calling his Welsh soldier Fluellen (Llewelyn). Thus "Meddygon Myddvai" would be *Anglicè* "Methugon Muthvai."

Parallels.—Other versions of the legend of the Van Pool are given in *Cambro-Briton*, ii. 315 ; W. Sikes, *British Goblins*, p. 40. Mr. E. Sidney Hartland has discussed these and others in a set of papers contributed to the first volume of *The Archæological Review* (now incorporated into *Folk-Lore*), the substance of which is now given in his *Science of Fairy Tales*, 274–332. (See also the references given in *Revue Celtique*, iv., 187 and 268). Mr. Hartland gives there an ecumenical collection of parallels to the several incidents that go to make up our story—(1) The bride-capture of the Swan-Maiden, (2) the recognition of the bride, (3) the taboo against causeless blows, (4) doomed to be broken, and (5) disappearance of the Swan-Maiden, with (6) her return as Guardian Spirit to her descendants. In each case Mr. Hartland gives what he considers to be the most primitive form of the incident. With reference to our present tale, he comes to the conclusion, if I understand him aright, that the lake-maiden was once regarded as a local divinity. The physicians of Myddvai were historic personages, renowned for their medical skill for some six centuries, till the race died out with John Jones, *fl.* 1743. To explain their skill and uncanny knowledge of herbs, the folk traced them to a supernatural ancestress, who taught them their craft in a place still called Pant-y-Meddygon ("Doctors' Dingle"). Their medical knowledge did not require any such remarkable origin, as Mr. Hartland has shown in a paper " On Welsh Folk-Medicine," contributed to *Y Cymmrodor*, vol. xii. On the other hand, the Swan-Maiden type of story is widespread through the Old World. Mr. Morris' " Land East of the Moon and West of the Sun," in *The Earthly Paradise*, is taken from the Norse version. Parallels are accumulated by the Grimms, ii. 432 ; Köhler on Gonzenbach, ii. 20 ; or Blade, 149 ; Stokes' *Indian Fairy Tales*, 243, 276 ; and Messrs. Jones and Koopf, *Magyar Folk-Tales*, 362–5. It remains to be proved that one of these versions did not travel to Wales, and become there localised. We shall see other instances of such localisation or specialisation of general legends.

VIII. THE SPRIGHTLY TAILOR.

Source.—*Notes and Queries* for December 21, 1861, to which it was communicated by " Cuthbert Bede," the author of *Verdant Green*, who collected it in Cantyre.

Parallels.—Miss Dempster gives the same story in her Sutherland Collection, No. vii. (referred to by Campbell in his Gaelic list, at end of vol. iv.) ; Mrs. John Faed, I am informed by a friend, knows the Gaelic version, as told by her nurse in her youth. Chambers' "Strange Visitor," *Pop. Rhymes of Scotland,* 64, of which I gave an Anglicised version in my *English Fairy Tales,* No. xxxii., is clearly a variant.

Remarks.—The Macdonald of Saddell Castle was a very great man indeed. Once, when dining with the Lord-Lieutenant, an apology was made to him for placing him so far away from the head of the table. "Where the Macdonald sits," was the proud response, "there is the head of the table."

IX. DEIRDRE.

Source.—*Celtic Magazine,* xiii. pp. 69, *seq.* I have abridged somewhat, made the sons of Fergus all faithful instead of two traitors, and omitted an incident in the house of the wild men called here "strangers." The original Gaelic was given in the *Transactions of the Inverness Gaelic Society* for 1887, p. 241, *seq.,* by Mr. Carmichael. I have inserted Deirdre's "Lament" from the *Book of Leinster.*

Parallels.—This is one of the three most sorrowful Tales of Erin, (the other two, *Children of Lir* and *Children of Tureen,* are given in Dr. Joyce's *Old Celtic Romances*), and is a specimen of the old heroic sagas of elopement, a list of which is given in the *Book of Leinster.* The "outcast child" is a frequent episode in folk and hero-tales : an instance occurs in my *English Fairy Tales,* No. xxxv., and Prof. Köhler gives many others in *Archiv. f. Slav. Philologie,* i. 288. Mr. Nutt adds tenth century Celtic parallels in *Folk-Lore,* vol. ii. The wooing of hero by heroine is a characteristic Celtic touch. See "Connla" here, and other examples given by Mr. Nutt in his notes to MacInnes' *Tales.* The trees growing from the lovers' graves occurs in the English ballad of *Lord Lovel* and has been studied in *Mélusine.*

Remarks.—The "Story of Deirdre" is a remarkable instance of the tenacity of oral tradition among the Celts. It has been preserved in no less than five versions (or six, including Macpherson's "Darthula") ranging from the twelfth to the nineteenth century. The earliest is in the twelfth century, *Book of Leinster,* to be dated about 1140 (edited in facsimile under the auspices of the Royal Irish Academy, i. 147, *seq.*). Then comes a fifteenth century version, edited and translated by Dr. Stokes in Windisch's *Irische Texte* II., ii. 109, *seq.,* "Death of the Sons of Uisnech." Keating in his *History of Ireland* gave another version in the seventeenth century. The Dublin Gaelic Society published an eighteenth century version in their *Transactions* for 1808. And lastly we have the version before us, collected only a few years ago, yet agreeing in all essential details with the version of the *Book of Leinster*. Such a record is unique in the history of oral tradition, outside Ireland, where, however, it is quite a customary experience in the study of the Finn-saga. It is now recognised that Macpherson had, or could have had, ample material for his *rechauffé* of the Finn or "Fingal" saga. His "Darthula" is a similar cobbling of our present story. I leave to Celtic specialists the task of settling the exact relations of these various texts. I content myself with pointing out the fact that in these latter days of a seemingly prosaic century in these British Isles there has been collected from the lips of the folk a heroic story like this of "Deirdre," full of romantic incidents, told with tender feeling and considerable literary skill. No other country in Europe, except perhaps Russia, could provide a parallel to this living on of Romance among the common folk. Surely it is a bounden duty of those who are in the position to put on record any such utterances of the folk-imagination of the Celts before it is too late.

X. MUNACHAR AND MANACHAR.

Source.—I have combined the Irish version given by Dr. Hyde in his *Leabhar Sgeul.*, and translated by him for Mr. Yeats' *Irish Folk and Fairy Tales*, and the Scotch version given in Gaelic and English by Campbell, No. viii.

Parallels.—Two English versions are given in my *Eng. Fairy Tales*, No. iv., "The Old Woman and her Pig," and xxxiv., "The Cat and the Mouse," where see notes for other variants in these isles. M. Cosquin, in his notes to No. xxxiv., of his *Contes de Lorraine*, t. ii. pp. 35–41, has drawn attention to an astonishing number of parallels scattered through all Europe and the East (*cf.*, too, Crane, *Ital. Pop. Tales*, notes, 372–5). One of the earliest allusions to the jingle is in *Don Quixote*, pt. I, c. xvi.: "Y asi como suele decirse *el gato al rato, el rato á la cuerda, la cuerda al palo,* daba el arriero á Sancho, Sancho á la moza, la moza á él, el ventero á la moza." As I have pointed out, it is used to this day by Bengali women at the end of each folk-tale they recite (L. B. Day, *Folk-Tales of Bengal*, Pref.).

Remarks.—Two ingenious suggestions have been made as to the origin of this curious jingle, both connecting it with religious ceremonies: (1) Something very similar occurs in Chaldaic at the end of the Jewish *Hagada*, or domestic ritual for the Passover night. It has, however, been shown that this does not occur in early MSS. or editions, and was only added at the end to amuse the children after the service, and was therefore only a translation or adaptation of a current German form of the jingle; (2) M. Basset, in the *Revue des Traditions populaires*, 1890, t. v. p. 549, has suggested that it is a survival of the old Greek custom at the sacrifice of the Bouphonia for the priest to contend that *he* had not slain the sacred beast, the axe declares that the handle did it, the handle transfers the guilt further, and so on. This is ingenious, but fails to give any reasonable account of the diffusion of the jingle in countries which have had no historic connection with classical Greece.

XI. GOLD TREE AND SILVER TREE.

Source.—*Celtic Magazine*, xiii. 213-8, Gaelic and English from Mr. Kenneth Macleod.

Parallels.—Mr. Macleod heard another version in which "Gold Tree" (anonymous in this variant) is bewitched to kill her father's horse, dog, and cock. Abroad it is the Grimm's *Schneewitchen* (No. 53), for the Continental variants of which see Köhler on Gonzenbach, *Sicil. Märchen*, Nos. 2-4, Grimm's notes on 53, and Crane, *Ital. Pop. Tales*, 331. No other version is known in the British Isles.

Remarks.—It is unlikely, I should say impossible, that this tale, with the incident of the dormant heroine, should have arisen independently in the Highlands: it is most likely an importation from abroad. Yet in it occurs a most "primitive" incident, the bigamous household of the hero: this is glossed over in Mr. Macleod's other variant. On the "survival" method of investigation this would possibly be used as evidence for polygamy in the Highlands. Yet if, as is probable, the story came from abroad, this trait may have come with it, and only implies polygamy in the original home of the tale.

XII. KING O'TOOLE AND HIS GOOSE.

Source.—S. Lover's *Stories and Legends of the Irish Peasantry*.

Remarks.—This is really a moral apologue on the benefits of keeping your word. Yet it is told with such humour and vigour, that the moral glides insensibly into the heart.

XIII. THE WOOING OF OLWEN.

Source.—The *Mabinogi* of Kulhwych and Olwen from the translation of Lady Guest, abridged.

Parallels.—Prof. Rhys, *Hibbert Lectures*, p. 486, considers that our tale is paralleled by Cuchulain's "Wooing of Emer," a translation of which by Prof. K. Meyer appeared in the *Archæological Review*, vol. i.   I fail to see much analogy.   On the other hand in his *Arthurian Legend*, p. 41, he rightly compares the tasks set by Yspythadon to those set to Jason.   They are indeed of the familiar type of the Bride Wager (on which see Grimm-Hunt, i. 399).   The incident of the three animals, old, older, and oldest, has a remarkable resemblance to the *Tettira Jataka* (ed. Fausböll, No. 37, transl. Rhys Davids, i. p. 310 *seq.*) in which the partridge, monkey, and elephant dispute as to their relative age, and the partridge turns out to have voided the seed of the Banyan-tree under which they were sheltered, whereas the elephant only knew it when a mere bush, and the monkey had nibbled the topmost shoots. This apologue got to England at the end of the twelfth century as the sixty-ninth fable, "Wolf, Fox, and Dove," of a rhymed prose collection of "Fox Fables" (*Mishle Shu'alim*), of an Oxford Jew, Berachyah Nakdan, known in the Records as "Benedict le Puncteur" (see my *Fables of Æsop*, i. p. 170).   Similar incidents occur in "Jack and his Snuff-box" in my *English Fairy Tales*, and in Dr. Hyde's "Well of D'Yerree-in-Dowan." The skilled companions of Kulhwych are common in European folk-tales (*Cf.* Cosquin, i. 123–5), and especially among the Celts (see Mr. Nutt's note in MacInnes' *Tales*, 445–8), among whom they occur very early, but not so early as Lynceus and the other skilled comrades of the Argonauts.

Remarks.—The hunting of the boar Trwyth can be traced back in Welsh tradition at least as early as the ninth century.   For it is referred to in the following passage of Nennius' *Historia Britonum* ed. Stevenson, p: 60, "Est aliud miraculum in regione quæ dicitur Buelt [Builth, co. Brecon] Est ibi cumulus lapidum et unus lapis super-positus super congestum cum vestigia canis in eo.   Quando venatus est porcum Troynt [*var. lec.* Troit] impressit Cabal, qui erat canis Arthuri militis, vestigium in lapide et Arthur postea congregavit congestum lapidum sub lapide in quo erat vestigium canis sui et vocatur Carn Cabal." Curiously enough there is still a mountain called Carn Cabal in the district of Builth, south of Rhayader Gwy in Breconshire.   Still more curiously a friend of Lady Guest's found on this a cairn with a stone two feet long by one foot wide in which there was an indentation 4 in. × 3 in. × 2 in. which could easily have been mistaken for a paw-print of a dog, as may be seen from the engraving given of it (Mabinogion, ed. 1874, p. 269).

The stone and the legend are thus at least one thousand years old. "There stands the stone to tell if I lie." According to Prof. Rhys (*Hibbert Lect.* 486–97) the whole story is a mythological one, Kulhwych's mother being the dawn, the clover blossoms that grow under Olwen's feet being comparable to the roses that sprung up where Aphrodite had trod, and Yspyddadon being the incarnation of the sacred hawthorn. Mabon, again (*l.c.* pp. 21, 28–9), is the Apollo Maponus discovered in Latin inscriptions at Ainstable in Cumberland and elsewhere (Hübner, *Corp. Insc. Lat. Brit.* Nos. 218, 332, 1345). Granting all this, there

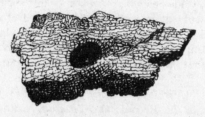

is nothing to show any mythological significance in the tale, though there may have been in the names of the *dramatis personæ*. I observe from the proceedings of the recent Eisteddfod that the bardic name of Mr. W. Abraham, M.P., is 'Mabon.' It scarcely follows that Mr. Abraham is in receipt of divine honours nowadays.

XIV. JACK AND HIS COMRADES.

Source.—Kennedy's *Legendary Fictions of the Irish Celts.*

Parallels.—This is the fullest and most dramatic version I know of the Grimm's "Town Musicians of Bremen" (No. 27). I have given an English (American) version in my *English Fairy Tales*, No. 5, in the notes to which would be found references to other versions known in the British Isles (*e.g.*, Campbell, No. 11) and abroad. *Cf.* remarks on No. vi.

XV. SHEE AN GANNON AND GRUAGACH GAIRE.

Source.—Curtin, *Myths and Folk-Lore of Ireland*, p. 114 *seq.* I have shortened the earlier part of the tale, and introduced into the

latter a few touches from Campbell's story of "Fionn's Enchantment," in *Revue Celtique*, t. i., 193 *seq.*

Parallels.—The early part is similar to the beginning of "The Sea-
Maiden" (No. xvii., which see). The latter part is practically the
same as the story of "Fionn's Enchantment," just referred to. It also
occurs in MacInnes' *Tales*, No. iii., "The King of Albainn" (see
Mr. Nutt's notes, 454). The head-crowned spikes are Celtic, *cf.* Mr.
Nutt's notes (MacInnes' *Tales*, 453).

Remarks.—Here again we meet the question whether the folk-tale
precedes the hero-tale about Finn or was derived from it, and again
the probability seems that our story has the priority as a folk-tale,
and was afterwards applied to the national hero, Finn. This is confirmed by the fact that a thirteenth century French romance, *Conte du
Graal*, has much the same incidents, and was probably derived from
a similar folk-tale of the Celts. Indeed, Mr. Nutt is inclined to think
that the original form of our story (which contains a mysterious
healing vessel) is the germ out of which the legend of the Holy Grail
was evolved (see his *Studies in the Holy Grail*, p. 202 *seq.*).

XVI. THE STORY-TELLER AT FAULT.

Source.—Griffin's *Tales from a Jury-Room*, combined with Campbell, No. xvii. *c*, "The Slim Swarthy Champion."

Parallels.—Campbell gives another variant, *l.c.* i. 318. Dr. Hyde
has an Irish version of Campbell's tale written down in 1762, from
which he gives the incident of the air-ladder (which I have had to
euphemise in my version) in his *Beside the Fireside*, p. 191, and other
passages in his Preface. The most remarkable parallel to this incident,
however, is afforded by the feats of Indian jugglers reported briefly by
Marco Polo, and illustrated with his usual wealth of learning by the
late Sir Henry Yule, in his edition, vol. i. p. 308 *seq.* The accom-
panying illustration (reduced from Yule) will tell its own tale: it is
taken from the Dutch account of the travels of an English sailor,
E. Melton, *Zeldzaame Reizen*, 1702, p. 468. It tells the tale in five acts,
all included in one sketch. Another instance quoted by Yule is
still more parallel, so to speak. The twenty-third trick performed
by some conjurors before the Emperor Jahangueir (*Memoirs*, p. 102)
is thus described: "They produced a chain of 50 cubits in length,
and in my presence threw one end of it towards the sky, where
it remained as if fastened to something in the air. A dog was then
brought forward, and being placed at the lower end of the chain, im-

mediately ran up, and, reaching the other end, immediately disappeared in the air. In the same manner a hog, a panther, a lion, and a tiger were successively sent up the chain." It has been suggested that the conjurors hypnotise the spectators, and make them believe they see these things. This is practically the suggestion of a wise Mohammedan, who is quoted by Yule as saying, " *Wallah!* 'tis my opinion there has been neither going up nor coming down ; 'tis all hocus-pocus," hocus-pocus being presumably the Mohammedan term for hypnotism.

Remarks.—Dr. Hyde (*l.c.* Pref. xxix.) thinks our tale cannot be older than 1362, because of a reference to one O'Connor Sligo which occurs in all its variants ; it is, however, omitted in our somewhat abridged version. Mr. Nutt (*ap.* Campbell, *The Fians*, Introd. xix.) thinks that this does not prevent a still earlier version having existed. I should have thought that the existence of so distinctly Eastern a trick in the tale, and the fact that it is a framework story (another Eastern characteristic), would imply that it is a rather late importation, with local allusions superadded (*cf.* notes on " Conal Yellow-claw," No. v.).

The passages in verse from pp. 137, 139, and the description of the

Beggarman, pp. 136, 140, are instances of a curious characteristic of Gaelic folk-tales called " runs." Collections of conventional epithets are used over and over again to describe the same incident, the beaching of a boat, sea-faring, travelling and the like, and are inserted in different tales. These " runs " are often similar in both the Irish and the Scotch form of the same tale or of the same incident. The vo umes of *Waifs and Strays* contain numerous examples of these " runs," which have been indexed in each volume. These " runs " are another confirmation of my view that the original form of the folk-tale was that of the *Cante-fable* (see note on "Connla" and on "Childe Rowland" in *English Fairy Tales*).

XVII. SEA-MAIDEN.

Source.—Campbell, *Pop. Tales*, No. 4. I have omitted the births of the animal comrades and transposed the carlin to the middle of the tale. Mr. Batten has considerably idealised the Sea-Maiden in his frontispiece. When she restores the husband to the wife in one of the variants, she brings him out of her mouth! " So the sea-maiden put up his head (*Who do you mean? Out of her mouth to be sure. She had swallowed him*)."

Parallels.—The early part of the story occurs in No. xv., " Shee an Gannon," and the last part in No. xix., " Fair, Brown, and Trembling " (both from Curtin), Campbell's No. 1. " The Young King " is much like it; also MacInnes' No. iv., " Herding of Cruachan " and No. viii., " Lod the Farmer's Son." The third of Mr. Britten's Irish folk-tales in the *Folk-Lore Journal* is a Sea-Maiden story. The story is obviously a favourite one among the Celts. Yet its main incidents occur with frequency in Continental folk-tales. Prof. Köhler has collected a number in his notes on Campbell's Tales in *Orient und Occident*, Bnd. ii. 115-8. The trial of the sword occurs in the saga of Sigurd, yet it is also frequent in Celtic saga and folk-tales (see Mr. Nutt's note, MacInnes' *Tales*, 473, and add. Curtin, 320). The hideous carlin and her three giant sons is also common form in Celtic. The external soul of the Sea-Maiden carried about in an egg, in a trout, in a hoodie, in a hind, is a remarkable instance of a peculiarly savage conception which has been studied by Major Temple, *Wide-awake Stories*, 404-5; by Mr. E. Clodd, in the " Philosophy of Punchkin," in *Folk-Lore Journal*, vol. ii., and by Mr. Frazer in his *Golden Bough*, vol. ii.

Remarks.—As both Prof. Rhys (*Hibbert Lect.*, 464) and Mr. Nutt (MacInnes' *Tales*, 477) have pointed out, practically the same story (that of Perseus and Andromeda) is told of the Ultonian hero, Cuchulain, in the *Wooing of Emer*, a tale which occurs in the Book of Leinster, a MS. of the twelfth century, and was probably copied from one of the eighth. Unfortunately it is not complete, and the Sea-Maiden incident is only to be found in a British Museum MS. of about 1300. In this Cuchulain finds that the daughter of Ruad is to be given as a tribute to the Fomori, who, according to Prof. Rhys, *Folk-Lore*, ii. 293, have something of the night*mare* about their etymology. Cuchulain fights *three* of them successively, has his wounds bound up by a strip of the maiden's garment, and then departs. Thereafter many boasted of having slain the Fomori, but the maiden believed them not till at last by a stratagem she recognises Cuchulain. I may add to this that in Mr. Curtin's *Myths*, 330, the threefold trial of the sword is told of Cuchulain. This would seem to trace our story back to the seventh or eighth century and certainly to the thirteenth. If so, it is likely enough that it spread from Ireland through Europe with the Irish missions (for the wide extent of which see map in Mrs. Bryant's *Celtic Ireland*). The very letters that have spread through all Europe except Russia, are to be traced to the script of these Irish monks : why not certain folk-tales ? There is a further question whether the story was originally told of Cuchulain as a hero-tale and then became departicularised as a folk-tale, or was the process *vice versâ*. Certainly in the form in which it appears in the *Tochmarc Emer* it is not complete, so that here, as elsewhere, we seem to have an instance of a folk-tale applied to a well-known heroic name, and becoming a hero-tale or saga.

XVIII. LEGEND OF KNOCKMANY.

Source.—W. Carleton, *Traits and Stories of the Irish Peasantry*.

Parallels.—Kennedy's "Fion MacCuil and the Scotch Giant," *Legend. Fict.*, 203–5.

Remarks.—Though the venerable names of Finn and Cucullin (Cuchulain) are attached to the heroes of this story, this is probably only to give an extrinsic interest to it. The two heroes could not have come together in any early form of their sagas, since Cuchulain's reputed date is of the first, Finn's of the third century A.D. (*cf.* however, MacDougall's *Tales*, notes, 272). Besides, the grotesque form of the legend is enough to remove it from the region of the hero-tale. On the other hand, there is a distinct reference to Finn's wisdom-tooth, which presaged the future to him (on this see *Revue Celtique*, v. 201, Joyce, *Old Celt. Rom.*, 434–5, and MacDougall, *l.c.* 274).

Cucullin's power-finger is another instance of the life-index or external soul, on which see remarks on Sea-Maiden. Mr. Nutt informs me that parodies of the Irish sagas occur as early as the sixteenth century, and the present tale may be regarded as a specimen.

XIX. FAIR, BROWN, AND TREMBLING.

Source.—Curtin, *Myths, &c., of Ireland*, 78 *seq.*

Parallels.—The latter half resembles the second part of the Sea-Maiden (No. xvii.), which see. The earlier portion is a Cinderella tale (on which see the late Mr. Ralston's article in *Nineteenth Century*, Nov. 1879, and Mr. Lang's treatment in his Perrault). Miss Roalie Cox is about to publish for the Folk-Lore Society a whole volume of variants of the Cinderella group of stories, which are remarkably well represented in these isles, nearly a dozen different versions being known in England, Ireland, and Scotland.

XX. JACK AND HIS MASTER.

Source.—Kennedy, *Fireside Stories of Ireland*, 74–80, " Shan an Omadhan and his Master."

Parallels.—It occurs also in Campbell, No. xlv., " Mac a Rusgaich." It is a European droll, the wide occurrence of which—" the loss of temper bet " I should call it—is bibliographised by M. Cosquin, *l.c.* ii. 50 (*cf.* notes on No. vi.).

XXI. BETH GELLERT.

Source.—I have paraphrased the well-known poem of Hon. W. R. Spencer, " Beth Gêlert, or the Grave of the Greyhound," first printed privately as a broadsheet in 1800 when it was composed (" August 11, 1800, Dolymalynllyn " is the colophon). It was published in Spencer's *Poems*, 1811, pp. 78–86. These dates, it will be seen, are of importance. Spencer states in a note : " The story of this ballad is traditionary in a village at the foot of Snowdon where Llewellyn the Great had a house. The Greyhound named Gêlert was given him by his father-in-law, King John, in the year 1205, and the place to this day is called Beth-Gêlert, or the grave of Gêlert." As a matter of fact, no trace of the tradition in connection with Bedd Gellert can be found before Spencer's time. It is not mentioned in Leland's *Itinerary*, ed. Hearne, v. p. 37 (" Beth Kellarth "), in Pennant's *Tour* (1770), ii. 176, or in Bingley's

Tour in Wales (1800). Borrow in his *Wild Wales*, p. 146, gives the legend, but does not profess to derive it from local tradition.

Parallels.—The only parallel in Celtdom is that noticed by Croker in his third volume, the legend of Partholan who killed his wife's greyhound from jealousy : this is found sculptured in stone at Ap Brune, co. Limerick. As is well known, and has been elaborately discussed by Mr. Baring-Gould (*Curious Myths of the Middle Ages*, p. 134 *seq.*), and Mr. W. A. Clouston (*Popular Tales and Fictions*, ii 166, *seq.*), the story of the man who rashly slew the dog (ichneumon, weasel, &c.) that had saved his babe from death, is one of those which have spread from East to West. It is indeed, as Mr. Clouston points out, still current in India, the land of its birth. There is little doubt that it is originally Buddhistic : the late Prof. S. Beal gave the earliest known version from the Chinese translation of the *Vinaya Pitaka* in the *Academy* of Nov. 4, 1882. The conception of an animal sacrificing itself for the sake of others is peculiarly Buddhistic ; the "hare in the moon" is an apotheosis of such a piece of self-sacrifice on the part of Buddha (*Sasa Jataka*). There are two forms that have reached the West, the first being that of an animal saving men at the cost of its own life. I pointed out an early instance of this, quoted by a Rabbi of the second century, in my *Fables of Æsop*, i. 105. This concludes with a strangely close parallel to Gellert ; "They raised a cairn over his grave, and the place is still called The Dog's Grave." The *Culex* attributed to Virgil seems to be another variant of this. The second form of the legend is always told as a moral apologue against precipitate action, and originally occurred in *The Fables of Bidpai* in its hundred and one forms, all founded on Buddhistic originals (*cf.* Benfey, *Pantschatantra*, Einleitung, § 201).* Thence, according to Benfey, it was inserted in the *Book of Sindibad*, another collection of Oriental Apologues framed on what may be called the Mrs. Potiphar formula. This came to Europe with the Crusades, and is known in its Western versions as the *Seven Sages of Rome*. The Gellert story occurs in all the Oriental and Occidental versions ; *e.g.*, it is the First Master's story in Wynkyn de Worde's (ed. G. L. Gomme, for the Villon Society.) From the *Seven Sages* it was taken into the particular branch of the *Gesta Romanorum* current in England and known as the English *Gesta*,

---

* It occurs in the same chapter as the story of La Perrette, which has been traced, after Benfey, by Prof. M. Müller in his "Migration of Fables" (*Sel. Essays*, i. 500–74); exactly the same history applies to Gellert.

where it occurs as c. xxxii., "Story of Folliculus." We have thus traced it to England whence it passed to Wales, where I have discovered it as the second apologue of " The Fables of Cattwg the Wise," in the Iolo MS. published by the Welsh MS. Society, p. 561, " The man who killed his Greyhound." (These Fables, Mr. Nutt informs me, are a pseudonymous production probably of the sixteenth century.) This concludes the literary route of the Legend of Gellert from India to Wales : Buddhistic *Vinaya Pitaka—Fables of Bidpai ;*— Oriental *Sindibad ;*—Occidental *Seven Sages of Rome ;*—" English " (Latin), *Gesta Romanorum ;*—Welsh, *Fables of Cattwg.*

Remarks.—We have still to connect the legend with Llewelyn and with Bedd Gelert. But first it may be desirable to point out why it is necessary to assume that the legend is a legend and not a fact. The saving of an infant's life by a dog, and the mistaken slaughter of the dog, are not such an improbable combination as to make it impossible that the same event occurred in many places. But what is impossible, in my opinion, is that such an event should have independently been used in different places as the typical instance of, and warning against, rash action. That the Gellert legend, before it was localised, was used as a moral apologue in Wales is shown by the fact that it occurs among the Fables of Cattwg, which are all of that character. It was also utilised as a proverb: " *Yr wy'n edivaru cymmaint a'r Gŵr a laddodd ei Vilgi* (" I repent as much as the man who slew his greyhound"). The fable indeed, from this point of view, seems greatly to have attracted the Welsh mind, perhaps as of especial value to a proverbially impetuous temperament. Croker (*Fairy Legends of Ireland,* vol. iii. p. 165) points out several places where the legend seems to have been localised in place-names—two places, called "Gwal y Vilast" (" Greyhound's Couch "), in Carmarthen and Glamorganshire ; " Llech y Asp" ("Dog's Stone"), in Cardigan, and another place named in Welsh " Spring of the Greyhound's Stone." Mr. Baring-Gould mentions that the legend is told of an ordinary tombstone, with a knight and a greyhound, in Abergavenny Church ; while the Fable of Cattwg is told of a man in Abergarwan. So widespread and well known was the legend that it was in Richard III.'s time adopted as the national crest. In the Warwick Roll, at the Herald's Office, after giving separate crests for England, Scotland, and Ireland, that for Wales is given as figured in the margin, and blazoned " on a coronet in a cradle or, a greyhound argent for Walys" (see

J. R. Planché, *Twelve Designs for the Costume of Shakespeare's Richard III.*, 1830, frontispiece). If this Roll is authentic, the popularity of the legend is thrown back into the fifteenth century. It still remains to explain how and when this general legend of rash action was localised and specialised at Bedd Gelert: I believe I have discovered this. There certainly was a local legend about a dog named Gelert at that place; E. Jones, in the first edition of his *Musical Relicks of the Welsh Bards*, 1784, p. 40, gives the following *englyn* or epigram:

> Claddwyd Cylart celfydd (ymlyniad)
>   Ymlaneau Efionydd
> Parod giuio i'w gynydd
> Parai'r dydd yr heliai Hŷdd;

which he Englishes thus:

> The remains of famed Cylart, so faithful and good,
>   The bounds of the cantred conceal;
> Whenever the doe or the stag he pursued
>   His master was sure of a meal.

No reference was made in the first edition to the Gellert legend, but in the second edition of 1794, p. 75, a note was added telling the legend, "There is a general tradition in North Wales that a wolf had entered the house of Prince Llewellyn. Soon after the Prince returned home, and, going into the nursery, he met his dog *Kill-hart*, all bloody and wagging his tail at him; Prince Llewellyn, on entering the room found the cradle where his child lay overturned, and the floor flowing with blood; imagining that the greyhound had killed the child, he immediately drew his sword and stabbed it; then, turning up the cradle, found under it the child alive, and the wolf dead. This so grieved the Prince, that he erected a tomb over his faithful dog's grave; where afterwards the parish church was built and goes by that name—*Bedd Cilhart*, or the grave of Kill-hart, in *Carnarvonshire*. From this incident is elicited a very common Welsh proverb [that given above which occurs also in 'The Fables of Cattwg;' it will be observed that it is quite indefinite.]" "Prince Llewellyn ab Jorwerth married Joan, [natural] daughter of King John, by *Agatha*, daughter of Robert Ferrers, Earl of Derby; and the dog was a present to the prince from his father-in-law about the year 1205." It was clearly from this note that the Hon. Mr. Spencer got his account; oral tradition does not indulge in dates *Anno Domini*. The application of the general legend of "the man who slew his greyhound" to the dog Cylart, was due to the learning of E. Jones, author of the *Musical Relicks*. I am convinced of this, for by a lucky chance I am enabled to give the real legend about Cylart, which is thus given in Carlisle's *Topographical Dictionary of Wales*, s.v., "Bedd Celert," published in 1811, the date of publication of Mr. Spencer's *Poems*. "Its name, according to tradition, implies *The Grave of Celert*, a Greyhound which belonged to Llywelyn, the last Prince of Wales: and a large Rock is still pointed out as the monument of this celebrated Dog, being on the spot where it was found dead, together with the stag which it had pursued from Carnarvon," which is thirteen miles distant. The cairn was thus a monument of a "record" run of a greyhound: the *englyn* quoted by Jones is suitable enough for this, while quite inadequate to record the later legendary exploits of Gêlert. Jones found an *englyn* devoted to *an* exploit of a dog named Cylart, and chose to interpret it in his second edition, 1794, as *the* exploit of a greyhound with which all the world (in Wales) were acquainted. Mr. Spencer took the legend from Jones (the reference to the date 1205 proves that), enshrined it in his somewhat *banal* verses, which were lucky enough to be copied into several reading-books, and thus became known to all English-speaking folk.

It remains only to explain why Jones connected the legend with Llewelyn. Llewelyn had local connection with Bedd Gellert, which was the seat of an Augustinian abbey, one of the oldest in Wales. An inspeximus of Edward I. given in Dugdale, *Monast. Angl.*, ed. pr. ii. 100a, quotes as the earliest charter of the abbey "Cartam Lewelini magni." The name of the abbey was "Beth Kellarth"; the name is thus given by Leland, *l.c.*, and as late as 1794 an engraving at the British Museum is entitled "Beth Kelert," while Carlisle gives it as "Beth Celert." The place was thus named after the abbey, not after the cairn or rock. This is confirmed by the fact of which Prof. Rhys had informed me, that the collocation of letters *rt* is un-Welsh. Under these circumstances it is not impossible, I think, that the earlier legend of the marvellous run of "Cylart" from Carnarvon was due to the etymologising fancy of some English-speaking Welshman who interpreted the name as Killhart, so that the simpler legend would be only a folk-etymology.

But whether Kellarth, Kelert, Cylart, Gêlert or Gellert ever existed and run a hart from Carnarvon to Bedd Gellert or no, there can be little doubt after the preceding that he was not the original hero of the fable of "the man that slew his greyhound," which came to Wales from Buddhistic India through channels which are perfectly traceable. It was Edward Jones who first raised him to that proud position, and William Spencer who securely installed him there, probably for all time. The legend is now firmly established at Bedd Gellert. There is said to be an ancient air, "Bedd Gelert," "as sung by the Ancient Britons"; it is given in a pamphlet published at Carnarvon in the "fifties," entitled *Gellert's Grave; or, Llewellyn's Rashness: a Ballad, by the Hon. W. R. Spencer, to which is added that ancient Welsh air, "Bedd Gelert," as sung by the Ancient Britons.* The air is from R. Roberts' "Collection of Welsh Airs," but what connection it has with the legend I have been unable to ascertain. This is probably another case of adapting one tradition to another. It is almost impossible to distinguish palœozoic and cainozoic strata in oral tradition. According to Murray's *Guide to N. Wales*, p. 125, the only authority for the cairn now shown is that of the landlord of the Goat Inn, "who felt compelled by the cravings of tourists to invent a grave." Some old men at Bedd Gellert, Prof. Rhys informs me, are ready to testify that they saw the cairn laid. They might almost have been present at the birth of the legend, which, if my affiliation of it is correct, is not yet quite 100 years old.

XXII. STORY OF IVAN.

Source.—Lluyd, *Archæologia Britannia*, 1707, the first comparative Celtic grammar and the finest piece of work in comparative philology hitherto done in England, contains this tale as a specimen of Cornish then still spoken in Cornwall. I have used the English version contained in *Blackwood's Magazine* as long ago as May 1818. I have taken the third counsel from the Irish version, as the original is not suited *virginibus puerisque*, though harmless enough in itself.

Parallels.—Lover has a tale, *The Three Advices*. It occurs also in modern Cornwall *ap.* Hunt, *Drolls of West of England*, 344, "The Tinner of Chyamor." Borrow, *Wild Wales*, 41, has a reference which seems to imply that the story had crystallised into a Welsh proverb. Curiously enough, it forms the chief episode of the so-called "Irish Odyssey" ("*Merugud Uilix maicc Leirtis*"—"Wandering of Ulysses M'Laertes"). It was derived, in all probability, from the *Gesta Romanorum*, c. 103, where two of the three pieces of advice are "Avoid a byeway," "Beware of a house where the housewife is younger than her husband." It is likely enough that this chapter, like others of the *Gesta*, came from the East, for it is found in some versions of " The Forty Viziers," and in the *Turkish Tales* (see Oesterley's parallels and *Gesta*, ed. Swan and Hooper, note 9).

XXIII. ANDREW COFFEY.

Source.—From the late D. W. Logie, written down by Mr. Alfred Nutt.

Parallels.—Dr. Hyde's " Teig O'Kane and the Corpse," and Kennedy's " Cauth Morrisy," *Legend. Fict.*, 158, are practically the same.

Remarks.—No collection of Celtic Folk-Tales would be representative that did not contain some specimen of the gruesome. The most effective ghoul story in existence is Lover's " Brown Man."

XXIV. BATTLE OF BIRDS.

Source.—Campbell (*Pop. Tales, W. Highlands*, No. ii.), with touches from the seventh variant and others, including the casket and key finish, from Curtin's " Son of the King of Erin " (*Myths, &c.*, 32 *seq.*). I have also added a specimen of the humorous end pieces added by Gaelic story-tellers ; on these tags see an interesting note in MacDougall's *Tales*, note on p. 112. I have found some difficulty in dealing with Campbell's excessive use of the second person singular, " If thou thouest him some two or three times, 'tis well," but beyond that it is wearisome. Practically, I have reserved *thou* for the speech of giants, who may be supposed to be somewhat old-fashioned. I fear, however, I have not been quite consistent, though the *you's* addressed to the apple-pips are grammatically correct as applied to the pair of lovers.

Parallels.—Besides the eight versions given or abstracted by Campbell and Mr. Curtin's, there is Carleton's " Three Tasks," Dr. Hyde's " Son of Branduf" (MS.) ; there is the First Tale of MacInnes (where see Mr. Nutt's elaborate notes, 431–43), two in the *Celtic Magazine*, vol. xii., " Grey Norris from Warland " (*Folk-Lore Journ.* i. 316), and Mr. Lang's Morayshire Tale, " Nicht Nought Nothing " (see *Eng. Fairy Tales*, No. vii.), no less than sixteen variants found among the Celts. It must have occurred early among them. Mr. Nutt found the feather-thatch incident in the *Agallamh na Senoraib* (" Discourse of Elders "), which is at least as old as the fifteenth century. Yet the story is to be found throughout the Indo-European world, as is shown by Prof. Köhler's elaborate list of parallels attached to

Mr. Lang's variant in *Revue Celtique,* iii. 374 ; and Mr. Lang, in his *Custom and Myth* ("A far travelled Tale"), has given a number of parallels from savage sources. And strangest of all, the story is practically the same as the classical myth of Jason and Medea.

Remarks.—Mr. Nutt, in his discussion of the tale (MacInnes, *Tales* 441), makes the interesting suggestion that the obstacles to pursuit, the forest, the mountain, and the river, exactly represent the boundary of the old Teutonic Hades, so that the story was originally one of the Descent to Hell. Altogether it seems likely that it is one of the oldest folk-tales in existence, and belonged to the story-store of the original Aryans, whoever they were, was passed by them with their language on to the Hellenes and perhaps to the Indians, was developed in its modern form in Scandinavia (where its best representative "The Master Maid" of Asbjörnsen is still found), was passed by them to the Celts and possibly was transmitted by these latter to other parts of Europe, perhaps by early Irish monks (see notes on "Sea-Maiden"). The spread in the Buddhistic world, and thence to the South Seas and Madagascar, would be secondary from India. I hope to have another occasion for dealing with this most interesting of all folk-tales in the detail it deserves.

XXV. BREWERY OF EGGSHELLS.

Source.—From the *Cambrian Quarterly Magazine,* 1830, vol. ii. p. 86 ; it is stated to be literally translated from the Welsh.

Parallels.—Another variant from Glamorganshire is given in *Y Cymmrodor,* vi. 209. Croker has the story under the title I have given the Welsh one in his *Fairy Legends,* 41. Mr. Hartland, in his *Science of Fairy Tales,* 113-6, gives the European parallels.

XXVI. LAD WITH THE GOAT SKIN.

Source.—Kennedy, *Legendary Fictions,* pp. 23-31. The Adventures of "Gilla na Chreck an Gour'."

Parallels.—"The Lad with the Skin Coverings" is a popular Celtic figure, *cf.* MacDougall's Third Tale, MacInnes' Second, and a reference in Campbell, iii. 147. According to Mr. Nutt (*Holy Grail,* 134), he is the original of Parzival. But the adventures in these tales are not the "cure by laughing" incident which forms the centre of our tale, and is Indo-European in extent (*cf.* references in *English Fairy Tales,* notes to No. xxvii.). "The smith who made hell too hot for him is Sisyphus," says Mr. Lang (Introd. to Grimm, p. xiii.) ; in Ireland he is Billy Dawson (Carleton, *Three Wishes*). In the Finn-Saga, Conan harries hell, as readers of *Waverley* may remember " ' Claw for claw, and devil take the shortest nails,' as Conan said to the Devil " (*cf.* Campbell, *The Fians*, 73, and notes, 283). Red-haired men in Ireland and elsewhere are always rogues (see Mr. Nutt's references, MacInnes' *Tales*, 477 ; to which add the case in "Lough Neagh," Yeats, *Irish Folk-Tales*, p. 210).

THE END.

More
Celtic Fairy Tales

Collected by
JOSEPH JACOBS

Illustrated by
JOHN D. BATTEN

Preface

OR the last time, for the present, I give the children of the British Isles a selection of Fairy Tales once or still existing among them. The story store of Great Britain and Ireland is, I hope, now adequately represented in the four volumes which have won me so many little friends, and of which this is the last.

My collections have dealt with the two folk-lore regions of these Isles on different scales. The "English" region, including Lowland Scotland and running up to the Highland line, is, I fancy, as fully represented in "English" and "More English Fairy Tales" as it is ever likely to be. But the Celtic district, including the whole of Ireland and the Gaelic-speaking part of Scotland, still offers a rich harvest to the collector, and will not be exhausted for many a long day. The materials already collected are far richer than those which the "English" region afford, and it has

Preface

accordingly been my aim in the two volumes devoted to the Celts, rather to offer specimens of the crop than to exhaust the field.

In the present volume I have proceeded on much the same lines as those which I laid down for myself in compiling its predecessor. In making my selection I have attempted to select the tales common both to Erin and Alba. I have included, as specimen of the Irish mediæval hero tales, one of the three sorrowful tales of Erin: "The Tale of the Children of Lir." For the "drolls" or "comic relief" of the volume, I have again drawn upon the inexhaustible Kennedy, while the great J. F. Campbell still stands out as the most prominent figure in the history of the Celtic Fairy Tale.

In my method of telling I have continued the practice which I adopted in the previous volume: where I considered the language too complicated for children, I have simplified; where an incident from another parallel version seemed to add force to the narrative I have inserted it; and in each case mentioned the fact in the corresponding notes. As former statements of mine on this point have somewhat misled my folk-lore friends, I should, perhaps, add that the alterations on this score have been much slighter than they have seemed, and have not affected anything of value to the science of folk-lore.

Preface

I fear I am somewhat of a heretic with regard to the evidential value of folk-tales regarded as *capita mortua* of anthropology. The ready transit of a folk-tale from one district to another of the same linguistic area, robs it to my mind of any anthropological or ethnographical value; but on this high topic I have discoursed elsewhere.

This book, like the others of this series, has only been rendered possible by the courtesy and complaisance of the various collectors from whom I have culled my treasures. In particular, I have to thank Mr. Larminie and Mr. Eliot Stock for permission to include that fine tale "Morraha" from the former's "West Irish Folk-tales," the chief addition to the Celtic store since the appearance of my last volume. I have again to thank Dr. Hyde for permission to use another tale from his delightful collection. Mr. Curtin has been good enough to place at my disposal another of the tales collected by him in Connaught, and my colleague, Mr. Duncan, has translated for me a droll from the Erse. Above all, I have to thank Mr. Alfred Nutt for constant supervision over my selection and over my comments upon it. Mr. Nutt, by his own researches, and by the encouragement and aid he has given to the researches of others on Celtic folk-lore, has done much to replace the otherwise irreparable loss of Campbell.

With this volume I part, at any rate for a time, from the

Preface

pleasant task which has engaged my attention for the last four years. For the "English" folk-lore district I have attempted to do what the brothers Grimm did for Germany, so far as that was possible at this late day. But for the Celtic area I can claim no such high function; here the materials are so rich that it would tax the resources of a whole clan of Grimms to exhaust the field, and those Celtic Grimms must be Celts themselves, or at any rate fully familiar with the Gaelic. Here then is a task for the newly revived local patriotism of Ireland and the Highlands. I have done little more than spy the land, and bring back some specimen bunches from the Celtic vine. It must be for others, Celts themselves, to enter in and possess the promised land.

1892

JOSEPH JACOBS.

SAY THIS

Three times, with your eyes shut

Ꮶoċuiᵹiꞃ bolaᷘ an Éiꞃeannaiᵹ binn bꞃeuᵹaiᵹ
ꝼaoi m'ꝼóibin ᷘuċaiᵹ

And you will see

What you will see

Contents

[For Nos. I–XXVI, see Book One at
the front of this volume.]

Contents

The Fate of the Children
of Lir

IT happened that the five Kings of Ireland
met to determine who should have the
head kingship over them, and King Lir
of the Hill of the White Field expected
surely he would be elected. When
the nobles went into council together
they chose for head king, Dearg, son of
Daghda, because his father had been so great a Druid
and he was the eldest of his father's sons. But Lir
left the Assembly of the Kings and went home to the
Hill of the White Field. The other kings would have
followed after Lir to give him wounds of spear and
wounds of sword for not yielding obedience to the man to
whom they had given the over-lordship. But Dearg the

king would not hear of it and said : "Rather let us bind him to us by the bonds of kinship, so that peace may dwell in the land.　Send over to him for wife the choice of the three maidens of the fairest form and best repute in Erin, the three daughters of Oilell of Aran, my own three bosom-nurslings."

So the messengers brought word to Lir that Dearg the king would give him a foster-child of his foster-children. Lir thought well of it, and set out next day with fifty chariots from the Hill of the White Field.　And he came to the Lake of the Red Eye near Killaloe.　And when Lir saw the three daughters of Oilell, Dearg the king said to him : "Take thy choice of the maidens, Lir."　"I know not," said Lir, "which is the choicest of them all ; but the eldest of them is the noblest, it is she I had best take."　"If so," said Dearg the king, "Ove is the eldest, and she shall be given to thee, if thou willest."　So Lir and Ove were married and went back to the Hill of the White Field.

And after this there came to them twins, a son and a daughter, and they gave them for names Fingula and Aod.　And two more sons came to them, Fiachra and Conn.　When they came Ove died, and Lir mourned bitterly for her, and but for his great love for his children he would have died of his grief.　And Dearg the king grieved for Lir and sent to him and said : "We grieve for Ove for thy sake ; but, that our friendship may not be rent asunder, I will give unto thee her sister, Oifa, for a wife."　So Lir agreed, and they were united, and he took her with him to his own house.　And at first Oifa felt affection and honour for the children of Lir and her sister, and indeed every one who saw the four children could not help giving them the love of his soul. Lir doted upon the children, and they always slept in beds in front of their father, who used to rise at early dawn every morning and lie down among his children. But thereupon the dart of jealousy passed into Oifa on account of this and she came to regard the children with hatred and enmity. One day her chariot was yoked for her and she took with her the four children of Lir in it. Fingula was not willing to go with her on the journey, for she had dreamed a dream in the night warning her against Oifa : but she was not to avoid her fate. And when the chariot came to the Lake of the Oaks, Oifa said to the people : " Kill the four children of Lir and I will give you your own reward of every kind in the world." But they refused and told her it was an evil thought she had. Then she would have raised a sword herself to kill and destroy the children, but her own womanhood and her weakness prevented her ; so she drove the children of Lir into the lake to bathe, and they did as Oifa told them. As soon as they were upon the lake she struck them with a Druid's wand of spells and wizardry and put them into the forms of four beautiful, perfectly white swans, and she sang this song over them :

> " Out with you upon the wild waves, children of the king !
> Henceforth your cries shall be with the flocks of birds."

And Fingula answered :

> " Thou witch ! we know thee by thy right name !
> Thou mayest drive us from wave to wave,
> But sometimes we shall rest on the headlands ;
> We shall receive relief, but thou punishment.
> Though our bodies may be upon the lake,
> Our minds at least shall fly homewards."

And again she spoke: "Assign an end for the ruin and woe which thou hast brought upon us."

Oifa laughed and said: "Never shall ye be free until the woman from the south be united to the man from the north, until Lairgnen of Connaught wed Deoch of Munster; nor shall any have power to bring you out of these forms. Nine hundred years shall you wander over the lakes and streams of Erin. This only I will grant unto you: that you retain your own speech, and there shall be no music in the world equal to yours, the plaintive music you shall sing." This she said because repentance seized her for the evil she had done.

And then she spake this lay:

> "Away from me, ye children of Lir,
> Henceforth the sport of the wild winds
> Until Lairgnen and Deoch come together,
> Until ye are on the north-west of Red Erin.

> "A sword of treachery is through the heart of Lir,
> Of Lir the mighty champion,
> Yet though I have driven a sword.
> My victory cuts me to the heart."

Then she turned her steeds and went on to the Hall of Dearg the king. The nobles of the court asked her where were the children of Lir, and Oifa said: "Lir will not trust them to Dearg the king." But Dearg thought in his own mind that the woman had played some treachery upon them, and he accordingly sent messengers to the Hall of the White Field.

Lir asked the messengers: "Wherefore are ye come?"

"To fetch thy children, Lir," said they.

"Have they not reached you with Oifa?" said Lir.

"They have not," said the messengers; "and Oifa said it was you would not let the children go with her."

Then was Lir melancholy and sad at heart, hearing these things, for he knew that Oifa had done wrong upon his children, and he set out towards the Lake of the Red Eye. And when the children of Lir saw him coming Fingula sang the lay:

> "Welcome the cavalcade of steeds
> Approaching the Lake of the Red Eye,
> A company dread and magical
> Surely seek after us.

> "Let us move to the shore, O Aod,
> Fiachra and comely Conn,
> No host under heaven can those horsemen be
> But King Lir with his mighty household."

Now as she said this King Lir had come to the shores of the lake and heard the swans speaking with human voices. And he spake to the swans and asked them who they were. Fingula answered and said: "We are thy own children, ruined by thy wife, sister of our own mother, through her ill mind and her jealousy." "For how long is the spell to be upon you?" said Lir. "None can relieve us till the woman from the south and the man from the north come together, till Lairgnen of Connaught wed Deoch of Munster."

Then Lir and his people raised their shouts of grief, crying, and lamentation, and they stayed by the shore of the lake listening to the wild music of the swans until the swans flew away, and King Lir went on to the Hall of Dearg the king. He told Dearg the king what Oifa had done to his children. And Dearg put his power upon Oifa and bade

her say what shape on earth she would think the worst of
all.   She said it would be in the form of an air-demon.
"It is into that form I shall put you," said Dearg the
king, and he struck her with a Druid's wand of spells and
wizardry and put her into the form of an air-demon.   And
she flew away at once, and she is still an air-demon, and
shall be so for ever.

But the children of Lir continued to delight the Milesian
clans with the very sweet fairy music of their songs, so
that no delight was ever heard in Erin to compare with
their music until the time came appointed for the leaving
the Lake of the Red Eye.

Then Fingula sang this parting lay :

"Farewell to thee, Dearg the king,
  Master of all Druid's lore !
Farewell to thee, our father dear,
  Lir of the Hill of the White Field !

"We go to pass the appointed time
  Away and apart from the haunts of men
In the current of the Moyle,
  Our garb shall be bitter and briny,

"Until Deoch come to Lairgnen.
  So come, ye brothers of once ruddy cheeks ;
Let us depart from this Lake of the Red Eye,
  Let us separate in sorrow from the tribe that has
    loved us."

And after they took to flight, flying highly, lightly, aerially
till they reached the Moyle, between Erin and Albain.

The men of Erin were grieved at their leaving, and it
was proclaimed throughout Erin that henceforth no swan
should be killed.   Then they stayed all solitary, all alone,
filled with cold and grief and regret, until a thick tempest

came upon them and Fingula said : "Brothers, let us appoint a place to meet again if the power of the winds separate us." And they said : "Let us appoint to meet, O sister, at the Rock of the Seals." Then the waves rose up and the thunder roared, the lightnings flashed, the sweeping tempest passed over the sea, so that the children of Lir were scattered from each other over the great sea. There came, however, a placid calm after the great tempest and Fingula found herself alone, and she said this lay :

> " Woe upon me that I am alive !
> My wings are frozen to my sides.
> O beloved three, O beloved three,
> Who hid under the shelter of my feathers,
> Until the dead come back to the living
> I and the three shall never meet again ! "

And she flew to the Lake of the Seals and soon saw Conn coming towards her with heavy step and drenched feathers, and Fiachra also, cold and wet and faint, and no word could they tell, so cold and faint were they : but she nestled them under her wings and said : "If Aod could come to us now our happiness would be complete." But soon they saw Aod coming towards them with dry head and preened feathers : Fingula put him under the feathers of her breast, and Fiachra under her right wing, and Conn under her left : and they made this lay :

> " Bad was our stepmother with us,
> She played her magic on us,
> Sending us north on the sea
> In the shapes of magical swans.
> " Our bath upon the shore's ridge
> Is the foam of the brine-crested tide,
> Our share of the ale feast
> Is the brine of the blue-crested sea."

One day they saw a splendid cavalcade of pure white
steeds coming towards them, and when they came near they
were the two sons of Dearg the king who had been seeking
for them to give them news of Dearg the king and Lir
their father. "They are well," they said, "and live
together happy in all except that ye are not with them, and
for not knowing where ye have gone since the day ye left
the Lake of the Red Eye." "Happy are not we," said
Fingula, and she sang this song:

> "Happy this night the household of Lir,
> Abundant their meat and their wine.
> But the children of Lir—what is their lot?
> For bed-clothes we have our feathers,
> And as for our food and our wine—
> The white sand and the bitter brine,
> Fiachra's bed and Conn's place
> Under the cover of my wings on the Moyle,
> Aod has the shelter of my breast,
> And so side by side we rest."

So the sons of Dearg the king came to the Hall of Lir
and told the king the condition of his children.

Then the time came for the children of Lir to fulfil their
lot, and they flew in the current of the Moyle to the Bay of
Erris, and remained there till the time of their fate, and
then they flew to the Hill of the White Field and found all
desolate and empty, with nothing but unroofed green raths
and forests of nettles—no house, no fire, no dwelling-place.
The four came close together, and they raised three shouts
of lamentation aloud, and Fingula sang this lay:

> "Uchone! it is bitterness to my heart
> To see my father's place forlorn—
> No hounds, no packs of dogs,
> No women, and no valiant kings

" No drinking-horns, no cups of wood,
   No drinking in its lightsome halls.
   Uchone ! I see the state of this house
   That its lord our father lives no more.

" Much have we suffered in our wandering years,
   By winds buffeted, by cold frozen ;
   Now has come the greatest of our pain—
   There lives no man who knoweth us in the house
     where we were born."

So the children of Lir flew away to the Glory Isle of
Brandan the saint, and they settled upon the Lake of the
Birds until the holy Patrick came to Erin and the holy
Mac Howg came to Glory Isle.

And the first night he came to the island the children of
Lir heard the voice of his bell ringing for matins, so that
they started and leaped about in terror at hearing it ; and
her brothers left Fingula alone. " What is it, beloved
brothers ? " said she. " We know not what faint, fearful
voice it is we have heard." Then Fingula recited this lay :

" Listen to the Cleric's bell,
   Poise your wings and raise
   Thanks to God for his coming,
   Be grateful that you hear him,

" He shall free you from pain,
   And bring you from the rocks and stones.
   Ye comely children of Lir
   Listen to the bell of the Cleric."

And Mac Howg came down to the brink of the shore
and said to them : " Are ye the children of Lir ? " " We
are indeed," said they. " Thanks be to God ! " said the
saint ; " it is for your sakes I have come to this Isle beyond
every other island in Erin. Come ye to land now and put
your trust in me." So they came to land, and he made

for them chains of bright white silver, and put a chain between Aod and Fingula and a chain between Conn and Fiachra.

It happened at this time that Lairgnen was prince of Connaught and he was to wed Deoch the daughter of the king of Munster. She had heard the account of the birds and she became filled with love and affection for them, and she said she would not wed till she had the wondrous birds of Glory Isle. Lairgnen sent for them to the Saint Mac Howg. But the Saint would not give them, and both Lairgnen and Deoch went to Glory Isle. And Lairgnen went to seize the birds from the altar: but as soon as he had laid hands on them their feathery coats fell off, and the three sons of Lir became three withered bony old men, and Fingula, a lean withered old woman without blood or flesh. Lairgnen started at this and left the place hastily, but Fingula chanted this lay :

> "Come and baptise us, O Cleric,
> Clear away our stains !
> This day I see our grave—
> Fiachra and Conn on each side,
> And in my lap, between my two arms,
> Place Aod, my beauteous brother."

After this lay, the children of Lir were baptised. And they died, and were buried as Fingula had said, Fiachra and Conn on either side, and Aod before her face. A cairn was raised for them, and on it their names were written in runes. And that is the fate of the children of Lir.

Jack the Cunning Thief

HERE was a poor farmer who had three sons, and on the same day the three boys went to seek their fortune. The eldest two were sensible, industrious young men ; the youngest never did much at home that was any use. He loved to be setting snares for rabbits, and tracing hares in the snow, and inventing all sorts of funny tricks to annoy people at first and then set them laughing.

The three parted at cross-roads, and Jack took the lonesomest. The day turned out rainy, and he was wet and weary, you may depend, at nightfall, when he came to a lonesome house a little off the road.

"What do you want?" said a blear-eyed old woman, that was sitting at the fire.

"My supper and a bed to be sure," said he.

"You can't get it," said she.

"What's to hinder me?" said he.

"The owners of the house is," said she, "six honest men that does be out mostly till three or four o'clock in the morning, and if they find you here they'll skin you alive at the very least."

"Well, I think," said Jack, "that their very most couldn't be much worse. Come, give me something out of the cupboard, for here I'll stay. Skinning is not much worse than catching your death of cold in a ditch or under a tree such a night as this."

Begonins she got afraid, and gave him a good supper; and when he was going to bed he said if she let any of the six honest men disturb him when they came home she'd sup sorrow for it. When he awoke in the morning, there were six ugly-looking spalpeens standing round his bed. He leaned on his elbow, and looked at them with great contempt.

"Who are you," said the chief, "and what's your business?"

"My name," says he, "is Master Thief, and my business just now is to find apprentices and workmen. If I find you any good, maybe I'll give you a few lessons."

Bedad they were a little cowed, and says the head man, "Well, get up, and after breakfast, we'll see who is to be the master, and who the journeyman."

They were just done breakfast, when what should they see but a farmer driving a fine large goat to market. "Will any of you," says Jack, "undertake to steal that goat from the owner before he gets out of the wood, and that without the smallest violence?"

"I couldn't do it," says one; and "I couldn't do it," says another.

"I'm your master," says Jack, "and I'll do it."

He slipped out, went through the trees to where there was a bend in the road, and laid down his right brogue in the very middle of it. Then he ran on to another bend, and laid down his left brogue and went and hid himself.

When the farmer sees the first brogue, he says to himself, " That would be worth something if it had the fellow, but it is worth nothing by itself."

He goes on till he comes to the second brogue.

" What a fool I was," says he, " not to pick up the other! I'll go back for it."

So he tied the goat to a sapling in the hedge, and returned for the brogue. But Jack, who was behind a tree had it already on his foot, and when the man was beyond the bend he picked up the other and loosened the goat, and led him off through the wood.

Ochone! the poor man couldn't find the first brogue, and when he came back he couldn't find the second, nor neither his goat.

" *Mile mollacht!* " says he, " what will I do after promising Johanna to buy her a shawl. I must only go and drive another beast to the market unknownst. I'd never hear the last of it if Joan found out what a fool I made of myself."

The thieves were in great admiration at Jack, and wanted him to tell them how he had done the farmer, but he wouldn't tell them.

By-and-by, they see the poor man driving a fine fat wether the same way.

" Who'll steal that wether," says Jack, " before it's out of the wood, and no roughness used ? "

" I couldn't," says one; and " I couldn't," says another.

" I'll try," says Jack. " Give me a good rope."

The poor farmer was jogging along and thinking of

his misfortune, when he sees a man hanging from the bough of a tree. "Lord save us!" says he, "the corpse wasn't there an hour ago." He went on about half a quarter of a mile, and there was another corpse again hanging over the road. "God between us and harm," said he, "am I in my right senses?" There was another turn about the same distance, and just beyond it the third corpse was hanging. "Oh, murdher!" said he; "I'm beside myself. What would bring three hung men so near one another? I must be mad. I'll go back and see if the others are there still."

He tied the wether to a sapling, and back he went. But when he was round the bend, down came the corpse, and loosened the wether, and drove it home through the wood to the robbers' house. You all may think how the poor farmer felt when he could find no one dead or alive going or coming, nor his wether, nor the rope that fastened him. "Oh, misfortunate day!" cried he, "what'll Joan say to me now? My morning gone, and the goat and wether lost! I must sell something to make the price of the shawl. Well, the fat bullock is in the nearest field. She won't see me taking it."

Well, if the robbers were not surprised when Jack came into the bawn with the wether! "If you do another trick like this," said the captain, "I'll resign the command to you."

They soon saw the farmer going by again, driving a fat bullock this time.

"Who'll bring that fat bullock here," says Jack, "and use no violence?"

"I couldn't," says one; and "I couldn't," says another.

"I'll try," says Jack, and away he went into the wood.

The farmer was about the spot where he saw the first brogue, when he heard the bleating of a goat off at his right in the wood.

He cocked his ears, and the next thing he heard was the maaing of a sheep.

"Blood alive!" says he, "maybe these are my own that I lost." There was more bleating and more maaing. "There they are as sure as a gun," says he, and he tied his bullock to a sapling that grew in the hedge, and away he went into the wood. When he got near the place where the cries came from, he heard them a little before him, and on he followed them. At last, when he was about half a mile from the spot where he tied the beast, the cries stopped altogether. After searching and searching till he was tired, he returned for his bullock; but there wasn't the ghost of a bullock there, nor any where else that he searched.

This time, when the thieves saw Jack and his prize coming into the bawn, they couldn't help shouting out, "Jack must be our chief." So there was nothing but feasting and drinking hand to fist the rest of the day. Before they went to bed, they showed Jack the cave where their money was hid, and all their disguises in another cave, and swore obedience to him.

One morning, when they were at breakfast, about a week after, said they to Jack, "Will you mind the house for us to-day while we are at the fair of Mochurry? We hadn't a spree for ever so long: you must get your turn whenever you like."

"Never say't twice," says Jack, and off they went.

After they were gone says Jack to the wicked housekeeper,
" Do these fellows ever make you a present ? "

" Ah, catch them at it ! indeed, and they don't, purshuin
to 'em."

" Well, come along with me, and I'll make you a rich
woman."

He took her to the treasure cave ; and while she was in
raptures, gazing at the heaps of gold and silver, Jack filled
his pockets as full as they could hold, put more into a
little bag, and walked out, locking the door on the old hag,
and leaving the key in the lock. He then put on a rich
suit of clothes, took the goat, and the wether, and the
bullock, and drove them before him to the farmer's
house.

Joan and her husband were at the door ; and when they saw the animals, they clapped their hands and laughed for joy.

" Do you know who owns them bastes, neighbours ? "

" Maybe we don't ! sure they're ours."

" I found them straying in the wood.   Is that bag with ten guineas in it that's hung round the goat's neck yours ? "

" Faith, it isn't."

" Well, you may as well keep it for a Godsend ; I don't want it."

" Heaven be in your road, good gentleman ! "

Jack travelled on till he came to his father's house in the dusk of the evening.   He went in.   " God save all here ! "

" God save you kindly, sir ! "

" Could I have a night's lodging here ? "

" Oh, sir, our place isn't fit for the likes of a gentleman such as yon."

" Oh, *musha*, don't you know your own son ? "

Well, they opened their eyes, and it was only a strife to see who'd have him in their arms first.

" But, Jack asthore, where did you get the fine clothes ? "

" Oh, you may as well ask me where I got all that money ? " said he, emptying his pockets on the table.

Well, they got in a great fright, but when he told them his adventures, they were easier in mind, and all went to bed in great content.

" Father," says Jack, next morning, " go over to the landlord, and tell him I wish to be married to his daughter."

"Faith, I'm afraid he'd only set the dogs at me. If he asks me how you made your money, what'll I say?"

"Tell him I am a master thief, and that there is no one equal to me in the three kingdoms; that I am worth a thousand pounds, and all taken from the biggest rogues unhanged. Speak to him when the young lady is by."

"It's a droll message you're sending me on : I'm afraid it won't end well."

The old man came back in two hours.

"Well, what news?"

"Droll news, enough. The lady didn't seem a bit unwilling : I suppose it's not the first time you spoke to her ; and the squire laughed, and said you would have to steal the goose off o' the spit in his kitchen next Sunday, and he'd see about it."

"O! that won't be hard, any way."

Next Sunday, after the people came from early Mass, the squire and all his people were in the kitchen, and the goose turning before the fire. The kitchen door opened, and a miserable old beggar man with a big wallet on his back put in his head.

"Would the mistress have anything for me when dinner is over, your honour?"

"To be sure. We have no room here for you just now ; sit in the porch for a while."

"God bless your honour's family, and yourself!"

Soon some one that was sitting near the window cried out, "Oh, sir, there's a big hare scampering like the divil round the bawn. Will we run out and pin him?"

"Pin a hare indeed! much chance you'd have; sit where you are."

That hare made his escape into the garden, but Jack that was in the beggar's clothes soon let another out of the bag.

"Oh, master, there he is still pegging round. He can't make his escape: let us have a chase. The hall door is locked on the inside, and Mr. Jack can't get in."

"Stay quiet, I tell you."

In a few minutes he shouted out again that the hare was there still, but it was the third that Jack was just after giving its liberty. Well, by the laws, they couldn't be kept in any longer. Out pegged every mother's son of them, and the squire after them.

"Will I turn the spit, your honour, while they're catching the *hareyeen*?" says the beggar.

"Do, and don't let any one in for your life."

"Faith, an' I won't, you may depend on it."

The third hare got away after the others, and when they all came back from the hunt, there was neither beggar nor goose in the kitchen.

"Purshuin' to you, Jack," says the landlord, "you've come over me this time."

Well, while they were thinking of making out another dinner, a messenger came from Jack's father to beg that the squire, and the mistress, and the young lady would step across the fields, and take share of what God sent. There was no dirty mean pride about the family, and they walked over, and got a dinner with roast turkey, and roast beef, and their own roast goose; and the squire had like to burst his waistcoat with laughing at the trick, and Jack's good clothes and good manners did not take away any liking the young lady had for him already.

While they were taking their punch at the old oak table in the nice clean little parlour with the sanded floor, says the squire, "You can't be sure of my daughter, Jack, unless you steal away my six horses from under the six men that will be watching them to-morrow night in the stable."

"I'll do more than that," says Jack, "for a pleasant look from the young lady"; and the young lady's cheeks turned as red as fire.

Monday night the six horses were in their stalls, and a man on every horse, and a good glass of whisky under every man's waistcoat, and the door was left wide open for Jack. They were merry enough for a long time, and joked and sung, and were pitying the poor fellow. But the small hours crept on, and the whisky lost its power, and they began to shiver and wish it was morning. A miserable old colliach, with half a dozen bags round her, and a beard half an inch long on her chin came to the door.

"Ah, then, tendher-hearted Christians," says she, "would you let me in, and allow me a wisp of straw in the corner; the life will be froze out of me, if you don't give me shelter."

Well, they didn't see any harm in that, and she made herself as snug as she could, and they soon saw her pull out a big black bottle, and take a sup. She coughed and smacked her lips, and seemed a little more comfortable, and the men couldn't take their eyes off her.

"Gorsoon," says she, "I'd offer you a drop of this, only you might think it too free-making."

"Oh, hang all impedent pride," says one, "we'll take it, and thankee."

So she gave them the bottle, and they passed it round, and the last man had the manners to leave half a glass in the bottom for the old woman. They all thanked her, and said it was the best drop ever passed their tongue.

"In throth, agras," said she, "it's myself that's glad to show how I value your kindness in giving me shelter; I'm not without another *buideal*, and you may pass it round while myself finishes what the dasent man left me."

Well, what they drank out of the other bottle only gave them a relish for more, and by the time the last man got to the bottom, the first man was dead asleep in the saddle, for the second bottle had a sleepy posset mixed with the whisky. The beggar woman lifted each man down, and laid him in the manger, or under the manger, snug and sausty, drew a stocking over every horse's hoof, and led them away without any noise to one of Jack's father's outhouses. The first thing the squire saw next morning was Jack riding up the avenue, and five horses stepping after the one he rode.

"Confound you, Jack!" says he, "and confound the numskulls that let you outwit them!"

He went out to the stable, and didn't the poor fellows look very lewd o' themselves, when they could be woke up in earnest!

"After all," says the squire, when they were sitting at breakfast, "it was no great thing to outwit such ninny-hammers. I'll be riding out on the common from one to three to-day, and if you can outwit me of the beast I'll be riding, I'll say you deserve to be my son-in-law."

"I'd do more than that," says Jack, "for the honour, if

there was no love at all in the matter," and the young lady held up her saucer before her face.

Well, the squire kept riding about and riding about till he was tired, and no sign of Jack. He was thinking of going home at last, when what should he see but one of his servants running from the house as if he was mad.

"Oh masther, masther," says he, as far as he could be heard, "fly home if you wish to see the poor mistress alive! I'm running for the surgeon. She fell down two flights of stairs, and her neck, or her hips, or both her arms are broke, and she's speechless, and it's a mercy if you find the breath in her. Fly as fast as the baste will carry you."

"But hadn't you better take the horse? It's a mile and a half to the surgeon's."

"Oh, anything you like, master. Oh, *Vuya, Vuya!* misthress *alanna*, that I should ever see the day! and your purty body disfigured as it is!"

"Here, stop your noise, and be off like wildfire! Oh, my darling, my darling, isn't this a trial?"

He tore home like a fury, and wondered to see no stir outside, and when he flew into the hall, and from that to the parlour, his wife and daughter that were sewing at the table screeched out at the rush he made, and the wild look that was on his face.

"Oh, my darling!" said he, when he could speak, "how's this? Are you hurt? Didn't you fall down the stairs? What happened at all? Tell me!"

"Why, nothing at all happened, thank God, since you rode out; where did you leave the horse?"

Well, no one could describe the state he was in for

about a quarter of an hour, between joy for his wife and anger with Jack, and *sharoose* for being tricked. He saw the beast coming up the avenue, and a little gorsoon in the saddle with his feet in the stirrup leathers. The servant didn't make his appearance for a week; but what did he care with Jack's ten golden guineas in his pocket.

Jack didn't show his nose till next morning, and it was a queer reception he met.

"That was all foul play you gave," says the squire. "I'll never forgive you for the shock you gave me. But then I am so happy ever since, that I think I'll give you only one trial more. If you will take away the sheet from under my wife and myself to-night, the marriage may take place to-morrow."

"We'll try," says Jack, "but if you keep my bride from me any longer, I'll steal her away if she was minded by fiery dragons."

When the squire and his wife were in bed, and the moon

shining in through the window, he saw a head rising over the sill to have a peep, and then bobbing down again.

"That's Jack," says the squire; "I'll astonish him a bit," says the squire, pointing a gun at the lower pane.

"Oh Lord, my dear!" says the wife, " sure, you wouldn't shoot the brave fellow?"

"Indeed, an' I wouldn't for a kingdom; there's nothing but powder in it."

Up went the head, bang went the gun, down dropped the body, and a great souse was heard on the gravel walk.

"Oh, Lord," says the lady, "poor Jack is killed or disabled for life."

"I hope not," says the squire, and down the stairs he ran. He never minded to shut the door, but opened the gate and ran into the garden. His wife heard his voice at the room door, before he could be under the window and back, as she thought.

"Wife, wife," says he from the door, " the sheet, the sheet! He is not killed, I hope, but he is bleeding like a pig. I must wipe it away as well as I can, and get some one to carry him in with me." She pulled it off the bed, and threw it to him. Down he ran like lightning, and he had hardly time to be in the garden, when he was back, and this time he came back in his shirt, as he went out.

"High hanging to you, Jack," says he, "for an arrant rogue!"

"Arrant rogue?" says she, "isn't the poor fellow all cut and bruised?"

" I didn't much care if he was. What do you think was

bobbing up and down at the window, and sossed down so heavy on the walk? A man's clothes stuffed with straw, and a couple of stones."

"And what did you want with the sheet just now, to wipe his blood if he was only a man of straw?"

"Sheet, woman! I wanted no sheet."

"Well, whether you wanted it or not, I threw it to you, and you standing outside o' the door."

"Oh, Jack, Jack, you terrible tinker!" says the squire, "there's no use in striving with you. We must do without the sheet for one night. We'll have the marriage to-morrow to get ourselves out of trouble."

So married they were, and Jack turned out a real good husband. And the squire and his lady were never tired of praising their son-in-law, "Jack the Cunning Thief."

Powel, Prince of Dyfed.

OWEL, Prince of Dyfed, was lord of the seven Cantrevs of Dyfed; and once upon a time Powel was at Narberth, his chief palace, where a feast had been prepared for him, and with him was a great host of men. And after the first meal, Powel arose to walk, and he went to the top of a mound that was above the palace, and was called Gorseth Arberth.

"Lord," said one of the court, "it is peculiar to the mound that whosoever sits upon it cannot go thence without either receiving wounds or blows, or else seeing a wonder."

"I fear not to receive wounds and blows in the midst of such a host as this; but as to the wonder, gladly would I see it. I will go, therefore, and sit upon the mound."

And upon the mound he sat. And while he sat there, they saw a lady, on a pure white horse of large size, with a garment of shining gold around her, coming along the highway that led from the mound; and the horse seemed to move at a slow and even pace, and to be coming up towards the mound.

"My men," said Powel, " is there any among you who knows yonder lady ? "

"There is not, lord," said they.

"Go one of you and meet her, that we may know who she is."

And one of them arose ; and as he came upon the road to meet her she passed by, and he followed as fast as he could, being on foot; and the greater was his speed, the farther was she from him. And when he saw that it profited him nothing to follow her, he returned to Pwyll, and said unto him, "Lord, it is idle for any one in the world to follow her on foot."

"Verily," said Powel, "go unto the palace, and take the fleetest horse that thou seest, and go after her."

And he took a horse and went forward. And he came to an open level plain, and put spurs to his horse ; and the more he urged his horse, the farther was she from him. Yet she held the same pace as at first. And his horse began to fail ; and when his horse's feet failed him, he returned to the place where Powel was.

"Lord," said he, "it will avail nothing for any one to follow yonder lady. I know of no horse in these realms swifter than this, and it availed me not to pursue her."

"Of a truth," said Powel, "there must be some illusion here. Let us go towards the palace." So to the palace they went, and they spent that day. And the next day they arose, and that also they spent until it was time to go to meat. And after the first meal, "Verily," said Powel, "we will go, the same party as yesterday, to the top of the mound. Do thou," said he to one of his young men, "take the swiftest horse that thou knowest in the field. And thus did the young man. They went towards the mound, taking the horse with them. And as they were sitting down they beheld the lady on the same horse, and in the same apparel, coming along the same road. "Behold," said Powel, "here is the lady of yesterday. Make ready, youth, to learn who she is."

"My lord," said he "that will I gladly do." And thereupon the lady came opposite to them. So the youth mounted his horse; and before he had settled himself in his saddle, she passed by, and there was a clear space between them. But her speed was no greater than it had been the day before. Then he put his horse into an amble, and thought, that, notwithstanding the gentle pace at which his horse went, he should soon overtake her. But this availed him not: so he gave his horse the reins. And still he came no nearer to her than when he went at a foot's pace. The more he urged his horse, the farther was she from him. Yet she rode not faster than before. When he saw that it availed not to follow her, he returned to the place where Powel was. "Lord," said he, "the horse can no more than thou hast seen."

"I see indeed that it avails not that any one should follow her. And by Heaven," said he, "she must needs have an errand to some one in this plain, if her haste would allow her to declare it. Let us go back to the palace." And to the palace they went, and they spent that night in songs and feasting, as it pleased them.

The next day they amused themselves until it was time to go to meat. And when meat was ended, Powel said, "Where are the hosts that went yesterday and the day before to the top of the mound?"

" Behold, lord, we are here," said they.

" Let us go," said he, " to the mound to sit there. And do thou," said he to the page who tended his horse, " saddle my horse well, and hasten with him to the road, and bring also my spurs with thee." And the youth did thus, They went and sat upon the mound. And ere they had been there but a short time, they beheld the lady coming by the same road, and in the same manner, and at the same pace. " Young man," said Powel, " I see the lady coming ; give me my horse." And no sooner had he mounted his horse than she passed him. And he turned after her, and followed her. And he let his horse go bounding playfully, and thought that at the second step or the third he should come up with her. But he came no nearer to her than at first. Then he urged his horse to his utmost speed, yet he found that it availed nothing to follow her. Then said Powel, " O maiden, " for the sake of him who thou best lovest, stay for me."

" I will stay gladly," said she, " and it were better for thy horse hadst thou asked it long since." So the maiden stopped, and she threw back that part of her head-dress which covered her face. And she fixed her eyes upon him, and began to talk with him.

" Lady," asked he, " whence comest thou, and whereunto dost thou journey ? "

" I journey on mine own errand," said she, " and right glad am I to see thee."

" My greeting be unto thee," said he. Then he thought that the beauty of all the maidens, and all the ladies that he had ever seen, was as nothing compared to her beauty. " Lady," he said, " wilt thou tell me aught concerning thy purpose ? "

"I will tell thee," said she. "My chief quest was to seek thee."

"Behold," said Powel, "this is to me the most pleasing quest on which thou couldst have come. And wilt thou tell me who thou art?"

· I · JOURNEY ·
· ON · MINE · OWN ·
· ERRAND ·

"I will tell thee, lord," said she. "I am Rhiannon, the daughter of Heveyth Hên, and they sought to give me to a husband against my will. But no husband would I have, and that because of my love for thee, neither will I yet

have one unless thou reject me. And hither have I come
to hear thy answer."

"By Heaven," said Powel, "behold this is my answer.
If I might choose among all the ladies and damsels in the
world, thee would I choose."

"Verily," said she, "if thou art thus minded, make a
pledge to meet me ere I am given to another."

"The sooner I may do so, the more pleasing will it be
unto me," said Powel, "and wheresoever thou wilt, there
will I meet with thee."

"I will that thou meet me this day twelvemonth, at the
palace of Heveyth. And I will cause a feast to be prepared,
so that it be ready against thou come."

"Gladly," said he, "will I keep this tryst."

"Lord," said she, "remain in health, and be mindful
that thou keep thy promise. And now I will go hence."

So they parted, and he went back to his hosts and to
them of his household. And whatsoever questions they
asked him respecting the damsel, he always turned the
discourse upon other matters. And when a year from that
time was gone, he caused a hundred knights to equip themselves, and to go with him to the palace of Heveyth Hên.
And he came to the palace, and there was great joy concerning him, with much concourse of people, and great
rejoicing, and vast preparations for his coming. And the
whole court was placed under his orders.

And the hall was garnished, and they went to meat, and
thus did they sit; Heveyth Hên was on one side of Powel,
and Rhiannon on the other. And all the rest according to
their rank. And they ate and feasted and talked, one with
another; and at the beginning of the carousal after the

meat, there entered a tall auburn-haired youth, of royal bearing, clothed in a garment of satin. And when he came into the hall he saluted Powel and his companions.

"The greeting of Heaven be unto thee, my soul," said Powel. "Come thou and sit down."

"Nay," said he, "a suitor am I; and I will do mine errand."

"Do so willingly," said Powel.

"Lord," said he, "my errand is unto thee; and it is to crave a boon of thee that I come."

"What boon soever thou mayest ask of me, as far as I am able, thou shalt have."

"Ah," said Rhiannon, "wherefore didst thou give that answer?"

"Has he not given it before the presence of these nobles?" asked the youth.

"My soul," said Powel, "what is the boon thou askest?"

"The lady whom best I love is to be thy bride this night; I come to ask her of thee, with the feast and the banquet that are in this place."

And Powel was silent because of the answer which he had given.

"Be silent as long as thou wilt," said Rhiannon. "Never did man make worse use of his wits than thou hast done."

"Lady," said he, "I knew not who he was."

"Behold, this is the man to whom they would have given me against my will," said she. "And he is Gwawl the son of Clud, a man of great power and wealth; and because of the word thou hast spoken, bestow me upon him, lest shame befall thee."

"Lady," said he, "I understand not thine answer. Never can I do as thou sayest."

"Bestow me upon him," said she, "and I will cause that I shall never be his."

"By what means will that be?" said Powel.

"In thy hand will I give thee a small bag," said she. "See that thou keep it well, and he will ask of thee the banquet and the feast, and the preparations, which are not in thy power. Unto the hosts and the household will I give the feast. And such will be thy answer respecting this. And as concerns myself, I will engage to become his bride this night twelvemonth. And at the end of the year be thou here," said she, "and bring this bag with thee and let thy hundred knights be in the orchard up yonder. And when he is in the midst of joy and feasting, come thou in by thyself, clad in ragged garments, and holding thy bag in thy hand, and ask nothing but a bagful of food; and I will cause that if all the meat and liquor that are in these seven cantrevs were put into it, it would be no fuller than before. And after a great deal has been put therein, he will ask thee whether thy bag will ever be full. Say thou then that it never will, until a man of noble birth and of great wealth arise and press the food in the bag with both his feet, saying, 'Enough has been put therein.' And I will cause him to go and tread down the food in the bag, and when he does so, turn thou the bag, so that he shall be up over his head in it, and then slip a knot upon the thongs of the bag. Let there be also a good bugle-horn about thy neck, and as soon as thou hast bound him in the bag, wind thy horn, and let it be a signal between thee and thy knights. And when they hear the sound of the horn, let them come down upon the palace."

"Lord," said Gwawl, "it is meet that I have an answer to my request."

"As much of that thou hast asked as it is in my power to give, thou shalt have," replied Powel.

"My soul," said Rhiannon unto him, "as for the feast and the banquet that are here, I have bestowed them upon the men of Dyved, and the household, and the warriors that are with us. These can I not suffer to be given to any. In a year from to-night a banquet shall be prepared for thee in this palace, that I may become thy bride."

So Gwawl went forth to his possessions, and Powel went also back to Dyved. And they both spent that year until it was the time for the feast at the palace of Heveyth Hên. Then Gwawl the son of Clud set out to the feast that was prepared for him, and he came to the palace and was received there with rejoicing. Powel also, the chief of Annuvyn, came to the orchard with his hundred knights, as Rhiannon had commanded him, having the bag with him. And Powel was clad in coarse and ragged garments, and wore large clumsy old shoes upon his feet. And when he knew that the carousal after the meat had begun, he went towards the hall, and when he came into the hall, he saluted Gwawl the son of Clud, and his company, both men and women.

"Heaven prosper thee!" said Gwawl, "and the greeting of Heaven be unto thee!"

"Lord," said he, "may Heaven reward thee!" I have an errand unto thee."

"Welcome be thine errand, and, if thou ask of me that which is just, thou shalt have it gladly."

"It is fitting," answered he. "I crave but from want ; and the boon that I ask is to have this small bag that thou seest filled with meat."

"A request within reason is this," said he, "and gladly shalt thou have it. Bring him food."

A great number of attendants arose, and began to fill the bag ; but for all that they put into it, it was no fuller than at first.

"My soul," said Gwawl, "will thy bag be ever full ?"

"It will not, I declare to Heaven," said he, "for all that

may be put into it, unless one possessed of lands and domains and treasure shall arise, and tread down with both his feet the food which is within the bag, and shall say, 'Enough has been put herein.'"

Then said Rhiannon unto Gwawl the son of Clud, "Rise up quickly."

"I will willingly arise," said he. So he rose up, and put his two feet into the bag. And Powel turned up the sides of the bag, so that Gwawl was over his head in it. And he shut it up quickly, and slipped a knot upon the thongs, and blew his horn. And thereupon behold his household came down upon the palace. And they seized all the host that had come with Gwawl, and cast them into his own prison. And Powel threw off his rags, and his old shoes, and his tattered array. And as they came in, every one of Powel's knights struck a blow upon the bag, and asked, "What is here?"

"A badger," said they. And in this manner they played, each of them striking the bag, either with his foot or with a staff. And thus played they with the bag. Every one as he came in asked, "What game are you playing at thus?"

"The game of Badger in the Bag," said they. And then was the game of Badger in the Bag first played.

"Lord," said the man in the bag, "if thou wouldest but hear me, I merit not to be slain in a bag."

Said Heveyth Hên, "Lord, he speaks truth. It were fitting that thou listen to him; for he deserves not this."

"Verily," said Powel, "I will do thy counsel concerning him."

"Behold, this is my counsel then," said Rhiannon. "Thou art now in a position in which it behoves thee to

satisfy suitors and minstrels : let him give unto them in thy stead, and take a pledge from him that he will never seek to revenge that which has been done to him. And this will be punishment enough."

" I will do this gladly," said the man in the bag.

"And gladly will I accept it," said Powel, " since it is the counsel of Heveyth and Rhiannon."

" Such, then, is our counsel," answered they.

" I accept it," said Powel.

" Seek thyself sureties."

" We will be for him," said Heveyth, "until his men be free to answer for him." And upon this he was let out of the bag, and his liege-men were liberated. " Demand now of Gwawl his sureties," said Heveyth ; "we know which should be taken for him." And Heveyth numbered the sureties.

Said Gwawl, " Do thou thyself draw up the covenant."

" It will suffice me that it be as Rhiannon said," answered Powel. So unto that covenant were all the sureties pledged.

" Verily, lord," said Gwawl, " I am greatly hurt, and I have many bruises. I have need to be anointed ; with thy leave I will go forth. I will leave nobles in my stead to answer for me in all that thou shalt require."

" Willingly," said Powel, " mayest thou do thus." So Gwawl went towards his own possessions.

And the hall was set in order for Powel and the men of his host, and for them also of the palace, and they went to the tables and sat down. And as they had sat that time twelvemonth, so sat they that night. And they ate and feasted, and spent the night in mirth and tranquillity.

And next morning, at the break of day, "My lord," said Rhiannon, "arise and begin to give thy gifts unto the minstrels. Refuse no one to-day that may claim thy bounty."

"Thus shall it be, gladly," said Powel, "both to-day and every day while the feast shall last." So Powel arose, and he caused silence to be proclaimed, and desired all the suitors and the minstrels to show and to point out what gifts were to their wish and desire. And this being done, the feast went on, and he denied no one while it lasted. And when the feast was ended, Powel said unto Heveyth, "My lord, with thy permission, I will set out for Dyved to-morrow."

"Certainly," said Heveyth. "May Heaven prosper thee! Fix also a time when Rhiannon may follow thee."

Said Powel, "We will go hence together."

"Willest thou this, lord?" said Heveyth.

"Yes," answered Powel.

And the next day they set forward towards Dyved, and journeyed to the palace of Narberth, where a feast was made ready for them. And there came to them great numbers of the chief men and the most noble ladies of the land, and of these there was none to whom Rhiannon did not give some rich gift, either a bracelet, or a ring, or a precious stone. And they ruled the land prosperously both that year and the next.

And in the fourth year a son was born to them, and women were brought to watch the babe at night. And the women slept, as did also Rhiannon. And when they awoke they looked where they had put the boy, and behold he was not there. And the women were frightened; and, having plotted together, they accused Rhiannon of having murdered her child before their eyes.

"For pity's sake," said Rhiannon, "the Lord God knows all things. Charge me not falsely. If you tell me this from fear, I assert before Heaven that I will defend you."

"Truly," said they, "we would not bring evil on ourselves for any one in the world."

"For pity's sake," said Rhiannon, "you will receive no evil by telling the truth." But for all her words, whether fair or harsh, she received but the same answer from the women.

And Powel the chief of Annuvyn arose, and his household and his hosts. And this occurrence could not be concealed; but the story went forth throughout the land, and all the nobles heard it. Then the nobles came to Powel, and besought him to put away his wife because of the great crime which she had done. But Powel answered them that they had no cause wherefore they might ask him to put away his wife.

So Rhiannon sent for the teachers and the wise men, and as she preferred doing penance to contending with the women, she took upon her a penance. And the penance that was imposed upon her was that she should remain in that palace of Narberth until the end of seven years, and that she should sit every day near unto a horse-block that was without the gate; and that she should relate the story to all who should come there whom she might suppose not to know it already; and that she should offer the guests and strangers, if they would permit her, to carry them upon her back into the palace. But it rarely happened that any would permit. And thus did she spend part of the year.

Now at that time Teirnyon Twryv Vliant was lord of

Gwent Is Coed, and he was the best man in the world.
And unto his house there belonged a mare than which
neither mare nor horse in the kingdom was more beautiful.
And on the night of every first of May she foaled, and no
one ever knew what became of the colt. And one night
Teirnyon talked with his wife: "Wife," said he, "it is very
simple of us that our mare should foal every year, and that
we should have none of her colts."

"What can be done in the matter?" said she.

"This is the night of the first of May," said he. "The
vengeance of Heaven be upon me, if I learn not what it is
that takes away the colts." So he armed himself, and began
to watch that night. Teirnyon heard a great tumult, and
after the tumult behold a claw came through the window
into the house, and it seized the colt by the mane. Then
Teirnyon drew his sword, and struck off the arm at the
elbow: so that portion of the arm, together with the colt,
was in the house with him. And then did he hear a tumult
and wailing both at once. And he opened the door, and
rushed out in the direction of the noise, and he could not
see the cause of the tumult because of the darkness of the
night; but he rushed after it and followed it. Then he
remembered that he had left the door open, and he returned.
And at the door behold there was an infant-boy in
swaddling clothes, wrapped around in a mantle of satin.
And he took up the boy, and behold he was very strong for
the age that he was of.

Then he shut the door, and went into the chamber where
his wife was. "Lady," said he, "art thou sleeping?"

"No, lord," said she: "I was asleep, but as thou camest
in I did awake."

"Behold, here is a boy for thee, if thou wilt," said he, "since thou hast never had one."

"My lord," said she, "what adventure is this?"

"It was thus," said Teirnyon.   And he told her how it all befell.

"Verily, lord," said she, "what sort of garments are there upon the boy?"

"A mantle of satin," said he.

"He is then a boy of gentle lineage," she replied.

And they caused the boy to be baptised, and the ceremony was performed there.   And the name which they gave unto him was Goldenlocks, because what hair was upon his head was as yellow as gold.   And they had the boy nursed in the court until he was a year old.   And before the year was over he could walk stoutly; and he was larger than a boy of three years old, even one of great growth and size. And the boy was nursed the second year, and then he was as large as a child six years old. And before the end of the fourth year, he would bribe the grooms to allow him to take the horses to water.

"My lord," said his wife unto Tiernyon, "where is the colt which thou didst save on the night that thou didst find the boy?"

"I have commanded the grooms of the horses," said he, "that they take care of him."

"Would it not be well, lord," said she, "if thou wert to cause him to be broken in, and given to the boy, seeing that on the same night that thou didst find the boy, the colt was foaled, and thou didst save him?"

"I will not oppose thee in this matter," said Tiernyon. "I will allow thee to give him the colt."

"Lord," said she, "may Heaven reward thee! I will give it him." So the horse was given to the boy. Then she went to the grooms and those who tended the horses, and commanded them to be careful of the horse, so that he might be broken in by the time that the boy could ride him.

And while these things were going forward, they heard tidings of Rhiannon and her punishment. And Teirnyon Twryv Vliant, by reason of the pity that he felt on hearing this story of Rhiannon and her punishment, inquired closely concerning it, until he had heard from many of those who came to his court. Then did Teirnyon, often lamenting the sad history, ponder with himself; and he looked steadfastly on the boy, and as he looked upon him, it seemed to him that he had never beheld so great a likeness between father and son as between the boy and Powel the chief of Annuvyn. Now the semblance of Powel was well known to him, for he had of yore been one of his followers. And thereupon he became grieved for the wrong that he did in keeping with him a boy whom he knew to be the son of another man. And the first time that he was alone with his wife he told her that it was not right that they should keep the boy with them, and suffer so excellent a lady as Rhiannon to be punished so greatly on his account, whereas the boy was the son of Powel the chief of Annuvyn. And Teirnyon's wife agreed with him that they should send the boy to Powel. "And three things, lord," said she, "shall we gain thereby—thanks and gifts for releasing Rhiannon from her punishment, and thanks from Powel for nursing his son and restoring him unto him ; and, thirdly, if the boy is of gentle nature, he will be our foster-son, and he will do for us all the good in his power." So it was settled according to this counsel.

And no later than the next day was Teirnyon equipped and two other knights with him. And the boy, as a fourth in their company, went with them upon the horse which Teirnyon had given him. And they journeyed towards Narberth, and it was not long before they reached that place. And as they drew near to the palace, they beheld Rhiannon sitting beside the horse-block. And when they were opposite to her, "Chieftain," said she, "go not farther thus : "I will bear every one of you into the palace. And this is my penance for slaying my own son, and devouring him."

"Oh, fair lady," said Teirnyon, "think not that I will be one to be carried upon thy back."

"Neither will I," said the boy.

"Truly, my soul," said Teirnyon, "we will not go." So they went forward to the palace, and there was great joy at their coming. And at the palace a feast was prepared because Powel was come back from the confines of Dyfed And they went into the hall and washed, and Powel rejoiced to see Teirnyon. And in this order they sat : Teirnyon between Powel and Rhiannon, and Teirnyon's two companions on the other side of Powel, with the boy between them. And after meat they began to carouse and discourse. And Teirnyon's discourse was concerning the adventure of the mare and the boy, and how he and his wife had nursed and reared the child as their own. "Behold here is thy son, lady," said Teirnyon. "And whosoever told that lie concerning thee has done wrong. When I heard of thy sorrow, I was troubled and grieved. And I believe that there is none of this host who will not perceive that the boy is the son of Powel," said Teirnyon.

"There is none," said they all, "who is not certain thereof."

"I declare to Heaven," said Rhiannon, "that if this be true, there is indeed an end to my trouble."

"Lady," said Pendaran Dyfed, "well hast thou named thy son Pryderi (end of trouble), and well becomes him the name of Pryderi son of Powel chief of Annuvyn."

"Look you," said Rhiannon : "will not his own name become him better ?"

"What name has he ?" asked Pendaran Dyfed.

"Goldenlocks is the name that we gave him."

"Pryderi," said Pendaran, "shall his name be."

"It were more proper," said Powel, "that the boy should take his name from the word his mother spoke when she received the joyful tidings of him." And thus was it arranged.

"Teirnyon," said Powel, "Heaven reward thee that thou hast reared the boy up to this time, and, being of gentle lineage, it were fitting that he repay thee for it."

"My lord," said Teirnyon, "it was my wife who nursed him, and there is no one in the world so afflicted as she at parting with him. It were well that he should bear in mind what I and my wife have done for him."

"I call Heaven to witness," said Powel, "that while I live I will support thee and thy possessions as long as I am able to preserve my own. And when he shall have power, he will more fitly maintain them than I. And if this counsel be pleasing unto thee and to my nobles, it shall be, that, as thou hast reared him up to the present time, I will give him to be brought up by Pendaran Dyfed from henceforth. And you shall be companions, and shall both be foster-fathers unto him."

"This is good counsel," said they all. So the boy was given to Pendaran Dyfed, and the nobles of the land were sent with him. And Teirnyon Twryv Vliant and his companions set out for his country and his possessions, with love and gladness. And he went not without being offered the fairest jewels, and the fairest horses, and the choicest dogs ; but he would take none of them.

Thereupon they all remained in their own dominions. And Pryderi the son of Powel the chief of Annuvyn was brought up carefully, as was fit, so that he became the fairest youth, and the most comely, and the best skilled in all good games, of any in the kingdom. And thus passed years and years until the end of Powel the chief of Annuvyn's life came, and he died.

Paddy O'Kelly and the Weasel

LONG time ago there was once a man of the name of Paddy O'Kelly, living near Tuam, in the county Galway. He rose up one morning early, and he did not know what time of day it was, for there was fine light coming from the moon. He wanted to go to the fair of Cauher-na-mart to sell a *sturk* of an ass that he had.

He had not gone more than three miles of the road when a great darkness came on, and a shower began falling. He saw a large house among trees about five hundred yards in from the road, and he said to himself that he would go to that house till the shower would be over. When he got to the house he found the door open before him, and in with him. He saw a large room to his left, and a fine fire in the grate. He sat down on a stool that was beside the wall, and began falling asleep, when he saw a big weasel coming to the fire with something yellow in his mouth, which it dropped on the hearth-stone, and then it went away. She soon came back again with the same thing in her mouth, and he saw that it was a guinea she had. She dropped it on the hearth-stone, and went away again. She was coming and going, until there was a great heap of guineas on the hearth. But at last, when she got her gone, Paddy rose up, thrust all the gold she had gathered into his pockets, and out with him.

He had not gone far till he heard the weasel coming after him, and she screeching as loud as a bag-pipes. She went before Paddy and got on the road, and she was twisting herself back and forwards, and trying to get a hold of his throat. Paddy had a good oak stick, and he kept her from him, until two men came up who were going to the same fair, and one of them had a good dog, and it routed the weasel into a hole in the wall.

Paddy went to the fair, and instead of coming home with the money he got for his old ass, as he thought would be the way with him in the morning, he went and bought a horse with some of the money he took from the weasel, and he came home riding. When he came to the place where the dog had routed the weasel into the hole in the wall, she came out before him, gave a leap, and caught the horse by the throat. The horse made off, and Paddy could not stop him, till at last he gave a leap into a big drain that was full up of water and black mud, and he was drowning and choking as fast as he could, until men who were coming from Galway came up and drove away the weasel.

Paddy brought the horse home with him, and put him into the cow's byre and fell asleep.

Next morning, the day on the morrow, Paddy rose up early, and went out to give his horse hay and oats. When he got to the door he saw the weasel coming out of the byre and she covered with blood.

"My seven thousand curses on you," said Paddy, " but I'm afraid you've done harm."

He went in and found the horse, a pair of milch cows, and two calves dead. He came out and set a dog he had after the weasel. The dog got a hold of her, and she got a hold of the dog. The dog was a good one, but he was forced to loose his hold of her before Paddy could come up. He kept his eye on her, however, all through, until he saw her creeping into a little hovel that was on the brink of a lake. Paddy came running, and when

he got to the little hut he gave the dog a shake to rouse him up and put anger on him, and then he sent him in. When the dog went in he began barking. Paddy went in after him, and saw an old hag in the corner. He asked her if she saw a weasel coming in there.

"I did not," said she; "I'm all destroyed with a plague of sickness, and if you don't go out quick, you'll catch it from me."

While Paddy and the hag were talking, the dog kept moving in all the time, till at last he gave a leap and caught the hag by the throat.   She screeched and said :

" Paddy Kelly, take off your dog, and I'll make you a rich man."

Paddy made the dog loose his hold, and said :

" Tell me who you are, or why did you kill my horse and my cows ? "

" And why did you bring away my gold that I was gathering for five hundred years throughout the hills and hollows of the world ? "

" I thought you were a weasel," said Paddy, " or I wouldn't touch your gold ; and another thing," says he, " if you're for five hundred years in this world, it's time for you to go to rest now."

" I committed a great crime in my youth," said the hag, " and now I am to be released from my sufferings if you can pay twenty pounds for a hundred and three-score masses for me."

" Where's the money ? " said Paddy.

" Go and dig under a bush that's over a little well in the corner of that field there without, and you'll get a pot filled with gold.   Pay the twenty pounds for the masses, and yourself shall have the rest.   When you'll lift the flag off the pot, you'll see a big black dog coming out ; but don't be afraid before him ; he is a son of mine.   When you get the gold, buy the house in which you saw me at first.   You'll get it cheap, for it has the name of there being a ghost in it.   My son will be down in the cellar. He'll do you no harm, but he'll be a good friend to you.   I shall be dead a month from this day, and when you get me dead, put a coal under this little hut and burn it. Don't tell a living soul anything about me—and the luck will be on you."

"What is your name?" said Paddy.

"Mary Kerwan," said the hag.

Paddy went home, and when the darkness of the night came on, he took with him a spade and went to the bush that was in the corner of the field, and began digging. It was not long till he found the pot, and when he took the flag off of it a big black dog leaped out, and off and away with him, and Paddy's dog after him.

Paddy brought home the gold, and hid it in the cow-house. About a month after that he went to the fair of Galway, and bought a pair of cows, a horse, and a dozen sheep. The neighbours did not know where he had got all the money; they said that he had a share with the good people.

One day Paddy dressed himself, and went to the gentle-man who owned the large house where he first saw the weasel, and asked to buy the house of him, and the land that was round about.

"You can have the house without paying any rent at all; but there is a ghost in it, and I wouldn't like you to go to live in it without my telling you, but I couldn't part with the land without getting a hundred pounds more than you have to offer me."

"Perhaps I have as much as you have yourself," said Paddy. "I'll be here to-morrow with the money, if you're ready to give me possession."

"I'll be ready," said the gentleman.

Paddy went home and told his wife that he had bought a large house and a holding of land.

"Where did you get the money ? " says the wife.

"Isn't it all one to you where I got it ? " says Paddy.

The day on the morrow Paddy went to the gentleman, gave him the money, and got possession of the house and land ; and the gentleman left him the furniture and everything that was in the house, into the bargain.

Paddy remained in the house that night, and when darkness came he went down to the cellar, and he saw a little man with his two legs spread on a barrel.

"God save you, honest man," says he to Paddy.

"The same to you," says Paddy.

"Don't be afraid of me, at all," says the little man. "I'll be a friend to you, if you are able to keep a secret."

"I am able, indeed ; I kept your mother's secret, and I'll keep yours as well."

"Maybe you're thirsty ? " said the little man.

"I'm not free from it," said Paddy.

The little man put a hand in his bosom and drew out a gold goblet. He gave it to Paddy, and said : "Draw wine out of that barrel under me."

Paddy drew the full up of the goblet, and handed it to the little man.

"Drink yourself first," says he.

Paddy drank, drew another goblet, and handed it to the little man, and he drank it.

"Fill up and drink again," said the little man. "I have a mind to be merry to-night."

The pair of them sat there drinking until they were half drunk. Then the little man gave a leap down to the floor, and said to Paddy :

"Don't you like music ? "

"I do, surely," said Paddy, "and I'm a good dancer, too."

"Lift up the big flag over there in the corner, and you'll get my pipes under it."

Paddy lifted the flag, got the pipes, and gave them to the little man. He squeezed the pipes on him, and began playing melodious music. Paddy began dancing till he was tired. Then they had another drink, and the little man said :

"Do as my mother told you, and I'll show you great riches. You can bring your wife in here, but don't tell her that I'm there, and she won't see me. Any time at all that ale or wine are wanting, come here and draw. Farewell, now ; go to sleep, and come again to me to-morrow night."

Paddy went to bed, and it wasn't long till he fell asleep.

On the morning of the day on the morrow, Paddy went home, and brought his wife and children to the big house, and they were very comfortable. That night Paddy went down to the cellar ; the little man welcomed him and asked him did he wish to dance ?

"Not till I get a drink," said Paddy.

"Drink your fill," said the little man ; "that barrel will never be empty as long as you live."

Paddy drank the full of the goblet, and gave a drink to the little man. Then the little man said to him :

"I am going to the Fortress of the Fairies to-night, to play music for the good people, and if you come with me you'll see fine fun. I'll give you a horse that you never saw the like of him before."

" I'll go with you, and welcome," said Paddy ; " but what excuse will I make to my wife ? "

" I'll bring you away from her side without her knowing it, when you are both asleep together, and I'll bring you back to her the same way," said the little man.

" I'm obedient," says Paddy ; " we'll have another drink before I leave you."

He drank drink after drink, till he was half drunk, and he went to bed with his wife.

When he awoke he found himself riding on a broom near Doon-na-shee, and the little man riding on another besom by his side.   When they came as far as the green hill of the Doon, the little man said a couple of words that Paddy did not understand.   The green hill opened, and the pair went into a fine chamber.

Paddy never saw before a gathering like that which was in the Doon.   The whole place was full up of little people, men and women, young and old.   They all welcomed little Donal—that was the name of the piper—and Paddy O'Kelly. The king and queen of the fairies came up to them, and said :

" We are all going on a visit to-night to Cnoc Matha, to the high king and queen of our people."

They all rose up then and went out.   There were horses ready for each one of them, and the *coash-t'ya bower* for the king and queen.   The king and queen got into the coach, each man leaped on his own horse, and be certain that Paddy was not behind.   The piper went out before them, and began playing them music, and then off and away with them.   It was not long till they came to Cnoc Matha. The hill opened, and the king of the fairy host passed in.

Finvara and Nuala were there, the arch-king and queen of the fairy host of Connacht, and thousands of little persons. Finvara came up and said :

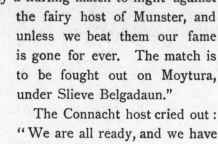

' "We are going to play a hurling match to-night against the fairy host of Munster, and unless we beat them our fame is gone for ever. The match is to be fought out on Moytura, under Slieve Belgadaun."

The Connacht host cried out : "We are all ready, and we have no doubt but we'll beat them."

"Out with ye all," cried the high king ; "the men of the hill of Nephin will be on the ground before us."

They all went out, and little Donal and twelve pipers more before them, playing melodious music. When they came to Moytura, the fairy host of Munster and the fairy men of the hill of Nephin were there before them.

Now it is necessary for the fairy host to have two live men beside them when they are fighting or at a hurling match, and that was the reason that little Donal took Paddy O'Kelly with him. There was a man they called the " *Yellow Stongirya*," with the fairy host of Munster, from Ennis, in the County Clare.

It was not long till the two hosts took sides ; the ball was thrown up between them, and the fun began in earnest.

They were hurling away, and the pipers playing music,
until Paddy O'Kelly saw the host of Munster getting the

strong hand, and he began helping the fairy host of Connacht. The *Ston-
girya* came up and
he made at Paddy
O'Kelly, but Paddy
turned him head
over heels. From
hurling the two hosts
began at fighting,
but it was not long
until the host of
Connacht beat the

other host.   Then the host of Munster made flying beetles
of themselves, and they began eating
every green thing that they came
up to.   They were destroying the
country before them until they came
as far as Cong.   Then there rose up
thousands of doves out of the hole,
and they swallowed down the beetles.

That hole has no other name until this day but Pull-na-gullam, the dove's hole.

When the fairy host of Connacht won their battle, they came back to Cnoc Matha joyous enough, and the king Finvara gave Paddy O'Kelly a purse of gold, and the little piper brought him home, and put him into bed beside his wife, and left him sleeping there.

A month went by after that without anything worth mentioning, until one night Paddy went down to the cellar, and the little man said to him : " My mother is dead ; burn the house over her."

" It is true for you," said Paddy. " She told me that she hadn't but a month to be in the world, and the month was up yesterday."

On the next morning of the next day Paddy went to the hut and he found the hag dead. He put a coal under the hut and burned it. He came home and told the little man that the hag was burnt. The little man gave him a purse and said to him : " This purse will never be empty as long as you are alive. Now, you will never see me more ; but have a loving remembrance of the weasel. She was the beginning and the prime cause of your riches." Then he went away and Paddy never saw him again.

Paddy O'Kelly and his wife lived for years after this in the large house, and when he died he left great wealth behind him, and a large family to spend it.

There now is the story for you, from the first word to the last, as I heard it from my grandmother.

The Black Horse

NCE there was a king and he had three sons, and when the king died, they did not give a shade of anything to the youngest son, but an old white limping garron.

"If I get but this," quoth he, "it seems that I had best go with this same."

He was going with it right before him, sometimes walking, sometimes riding. When he had been riding a good while he thought that the garron would need a while of eating, so he came down to earth, and what should he see coming out of the heart of the western airt towards him but a rider riding high, well, and right well.

"All hail, my lad," said he.

"Hail, king's son," said the other.

"What's your news?" said the king's son.

"I have got that," said the lad who came. "I am after breaking my heart riding this ass of a horse; but will you give me the limping white garron for him?"

"No," said the prince; "it would be a bad business for me."

"You need not fear," said the man that came, "there is no saying but that you might make better use of him than I. He has one value, there is no single place that you can think of in the four parts of the wheel of the world that the black horse will not take you there."

So the king's son got the black horse, and he gave the limping white garron.

Where should he think of being when he mounted but in the Realm Underwaves. He went, and before sunrise on the morrow he was there. What should he find when he got there but the son of the King Underwaves holding a Court, and the people of the realm gathered to see if there was any one who would undertake to go to seek the daughter of the King of the Greeks to be the prince's wife. No one came forward, when who should come up but the rider of the black horse.

"You, rider of the black horse," said the prince, "I lay you under crosses and under spells to have the daughter of the King of the Greeks here before the sun rises to-morrow."

He went out and he reached the black horse and leaned his elbow on his mane, and he heaved a sigh.

"Sigh of a king's son under spells!" said the horse; "but have no care; we shall do the thing that was set before you." And so off they went.

"Now," said the horse, "when we get near the great town of the Greeks, you will notice that the four feet of a horse never went to the town before. The king's daughter will see me from the top of the castle looking out of a window, and she will not be content without a turn of a ride upon me. Say that she may have that, but the horse will suffer no man but you to ride before a woman on him."

They came near the big town, and he fell to horseman-ship; and the princess was looking out of the windows, and noticed the horse. The horsemanship pleased her, and she came out just as the horse had come.

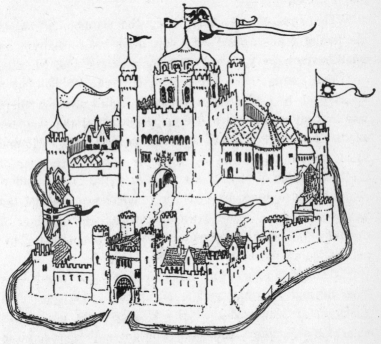

"Give me a ride on the horse," said she.

"You shall have that," said he, "but the horse will let no man ride him before a woman but me."

"I have a horseman of my own," said she.

"If so, set him in front," said he.

Before the horseman mounted at all, when he tried to get up, the horse lifted his legs and kicked him off.

"Come then yourself and mount before me," said she; "I won't leave the matter so."

He mounted the horse and she behind him, and before she glanced from her she was nearer sky than earth. He was in Realm Underwaves with her before sunrise.

"You are come," said Prince Underwaves.

"I am come," said he.

"There you are, my hero," said the prince. "You are the son of a king, but I am a son of success. Anyhow, we shall have no delay or neglect now, but a wedding."

"Just gently," said the princess; "your wedding is not so short a way off as you suppose. Till I get the silver cup that my grandmother had at her wedding, and that my mother had as well, I will not marry, for I need to have it at my own wedding."

"You, rider of the black horse," said the Prince Underwaves, "I set you under spells and under crosses unless the silver cup is here before dawn to-morrow."

Out he went and reached the horse and leaned his elbow on his mane, and he heaved a sigh.

"Sigh of a king's son under spells!" said the horse; "mount and you shall get the silver cup. The people of the realm are gathered about the king to-night, for he has missed his daughter, and when you get to the palace go in and leave me without; they will have the cup there going round the company. Go in and sit in their midst. Say nothing, and seem to be as one of the people of the place. But when the cup comes round to you, take it under your oxter, and come out to me with it, and we'll go."

Away they went and they got to Greece, and he went in to the palace and did as the black horse bade. He took the cup and came out and mounted, and before sunrise he was in the Realm Underwaves.

"You are come," said Prince Underwaves.

"I am come," said he.

"We had better get married now," said the prince to the Greek princess.

"Slowly and softly," said she. "I will not marry till I get the silver ring that my grandmother and my mother wore when they were wedded."

"You, rider of the black horse," said the Prince Underwaves, "do that. Let's have that ring here to-morrow at sunrise."

The lad went to the black horse and put his elbow on his crest and told him how it was.

"There never was a matter set before me harder than this matter which has now been set in front of me," said the horse, "but there is no help for it at any rate. Mount me. There is a snow mountain and an ice mountain and a mountain of fire between us and the winning of that ring. It is right hard for us to pass them."

Thus they went as they were, and about a mile from the snow mountain they were in a bad case with cold. As they came near it he struck the horse, and with the bound he gave the black horse was on the top of the snow mountain; at the next bound he was on the top of the ice mountain; at the third bound he went through the mountain of fire. When he had passed the mountains he was dragging at the horse's neck, as though he were about to lose himself. He went on before him down to a town below.

"Go down," said the black horse, "to a smithy; make an iron spike for every bone end in me."

Down he went as the horse desired, and he got the spikes made, and back he came with them.

"Stick them into me," said the horse, "every spike of them in every bone end that I have."

That he did ; he stuck the spikes into the horse.

" There is a loch here," said the horse, " four miles long and four miles wide, and when I go out into it the loch will take fire and blaze. If you see the Loch of Fire going out before the sun rises, expect me, and if not, go your way."

Out went the black horse into the lake, and the lake became flame. Long was he stretched about the lake, beating his palms and roaring. Day came, and the loch did not go out.

But at the hour when the sun was rising out of the water the lake went out.

And the black horse rose in the middle of the water with one single spike in him, and the ring upon its end.

He came on shore, and down he fell beside the loch.

Then down went the rider. He got the ring, and he dragged the horse down to the side of a hill. He fell to sheltering him with his arms about him, and as the sun was rising he got better and better, till about. midday, when he rose on his feet.

" Mount," said the horse, "and let us begone."

He mounted on the black horse, and away they went.

He reached the mountains, and he leaped the horse at the fire mountain and was on the top. From the mountain of fire he leaped to the mountain of ice, and from the mountain of ice to the mountain of snow. He put the mountains past him, and by morning he was in realm under the waves.

"You are come," said the prince.

"I am," said he.

"That's true," said Prince Underwaves. "A king's son are you, but a son of success am I. We shall have no more mistakes and delays, but a wedding this time."

"Go easy," said the Princess of the Greeks. "Your wedding is not so near as you think yet. Till you make a castle, I won't marry you. Not to your father's castle nor to your mother's will I go to dwell; but make me a castle for which your father's castle will not make washing water."

"You, rider of the black horse, make that," said Prince Underwaves, "before the morrow's sun rises."

The lad went out to the horse and leaned his elbow on his neck and sighed, thinking that this castle never could be made for ever.

"There never came a turn in my road yet that is easier for me to pass than this," said the black horse.

Glance that the lad gave from him he saw all that there were, and ever so many wrights and stone masons at work, and the castle was ready before the sun rose.

He shouted at the Prince Underwaves, and he saw the castle. He tried to pluck out his eye, thinking that it was a false sight.

"Son of King Underwaves," said the rider of the black horse, "don't think that you have a false sight; this is a true sight."

"That's true," said the prince. "You are a son of success, but I am a son of success too. There will be no more mistakes and delays, but a wedding now."

"No," said she. "The time is come. Should we not go to look at the castle? There's time enough to get married before the night comes."

They went to the castle and the castle was without a "but"——

"I see one," said the prince. "One want at least to be made good. A well to be made inside, so that water may not be far to fetch when there is a feast or a wedding in the castle."

"That won't be long undone," said the rider of the black horse.

The well was made, and it was seven fathoms deep and two or three fathoms wide, and they looked at the well on the way to the wedding.

"It is very well made," said she, "but for one little fault yonder."

"Where is it?" said Prince Underwaves.

"There," said she.

He bent him down to look. She came out, and she put her two hands at his back, and cast him in.

"Be thou there," said she. "If I go to be married, thou art not the man; but the man who did each exploit that has been done, and, if he chooses, him will I have."

Away she went with the rider of the little black horse to the wedding.

And at the end of three years after that so it was that he first remembered the black horse or where he left him.

He got up and went out, and he was very sorry for his neglect of the black horse. He found him just where he left him.

"Good luck to you, gentleman," said the horse. "You seem as if you had got something that you like better than me."

"I have not got that, and I won't; but it came over me to forget you," said he.

"I don't mind," said the horse, "it will make no difference. Raise your sword and smite off my head."

"Fortune will now allow that I should do that," said he.

"Do it instantly, or I will do it to you," said the horse.

So the lad drew his sword and smote off the horse's head; then he lifted his two palms and uttered a doleful cry.

What should he hear behind him but "All hail, my brother-in-law."

He looked behind him, and there was the finest man he ever set eyes upon.

"What set you weeping for the black horse?" said he.

"This," said the lad, "that there never was born of man or beast a creature in this world that I was fonder of."

"Would you take me for him?" said the stranger.

"If I could think you the horse, I would; but if not, I would rather the horse," said the rider.

"I am the black horse," said the lad, "and if I were not, how should you have all these things that you went to seek in my father's house. Since I went under spells, many a man have I ran at before you met me. They had but one word amongst them: they could not keep me, nor manage me, and they never kept me a couple of days. But when I fell in with you, you kept me till the time ran out that was to come from the spells. And now you shall go home with me, and we will make a wedding in my father's house."

The Vision of MacConglinney

CATHAL, King of Munster, was a good king and a great warrior. But there came to dwell within him a lawless evil beast, that afflicted him with hunger that ceased not, and might not be satisfied, so that he would devour a pig, a cow, and a bull calf and three-score cakes of pure wheat, and a vat of new ale, for his breakfast, whilst as for his great feast, what he ate there passes account or reckoning. He was like this for three half-years, and during that time it was the ruin of Munster he was, and it is likely he would have ruined all Ireland in another half-year.

Now there lived in Armagh a famous young scholar and his name was Anier MacConglinney. He heard of the strange disease of King Cathal, and of the abundance of food and drink, of whitemeats, ale and mead, there were always to be found at the king's court. Thither then was he minded to go to try his own fortune, and to see of what help he could be to the king.

He arose early in the morning and tucked up his shirt

and wrapped him in the folds of his white cloak. In his right hand he grasped his even-poised knotty staff, and going right-hand-wise round his home, he bade farewell to his tutors and started off.

He journeyed across all Ireland till he came to the house of Pichan. And there he stayed and told tales, and made all merry. But Pichan said:

"Though great thy mirth, son of learning, it does not make me glad."

"And why?" asked MacConglinney.

"Knowest thou not, scholar, that Cathal is coming here to-night with all his host. And if the great host is troublesome, the king's first meal is more troublesome still; and troublesome though the first be, most troublesome of all is the great feast. Three things are wanted for this last: a bushel of oats, and a bushel of wild apples, and a bushel of flour cakes."

"What reward would you give me if I shield you from the king from this hour to the same hour to-morrow?"

"A white sheep from every fold between Carn and Cork."

"I will take that," said MacConglinney.

Cathal, the king, came with the companies, and a host of horse of the Munster men. But Cathal did not let the thong of his shoe be half loosed before he began supplying his mouth with both hands from the apples round about him. Pichan and all the men of Munster looked on sadly and sorrowfully. Then rose MacConglinney, hastily and impatiently, and seized a stone, against which swords were used to be sharpened; this he thrust into his mouth and began grinding his teeth against the stone.

"What makes thee mad, son of learning?" asked Cathal.

"I grieve to see you eating alone," said the scholar.

Then the king was ashamed and flung him the apples, and it is said that for three half-years he had not performed such an act of humanity.

"Grant me a further boon," said MacConglinney.

"It is granted, on my troth," said the king.

"Fast with me the whole night," said the scholar.

And grievous though it was to the king, he did so, for he had passed his princely troth, and no King of Munster might transgress that.

In the morning MacConglinney called for juicy old bacon, and tender corned beef, honey in the comb, and English salt on a beautiful polished dish of white silver. A fire he lighted of oak wood without smoke, without fumes, without sparks.

And sticking spits into the portion of meat, he set to work to roast them. Then he shouted, "Ropes and cords here."

Ropes and cords were given to him, and the strongest of the warriors.

And they seized the king and bound him securely, and made him fast with knots and hooks and staples. When the king was thus fastened, MacConglinney sat himself down before him, and taking his knife out of his girdle, he carved the portion of meat that was on the spits, and every morsel he dipped in the honey, and, passing it in front of the king's mouth, put it in his own.

When the king saw that he was getting nothing, and he had been fasting for twenty-four hours, he roared and bellowed, and commanded the killing of the scholar. But that was not done for him.

"Listen, King of Munster," said MacConglinney, "a vision appeared to me last night, and I will relate it to you."

He then began his vision, and as he related it he put morsel after morsel past Cathal's mouth into his own.

> "A lake of new milk I beheld
> In the midst of a fair plain,
> Therein a well-appointed house,
> Thatched with butter.
> Puddings fresh boiled,
> Such were its thatch-rods,
> Its two soft door posts of custard,
> Its beds of glorious bacon.
> Cheeses were the palisades,
> Sausages the rafters.
> Truly 'twas a rich filled house,
> In which was great store of good feed.

Such was the vision I beheld, and a voice sounded into my ears. 'Go now, thither, MacConglinney, for you have no power of eating in you.' 'What must I do,' said I, for the sight of that had made me greedy. Then the voice bade me go to the hermitage of the Wizard Doctor, and there I should find appetite for all kinds of savoury tender sweet food, acceptable to the body.

"There in the harbour of the lake before me I saw a juicy little coracle of beef; its thwarts were of curds, its prow of lard; its stern of butter; its oars were flitches of venison. Then I rowed across the wide expanse of the New Milk Lake, through seas of broth, past river mouths of meat, over swelling boisterous waves of butter milk, by perpetual pools of savoury lard, by islands of cheese, by headlands of old curds, until I reached the firm level land between Butter Mount and Milk Lake, in the land of O'Early-eating, in front of the hermitage of the Wizard Doctor.

" Marvellous, indeed, was the hermitage. Around it were seven-score hundred smooth stakes of old bacon, and instead of thorns above the top of every stake was fixed juicy lard. There was a gate of cream, whereon was a bolt of sausage. And there I saw the doorkeeper, Bacon Lad, son of Butterkins, son of Lardipole, with his smooth sandals of old bacon, his legging of pot-meat round his shins, his tunic of corned beef, his girdle of salmon skin round him, his hood of flummery about him, his steed of bacon under him, with its four legs of custard, its four hoofs of oaten bread, its ears of curds, its two eyes of honey in its head ; in his hand a whip, the cords whereof were four-and-twenty fair white puddings, and every juicy drop that fell from each of these puddings would have made a meal for an ordinary man.

" On going in I beheld the Wizard Doctor with his two gloves of rump steak on his hands, setting in order the house, which was hung all round with tripe, from roof to floor.

" I went into the kitchen, and there I saw the Wizard Doctor's son, with his fishing hook of lard in his hand, and the line was made of marrow, and he was angling in a lake of whey. Now he would bring up a flitch of ham, and now a fillet of corned beef. And as he was angling, he fell in, and was drowned.

" As I set my foot across the threshold into the house, I saw a pure white bed of butter, on which I sat down, but

I sank down into it up to the tips of my hair.   Hard work had the eight strongest men in the house to pull me out by the top of the crown of my head.

"Then I was taken in to the Wizard Doctor.   'What aileth thee?' said he.

"My wish would be, that all the many wonderful viands of the world were before me, that I might eat my fill and satisfy my greed.   But alas! great is the misfortune to me, who cannot obtain any of these.

"'On my word,' said the Doctor, 'the disease is grievous.   But thou shall take home with thee a medicine to cure thy disease, and shalt be for ever healed therefrom.'

"'What is that?' asked I.

"'When thou goest home to-night, warm thyself before a glowing red fire of oak, made up on a dry hearth, so that its embers may warm thee, its blaze may not burn thee, its smoke may not touch thee.   And make for thyself thrice nine morsels, and every morsel as big as an heath fowl's egg, and in each morsel eight kinds of grain, wheat and barley, oats and rye, and therewith eight condiments, and to every condiment eight sauces.   And when thou hast prepared thy food, take a drop of drink, a tiny drop, only as much as twenty men will drink, and let it be of thick milk, of yellow bubbling milk, of milk that will gurgle as it rushes down thy throat.'

"'And when thou hast done this, whatever disease thou hast, shall be removed.   Go now,' said he, 'in the name of cheese, and may the smooth juicy bacon protect thee, may yellow curdy cream protect, may the cauldron full of pottage protect thee.'"

Now, as MacConglinney recited his vision, what with the pleasure of the recital and the recounting of these many pleasant viands, and the sweet savour of the honeyed morsels roasting on the spits, the lawless beast that dwelt

within the king, came forth until it was licking its lips outside its head.

Then MacConglinney bent his hand with the two spits of food, and put them to the lips of the king, who longed to swallow them, wood, food, and all. So he took them an arm's length away from the king, and the lawless beast

jumped from the throat of Cathal on to the spit. MacConglinney put the spit into the embers, and upset the cauldron
of the royal house over the spit. The house was emptied,
so that not the value of a cockchafer's leg was left in it, and
four huge fires were kindled here and there in it. When
the house was a tower of red flame and a huge blaze, the
lawless beast sprang to the rooftree of the palace, and from
thence he vanished, and was seen no more.

As for the king, a bed was prepared for him on a downy
quilt, and musicians and singers entertained him going from
noon till twilight. And when he awoke, this is what he
bestowed upon the scholar—a cow from every farm, and a
sheep from every house in Munster. Moreover, that so
long as he lived, he should carve the king's food, and sit
at his right hand.

Thus was Cathal, King of Munster, cured of his craving,
and MacConglinney honoured.

Dream of Owen O'Mulready

HERE was a man long ago living near Ballaghadereen named Owen O'Mulready, who was a workman for the gentleman of the place, and was a prosperous, quiet, contented man. There was no one but himself and his wife Margaret, and they had a nice little house and enough potatoes in the year, in addition to their share of wages, from their master. There wasn't a want or anxiety on Owen, except one desire, and that was to have a dream—for he had never had one.

One day when he was digging potatoes, his master—James Taafe—came out to his ridge, and they began talking, as was the custom with them. The talk fell on dreams, and said Owen that he would like better than anything if he could only have one.

"You'll have one to-night," says his master, "if you do as I tell you."

"Musha, I'll do it, and welcome," says Owen.

"Now," says his master, "when you go home to-night, draw the fire from the hearth, put it out, make your bed in its place and sleep there to-night, and you'll get your enough of dreaming before the morning."

Owen promised to do this. When, however, he began to draw the fire out, Margaret thought that he had lost his senses, so he explained everything James Taafe had said to him, had his own way, and they went to lie down together on the hearth.

Not long was Owen asleep when there came a knock at the door.

"Get up, Owen O'Mulready, and go with a letter from the master to America."

Owen got up, and put his feet into his boots, saying to himself, " It's late you come, messenger."

He took the letter, and he went forward and never tarried till he came to the foot of Sliabh Charn, where he met a cow-boy, and he herding cows.

"The blessing of God be with you, Owen O'Mulready," says the boy.

"The blessing of God and Mary be with you, my boy," says Owen. "Every one knows me, and I don't know any one at all."

"Where are you going this time of night?" says the boy.

"I'm going to America, with a letter from the master; is this the right road?" says Owen.

"It is; keep straight to the west; but how are you going to get over the water?" says the boy.

"Time enough to think of that when I get to it," replied Owen.

He went on the road again, till he came to the brink of the sea; there he saw a crane standing on one foot on the shore.

"The blessing of God be with you, Owen O'Mulready," says the crane.

"The blessing of God and Mary be with you, Mrs. Crane," says Owen. "Everybody knows me, and I don't know any one."

"What are you doing here?"

Owen told her his business, and that he didn't know how he'd get over the water.

"Leave your two feet on my two wings, and sit on my back, and I'll take you to the other side," says the crane.

"What would I do if tiredness should come on you before we got over?" says Owen.

"Don't be afraid, I won't be tired or wearied till I fly over."

Then Owen went on the back of the crane, and she arose over the sea and went forward, but she hadn't flown more than half-way, when she cried out:

"Owen O'Mulready get off me; I'm tired."

"That you may be seven times worse this day twelve-months, you rogue of a crane," says Owen; "I can't get off you now, so don't ask me."

"I don't care," replied the crane, "if you'll rise off me a while till I'll take a rest."

With that they saw threshers over their heads, and Owen shouted:

"Och! thresher, thresher, leave down your flail at me, that I may give the crane a rest!"

The thresher left down the flail, but when Owen took a hold with his two hands, the crane went from him laughing and mocking.

" My share of misfortunes go with you ! " said Owen, " It's you've left me in a fix hanging between the heavens and the water in the middle of the great sea."

It wasn't long till the thresher shouted to him to leave go the flail.

" I won't let it go," said Owen ; " shan't I be drowned ? "

" If you don't let it go, I'll cut the whang."

" I don't care," says Owen ; " I have the flail ; " and

with that he looked away from him, and what should he
see but a boat a long way off.

" O sailor dear, sailor, come, come ; perhaps you'll take
my lot of bones," said Owen.

" Are we under you now ? " says the sailor.

" Not yet, not yet," says Owen.

" Fling down one of your shoes, till we see the way it
falls," says the captain.

Owen shook one foot, and down fell the shoe.

" Uill, uill, puil, uil liu——who is killing me ? " came a
scream from Margaret in the bed. " Where are you,
Owen ? "

" I didn't know whether 'twas you were in it, Margaret."

"Indeed, then it is," says she, "who else would it
be ? "

She got up and lit the candle. She found Owen half-
way up the chimney, climbing by the hands on the crook,
and he black with soot ! He had one shoe on, but the
point of the other struck Margaret, and 'twas that which
awoke her.

Owen came down off the crook and washed himself, and
from that out there was no envy on him ever to have a
dream again.

Morraha

ORRAHA rose in the morning and washed his hands and face, and said his prayers, and ate his food; and he asked God to prosper the day for him. So he went down to the brink of the sea, and he saw a currach, short and green, coming towards him; and in it there was but one youthful champion, and he was playing hurly from prow to stern of the currach. He had a hurl of gold and a ball of silver; and he stopped not till the currach was in on the shore; and he drew her up on the green grass, and put fastenings on her for a year and a day, whether he should be there all that time or should only be on land for an hour by the clock. And Morraha saluted the young man courteously; and the other saluted him in the same fashion, and asked him would he play a game of cards with him; and Morraha said that he had not the wherewithal; and the other answered that he was never without a candle or the making of it; and he put his hand in his pocket and drew out a table and two chairs and a

pack of cards, and they sat down on the chairs and went to card-playing. The first game Morraha won, and the Slender Red Champion bade him make his claim ; and he asked that the land above him should be filled with stock of sheep in the morning. It was well ; and he played no second game, but home he went.

The next day Morraha went to the brink of the sea, and the young man came in the currach and asked him would he play cards ; they played, and Morraha won. The young man bade him make his claim ; and he asked that the land above should be filled with cattle in the morning. It was well ; and he played no other game, but went home.

On the third morning Morraha went to the brink of the sea, and he saw the young man coming. He drew up his boat on the shore and asked him would he play cards. They played, and Morraha won the game ; and the young man bade him give his claim. And he said he would have a castle and a wife, the finest and fairest in the world ; and they were his. It was well ; and the Red Champion went away.

On the fourth day his wife asked him how he had found her. And he told her. "And I am going out," said he, "to play again to-day."

"I forbid you to go again to him. If you have won so much, you will lose more ; have no more to do with him."

But he went against her will, and he saw the currach coming ; and the Red Champion was driving his balls from end to end of the currach ; he had balls of silver and a hurl of gold, and he stopped not till he drew his boat on the shore, and made her fast for a year and a day. Morraha and he saluted each other; and he asked Morraha if he would play a game of cards, and they played, and he won. Morraha said to him, "Give your claim now."

Said he, "You will hear it too soon. I lay on you bonds of the art of the Druid, not to sleep two nights in one house, nor finish a second meal at the one table, till you bring me the sword of light and news of the death of Anshgayliacht."

He went home to his wife and sat down in a chair, and gave a groan, and the chair broke in pieces.

"That is the groan of the son of a king under spells," said his wife; "and you had better have taken my counsel than that the spells should be on you."

He told her he had to bring news of the death of Anshgayliacht and the sword of light to the Slender Red Champion.

"Go out," said she, "in the morning of the morrow, and take the bridle in the window. and shake it; and whatever beast, handsome or ugly, puts its head in it, take that one with you. Do not speak a word to her till she speaks to you; and take with you three pint bottles of ale and three sixpenny loaves, and do the thing she tells you; and when she runs to my father's land, on a height above the castle, she will shake herself, and the bells will ring, and my father will say, 'Brown Allree is in the land. And if the son of a king or queen is there, bring him to me on your shoulders; but if it is the son of a poor man, let him come no further.'"

He rose in the morning, and took the bridle that was in the window, and went out and shook it; and Brown Allree came and put her head in it. He took the three loaves and three bottles of ale, and went riding; and when he was riding she bent her head down to take hold of her feet with her mouth, in hopes he would speak in ignorance; but he spoke not a word during the time, and the mare at last spoke to him, and told him to dismount and give her her dinner. He gave her the sixpenny loaf toasted, and a bottle of ale to drink.

"Sit up now riding, and take good heed of yourself: there are three miles of fire I have to clear at a leap."

She cleared the three miles of fire at a leap, and asked if he were still riding, and he said he was. Then they went on, and she told him to dismount and give her a meal; and he did so, and gave her a sixpenny loaf and a bottle; she consumed them and said to him there were before them three miles of hill covered with steel thistles, and that she must clear it. She cleared the hill with a leap, and she asked him if he were still riding, and he said he was. They went on, and she went not far before she told him to give her a meal, and he gave her the bread and the bottleful. She went over three miles of sea with a leap, and she came then to the land of the King of France; she went up on a height above the castle, and she shook herself and neighed, and the bells rang; and the king said that it was Brown Allree was in the land.

"Go out," said he; "and if it is the son of a king or queen, carry him in on your shoulders; if it is not, leave him there."

They went out; and the stars of the son of a king were on his breast; they lifted him high on their shoulders and bore him in to the king. They passed the night cheerfully, playing and drinking, with sport and with diversion, till the whiteness of the day came upon the morrow morning.

Then the young king told the cause of his journey, and he asked the queen to give him counsel and good luck, and she told him everything he was to do.

"Go now," said she, "and take with you the best mare in the stable, and go to the door of Rough Niall of the Speckled Rock, and knock, and call on him to give you news of the death of Anshgayliacht and the sword of light : and let the horse's back be to the door, and apply the spurs, and away with you."

In the morning he did so, and he took the best horse from the stable and rode to the door of Niall, and turned the horse's back to the door, and demanded news of the death of Anshgayliacht and the sword of light ; then he applied the spurs, and away with him.   Niall followed him hard, and, as he was passing the gate, cut the horse in two. His wife was there with a dish of puddings and flesh, and she threw it in his eyes and blinded him, and said, "Fool! whatever kind of man it is that's mocking you, isn't that a fine condition you have got your father's horse into ? "

On the morning of the next day Morraha rose, and took another horse from the stable, and went again to the door of Niall, and knocked and demanded news of the death of Anshgayliacht and the sword of light, and applied the spurs to the horse and away with him.   Niall followed, and as Morraha was passing, the gate cut the horse in two and took half the saddle with him ; but his wife met him and threw flesh in his eyes and blinded him.

On the third day, Morraha went again to the door of

Niall; and Niall followed him, and as he was passing the gate, cut away the saddle from under him and the clothes from his back. Then his wife said to Niall:

"The fool that's mocking you, is out yonder in the little currach, going home; and take good heed to yourself, and don't sleep one wink for three days."

For three days the little currach kept in sight, but then Niall's wife came to him and said:

"Sleep as much as you want now. He is gone."

He went to sleep, and there was heavy sleep on him, and Morraha went in and took hold of the sword that was on the bed at his head. And the sword thought to draw itself out of the hand of Morraha; but it failed. Then it gave a cry, and it wakened Niall, and Niall said it was a rude and rough thing to come into his house like that; and said Morraha to him:

"Leave your much talking, or I will cut the head off you. Tell me the news of the death of Anshgayliacht."

"Oh, you can have my head."

"But your head is no good to me; tell me the story."

"Oh," said Niall's wife, "you must get the story."

"Well," said Niall, "let us sit down together till I tell the story. I thought no one would ever get it; but now it will be heard by all."

THE STORY.

When I was growing up, my mother taught me the language of the birds; and when I got married, I used to be listening to their conversation; and I would be laughing; and my wife would be asking me what was the reason of my laughing, but I did not like to tell her, as women are always asking questions. We went out walking one fine morning, and the birds were arguing with one another. One of them said to another :

"Why should you be comparing yourself with me, when there is not a king nor knight that does not come to look at my tree ?"

"What advantage has your tree over mine, on which there are three rods of magic mastery growing ?"

When I heard them arguing, and knew that the rods were there, I began to laugh.

"Oh," asked my wife, " why are you always laughing ? I believe it is at myself you are jesting, and I'll walk with you no more."

"Oh, it is not about you I am laughing. It is because I understand the language of the birds."

Then I had to tell her what the birds were saying to one another ; and she was greatly delighted, and she asked me to go home, and she gave orders to the cook to have breakfast ready at six o'clock in the morning. I did not know why she was going out early, and breakfast was ready in the morning at the hour she appointed. She asked me to go out walking. I went with her. She went to the tree, and asked me to cut a rod for her.

"Oh, I will not cut it. Are we not better without it ?"

"I will not leave this until I get the rod, to see if there is any good in it."

I cut the rod and gave it to her. She turned from me and struck a blow on a stone, and changed it ; and she struck a second blow on me, and made of me a black raven, and she went home and left me after her. I thought she would come back ; she did not come, and I had to go into

a tree till morning. In the morning, at six o'clock, there
was a bellman out, proclaiming that every one who killed a
raven would get a fourpenny-bit. At last you could not
find man or boy without a gun, nor, if you were to walk
three miles, a raven that was not killed. I had to make

a nest in the top of the parlour chimney, and hide myself
all day till night came, and go out to pick up a bit to
support me, till I spent a month. Here she is herself to
say if it is a lie I am telling.

"It is not," said she.

Then I saw her out walking. I went up to her, and I

thought she would turn me back to my own shape, and she struck me with the rod and made of me an old white horse, and she ordered me to be put to a cart with a man, to draw stones from morning till night. I was worse off then. She spread abroad a report that I had died suddenly in my bed, and prepared a coffin, and waked and buried me. Then she had no trouble. But when I got tired I began to kill every one who came near me, and I used to go into the haggard every night and destroy the stacks of corn; and when a man came near me in the morning I would follow him till I broke his bones. Every one got afraid of me. When she saw I was doing mischief she came to meet me, and I thought she would change me. And she did change me, and made a fox of me. When I saw she was doing me every sort of damage I went away from her. I knew there was a badger's hole in the garden, and I went there till night came, and I made great slaughter among the geese and ducks. There she is herself to say if I am telling a lie.

" Oh! you are telling nothing but the truth, only less than the truth."

When she had enough of my killing the fowl she came out into the garden, for she knew I was in the badger's hole. She came to me and made me a wolf. I had to be off, and go to an island, where no one at all would see me, and now and then I used to be killing sheep, for there were not many of them, and I was afraid of being seen and hunted; and so I passed a year, till a shepherd saw me among the sheep and a pursuit was made after me. And when the dogs came near me there was no place for me to escape to from them; but I recognised the sign of the king among the men, and I made for him, and the king cried out to stop the hounds. I took a leap upon the front of the king's saddle, and the woman behind cried out, " My king and my lord, kill him, or he will kill you ! "

" Oh ! he will not kill me. He knew me ; he must be pardoned."

The king took me home with him, and gave orders I should be well cared for. I was so wise, when I got food, I would not eat one morsel until I got a knife and fork. The man told the king, and the king came to see if it was true, and I got a knife and fork, and I took the knife in one paw and the fork in the other, and I bowed to the king. The king gave orders to bring him drink, and it came ; and the king filled a glass of wine and gave it to me.

I took hold of it in my paw and drank it, and thanked the king.

" On my honour," said he, " it is some king or other has lost him, when he came on the island ; and I will keep him, as he is trained ; and perhaps he will serve us yet."

And this is the sort of king he was,—a king who had not a child living. Eight sons were born to him and three daughters, and they were stolen the same night they were born. No matter what guard was placed over them, the child would be gone in the morning. A twelfth child now came to the queen, and the king took me with him to watch the baby. The women were not satisfied with me.

" Oh," said the king, " what was all your watching ever good for ? One that was born to me I have not ; I will leave this one in the dog's care, and he will not let it go."

A coupling was put between me and the cradle, and when every one went to sleep I was watching till the person woke who attended in the daytime ; but I was there only two nights ; when it was near the day, I saw a hand coming down through the chimney, and the hand was so big that it took round the child altogether, and thought to take him away. I caught hold of the hand above the wrist, and as I was fastened to the cradle, I did not let go my hold till I cut the hand from the wrist, and there was a howl from the person without. I laid the hand in the cradle with the child, and as I was tired I fell asleep ; and when I awoke, I had neither child nor hand ; and I began to howl, and the king heard me, and he cried out that something was wrong with me, and he sent servants to see what was the matter with me, and when the messenger came he saw me covered with blood, and he could not see the child ; and he went to the king and told him the child was not to be got. The king came and saw the cradle coloured with the blood, and he cried out " where was the child gone ? " and every one said it was the dog had eaten it.

The king said : " It is not : loose him, and he will get the pursuit himself."

When I was loosed, I found the scent of the blood till I came to a door of the room in which the child was. I went back to the king and took hold of him, and went back again and began to tear at the door. The king followed me and asked for the key. The servant said it was in the room of the stranger woman. The king caused search to be made for her, and she was not to be found. " I will break the door," said the king, " as I can't get the key." The king broke the door, and I went in, and went to the trunk, and the king asked for a key to unlock it. He got no key, and he broke the lock. When he opened the trunk, the child and the hand were stretched side by side, and the child was asleep. The king took the hand and ordered a woman to come for the child, and he showed the hand to every one in the house. But the stranger woman was gone, and she did not see the king ;—and here she is herself to say if I am telling lies of her.

"Oh, it's nothing but the truth you have!"

The king did not allow me to be tied any more. He said there was nothing so much to wonder at as that I cut the hand off, as I was tied.

The child was growing till he was a year old. He was beginning to walk, and no one cared for him more than I did. He was growing till he was three, and he was running out every minute ; so the king ordered a silver chain to be put between me and the child, that he might not go away from me. I was out with him in the garden every day, and the king was as proud as the world of the child. He would be watching him everywhere we went, till the child grew so wise that he would loose the chain and get off. But one day that he loosed it I failed to find him ; and I ran into the house and searched the house, but there was no getting him for me. The king cried to go out and find the child, that had got loose from the dog. They went searching for him, but could not find him. When they failed altogether to find him, there remained no more favour with the king towards me, and every one disliked me, and I grew weak, for I did not get a morsel to eat half the time. When summer came, I said I would try and go

home to my own country.   I went away one fine morning,
and I went swimming, and God helped me till I came home.
I went into the garden, for I knew there was a place in the
garden where I could hide myself, for fear my wife should
see me.   In the morning I saw her out walking, and the
child with her, held by the hand.   I pushed out to see the

child, and as he was looking about him everywhere, he saw
me and called out, "I see my shaggy papa.   Oh!" said he;
"oh, my heart's love, my shaggy papa, come here till I see
you!"

I was afraid the woman would see me, as she was asking
the child where he saw me, and he said I was up in a tree;
and the more the child called me, the more I hid myself.

The woman took the child home with her, but I knew he would be up early in the morning.

I went to the parlour-window, and the child was within, and he playing. When he saw me he cried out, "Oh! my heart's love, come here till I see you, shaggy papa." I broke the window and went in, and he began to kiss me. I saw the rod in front of the chimney, and I jumped up at the rod and knocked it down. "Oh! my heart's love, no one would give me the pretty rod," said he. I hoped he would strike me with the rod, but he did not. When I saw the time was short I raised my paw, and I gave him a scratch below the knee. "Oh! you naughty, dirty, shaggy papa, you have hurt me so much, I'll give you a blow of the rod." He struck me a light blow, and so I came back to my own shape again. When he saw a man standing before him he gave a cry, and I took him up in my arms. The servants heard the child. A maid came in to see what was the matter with him. When she saw me she gave a cry out of her, and she said, "Oh, if the master isn't come to life again!"

Another came in, and said it was he really. When the mistress heard of it, she came to see with her own eyes, for she would not believe I was there ; and when she saw me she said she'd drown herself. But I said to her, "If you yourself will keep the secret, no living man will ever get the story from me until I lose my head." Here she is herself to say if I am telling the truth. "Oh, it's nothing but truth you are telling."

When I saw I was in a man's shape, I said I would take the child back to his father and mother, as I knew the grief they were in after him. I got a ship, and took

the child with me; and as I journeyed I came to land
on an island, and I saw not a living soul on it, only a
castle dark and gloomy. I went in to see was there any
one in it. There was no one but an old hag, tall and
frightful, and she asked me, "What sort of person are
you?" I heard some one groaning in another room, and
I said I was a doctor, and I asked her what ailed the
person who was groaning.

"Oh," said she, "it is my son, whose hand has been
bitten from his wrist by a dog."

I knew then that it was he who had taken the child from
me, and I said I would cure him if I got a good reward.

"I have nothing; but there are eight young lads and
three young women, as handsome as any one ever laid eyes
on, and if you cure him I will give you them."

"Tell me first in what place his hand was cut from
him?"

"Oh, it was out in another country, twelve years ago."

"Show me the way, that I may see him."

She brought me into a room, so that I saw him, and his
arm was swelled up to the shoulder. He asked me if I
would cure him; and I said I would cure him if he would
give me the reward his mother promised.

"Oh, I will give it; but cure me."

"Well, bring them out to me."

The hag brought them out of the room. I said I should
burn the flesh that was on his arm. When I looked on
him he was howling with pain. I said that I would not
leave him in pain long. The wretch had only one eye in
his forehead. I took a bar of iron, and put it in the fire till
it was red, and I said to the hag, "He will be howling at

first, but will fall asleep presently, and do not wake him
till he has slept as much as he wants. I will close the
door when I am going out." I took the bar with me, and
I stood over him, and I turned it across through his eye as
far as I could. He began to bellow, and tried to catch me,
but I was out and away, having closed the door. The hag
asked me, "Why is he bellowing?"

"Oh, he will be quiet presently, and will sleep for a good
while, and I'll come again to have a look at him; but bring
me out the young men and the young women."

I took them with me, and I said to her, "Tell me where
you got them."

"My son brought them with him, and they are all the
children of one king."

I was well satisfied, and I had no wish for delay to get
myself free from the hag, so I took them on board the ship,
and the child I had myself. I thought the king might leave
me the child I nursed myself; but when I came to land,
and all those young people with me, the king and queen
were out walking. The king was very aged, and the queen
aged likewise. When I came to converse with them, and
the twelve with me, the king and queen began to cry. I
asked, "Why are you crying?"

"It is for good cause I am crying. As many children as
these I should have, and now I am withered, grey, at the
end of my life, and I have not one at all."

I told him all I went through, and I gave him the child
in his hand, and "These are your other children who were
stolen from you, whom I am giving to you safe. They are
gently reared."

When the king heard who they were he smothered them

with kisses and drowned them with tears, and dried them with fine cloths silken and the hair of his own head, and so also did their mother, and great was his welcome for me, as it was I who found them all. The king said to me, " I will give you the last child, as it is you who have earned him best ; but you must come to my court every year, and the child with you, and I will share with you my possessions.

"I have enough of my own, and after my death I will leave it to the child."

I spent a time, till my visit was over, and I told the king all the troubles I went through, only I said nothing about my wife. And now you have the story.

And now when you go home, and the Slender Red Champion asks you for news of the death of Anshgayliacht and for the sword of light, tell him the way in which his brother was killed, and say you have the sword ; and he will ask the sword from you. Say you to him, " If I promised to bring it to you, I did not promise to bring it for you ;" and then throw the sword into the air and it will come back to me.

He went home, and he told the story of the death of Anshgayliacht to the Slender Red Champion, " And here," said he, " is the sword." The Slender Red Champion asked for the sword ; but he said : " If I promised to bring it to you, I did not promise to bring it for you ;" and he threw it into the air and it returned to Blue Niall.

The Story of the McAndrew Family

ALONG time ago, in the County Mayo, there lived a rich man of the name of McAndrew. He owned cows and horses without number, not to mention ducks and geese and pigs; and his land extended as far as the eye could reach on the four sides of you.

McAndrew was a lucky man, the neighbours all said; but as for himself, when he looked on his seven big sons growing up like weeds and with scarcely any more sense, he felt sore enough, for of all the stupid omadhauns the seven McAndrew brothers were the stupidest.

When the youngest grew to be a man, the father built a house for each of them, and gave every one a piece of land and a few cows, hoping to make men of them before he died, for, as the old man said :

"While God spares my life, I'll be able to have an eye to them, and maybe they will learn from experience."

The seven young McAndrews were happy enough. Their fields were green, their cows were fat and sleek, and they thought they would never see a poor day.

All went well for a time, and the day of the Fair of Killalla was as fine a day as ever shone in Ireland, when the whole seven got ready to be off, bright and early, in the morning.

Each one of them drove before him three fine cows, and a finer herd, when they were all together, was never seen in the country far or near.

Now, there was a smart farmer, named O'Toole, whose fields were nearing on the McAndrews', and he had many a time set his heart on the fine cattle belonging to his easy-going neighbours; so when he saw them passing with their twenty-one cows he went out and hailed them.

"Where are ye going to, this fine morning?"

"It's to the Fair of Killalla we're going, to sell these fine cows our father gave us," they all answered together.

"And are ye going to sell cows that the Evil Eye has long been set on? Oh, Con and Shamus, I would never belave it of ye, even if that spalpeen of a Pat would do such a thing; any one would think that the spirit of the good mother that bore ye would stretch out a hand and kape ye from committing such a mortal sin."

This O'Toole said to the three eldest, who stood trembling, while the four younger ones stuck their knuckles into their eyes and began to cry.

"Oh, indade, Mr. O'Toole, we never knew that the cows were under the Evil Eye. How did ye find it out? Oh,

sorra the day when such a fine lot of cattle should go to
the bad," answered Con.

"Indade ye may well ask it, whin
it's meself that was always a good
neighbour and kept watch on auld
Judy, the witch, when she used to
stand over there laughing at the
ravens flying over the cows. Do ye
mind the time yer father spoke ugly
to her down by the cross-roads?
She never forgot it, and now yer twenty-one fine cows will
never be worth the hides on their backs."

"Worra, worra, worra," roared the seven McAndrews, so
loud that pretty Katie O'Toole bobbed her head out of the
window, and the hindermost cows began to caper like mad.

"The spell has come upon them!" cried Shamus. "Oh!
what'll we do?　What'll we do?"

"Hould yer whist, man alive," said O'Toole. "I'm a
good neighbour, as I said before, so to give ye a lift in the
world I'll take the risk on meself and buy the cows from ye
for the price of their hides.　Sure no harm can be done

to the hides for making leather, so I'll
give ye a shilling apiece, and that's
better than nothing.　Twenty-one
bright shillings going to the fair may
make yer fortune."

It seemed neck or nothing with the
McAndrews, and they accepted the
offer, thanking O'Toole for his
generosity, and helped him drive the cows into his field.
Then they set off for the fair.

They had never been in a fair before, and when they saw the fine sights they forgot all about the cows, and only remembered that they had each a shilling to spend.

Every one knew the McAndrews, and soon a crowd gathered round them, praising their fine looks and telling them what a fine father they had to give them so much money, so that the seven omadhauns lost their heads entirely, and treated right and left until there wasn't a farthing left of the twenty-one shillings. Then they staggered home a little the worse for the fine whisky they drank with the boys.

It was a sorry day for old McAndrew when his seven sons came home without a penny of the price of their twenty-one fine cows, and he vowed he'd never give them any more.

So one day passed with another, and the seven young McAndrews were as happy as could be until the fine old father fell sick and died.

The eldest son came in for all the father had, so he felt like a lord. To see him strut and swagger was a sight to make a grum growdy laugh.

One day, to show how fine he could be, he dressed in his best, and with a purse filled with gold pieces started off for the market town.

When he got there, in he walked to a public-house, and called for the best of everything, and to make a fine fellow of himself he tripled the price of everything to the landlord. As soon as he got through his eye suddenly caught sight of a little keg, all gilded over to look like gold, that hung outside the door for a sign. Con had never heeded it before, and he asked the landlord what it was.

Now the landlord, like many another, had it in mind that he might as well get all he could out of a McAndrew, and he answered quickly :

" You stupid omadhaun, don't you know what that is ? It's a mare's egg."

" And will a foal come out of it ? "

" Of course ; what a question to ask a dacent man ! "

" I niver saw one before," said the amazed McAndrew.

" Well, ye see one now, Con, and take a good look at it."

" Will ye sell it ? "

" Och, Con McAndrew, do ye think I want to sell that fine egg afther kaping it so long hung up there before the sun—when it is ready to hatch out a foal that will be worth twenty good guineas to me ? "

" I'll give ye twenty guineas for it," answered Con.

" Thin it's a bargain," said the landlord ; and he took down the keg and handed it to Con, who handed out the twenty guineas, all the money he had.

" Be careful of it, and carry it as aisy as ye can, and when ye get home hang it up in the sun."

Con promised, and set off home with his prize.

Near the rise of a hill he met his brothers.

" What have ye, Con ? "

" The most wonderful thing in the world—a mare's egg."

" Faith, what is it like ? " asked Pat, taking it from Con.

" Go aisy, can't ye ?   It's very careful ye have to be "

But the brothers took no heed to Con, and before one could say, " whist," away rolled the keg down the hill, while all seven ran after it ; but before any one could catch it, it rolled into a clump of bushes, and in an instant out hopped a hare.

"Bedad, there's the foal," cried Con, and all seven gave chase; but there was no use trying to catch a hare.

"That's the foinest foal that ever was, if he was five year old the devil himself could not catch him," Con said; and with that the seven omadhauns gave up the chase and went quietly home.

As I said before, every one had it in mind to get all he could out of the McAndrews.

Every one said, "One man might as well have it as another, for they're bound to spend every penny they have."

So their money dwindled away; then a fine horse would go for a few bits of glass they took for precious stones, and by-and-by a couple of pigs or a pair of fine geese for a bit of ribbon to tie on a hat; and at last their land began to go.

One day Shamus was sitting by his fireplace warming himself, and to make a good fire he threw on a big heap of turf so that by-and-by it got roaring hot, and instead of feeling chilly as he had before, Shamus got as hot as a spare-rib on a spit. Just then in came his youngest brother.

"That's a great fire ye have here, Shamus."

"It is, indade, and too near it is to me; run like a good boy to Giblin, the mason, and see if he can't move the chimney to the other side of the room."

The youngest McAndrew did as he was bid, and soon in came Giblin, the mason.

"Ye're in a sad plight, Shamus, roasting alive; what can I do for ye?"

"Can ye move the chimney over beyant?"

"Faith, I can, but ye will have to move a bit; just go out for a walk with yer brother, and the job will be done when ye come back."

Shamus did as he was bid, and Giblin took the chair the omadhaun was sitting on and moved it away from the fire, and then sat down for a quiet laugh for himself and to consider on the price he'd charge for the job.

When Shamus came back, Giblin led him to the chair, saying:

"Now, isn't that a great deal better?"

"Ye're a fine man, Giblin, and ye did it without making a bit of dirt; what'll I give ye for so fine a job?"

"If ye wouldn't mind, I'd like the meadow field nearing on mine. It's little enough for a job like that."

"It's yours and welcome, Giblin;" and without another word the deed was drawn.

That was the finest of the McAndrew fields, and the only pasture land left to Shamus.

It was not long before it came about that first one and

then another lost the house he lived in, until all had to live together in the father's old place.

O'Toole and Giblin had encroached field by field, and there was nothing left but the old house and a strip of garden that none of them knew how to till.

It was hard times for the seven McAndrews, but they were happy and contented as long as they had enough to eat, and that they had surely, for the wives of the men who got away all their fine lands and cattle, had sore hearts when they saw their men enriched at the expense of the omadhauns, and every day, unbeknown to their husbands, they carried them meat and drink.

O'Toole and Giblin now had their avaricious eyes set on the house and garden, and they were on the watch for a chance to clutch them, when luck, or something worse, threw the chance in the way of O'Toole.

He was returning from town one day just in the cool of the afternoon, when he spied the seven brothers by the roadside, sitting in a circle facing each other.

"What may ye be doing here instead of earning yer salt, ye seven big sturks?"

"We're in a bad fix, Mr. O'Toole," answered Pat. "We can't get up."

"What's to hinder ye from getting up? I'd like to know."

"Don't ye see our feet are all here together in the middle, and not for the life of us can we each tell our own. You see if one of us gets up he don't know what pair of feet to take with him.'

O'Toole was never so ready to laugh before in his life, but he thought:

"Now's me chance to get the house and garden before Giblin, the mason, comes round;" so he looked very grave and said: "I suppose it is hard to tell one man's feet from another's when they're all there in a heap, but I think I can help you as I have many a time before. It would be a sorry day for ye if ye did not have me for a neighbour. What will ye give me if I help you find yer feet?"

"Anything, anything we have, so that we can get up from here," answered the whole seven together.

"Will ye give me the house and garden?"

"Indade we will; what good is a house and garden, if we have to sit here all the rest of our lives?"

"Then it's a bargain," said O'Toole; and with that he went over to the side of the road and pulled a good stout rod. Then he commenced to belabour the poor McAndrews over the heads, feet, shoulders, and any place he could get in a stroke, until with screeches of pain they all jumped up, every one finding his own feet, and away they ran.

So O'Toole got the last of the property of the McAndrews, and there was nothing left for them but to go and beg.

The Farmer of Liddesdale

HERE was in Liddesdale (in Morven) a Farmer who suffered great loss within the space of one year. In the first place, his wife and children died, and shortly after their death the Ploughman left him. The hiring-markets were then over, and there was no way of getting another ploughman in place of the one that left. When spring came his neighbours began ploughing; but he had not a man to hold the plough, and he knew not what he should do. The time was passing, and he was therefore losing patience. At last he said to himself, in a fit of passion, that he would engage the first man that came his way, whoever he should be.

Shortly after that a man came to the house. The Farmer met him at the door, and asked him whither was he going, or what was he seeking? He answered that he was a ploughman, and that he wanted an engagement. "I want a ploughman, and if we agree about the wages, I will engage thee. What dost thou ask from this day to the day when the crop will be gathered in?" "Only as much of the corn when it shall be dry as I can carry with me in one burden-withe." "Thou shalt get that," said the Farmer, and they agreed.

Next morning the Farmer went out with the Ploughman, and showed him the fields which he had to plough. Before they returned, the Ploughman went to the wood, and having cut three stakes, came back with them, and placed one of them at the head of each one of the fields. After he had done that he said to the Farmer, "I will do the work now alone, and the ploughing need no longer give thee anxiety."

Having said this, he went home and remained idle all that day. The next day came, but he remained idle as on the day before. After he had spent a good while in that manner, the Farmer said to him that it was time for him to begin work now, because the spring was passing away, and the neighbours had half their work finished. He replied, "Oh, our land is not ready yet." "How dost thou think that?" "Oh, I know it by the stakes."

If the delay of the Ploughman made the Farmer wonder, this answer made him wonder more. He resolved that he would keep his eye on him, and see what he was doing.

The Farmer rose early next morning, and saw the Ploughman going to the first field. When he reached the field, he pulled the stake at its end out of the ground, and put it to his nose. He shook his head and put the stake back in the ground. He then left the first field and went to the rest. He tried the stakes, shook his head, and returned home. In the dusk he went out the second time to the fields, tried the stakes, shook his head, and after putting them again in the ground, went home. Next morning he went out to the fields the third time. When he reached the first stake he pulled it out of the ground and put it to his nose as he did on the foregoing days. But no sooner had he done that than he threw the stake from him, and stretched away for the houses with all his might.

He got the horses, the withes, and the plough, and when he reached the end of the first field with them, he thrust the plough into the ground, and cried :

"My horses and my leather-traces, and mettlesome lads,
    The earth is coming up !"

He then began ploughing, kept at it all day at a terrible rate, and before the sun went down that night there was not a palm-breadth of the three fields which he had not ploughed, sowed, and harrowed. When the Farmer saw this he was exceedingly well pleased, for he had his work finished as soon as his neighbours.

The Ploughman was quick and ready to do everything that he was told, and so he and the Farmer agreed well until the harvest came. But on a certain day when the reaping was over, the Farmer said to him that he thought the corn was dry enough for putting in. The Ploughman tried a sheaf or two, and answered that it was not dry yet. But shortly after that day he said that it was now ready. "If it is," said the Farmer, "we better begin putting it in." "We will not until I get my share out of it first," said the Ploughman. He then went off to the wood, and in a short time returned, having in his hand a withe scraped and twisted. He stretched the withe on the field, and began to put the corn in it. He continued putting sheaf after sheaf in the withe until he had taken almost all the sheaves that were on the field.   The Farmer asked of him what he meant ?   "Thou didst promise me as wages as much corn as I could carry with me in one burden-withe, and here I have it now," said the Ploughman, as he was shutting the withe.

The Farmer saw that he would be ruined by the Ploughman, and therefore said :

> "'Twas in the Màrt I sowed,
> 'Twas in the Màrt I baked,
> 'Twas in the Màrt I harrowed.
> Thou Who hast ordained the three Màrts,
> Let not my share go in one burden-withe."

Instantly the withe broke, and it made a loud report, which echo answered from every rock far and near.   Then the corn spread over the field, and the Ploughman went away in a white mist in the skies, and was seen no more.

The Greek Princess and the Young Gardener

THERE was once a king, but I didn't hear what country he was over, and he had one very beautiful daughter. Well, he was getting old and sickly, and the doctors found out that the finest medicine in the world for him was the apples of a tree that grew in the orchard just under his window. So you may be sure he had the tree well minded, and used to get the apples counted from the time they were the size of small marbles. One harvest, just as they were beginning to turn ripe, the king was awakened one night by the flapping of wings outside in the orchard ; and when he looked out, what did he see but a bird among the branches of his tree. Its feathers were so bright that they made a light all round them, and the minute it saw the king in his night-cap and night-shirt it picked off an apple, and flew away. "Oh, botheration to that thief of a gardener !" says the king, "this is a nice way he's watching my precious fruit."

He didn't sleep a wink the rest of the night; and as soon as any one was stirring in the palace, he sent for the gardener, and abused him for his neglect.

"Please your Majesty!" says he, "not another apple you shall lose. My three sons are the best shots at the bow and arrow in the kingdom, and they and myself will watch in turn every night."

When the night came, the gardener's eldest son took his post in the garden, with his bow strung and his arrow between his fingers, and watched, and watched. But at the dead hour, the king, that was wide awake, heard the flapping of wings, and ran to the window. There was the bright bird in the tree, and the boy fast asleep, sitting with his back to the wall, and his bow on his lap.

"Rise, you lazy thief!" says the king, "there's the bird again, botheration to her!"

Up jumped the poor fellow; but while he was fumbling with the arrow and the string, away was the bird with the nicest apple on the tree. Well, to be sure, how the king fumed and fretted, and how he abused the gardener and the boy, and what a twenty-four hours he spent till midnight came again!

He had his eye this time on the second son of the gardener; but though he was up and lively enough when the clock began to strike twelve, it wasn't done with the last bang when he saw him stretched like one dead on the long grass, and saw the bright bird again, and heard the flap of her wings, and saw her carry away the third apple. The poor fellow woke with the roar the king let at him, and even was in time enough to let fly an arrow after the bird. He did not hit her, you may depend; and though the king was mad enough, he saw the poor fellows were under *pishtrogues*, and could not help it.

Well, he had some hopes out of the youngest, for he was a brave, active young fellow, that had everybody's good word. There he was ready, and there was the king watching him, and talking to him at the first stroke of twelve. At the last clang, the brightness coming before the bird lighted up the wall and the trees, and the rushing of the wings was heard as it flew into the branches; but at the same instant the crack of the arrow on her side might be heard a quarter of a mile off. Down came the arrow and a large bright feather along with it, and away was the bird, with a screech that was enough to break the drum of your ear. She hadn't time to carry off an apple; and bedad, when the feather was thrown up into the king's room it was heavier than lead, and turned out to be the finest beaten gold.

Well, there was great *cooramuch* made about the youngest boy next day, and he watched night after night for a week, but not a mite of a bird or bird's feather was to be seen, and then the king told him to go home and sleep. Every one admired the beauty of the gold feather beyond anything, but the king was fairly bewitched. He was turning it round and round, and rubbing it against his forehead and his nose the live-long day; and at last he proclaimed that he'd give his daughter and half his kingdom to whoever would bring him the bird with the gold feathers, dead or alive.

The gardener's eldest son had great conceit of himself, and away he went to look for the bird. In the afternoon he sat down under a tree to rest himself, and eat a

bit of bread and cold meat that he had in his wallet, when
up comes as fine a looking fox as you'd see in the burrow
of Munfin. "Musha, sir," says he, "would you spare a
bit of that meat to a poor body that's hungry?"

"Well," says the other, "you must have the divil's own
assurance, you common robber, to ask me such a question.
Here's the answer," and he let fly at the *moddhereen rua.*

The arrow scraped from his side up over his back, as if
he was made of hammered iron, and stuck in a tree a
couple of perches off.

"Foul play," says the fox; "but I respect your young
brother, and will give a bit of advice. At nightfall you'll
come into a village. One side of the street you'll see a
large room lighted up, and filled with young men and
women, dancing and drinking. The other side you'll see a
house with no light, only from the fire in the front room,
and no one near it but a man and his wife, and their child.
Take a fool's advice, and get lodging there." With that he
curled his tail over his crupper, and trotted off.

The boy found things as the fox said, but *begonies* he
chose the dancing and drinking, and there we'll leave him.
In a week's time, when they got tired at home waiting for
him, the second son said he'd try his fortune, and off he set.
He was just as ill-natured and foolish as his brother, and
the same thing happened to him. Well, when a week was
over, away went the youngest of all, and as sure as the
hearth-money, he sat under the same tree, and pulled out
his bread and meat, and the same fox came up and saluted
him. Well, the young fellow shared his dinner with the
moddhereen, and he wasn't long beating about the bush, but
told the other he knew all about his business.

" I'll help you," says he, " if I find you're biddable. So just at nightfall you'll come into a village. . . . . Good-bye till to-morrow."

It was just as the fox said, but the boy took care not to go near dancer, drinker, fiddler, or piper. He got welcome in the quiet house to supper and bed, and was on his journey next morning before the sun was the height of the trees.

He wasn't gone a quarter of a mile when he saw the fox coming out of a wood that was by the roadside.

" Good-morrow, fox," says one.

" Good-morrow, sir," says the other.

" Have you any notion how far you have to travel till you find the golden bird ? "

" Dickens a notion have I ;—how could I ? "

" Well, I have. She's in the King of Spain's palace, and that's a good two hundred miles off."

" Oh, dear ! we'll be a week going."

" No, we won't. Sit down on my tail, and we'll soon make the road short."

" Tail, indeed ! that 'ud be the droll saddle, my poor *moddhereen*."

" Do as I tell you, or I'll leave you to yourself."

Well, rather than vex him he sat down on the tail that was spread out level like a wing, and away they went like thought. They overtook the wind that was before them, and the wind that came after didn't overtake them. In the afternoon, they stopped in a wood near the King of Spain's palace, and there they stayed till nightfall.

" Now," says the fox, " I'll go before you to make the minds of the guards easy, and you'll have nothing to do but go from lighted hall to another lighted hall till you find the golden bird in the last. If you have a head on you, you'll bring himself and his cage outside the door, and no one then can lay hands on him or you. If you haven't a head I can't help you, nor no one else." So he went over to the gates.

In a quarter of an hour the boy followed, and in the first hall he passed he saw a score of armed guards standing upright, but all dead asleep. In the next he saw a dozen, and in the next half a dozen, and in the next three, and in the room beyond that there was no guard at all, nor lamp, nor candle, but it was as bright as day; for there was the golden bird in a common wood and wire cage, and on the table were the three apples turned into solid gold.

On the same table was the most lovely golden cage eye ever beheld, and it entered the boy's head that it would be a thousand pities not to put the precious bird into it, the common cage was so unfit for her. Maybe he thought of the money it was worth; anyhow he made the exchange, and he had soon good reason to be sorry for it. The instant the shoulder of the bird's wing touched the golden wires, he let such a *squawk* out of him as was enough to break all the panes of glass in the windows, and at the same minute the three men, and the half-dozen, and the dozen, and the score men, woke up and clattered their swords and spears, and surrounded the poor boy, and jibed, and cursed, and swore at home, till he didn't know whether it's his foot or head he was standing on. They called the king, and told him what happened, and he put on a very grim face. "It's on a gibbet you ought to be this moment," says he, "but I'll give you a chance of your life, and of the golden bird, too. I lay you under prohibitions, and restrictions, and death, and destruction, to go and bring me the King of *Moroco's* bay filly that outruns the wind, and leaps over the walls of castle-bawns. When you fetch

her into the bawn of this palace, you must get the golden bird, and liberty to go where you please."

Out passed the boy, very down-hearted, but as he went along, who should come out of a brake but the fox again.

"Ah, my friend," says he, "I was right when I suspected you hadn't a head on you; but I won't rub your hair again' the grain. Get on my tail again, and when we come to the King of Morōco's palace, we'll see what we can do."

So away they went like thought. The wind that was before them they would overtake; the wind that was behind them would not overtake them.

Well, the nightfall came on them in a wood near the palace, and says the fox, " I'll go and make things easy for you at the stables, and when you are leading out the filly, don't let her touch the door, nor doorposts, nor anything but the ground, and that with her hoofs; and if you haven't a head on you once you are in the stable, you'll be worse off than before."

So the boy delayed for a quarter of an hour, and then he went into the big bawn of the palace. There were two rows of armed men reaching from the gate to the stable, and every man was in the depth of deep sleep, and through them went the boy till he got into the stable. There was the filly, as handsome a beast as ever stretched leg, and there was one stable-boy with a currycomb in his hand, and another with a bridle, and another with a sieve of oats, and another with an armful of hay, and all as if they were cut out of stone. The filly was the only live thing in the place except himself. She had a common wood and leather saddle on her back, but a golden saddle with the nicest work on it was hung from the post, and he thought it the greatest pity not to put it in place of the other. Well, I believe there was some *pishrogues* over it for a saddle; anyhow, he took off the other, and put the gold one in its place.

Out came a squeal from the filly's throat when she felt the strange article, that might be heard from Tombrick to

Bunclody, and all as ready were the armed men and the
stable-boys to run and surround the *omadhan* of a boy, and
the King of Moróco was soon there along with the rest,
with a face on him as black as the sole of your foot. After
he stood enjoying the abuse the poor boy got from everybody for some time, he says to him, " You deserve high
hanging for your impudence, but I'll give you a chance for
your life and the filly, too.   I lay on you all sorts of prohibitions, and restrictions, and death, and destruction to go
bring me Princess Golden Locks, the King of Greek's
daughter.   When you deliver her into my hand, you may
have the 'daughter of the wind,' and welcome.   Come in
and take your supper and your rest, and be off at the flight
of night."

The poor boy was down in the mouth, you may suppose,
as he was walking away next morning, and very much
ashamed when the fox looked up in his face after coming
out of the wood.

" What a thing it is," says he, " not to have a head when
a body wants it worst ; and here we have a fine long
journey before us to the King of Greek's palace.   The
worse luck now, the same always.   Here, get on my tail,
and we'll be making the road shorter."

So he sat on the fox's tail, and swift as thought they
went.   The wind that was before them they would overtake it, the wind that was behind them would not overtake
them, and in the evening they were eating their bread and
cold meat in the wood near the castle.

" Now," says the fox, when they were done, " I'll go
before you to make things easy.   Follow me in a quarter
of an hour.   Don't let Princess Golden Locks touch the

jambs of the doors with her hands, or hair, or clothes, and if you're asked any favour, mind how you answer. Once she's outside the door, no one can take her from you."

Into the palace walked the boy at the proper time, and there were the score, and the dozen, and the half-dozen, and the three guards all standing up or leaning on their arms, and all dead asleep, and in the farthest room of all was the Princess Golden Locks, as lovely as Venus herself. She was asleep in one chair, and her father, the King of Greek, in another. He stood before her for ever so long with the love sinking deeper into his heart every minute, till at last he went down on one knee, and took her darling white hand in his hand, and kissed it.

When she opened her eyes, she was a little frightened, but I believe not very angry, for the boy, as I call him, was a fine handsome young fellow, and all the respect and love that ever you could think of was in his face. She asked him what he wanted, and he stammered, and blushed, and began his story six times, before she understood it.

"And would you give me up to that ugly black King of Moróco ?" says she.

"I am obliged to do so," says he, "by prohibitions, and restrictions, and death, and destruction, but I'll have his life and free you, or lose my own. If I can't get you for my wife, my days on the earth will be short."

"Well," says she, "let me take leave of my father at any rate."

"Ah, I can't do that," says he, "or they'd all waken, and myself would be put to death, or sent to some task worse than any I got yet."

But she asked leave at any rate to kiss the old man ;

that wouldn't waken him, and then she'd go.   How could
he refuse her, and his heart tied up in every curl of her
hair? But, bedad, the moment her lips touched her father's,
he let a cry, and every one of the score, the dozen guards
woke up, and clashed their arms, and were going to make
gibbets of the foolish boy.

But the king ordered them to hold their hands, till he'd
be *insensed* of what it was all about, and when he heard the
boy's story he gave him a chance for his life.

"There is," says he, "a great heap of clay in front of
the palace, that won't let the sun shine on the walls in the
middle of summer.   Every one that ever worked at it found
two shovelfuls added to it for every one they threw away.
Remove it, and I'll let my daugher go with you.   If you're
the man I suspect you to be, I think she'll be in no danger
of being wife to that yellow *Molott*."

Early next morning was the boy tackled to his work,
and for every shovelful he flung away two came back on
him, and at last he could hardly get out of the heap that
gathered round him.   Well, the poor fellow scrambled out
some way, and sat down on a sod, and he'd have cried
only for the shame of it.   He began at it in ever so many
places, and one was still worse than the other, and in the
heel of the evening, when he was sitting with his head
between his hands, who should be standing before him but
the fox.

"Well, my poor fellow," says he, "you're low enough.
Go in: I won't say anything to add to your trouble.   Take
your supper and your rest: to-morrow will be a new
day."

"How is the work going off?" says the king, when they
were at supper.

" Faith, your Majesty," says the poor boy, " it's not going off, but coming on it is. I suppose you'll have the trouble of digging me out at sunset to-morrow, and waking me."

"I hope not," says the princess, with a smile on her kind face ; and the boy was as happy as anything the rest of the evening.

He was wakened up next morning with voices shouting, and bugles blowing, and drums beating, and such a hulli-bulloo he never heard in his life before. He ran out to see what was the matter, and there, where the heap of clay was the evening before, were soldiers, and servants, and lords, and ladies, dancing like mad for joy that it was gone.

"Ah, my poor fox !" says he to himself, "this is your work."

Well, there was little delay about his return. The king was going to send a great retinue with the princess and himself, but he wouldn't let him take the trouble.

"I have a friend," says he, "that will bring us both to the King of Moróco's palace in a day, d—— fly away with him !"

There was great crying when she was parting from her father.

"Ah !" says he, "what a lonesome life I'll have now ! Your poor brother in the power of that wicked witch, and kept away from us, and now you taken from me in my old age !"

Well, they both were walking on through the wood, and he telling her how much he loved her ; out walked the fox from behind a brake, and in a short time he and she were sitting on the brush, and holding one another fast for fear of slipping off, and away they went like thought. The wind that was before them they would overtake it, and in the evening he and she were in the big bawn of the King of Morōco's castle.

"Well," says he to the boy, "you've done your duty well; bring out the bay filly. I'd give the full of the bawn of such fillies, if I had them, for this handsome princess. Get on your steed, and here is a good purse of guineas for the road."

"Thank you," says he. "I suppose you'll let me shake hands with the princess before I start."

"Yes, indeed, and welcome."

Well, he was some little time about the hand-shaking, and before it was over he had her fixed snug behind him; and while you could count three, he, and she, and the filly were through all the guards, and a hundred perches away. On they went, and next morning they were in the wood near the King of Spain's palace, and there was the fox before them.

"Leave your princess here with me," says he, "and go get the golden bird and the three apples. If you don't bring us back the filly along with the bird, I must carry you both home myself."

Well, when the King of Spain saw the boy and the filly in the bawn, he made the golden bird, and the golden cage, and the golden apples be brought out and handed to him, and was very thankful and very glad of his prize. But the boy could not part with the nice beast without petting it and rubbing it; and while no one was expecting such a thing, he was up on its back, and through the guards, and a hundred perches away, and he wasn't long till he came to where he left his princess and the fox.

They hurried away till they were safe out of the King of Spain's land, and then they went on easier; and if I was to tell you all the loving things they said to one another, the story wouldn't be over till morning. When they were passing the village of the dance house, they found his two brothers begging, and they brought them along. When they came to where the fox appeared first, he begged the young man to cut off his head and his tail. He would not do it for him; he shivered at the very thought, but the eldest brother was ready enough. The head and tail vanished with the blows, and the body changed into the finest young man you could see, and who was he but the princess's brother that was bewitched. Whatever joy they had before, they had twice as much now, and when they arrived at the palace bonfires were set blazing, oxes roasting, and puncheons of wine put out in the lawn.

The young Prince of Greece was married to the king's daughter, and the prince's sister to the gardener's son. He and she went a shorter way back to her father's house, with many attendants, and the king was so glad of the golden bird and the golden apples, that he had sent a waggon full of gold and a waggon full of silver along with them.

The Russet Dog

H, he's a rare clever fellow, is the Russet Dog, the Fox, I suppose you call him. Have you ever heard the way he gets rid of his fleas? He hunts about and he hunts about till he finds a lock of wool: then he takes it in his mouth, and down he goes to the river and turns his tail to the stream, and goes in backwards. And as the water comes up to his haunches the little fleas come forward, and the more he dips into the river the more they come forward, till at last he has got nothing but his snout and the lock of wool above water; then the little fleas rush into his snout and into the lock of wool. Down he dips his nose, and as soon as he feels his nose free of them, he lets go the lock of wool, and so he is free of his fleas. Ah, but that is nothing to the way in which he catches ducks for his dinner. He will gather some heather, and put his head in the midst of it, and then will slip down stream to the place where the ducks are swimming, for all the world like a piece of floating heather. Then he lets go, and—gobble, gobble, gobble, till not a duck is left alive.   And he is as brave as he is clever.   It is said that once he found the bagpipes lying all alone, and being very hungry began to gnaw at them : but as soon as he made a hole in the bag, out came a squeal.   Was the Russet Dog afraid?   Never a bit: all he said was: "Here's music with my dinner."

Now a Russet Dog had noticed for some days a family of wrens, off which he wished to dine.   He might have been satisfied with one, but he was determined to have the whole lot—father and eighteen sons—but all so like that he could not tell one from the other, or the father from the children.

"It is no use to kill one son," he said to himself, "because the old cock will take warning and fly away with the seventeen.   I wish I knew which is the old gentleman."

He set his wits to work to find out, and one day seeing them all threshing in a barn, he sat down to watch them; still he could not be sure.

"Now I have it," he said; "well done the old man's stroke!   He hits true," he cried.

"Oh!" replied the one he suspected of being the head of the family, "if you had seen my grandfather's strokes, you might have said that."

The sly fox pounced on the cock, ate him up in a trice, and then soon caught and disposed of the eighteen sons, all flying in terror about the barn.

For a long time a Tod-hunter had been very anxious to catch our friend the fox, and had stopped all the earths in cold weather. One evening he fell asleep in his hut ; and when he opened his eyes he saw the fox sitting very demurely at the side of the fire. It had entered by the hole under the door provided for the convenience of the dog, the cat, the pig, and the hen.

"Oh! ho!" said the Tod-hunter, "now I have you." And he went and sat down at the hole to prevent Reynard's escape.

"Oh! ho!" said the fox, " I will soon make that stupid

fellow get up." So he found the man's shoes, and putting them into the fire, wondered if that would make the enemy move.

" I shan't get up for that, my fine gentleman," cried the Tod-hunter.

Stockings followed the shoes, coat and trousers shared the same fate, but still the man sat over the hole. At last the fox having set the bed and bedding on fire, put a light to the straw on which his jailer lay, and it blazed up to the ceiling.

"No! that I cannot stand," shouted the man, jumping up; and the fox, taking advantage of the smoke and confusion, made good his exit.

But Master Rory did not always have it his own way. One day he met a cock, and they began talking.

"How many tricks canst thou do?" said the fox.

"Well," said the cock, "I could do three; how many canst thou do thyself?"

"I could do three score and thirteen," said the fox.

"What tricks canst thou do?" said the cock.

"Well," said the fox, "my grandfather used to shut one eye and give a great shout."

"I could do that myself," said the cock.

"Do it," said the fox. And the cock shut one eye and crowed as loud as ever he could, but he shut the eye that was next the fox, and the fox gripped him by the neck and ran away with him. But the wife to whom the cock belonged saw him and cried out, "Let go the cock; he's mine."

"Say, 'Oh sweet-tongued singer, it is my own cock,' wilt thou not?" said the cock to the fox.

Then the fox opened his mouth to say as the cock did, and he dropped the cock, and he sprung up on the top of a house, and shut one eye and gave a loud crow.

But it was through that very fox that Master Wolf lost his tail. Have you never heard about that?

One day the wolf and the fox were out together, and they stole a dish of crowdie. Now in those days the wolf was the biggest beast of the two, and he had a long tail like a greyhound and great teeth.

The fox was afraid of him, and did not dare to say a word when the wolf ate the most of the crowdie, and left only a little at the bottom of the dish for him, but he determined to punish him for it; so the next night when they were out together the fox pointed to the image of the moon in a pool left in the ice, and said:

"I smell a very nice cheese, and there it is, too."

"And how will you get it?" said the wolf.

"Well, stop you here till I see if the farmer is asleep, and if you keep your tail on it, nobody will see you or know that it is there. Keep it steady. I may be some time coming back."

So the wolf lay down and laid his tail on the moonshine

in the ice, and kept it for an hour till it was fast. Then the fox, who had been watching, ran in to the farmer and said: "The wolf is there; he will eat up the children—the wolf! the wolf!"

Then the farmer and his wife came out with sticks to kill the wolf, but the wolf ran off leaving his tail behind him, and that's why the wolf is stumpy-tailed to this day, though the fox has a long brush.

One day shortly after this Master Rory chanced to see a fine cock and fat hen, off which he wished to dine, but at his approach they both jumped up into a tree. He did not lose heart, but soon began to make talk with them, inviting them at last to go a little way with him.

"There was no danger," he said, "nor fear of his hurting them, for there was peace between men and beasts, and among all animals."

At last after much parleying the cock said to the hen, "My dear, do you not see a couple of hounds coming across the field?"

"Yes," said the hen, "and they will soon be here."

"If that is the case, it is time I should be off," said the sly fox, "for I am afraid these stupid hounds may not have heard of the peace."

And with that he took to his heels and never drew breath till he reached his den.

Now Master Rory had not finished with his friend the wolf. So he went round to see him when his stump got better.

"It is lucky you are," he said to the wolf. "How much better you will be able to run now you haven't got all that to carry behind you."

"Away from me, traitor!" said the wolf.

But Master Rory said: "Is it a traitor I am, when all I have come to see you for is to tell you about a keg of butter I have found?"

After much grumbling the wolf agreed to go with Master Rory.

So the Russet Dog and the wild dog, the fox and the wolf, were going together; and they went round about the sea-shore, and they found the keg of butter, and they buried it.

On the morrow the fox went out, and when he returned in he said that a man had come to ask him to a baptism. He arrayed himself in excellent attire, and he went away, and where should he go but to the butter keg; and when he came home the wolf asked him what the child's name was; and he said it was HEAD OFF.

On the morrow he said that a man had sent to ask him to a baptism, and he reached the keg and he took out about half. The wolf asked when he came home what the child's name was.

"Well," said he, "it is a queer name that I myself would not give to my child, if I had him; it is HALF AND HALF."

On the morrow he said that there was a man there came to ask him to a baptism again; off he went and he reached the keg, and he ate it all up. When he came home the wolf asked him what the child's name was, and he said it was ALL GONE.

On the morrow he said to the wolf that they ought to bring the keg home. They went, and when they reached the keg there was not a shadow of the butter in it.

"Well, thou wert surely coming here to watch this, though I was not," quoth the fox.

The other one swore that he had not come near it.

"Thou needst not be swearing that thou didst not come here ; I know that thou didst come, and that it was thou that took it out ; but I will know it from thee when thou goest home, if it was thou that ate the butter," said the fox.

Off they went, and when they got home he hung the wolf by his hind legs, with his head dangling below him, and he had a dab of the butter and he put it under the wolf's mouth, as if it was out of the wolf's belly that it came.

"Thou red thief ! " said he, "I said before that it was thou that ate the butter."

They slept that night, and on the morrow when they rose the fox said :

"Well, then, it is silly for ourselves to be starving to death in this way merely for laziness ; we will go to a town-land, and we will take a piece of land in it."

They reached the town-land, and the man to whom it belonged gave them a piece of land the worth of seven Saxon pounds.

It was oats that they set that year, and they reaped it and they began to divide it.

"Well, then," said the fox, "wouldst thou rather have the root or the tip ? thou shalt have thy choice."

"I'd rather the root," said the wolf.

Then the fox had fine oaten bread all the year, and the other one had fodder.

On the next year they set a crop ; and it was potatoes that they set, and they grew well.

"Which wouldst thou like best, the root or the crop this year?" said the fox.

"Indeed, thou shalt not take the twist out of me any more; I will have the top this year," quoth the wolf.

"Good enough, my hero," said the fox.

Thus the wolf had the potato tops, and the fox the potatoes. But the wolf used to keep stealing the potatoes from the fox.

"Thou hadst best go yonder, and read the name that I have in the hoofs of the grey mare," quoth the fox.

Away went the wolf, and he begun to read the name; and on a time of these times the white mare drew up her leg, and she broke the wolf's head.

"Oh!" said the fox, "it is long since I heard my name. Better to catch geese than to read books."

He went home, and the wolf was not troubling him any more.

But the Russet Dog found his match at last, as I shall tell you.

One day the fox was once going over a loch, and there met him a little bonnach, and the fox asked him where he was going. The little bonnach told him he was going to such a place.

"And whence camest thou?" said the fox.

"I came from Geeogan, and I came from Cooaigean, and I came from the slab of the bonnach stone, and I came from the eye of the quern, and I will come from thee if I may," quoth the little bonnach.

"Well, I myself will take thee over on my back," said the fox.

"Thou'lt eat me, thou'lt eat me," quoth the little bonnach.

"Come then on the tip of my tail," said the fox.

"Oh no! I will not; thou wilt eat me," said the little bonnach.

"Come into my ear," said the fox.

"I will not go; thou wilt eat me," said the little bonnach.

"Come into my mouth," said the fox.

"Thou wilt eat me that way at all events," said the little bonnach.

"Oh no, I will not eat thee," said the fox. "When I am swimming I cannot eat anything at all."

He went into the fox's mouth.

"Oh! ho!" said the fox, "I may do my own pleasure on thee now. It was long ago said that a hard morsel is no good in the mouth."

The fox ate the little bonnach. Then he went to a loch, and he caught hold of a duck that was in it, and he ate that.

He went up to a hillside, and he began to stroke his sides on the hill.

"Oh, king! how finely a bullet would spank upon my rib just now."

Who was listening but a hunter.

"Ill try that upon thee directly," said the hunter.

"Bad luck to this place," quoth the fox, "in which a creature dares not say a word in fun that is not taken in earnest."

The hunter put a bullet in his gun, and he fired at him and killed him, and that was the end of the Russet Dog.

Smallhead and the King's Sons

LONG ago there lived in Erin a woman who married a man of high degree and had one daughter. Soon after the birth of the daughter the husband died.

The woman was not long a widow when she married a second time, and had two daughters. These two daughters hated their half-sister, thought she was not so wise as another, and nick-named her Smallhead. When the elder of the two sisters was fourteen years old their father died. The mother was in great grief then, and began to pine away. She used to sit at home in the corner and never left the house. Smallhead was kind to her mother, and the mother was fonder of her eldest daughter than of the other two, who were ashamed of her.

At last the two sisters made up in their minds to kill their mother. One day, while their half-sister was gone, they put the mother in a pot, boiled her, and threw the bones outside. When Smallhead came home there was no sign of the mother.

"Where is my mother?" asked she of the other two.

"She went out somewhere. How should we know where she is?"

"Oh, wicked girls! you have killed my mother," said Smallhead.

Smallhead wouldn't leave the house now at all, and the sisters were very angry.

"No man will marry either one of us," said they, "if he sees our fool of a sister."

Since they could not drive Smallhead from the house they made up their minds to go away themselves. One fine morning they left home unknown to their half-sister and travelled on many miles. When Smallhead discovered that her sisters were gone she hurried after them and never stopped till she came up with the two. They had to go home with her that day, but they scolded her bitterly.

The two settled then to kill Smallhead, so one day they took twenty needles and scattered them outside in a pile of straw. "We are going to that hill beyond," said they, "to stay till evening, and if you have not all the needles that are in that straw outside gathered and on the tables before us, we'll have your life."

Away they went to the hill. Smallhead sat down, and was crying bitterly when a short grey cat walked in and spoke to her.

"Why do you cry and lament so?" asked the cat.

"My sisters abuse me and beat me," answered Smallhead. " This morning they said they would kill me in the evening unless I had all the needles in the straw outside gathered before them."

" Sit down here," said the cat, " and dry your tears."

The cat soon found the twenty needles and brought them to Smallhead. " Stop there now," said the cat, "and listen to what I tell you. I am your mother ; your sisters killed me and destroyed my body, but don't harm them ; do them good, do the best you can for them, save them : obey my words and it will be better for you in the end."

The cat went away for herself, and the sisters came home in the evening. The needles were on the table before them. Oh, but they were vexed and angry when they saw the twenty needles, and they said some one was helping their sister !

One night when Smallhead was in bed and asleep they started away again, resolved this time never to return. Smallhead slept till morning. When she saw that the sisters were gone she followed, traced them from place to place, inquired here and there day after day, till one evening some person told her that they were in the house of an old hag, a terrible enchantress, who had one son and three daughters : that the house was a bad place to be in, for the old hag had more power of witchcraft than any one and was very wicked.

Smallhead hurried away to save her sisters, and facing the house knocked at the door, and asked lodgings for God's sake.

" Oh, then," said the hag, " it is hard to refuse any one lodgings, and besides on such a wild, stormy night.

I wonder if you are anything to the young ladies who came the way this evening ? "

The two sisters heard this and were angry enough that Smallhead was in it, but they said nothing, not wishing the old hag to know their relationship. After supper the hag told the three strangers to sleep in a room on the right side of the house. When her own daughters were going to bed Smallhead saw her tie a ribbon around the neck of each one of them, and heard her say : " Do you sleep in the left-hand bed." Smallhead hurried and said to her sisters : " Come quickly, or I'll tell the woman who you are."

They took the bed in the left-hand room and were in it before the hag's daughters came.

" Oh," said the daughers, "the other bed is as good.' So they took the bed in the right-hand room. When Smallhead knew that the hag's daughters were asleep she rose, took the ribbons off their necks, and put them on her sister's necks and on her own. She lay awake and watched them. After a while she heard the hag say to her son :

" Go, now, and kill the three girls ; they have the clothes and money."

" You have killed enough in your life and so let these go," said the son.

But the old woman would not listen. The boy rose up, fearing his mother, and taking a long knife, went to the right-hand room and cut the throats of the three girls without ribbons. He went to bed then for himself, and when Smallhead found that the old hag was asleep she roused her sisters, told what had happened, made them dress quickly and follow her. Believe me, they were willing and glad to follow her this time.

The three travelled briskly and came soon to a bridge, called at that time "The Bridge of Blood." Whoever had killed a person could not cross the bridge. When the three girls came to the bridge the two sisters stopped: they could not go a step further. Smallhead ran across and went back again.

"If I did not know that you killed our mother," said she, "I might know it now, for this is the Bridge of Blood."

She carried one sister over the bridge on her back and then the other. Hardly was this done when the hag was at the bridge.

"Bad luck to you, Smallhead!" said she, "I did not know that it was you that was in it last evening. You have killed my three daughters."

"It wasn't I that killed them, but yourself," said Smallhead.

The old hag could not cross the bridge, so she began to curse, and she put every curse · on Smallhead that she could remember. The sisters travelled on till they came to a King's castle. They heard that two servants were needed in the castle.

"Go now," said Smallhead to the two sisters, "and ask for service. Be faithful and do well. You can never go back by the road you came."

The two found employment at the King's castle. Smallhead took lodgings in the house of a blacksmith near by.

"I should be glad to find a place as kitchen-maid in the castle," said Smallhead to the blacksmith's wife.

"I will go to the castle and find a place for you if I can," said the woman.

The blacksmith's wife found a place for Smallhead as kitchen-maid in the castle, and she went there next day.

"I must be careful," thought Smallhead, "and do my best. I am in a strange place. My two sisters are here in the King's castle. Who knows, we may have great fortune yet."

She dressed neatly and was cheerful. Every one liked her, liked her better than her sisters, though they were beautiful. The King had two sons, one at home and the other abroad. Smallhead thought to herself one day: "It is time for the son who is here in the castle to marry. I will speak to him the first time I can." One day she saw him alone in the garden, went up to him, and said:

"Why are you not getting married, it is high time for you?"

He only laughed and thought she was too bold, but then thinking that she was a simple-minded girl who wished to be pleasant, he said:

"I will tell you the reason: My grandfather bound my father by an oath never to let his oldest son marry until he could get the Sword of Light, and I am afraid that I shall be long without marrying."

"Do you know where the Sword of Light is, or who has it?" asked Smallhead.

"I do," said the King's son, "an old hag who has great power and enchantment, and she lives a long distance from this, beyond the Bridge of Blood. I cannot go there myself, I cannot cross the bridge, for I have killed men in battle. Even if I could cross the bridge I would not go, for many is the King's son that hag has destroyed or enchanted."

"Suppose some person were to bring the Sword of Light, and that person a woman, would you marry her?"

"I would, indeed," said the King's son.

"If you promise to marry my elder sister I will strive to bring the Sword of Light."

"I will promise most willingly," said the King's son.

Next morning early, Smallhead set out on her journey. Calling at the first shop she bought a stone weight of salt, and went on her way, never stopping or resting till she reached the hag's house at nightfall. She climbed to the gable, looked down, and saw the son making a great pot of stirabout for his mother, and she hurrying him. "I am as hungry as a hawk!" cried she.

Whenever the boy looked away, Smallhead dropped salt down, dropped it when he was not looking, dropped it till she had the whole stone of salt in the stirabout. The old hag waited and waited till at last she cried out: "Bring the stirabout. I am starving! Bring the pot. I will eat from the pot. Give the milk here as well."

The boy brought the stirabout and the milk, the old woman began to eat, but the first taste she got she spat out and screamed: "You put salt in the pot in place of meal!"

"I did not, mother."

"You did, and it's a mean trick that you played on me. Throw this stirabout to the pig outside and go for water to the well in the field."

"I cannot go," said the boy, "the night is too dark; I might fall into the well."

"You must go and bring the water; I cannot live till morning without eating."

"I am as hungry as yourself," said the boy, "but how can I go to the well without a light? I will not go unless you give me a light."

"If I give you the Sword of Light there is no knowing who may follow you; maybe that devil öf a Smallhead is outside."

But sooner than fast till morning the old hag gave the Sword of Light to her son, warning him to take good care of it. He took the Sword of Light and went out. As he saw no one when he came to the well he left the sword on the top of the steps going down to the water, so as to have good light. He had not gone down many steps when Smallhead had the sword, and away she ran over hills, dales, and valleys towards the Bridge of Blood.

The boy shouted and screamed with all his might. Out ran the hag. "Where is the sword?" cried she.

"Some one took it from the step."

Off rushed the hag, following the light, but she didn't come near Smallhead till she was over the bridge.

"Give me the Sword of Light, or bad luck to you," cried the hag.

"Indeed, then, I will not; I will keep it, and bad luck to yourself," answered Smallhead.

On the following morning she walked up to the King's son and said:

"I have the Sword of Light; now will you marry my sister?"

"I will," said he.

The King's son married Smallhead's sister and got the

Sword of Light. Smallhead stayed no longer in the kitchen —the sister didn't care to have her in kitchen or parlour.

The King's second son came home. He was not long in the castle when Smallhead said to herself, "Maybe he will marry my second sister."

She saw him one day in the garden, went toward him ; he said something, she answered, then asked : "Is it not time for you to be getting married like your brother ? "

" When my grandfather was dying," said the young man, " he bound my father not to let his second son marry till he had the Black Book. This book used to shine and give brighter light than ever the Sword of Light did, and I suppose it does yet. The old hag beyond the Bridge of Blood has the book, and no one dares to go near her, for many is the King's son killed or enchanted by that woman."

" Would you marry my second sister if you were to get the Black Book ? "

" I would, indeed ; I would marry any woman if I got the Black Book with her. The Sword of Light and the Black Book were in our family till my grandfather's time, then they were stolen by that cursed old hag."

" I will have the book," said Smallhead, " or die in the trial to get it."

Knowing that stirabout was the main food of the hag, Smallhead settled in her mind to play another trick. Taking a bag she scraped the chimney, gathered about a stone of soot, and took it with her. The night was dark and rainy. When she reached the hag's house, she climbed up the gable to the chimney and found that the son was making stirabout for his mother. She dropped the soot down by degrees till at last the whole stone of soot was in the pot; then she scraped around the top of the chimney till a lump of soot fell on the boy's hand.

"Oh, mother," said he, "the night is wet and soft, the soot is falling."

"Cover the pot," said the hag. "Be quick with that stirabout, I am starving."

The boy took the pot to his mother.

"Bad luck to you," cried the hag the moment she tasted the stirabout, "this is full of soot; throw it out to the pig."

"If I throw it out there is no water inside to make more, and I'll not go in the dark and rain to the well."

"You must go!" screamed she.

"I'll not stir a foot out of this unless I get a light," said the boy.

"Is it the book you are thinking of, you fool, to take it and lose it as you did the sword? Smallhead is watching you."

"How could Smallhead, the creature, be outside all the time? If you have no use for the water you can do without it."

Sooner than stop fasting till morning, the hag gave her son the book, saying: "Do not put this down or let it from your hand till you come in, or I'll have your life."

The boy took the book and went to the well. Smallhead followed him carefully. He took the book down into the well with him, and when he was stooping to dip water she snatched the book and pushed him into the well, where he came very near drowning.

Smallhead was far away when the boy recovered, and

began to scream and shout to his mother. She came in a hurry, and finding that the book was gone, fell into such a rage that she thrust a knife into her son's heart and ran after Smallhead, who had crossed the bridge before the hag could come up with her.

When the old woman saw Smallhead on the other side of the bridge facing her and dancing with delight, she screamed :

"You took the Sword of Light and the Black Book, and your two sisters are married. Oh, then, bad luck to you. I will put my curse on you wherever you go. You have all my children killed, and I a poor, feeble, old woman."

"Bad luck to yourself," said Smallhead. "I am not afraid of a curse from the like of you. If you had lived an honest life you wouldn't be as you are to-day."

"Now, Smallhead," said the old hag, "you have me robbed of everything, and my children destroyed. Your two sisters are well married. Your fortune began with my ruin. Come, now, and take care of me in my old age. I'll take my curse from you, and you will have good luck. I bind myself never to harm a hair of your head."

Smallhead thought awhile, promised to do this, and said : "If you harm me, or try to harm me, it will be the worse for yourself."

The old hag was satisfied and went home. Smallhead went to the castle and was received with great joy. Next morning she found the King's son in the garden, and said : "If you marry my sister to-morrow, you will have the Black Book."

"I will marry her gladly," said the King's son.

Next day the marriage was celebrated and the King's

son got the book. Smallhead remained in the castle about a week, then she left good health with her sisters and went to the hag's house. The old woman was glad to see her and showed the girl her work. All Smallhead had to do was to wait on the hag and feed a large pig that she had.

"I am fatting that pig," said the hag; "he is seven years old now, and the longer you keep a pig the harder his meat is: we'll keep this pig a while longer, and then we'll kill and eat him."

Smallhead did her work; the old hag taught her some things, and Smallhead learned herself far more than the hag dreamt of. The girl fed the pig three times a day, never thinking that he could be anything but a pig. The hag had sent word to a sister that she had in the Eastern World, bidding her come and they would kill the pig and have a great feast. The sister came, and one day when the hag was going to walk with her sister she said to Smallhead:

"Give the pig plenty of meal to-day; this is the last food he'll have; give him his fill."

The pig had his own mind and knew what was coming. He put his nose under the pot and threw it on Smallhead's toes, and she barefoot. With that she ran into the house for a stick, and seeing a rod on the edge of the loft, snatched it and hit the pig.

That moment the pig was a splendid young man.

Smallhead was amazed.

"Never fear," said the young man, "I am the son of a King that the old hag hated, the King of Munster. She stole me from my father seven years ago and enchanted me—made a pig of me."

Smallhead told the King's son, then, how the hag had treated her. "I must make a pig of you again," said she,

"for the hag is coming. Be patient and I'll save you, if you promise to marry me."

"I promise you," said the King's son.

With that she struck him, and he was a pig again. She put the switch in its place and was at her work when the two sisters came. The pig ate his meal now with a good heart, for he felt sure of rescue.

"Who is that girl you have in the house, and where did you find her?" asked the sister.

"All my children died of the plague, and I took this girl to help me. She is a very good servant."

At night the hag slept in one room, her sister in another, and Smallhead in a third. When the two sisters were sleeping soundly Smallhead rose, stole the hag's magic book, and then took the rod. She went next to where the pig was, and with one blow of the rod made a man of him.

With the help of the magic book Smallhead made two doves of herself and the King's son, and they took flight through the air and flew on without stopping. Next morning the hag called Smallhead, but she did not come. She hurried out to see the pig. The pig was gone. She ran to her book. Not a sign of it.

"Oh!" cried she, "that villain of a Smallhead has robbed me. She has stolen my book, made a man of the pig, and taken him away with her."

What could she do but tell her whole story to the sister. "Go you," said she, " and follow them. You have more enchantment than Smallhead has."

"How am I to know them?" asked the sister.

"Bring the first two strange things that you find; they will turn themselves into something wonderful."

The sister then made a hawk of herself and flew away as swiftly as any March wind.

"Look behind," said Smallhead to the King's son some hours later; "see what is coming."

"I see nothing," said he, "but a hawk coming swiftly."

"That is the hag's sister. She has three times more enchantment than the hag herself. But fly down on the ditch and be picking yourself as doves do in rainy weather, and maybe she'll pass without seeing us."

The hawk saw the doves, but thinking them nothing wonderful, flew on till evening, and then went back to her sister.

"Did you see anything wonderful?"

"I did not; I saw only two doves, and they picking themselves."

"You fool, those doves were Smallhead and the King's son. Off with you in the morning and don't let me see you again without the two with you."

Away went the hawk a second time, and swiftly as Smallhead and the King's son flew, the hawk was gaining on them. Seeing this Smallhead and the King's son dropped down into a large village, and, it being market-day, they made two heather brooms of themselves. The two brooms began to sweep the road without any one holding them, and swept toward each other. This was a great wonder. Crowds gathered at once around the two brooms.

The old hag flying over in the form of a hawk saw this and thinking that it must be Smallhead and the King's son were in it, came down, turned into a woman, and said to herself:

"I'll have those two brooms."

She pushed forward so quickly through the crowd that

she came near knocking down a man standing before her. The man was vexed.

"You cursed old hag!" cried he, "do you want to knock us down?" With that he gave her a blow and drove her against another man, that man gave her a push that sent her spinning against a third man, and so on till between them all they came near putting the life out of her, and pushed her away from the brooms. A woman in the crowd called out then:

"It would be nothing but right to knock the head off that old hag, and she trying to push us away from the mercy of God, for it was God who sent the brooms to sweep the road for us."

"True for you," said another woman. With that the people were as angry as angry could be, and were ready to kill the hag. They were going to take the head off the hag when she made a hawk of herself and flew away, vowing never to do another stroke of work for her sister. She might do her own work or let it alone.

When the hawk disappeared the two heather brooms rose and turned into doves. The people felt sure when they saw the doves that the brooms were a blessing from heaven, and it was the old hag that drove them away.

On the following day Smallhead and the King's son saw his father's castle, and the two came down not too far from it in their own forms. Smallhead was a very beautiful woman now, and why not? She had the magic and didn't spare it. She made herself as beautiful as ever she could: the like of her was not to be seen in that kingdom or the next one.

The King's son was in love with her that minute, and

did not wish to part with her, but she would not go with him.

"When you are at your father's castle," said Smallhead, "all will be overjoyed to see you, and the king will give a great feast in your honour. If you kiss any one or let any living thing kiss you, you'll forget me for ever."

"I will not let even my own mother kiss me," said he.

The King's son went to the castle. All were overjoyed; they had thought him dead, had not seen him for seven years. He would let no one come near to kiss him. "I am bound by oath to kiss no one," said he to his mother. At that moment an old grey hound came in, and with one spring was on his shoulder licking his face: all that the King's son had gone through in seven years was forgotten in one moment.

Smallhead went toward a forge near the castle. The smith had a wife far younger than himself, and a step-daughter. They were no beauties. In the rear of the forge was a well and a tree growing over it. "I will go up in that tree," thought Smallhead. "and spend the night in it." She went up and sat just over the well. She was not long in the tree when the moon came out high above the hill tops and shone on the well. The blacksmith's stepdaughter, coming for water, looked down in the well, saw the face of the woman above in the tree, thought it her own face, and cried:

"Oh, then, to have me bringing water to a smith, and I such a beauty. I'll never bring another drop to him." With that she cast the pail in the ditch and ran off to find a king's son to marry.

When she was not coming with the water, and the

blacksmith waiting to wash after his day's work in the forge, he sent the mother. The mother had nothing but a pot to get the water in, so off she went with that, and coming to the well saw the beautiful face in the water.

"Oh, you black, swarthy villain of a smith," cried she, "bad luck to the hour that I met you, and I such a beauty. I'll never draw another drop of water for the life of you!"

She threw the pot down, broke it, and hurried away to find some king's son.

When neither mother nor daughter came back with water the smith himself went to see what was keeping them. He saw the pail in the ditch, and, catching it, went to the well; looking down, he saw the beautiful face of a woman in the water. Being a man, he knew that it was not his own face that was in it, so he looked up, and there in the tree saw a woman. He spoke to her and said:

"I know now why my wife and her daughter did not bring water. They saw your face in the well, and, thinking themselves too good for me, ran away. You must come now and keep the house till I find them."

"I will help you," said Smallhead. She came down, went to the smith's house, and showed the road that the women took. The smith hurried after them, and found the two in a village ten miles away. He explained their own folly to them, and they came home.

The mother and daughter washed fine linen for the castle. Smallhead saw them ironing one day, and said:

"Sit down: I will iron for you."

She caught the iron, and in an hour had the work of the day done.

The women were delighted. In the evening the daughter took the linen to the housekeeper at the castle.

" Who ironed this linen ? " asked the housekeeper.

" My mother and I."

" Indeed, then, you did not. You can't do the like of that work, and tell me who did it."

The girl was in dread now and answered :

" It is a woman who is stopping with us who did the ironing."

The housekeeper went to the Queen and showed her the linen.

" Send that woman to the castle," said the Queen.

Smallhead went : the Queen welcomed her, wondered at her beauty ; put her over all the maids in the castle. Smallhead could do anything ; everybody was fond of her. The King's son never knew that he had seen her before, and she lived in the castle a year ; what the Queen told her she did.

The King had made a match for his son with the daughter of the King of Ulster. There was a great feast in the castle in honour of the young couple, the marriage, was to be a week later. The bride's father brought many of his people who were versed in all kinds of tricks and enchantment.

The King knew that Smallhead could do many things, for neither the Queen nor himself had asked her to do a thing that she did not do in a twinkle.

" Now," said the King to the Queen, " I think she can do something that his people cannot do." He summoned Smallhead and asked :

" Can you amuse the strangers ? "

" I can if you wish me to do so."

When the time came and the Ulster men had shown their best tricks, Smallhead came forward and raised the window, which was forty feet from the ground. She had a small ball of thread in her hand; she tied one end of the thread to the window, threw the ball out and over a wall near the castle; then she passed out the window, walked on the thread and kept time to music from players that no man could see. She came in; all cheered her and were greatly delighted.

"I can do that," said the King of Ulster's daughter, and sprang out on the string; but if she did she fell and broke her neck on the stones below. There were cries, there was lamentation, and, in place of a marriage, a funeral.

The King's son was angry and grieved and wanted to drive Smallhead from the castle in some way.

"She is not to blame," said the King of Munster, who did nothing but praise her.

Another year passed: the King got the daughter of the King of Connacht for his son. There was a great feast before the wedding day, and as the Connacht people are full of enchantment and witchcraft, the King of Munster called Smallhead and said:

" Now show the best trick of any."

" I will," said Smallhead.

When the feast was over and the Connacht men had shown their tricks the King of Munster called Smallhead.

She stood before the company, threw two grains of wheat on the floor, and spoke some magic words. There was a hen and a cock there before her of beautiful plumage; she threw a grain of wheat between them; the hen sprang to eat the wheat, the cock gave her a blow of his bill, the hen drew back, looked at him, and said :

"Bad luck to you, you wouldn t do the like of that when I was serving the old hag and you her pig, and I made a man of you and gave you back your own form.

The King's son looked at her and thought, " There must be something in this."

Smallhead threw a second grain. The cock pecked the hen again. "Oh," said the hen, "you would not do that the day the hag's sister was hunting us, and we two doves."

The King's son was still more astonished.

She threw a third grain. The cock struck the hen, and she said, "You would not do that to me the day I made two heather brooms out of you and myself." She threw a fourth grain. The cock pecked the hen a fourth time. "You would not do that the day you promised not to let any living thing kiss you or kiss any one yourself but me—you let the hound kiss you and you forgot me."

The King's son made one bound forward, embraced and kissed Smallhead, and told the King his whole story from beginning to end.

" This is my wife," said he ; " I'll marry no other woman."

" Whose wife will my daughter be ? " asked the King of Connacht.

" Oh, she will be the wife of the man who will marry her," said the King of Munster, "my son gave his word to this woman before he saw your daughter, and he must keep it."

So Smallhead married the King of Munster's son.

The Legend of Knockgrafton.

HERE was once a poor man who lived in the fertile glen of Aherlow, at the foot of the gloomy Galtee mountains, and he had a great hump on his back: he looked just as if his body had been rolled up and placed upon his shoulders; and his head was pressed down with the weight so much that his chin, when he was sitting, used to rest upon his knees for support. The country people were rather shy of meeting him in any lonesome place, for though, poor creature, he was as harmless and as inoffensive as a new-born infant, yet his deformity was so great that he scarcely appeared to be a human creature, and some ill-minded persons had set strange stories about him afloat. He was said to have a great knowledge of herbs and charms; but certain it was that he had a mighty skilful hand in plaiting straw and rushes into

hats and baskets, which was the way he made his liveli-
hood.

Lusmore, for that was the nickname put upon him by
reason of his always wearing a sprig of the fairy cap, or
lusmore (the foxglove), in his little straw hat, would ever
get a higher penny for his plaited work than any one else,
and perhaps that was the reason why some one, out of
envy, had circulated the strange stories about him.   Be
that as it may, it happened that he was returning one
evening from the pretty town of Cahir towards Cappagh,
and as little Lusmore walked very slowly, on account of
the great hump upon his back, it was quite dark when he
came to the old moat of Knockgrafton, which stood on the
right-hand side of his road.   Tired and weary was he, and
noways comfortable in his own mind at thinking how much
farther he had to travel, and that he should be walking all
the night ; so he sat down under the moat to rest himself,
and began looking mournfully enough upon the moon.

Presently there rose a wild strain of unearthly melody
upon the ear of little Lusmore ; he listened, and he thought
that he had never heard such ravishing music before.   It
was like the sound of many voices, each mingling and
blending with the other so strangely that they seemed to
be one, though all singing different strains, and the words
of the song were these—

Da Luan, Da Mort, Da Luan, Da Mort, Da Luan, Da Mort ;

when there would be a moment's pause, and then the round
of melody went on again.

Lusmore listened attentively, scarcely drawing his breath
lest he might lose the slightest note.   He now plainly

perceived that the singing was within the moat; and
though at first it had charmed him so much, he began to
get tired of hearing the same round sung over and over
so often without any change; so availing himself of the

pause when the *Da Luan, Da Mort,* had been sung three
times, he took up the tune, and raised it with the words
augus Da Cadine, and then went on singing with the voices
inside of the moat, *Da Luan, Da Mort,* finishing the melody,
when the pause again came, with *augus Da Cadine.*

The fairies within Knockgrafton, for the song was a fairy
melody, when they heard this addition to the tune, were so
much delighted that, with instant resolve, it was determined

to bring the mortal among them, whose musical skill so far exceeded theirs, and little Lusmore was conveyed into their company with the eddying speed of a whirlwind.

Glorious to behold was the sight that burst upon him as he came down through the moat, twirling round and round, with the lightness of a straw, to the sweetest music that kept time to his motion. The greatest honour was then paid him, for he was put above all the musicians, and he had servants tending upon him, and everything to his heart's content, and a hearty welcome to all ; and, in short, he was made as much of as if he had been the first man in the land.

Presently Lusmore saw a great consultation going forward among the fairies, and, notwithstanding all their civility, he felt very much frightened, until one stepping out from the rest came up to him and said,—

> " Lusmore ! Lusmore !
> Doubt not, nor deplore,
> For the hump which you bore
> On your back is no more ;
> Look down on the floor,
> And view it, Lusmore ! "

When these words were said, poor little Lusmore felt himself so light, and so happy, that he thought he could have bounded at one jump over the moon, like the cow in the history of the cat and the fiddle ; and he saw, with inexpressible pleasure, his hump tumble down upon the ground from his shoulders. He then tried to lift up his head, and he did so with becoming caution, fearing that he might knock it against the ceiling of the grand hall, where he was ; he looked round and round again with greatest wonder and delight upon everything, which appeared more and more beautiful; and, overpowered at beholding such a resplendent scene, his head grew dizzy, and his eyesight became dim. At last he fell into a sound sleep, and when he awoke he found that it was broad daylight, the sun shining brightly, and the birds singing sweetly; and that he was lying just at the foot of the moat of Knockgrafton, with the cows and sheep grazing peacefully round about him. The first thing Lusmore did, after saying his prayers, was to put his hand behind to feel for his hump, but no sign of one was there on his back, and he looked at himself with great pride, for he had now become a well-shaped dapper little fellow, and more than that, found himself in a full suit of new clothes, which he concluded the fairies had made for him.

Towards Cappagh he went, stepping out as lightly, and springing up at every step as if he had been all his life a dancing-master. Not a creature who met Lusmore knew him without his hump, and he had a great work to persuade every one that he was the same man—in truth he was not, so far as outward appearance went.

Of course it was not long before the story of Lusmore's hump got about, and a great wonder was made of it. Through the country, for miles round, it was the talk of every one, high and low.

One morning, as Lusmore was sitting contented enough, at his cabin door, up came an old woman to him, and asked him if he could direct her to Cappagh.

"I need give you no directions, my good woman," said Lusmore, "for this is Cappagh; and whom may you want here?"

"I have come," said the woman, "out of Decie's country,

in the county of Waterford looking after one Lusmore, who, I have heard tell, had his hump taken off by the fairies ; for there is a son of a gossip of mine who has got a hump on him that will be his death ; and maybe if he could use the same charm as Lusmore, the hump may be taken off him. And now I have told you the reason of my coming so far : 'tis to find out about this charm, if I can."

Lusmore, who was ever a good-natured little fellow, told the woman all the particulars, how he had raised the tune for the fairies at Knockgrafton, how his hump had been removed from his shoulders, and how he had got a new suit of clothes into the bargain.

The woman thanked him very much, and then went away quite happy and easy in her own mind. When she came back to her gossip's house, in the county of Waterford, she told her everything that Lusmore had said, and they put the little hump-backed man, who was a peevish and cunning creature from his birth, upon a car, and took him all the way across the country. It was a long journey, but they did not care for that, so the hump was taken from off him ; and they brought him, just at nightfall, and left him under the old moat of Knockgrafton.

Jack Madden, for that was the humpy man's name, had not been sitting there long when he heard the tune going on within the moat much sweeter than before ; for the fairies were singing it the way Lusmore had settled their music for them, and the song was going on ; *Da Luan, Da Mort, Da Luan, Da Mort, Da Luan, Da Mort, augus Da Cadine*, without ever stopping. Jack Madden, who was in a great hurry to get quit of his hump, never thought of waiting until the fairies had done, or watching for a fit opportunity to raise the tune higher again than Lusmore had; so having heard them sing it over seven times without stopping, out he bawls, never minding the time or the humour of the tune, or how he could bring his words in properly, *augus Da Cadine, augus Da Hena*, thinking that if one day was good, two were better; and that if Lusmore had one new suit of clothes given him, he should have two.

No sooner had the words passed his lips than he was taken up and whisked into the moat with prodigious force; and the fairies came crowding round about him with great anger, screeching, and screaming, and roaring out, " Who spoiled our tune? who spoiled our tune ? " and one stepped up to him, above all the rest and said :

> " Jack Madden ! Jack Madden !
> Your words came so bad in
> The tune we felt glad in ;—
> This castle you're had in,
> That your life we may sadden ;
> Here's two humps for Jack Madden ! "

And twenty of the strongest fairies brought Lusmore's hump and put it down upon poor Jack's back, over his own, where it became fixed as firmly as if it was nailed on with twelve-penny nails, by the best carpenter that ever drove one. Out of their castle they then kicked him; and, in the morning, when Jack Madden's mother and her gossip came to look after their little man, they found him half dead, lying at the foot of the moat, with the other hump upon his back. Well to be sure, how they did look at each other! but they were afraid to say anything, lest a hump might be put upon their own shoulders. Home they brought the unlucky Jack Madden with them, as downcast in their hearts and their looks as ever two gossips were ; and what through the weight of his other hump, and the long journey, he died soon after, leaving they say his heavy curse to any one who would go to listen to fairy tunes again.

Elidore.

THE days of Henry Beauclerc of England there was a little lad named Elidore, who was being brought up to be a cleric. Day after day he would trudge from his mother's house, and she was a widow, up to the monks' Scriptorium. There he would learn his A B C, to read it and to write it. But he was a lazy little rogue was this Elidore, and as fast as he learned to write one letter, he forgot another; so it was very little progress he was making. Now when the good monks saw this they remembered the saying of the Book : " Spare the rod and spoil the child," and whenever Elidore forgot a letter they tried to make him remember it with the rod. At first they used it seldom and lightly, but Elidore was not a boy to be driven, and the more they thwacked him the less he learned : so the thwackings became more frequent and more severe, till Elidore could not stand them any longer. So one day when he was twelve years old he upped with him and offed with him into the great forest near St. David's. There for two long days and two long nights he wandered about eating nothing but hips and haws. At last he found himself at the mouth of a cave, at the side of a river, and there he sank down, all tired and exhausted. Suddenly two little pigmies appeared to him and said: "Come with us, and we will lead you

into a land full of games and sports:" so Elidore raised himself and went with these two; at first through an underground passage all in the dark, but soon they came out into a most beautiful country, with rivers and meadows, woods and plains, as pleasant as can be; only this there was curious about it, that the sun never shone and clouds were always over the sky, so that neither sun was seen by day, nor moon and stars at night.

The two little men led Elidore before their king, who asked why and whence he came. Elidore told him, and the king said : " Thou shalt attend on my son," and waved him away. So for a long time Elidore waited on the king's son, and joined in all the games and sports of the little men.

They were little, but they were not dwarfs, for all their limbs were of suitable size one with another. Their hair was fair, and hung upon their shoulders like that of women. They had little horses, about the size of greyhounds ; and did not eat flesh, fowl, or fish, but lived on milk flavoured with saffron. And as they had such curious ways, so they had strange thoughts. No oath took they, but never a lie they spoke. They would jeer and scoff at men for their struggles, lying, and treachery. Yet though they were so good they worshipped none, unless you might say they were worshippers of Truth.

After a time Elidore began to long to see boys and men of his own size, and he begged permission to go and visit his mother. So the King gave him permission : so the little men led him along the passage, and guided him through the forest, till he came near his mother's cottage, and when he entered, was not she rejoiced to see her dear son again ? " Where have you been ? What have you done ? " she cried ; and he had to tell her all that had happened to him. She begged of him to stay with her, but he had promised the King to go back. And soon he returned, after making his mother promise not to tell where he was, or with whom. Henceforth Elidore

lived, partly with the little men, and partly with his mother.
Now one day, when he was with his mother, he told her of
the yellow balls they used in their play, and which she felt
sure must be of gold. So she begged of him that the next
time he came back to her he would bring with him one of
these balls. When the time came for him to go back to
his mother again, he did not wait for the little men to guide
him back, as he now knew the road. But seizing one of
the yellow balls with which he used to play, he rushed home
through the passage. Now as he got near his mother's
house he seemed to hear tiny footsteps behind him, and he
rushed up to the door as quickly as he could. Just as he
reached it his foot slipped, and he fell down, and the ball
rolled out of his hand, just to the feet of his mother. At
that moment two little men rushed forward, seized the
ball and ran away, making faces, and spitting at the boy as
they passed him. Elidore remained with his mother for a
time ; but he missed the play and games of the little men,
and determined to go back to them. But when he came to
where the cave had been, near the river where the underground passage commenced, he could not find it again, and
though he searched again and again in the years to come,
he could not get back to that fair country. So after a time
he went back to the monastery, and became in due course a
monk. And men used to come and seek him out, and ask
him what had happened to him when he was in the Land of
the Little Men. Nor could he ever speak of that happy
time without shedding tears.

Now it happened once, when this Elidore was old, that
David, Bishop of St. David's, came to visit his monastery
and ask him about the manners and customs of the little

men, and above all, he was curious to know what language they spoke ; and Elidore told him some of their words. When they asked for water, they would say : *Udor udorum* ; and when they wanted salt, they would say : *Hapru udorum*. And from this, the Bishop, who was a learned man, discovered that they spoke some sort of Greek. For *Udor* is Greek for *Water*, and *Hap* for *Salt*.

Hence we know that the Britons came from Troy, being descendants from Brito, son of Priam, King of Troy.

The Leeching of Kayn's Leg.

HERE were five hundred blind men, and five hundred deaf men, and five hundred limping men, and five hundred dumb men, and five hundred cripple men. The five hundred deaf men had five hundred wives, and the five hundred limping men had five hundred wives, and the five hundred dumb men had five hundred wives, and the five hundred cripple men had five hundred wives. Each five hundred of these had five hundred children and five hundred dogs. They were in the habit of going about in one band, and were called the Sturdy Strolling Beggarly Brotherhood. There was a knight in Erin called O'Cronicert, with whom they spent a day and a year; and they ate up all that he had, and made a poor man of him, till he had nothing left but an old tumble-down black house, and an old lame white horse. There was a king in Erin called Brian Boru; and O'Cronicert went to him for help. He cut a cudgel of grey oak on the outskirts of the wood, mounted the old lame white horse, and set off at speed through wood and over moss and

rugged ground, till he reached the king's house. When he arrived he went on his knees to the king ; and the king said to him, " What is your news, O'Cronicert ? "

" I have but poor news for you, king."

" What poor news have you ? " said the king.

" That I have had the Sturdy Strolling Beggarly Brotherhood for a day and a year, and they have eaten all that I had, and made a poor man of me," said he.

" Well ! " said the king, " I am sorry for you ; what do you want ? "

" I want help," said O'Cronicert ; " anything that you may be willing to give me."

The king promised him a hundred cows. He went to the queen, and made his complaint to her, and she gave him another hundred. He went to the king's son, Murdoch Mac Brian, and he got another hundred from him. He got food and drink at the king's ; and when he was going away he said, " Now I am very much obliged to you. This will set me very well on my feet. After all that I have got there is another thing that I want."

" What is it ? " said the king.

" It is the lap-dog that is in and out after the queen that I wish for."

" Ha ! " said the king, " it is your mightiness and pride that has caused the loss of your means ; but if you become a good man you shall get this along with the rest."

O'Cronicert bade the king good-bye, took the lap-dog, leapt on the back of the old lame white horse, and went off at speed through wood, and over moss and rugged ground. After he had gone some distance through the wood a roebuck leapt up and the lap-dog went after it. In a moment the deer started up as a woman behind O'Cronicert, the handsomest that eye had ever seen from the beginning of the universe till the end of eternity. She said to him, "Call your dog off me."

"I will do so if you promise to marry me," said O'Cronicert.

"If you keep three vows that I shall lay upon you I will marry you," said she.

"What vows are they?" said he.

"The first is that you do not go to ask your worldly king to a feast or a dinner without first letting me know," said she.

"Hoch!" said O'Cronicert, "do you think that I cannot keep that vow? I would never go to invite my worldly king without informing you that I was going to do so. It is easy to keep that vow."

"You are likely to keep it!" said she.

"The second vow is," said she, "that you do not cast up to me in any company or meeting in which we shall be together, that you found me in the form of a deer."

"Hoo!" said O'Cronicert, "you need not to lay that vow upon me. I would keep it at any rate."

"You are likely to keep it!" said she.

"The third vow is," said she, "that you do not leave me in the company of only one man while you go out." It was agreed between them that she should marry him.

They reached the old tumble-down black house. Grass they cut in the clefts and ledges of the rocks; a bed they made and laid down. O'Cronicert's wakening from sleep was the lowing of cattle and the bleating of sheep and the neighing of mares, while he himself was in a bed of gold on wheels of silver, going from end to end of the Tower of Castle Town.

" I am sure that you are surprised," said she.

" I am indeed," said he.

" You are in your own room," said she.

" In my own room," said he. " I never had such a room."

" I know well that you never had," said she ; " but you have it now. So long as you keep me you shall keep the room."

He then rose, and put on his clothes, and went out. He took a look at the house when he went out ; and it was a palace, the like of which he had never seen, and the king himself did not possess. He then took a walk round the farm ; and he never saw so many cattle, sheep, and horses as were on it. He returned to the house, and said to his wife that the farm was being ruined by other people's cattle and sheep. " It is not," said she : " your own cattle and sheep are on it."

" I never had so many cattle and sheep," said he.

" I know that," said she ; " but so long as you keep me you shall keep them. There is no good wife whose tocher does not follow her."

He was now in good circumstances, indeed wealthy. He had gold and silver, as well as cattle and sheep. He went about with his gun and dogs hunting every day, and was a great man. It occurred to him one day that he would go to invite the King of Erin to dinner, but he did not tell his wife that he was going. His first vow was now broken. He sped away to the King of Erin, and invited him and his great court to dinner. The King of Erin said to him,

"Do you intend to take away the cattle that 1 promised you?"

"Oh! no, King of Erin,' said O'Cronicert; "I could give you as many to-day."

"Ah!" said the king, "how well you have got on since I saw you last!"

"I have indeed," said O'Cronicert! "I have fallen in with a rich wife who has plenty of gold and silver, and of cattle and sheep."

"I am glad of that," said the King of Erin.

O'Cronicert said, "I shall feel much obliged if you will go with me to dinner, yourself and your great court."

"We will do so willingly," said the king.

They went with him on that same day. It did not occur to O'Cronicert how a dinner could be prepared for the king without his wife knowing that he was coming. When they were going on, and had reached the place where O'Cronicert had met the deer, he remembered that his vow was broken, and he said to the king, "Excuse me; I am going on before to the house to tell that you are coming."

The king said, "We will send off one of the lads."

"You will not," said O'Cronicert; "no lad will serve the purpose so well as myself."

He set off to the house; and when he arrived his wife was diligently preparing dinner. He told her what he had done, and asked her pardon. "I pardon you this time," said she: "I know what you have done as well as you do yourself. The first of your vows is broken."

The king and his great court came to O'Cronicert's house; and the wife had everything ready for them as befitted a king and great people; every kind of drink and food. They spent two or three days and nights at dinner, eating and drinking. They were praising the dinner highly, and O'Cronicert himself was praising it ; but his wife was not. O'Cronicert was angry that she was not praising it and he went and struck her in the mouth with his fist and knocked out two of her teeth. "Why are you not praising the dinner like the others, you contemptible deer ? " said he.

"I am not," said she : "I have seen my father's big dogs having a better dinner than you are giving to-night to the King of Erin and his court."

O'Cronicert got into such a rage that he went outside of the door. He was not long standing there when a man came riding on a black horse, who in passing caught O'Cronicert by the collar of his coat, and took him up behind him : and they set off. The rider did not say a word to O'Cronicert. The horse was going so swiftly that O'Cronicert thought the wind would drive his head off. They arrived at a big, big palace, and came off the black horse. A stableman came out, and caught the horse, and took it in. It was with wine that he was cleaning the horse's feet. The rider of the black horse said to O'Cronicert, "Taste the wine to see if it is better than the wine that you are giving to Brian Boru and his court to-night."

O'Cronicert tasted the wine, and said, "This is better wine."

The rider of the black horse said, "How unjust was the fist a little ago ! The wind from your fist carried the two teeth to me."

He then took him into that big, handsome, and noble house, and into a room that was full of gentlemen eating and drinking, and he seated him at the head of the table, and gave him wine to drink, and said to him, " Taste that wine to see if it is better than the wine that you are giving to the King of Erin and his court to-night."

" This is better wine," said O'Cronicert.

" How unjust was the fist a little ago ! " said the rider of the black horse.

When all was over the rider of the black horse said, " Are you willing to return home now ? "

" Yes," said O'Cronicert, " very willing."

They then rose, and went to the stable : and the black horse was taken out ; and they leaped on its back, and went away.   The rider of the black horse said to O'Cronicert, after they had set off, " Do you know who I am ? "

" I do not," said O'Cronicert.

" I am a brother-in-law of yours," said the rider of the black horse ; and though my sister is married to you there is not a king or knight in Erin who is a match for her. Two of your vows are now broken ; and if you break the other vow you shall lose your wife and all that you possess."

They arrived at O'Cronicert's house ; and O'Cronicert said, " I am ashamed to go in, as they do not know where I have been since night came."

" Hoo ! " said the rider, " they have not missed you at all.   There is so much conviviality among them, that they have not suspected that you have been anywhere.   Here are the two teeth that you knocked out of the front of your wife's mouth.   Put them in their place, and they will be as strong as ever."

" Come in with me," said O'Cronicert to the rider of the black horse.

"I will not : I disdain to go in," said the rider of the black horse.

The rider of the black horse bade O'Cronicert good-bye, and went away.

O'Cronicert went in ; and his wife met him as she was busy waiting on the gentlemen. He asked her pardon, and put the two teeth in the front of her mouth, and they were as strong as ever. She said, "Two of your vows are now broken." No one took notice of him when he went in, or said "Where have you been ? " They spent the night in eating and drinking, and the whole of the next day,

In the evening the king said, " I think that it is time for us to be going ; " and all said that it was. O'Cronicert said, " You will not go to-night. I am going to get up a dance. You will go to-morrow."

" Let them go," said his wife.

" I will not," said he.

The dance was set a–going that night. They were playing away at dancing and music till they became warm and hot with perspiration. They were going out one after another to cool themselves at the side of the house. They all went out except O'Cronicert and his wife, and a man called Kayn Mac Loy. O'Cronicert himself went out, and left his wife and Kayn Mac Loy in the house, and when she saw that he had broken his third vow she gave a spring through a room, and became a big filly, and gave Kayn Mac Loy a kick with her foot, and broke his thigh in two. She gave another spring, and smashed the door and went away, and was seen no more. She took with her the Tower of Castle Town as an armful on her shoulder and a light burden on her back, and she left Kayn Mac Loy in the old tumble-down black house in a pool of rain-drip on the floor.

At daybreak next day poor O'Cronicert could only see the old house that he had before. Neither cattle nor sheep, nor any of the fine things that he had was to be seen. One awoke in the morning beside a bush, another beside a dyke, and another beside a ditch. The king only had the honour of having O'Cronicert's little hut over his head. As they were leaving, Murdoch Mac Brian remembered that he had left his own foster-brother Kayn Mac Loy behind, and said there should be no separation in life between them and that he would go back for him. He found Kayn in the old tumble-down black house, in the middle of the floor, in a pool of rain-water, with his leg broken ; and he said the earth should make a nest in his sole and the sky a nest in his head if he did not find a man to cure Kayn's leg.

They told him that on the Isle of Innisturk was a herb that would heal him.

So Kayn Mac Loy was then borne away, and sent to the island, and he was supplied with as much food as would keep him for a month, and with two crutches on which he would be going out and in as he might desire. At last the food was spent, and he was destitute, and he had not found the herb. He was in the habit of going down to the shore, and gathering shell-fish, and eating it.

As he was one day on the shore, he saw a big, big man landing on the island, and he could see the earth and the sky between his legs. He set off with the crutches to try if he could get into the hut before the big man would come upon him. Despite his efforts, the big man was between him and the door, and said to him, "Unless you deceive me, you are Kayn Mac Loy."

Kayn Mac Loy said, "I have never deceived a man: I am he."

The big man said to him:

"Stretch out your leg, Kayn, till I put a salve of herbs and healing to it. Salve and binding herb and the poultice are cooling; the worm is channering. Pressure and haste hard bind me, for I must hear Mass in the great church at Rome, and be in Norway before I sleep.

Kayn Mac Loy said:

"May it be no foot to Kayn or a foot to any one after one, or I be Kayn son of Loy, if I stretch out my foot for you to put a salve of herbs and healing on it, till you tell me why you have no church of your own in Norway, so as, as now, to be going to the great church of Rome to Rome to-morrow.

Unless you deceive me you are Machkan-an-Athar, the son of the King of Lochlann."

The big man said, "I have never deceived any man: I am he. I am now going to tell you why we have not a church in Lochlann. Seven masons came to build a church, and they and my father were bargaining about the building of it. The agreement that the masons wanted was that my mother and sister would go to see the interior of the church when it would be finished. My father was glad to get the church built so cheaply. They agreed accordingly; and the masons went in the morning to the place where the church was to be built. My father pointed out the spot for the foundation. They began to build in the morning, and the church was finished before the evening. When it was

finished they requested my mother and sister to go to see
its interior.   They had no sooner entered than the doors
were shut ; and the church went away into the skies in the
form of a tuft of mist.

"Stretch out your leg, Kayn, till I put a salve of herbs and
healing to it. Salve and binding herb and the poultice are
cooling; the worm is channering. Pressure and haste hard
bind me, for I must hear Mass in the great church at Rome,
and be in Norway before I sleep.

Kayn Mac Loy said :

"May it be no foot to Kayn or a foot to any one after one,
or I be Kayn son of Loy, if I stretch out my foot for you to
put a salve of herbs and healing on it, till you tell me if you
heard what befell your mother and sister."

"Ah!" said the big man, "the mischief is upon you; that tale is long to tell; but I will tell you a short tale about the matter. On the day on which they were working at the church I was away in the hill hunting game; and when I came home in the evening my brother told me what had happened, namely, that my mother and sister had gone away in the form of a tuft of mist. I became so cross and angry that I resolved to destroy the world till I should find out where my mother and sister were. My brother said to me that I was a fool to think of such a thing. 'I'll tell you,' said he, 'what you'll do. You will first go to try to find out where they are. When you find out where they are you will demand them peaceably, and if you do not get them peaceably you will fight for them.'

"I took my brother's advice, and prepared a ship to set off with. I set off alone, and embraced the ocean. I was overtaken by a great mist, and I came upon an island, and there was a large number of ships at anchor near it; I went in amongst them, and went ashore. I saw there a big, big woman reaping rushes; and when she would raise her head she would throw her right breast over her shoulder and when she would bend it would fall down between her legs. I came once behind her, and caught the breast with my mouth, and said to her, 'You are yourself witness, woman, that I am the foster-son of your right breast.' 'I perceive that, great hero,' said the old woman, 'but my advice to you is to leave this island as fast as you can.' 'Why?' said I. 'There is a big giant in the cave up there,' said she, 'and every one of the ships that you see he has taken in from the ocean with his breath, and he has killed and eaten the men. He is asleep at present, and when he wakens he will have you in a similar manner. A large iron door and an oak door are on the cave. When the giant draws in his breath the doors open, and when he emits his breath the doors shut; and they are shut as fast as though seven small bars, and seven large bars, and seven locks were on them. So fast are they that seven crowbars could not force them open.' I said to the old woman, 'Is there any way of destroying him?' 'I'll tell you,' said she, 'how it can be done. He has a weapon above the door that is called the short spear: and if you succeed in taking off his head with the first blow it will be well; but if you do not, the case will be worse than it was at first.'

"I set off, and reached the cave, the two doors of which opened. The giant's breath drew me into the cave; and stools, chairs, and pots were by its action · dashing against each other, and like to break my legs. The door shut when I went in, and was shut as fast as though seven small bars, and seven large bars, and seven locks were on it; and seven crowbars could not force it open; and I was a prisoner in the cave. The giant drew in his breath again, and the doors opened. I gave a look upwards, and saw the short spear, and laid hold of it. I drew the short spear, and I warrant you that I dealt him such a blow with it as did not require to be repeated; I swept the head off him. I took the head down to the old woman, who was reaping the rushes, and said to her, 'There is the giant's head for you.' The old woman said, 'Brave man! I knew that you were a hero. This island had need of your coming to it to-day. Unless you deceive me, you are Mac Connachar son of the King of Lochlann.' 'I have never deceived a man. I am he,' said I. 'I am a soothsayer,' said she, 'and know the

object of your journey.   You are going in quest of your
mother and sister.'   'Well,' said I, 'I am so far on the
way if I only knew where to go for them.'   'I'll tell you
where they are,' said she ; ' they are in the kingdom of the
Red Shield, and the King of the Red Shield is resolved
to marry your mother, and his son is resolved to marry
your sister.   I'll tell you how the town is situated.   A
canal of seven times seven paces breadth surrounds it.   On
the canal there is a drawbridge, which is guarded during
the day by two creatures that no weapon can pierce, as
they are covered all over with scales, except two spots
below the neck in which their death-wounds lie.   Their
names are Roar and Rustle.   When night comes the bridge
is raised, and the monsters sleep.   A very high and big
wall surrounds the king's palace.'

"Stretch out your leg, Kayn, till I put a salve of herbs and
healing to it. Salve and binding herb and the poultice are
cooling; the worm is channering. Pressure and haste hard
bind me, for I must hear Mass in the great church at Rome,
and be in Norway before I sleep.

Kayn Mac Loy said :

"May it be no foot to Kayn or a foot to any one after one,
or I be Kayn son of Loy, if I stretch out my foot for you to
put a salve of herbs and healing on it, till you tell me if you
went farther in search of your mother and sister, or if you
returned home, or what befell you."

"Ah !" said the big man, "the mischief is upon you ;
that tale is long to tell ; but I will tell you another tale.   I
set off, and reached the big town of the Red Shield ; and it
was surrounded by a canal, as the old woman told me ;

and there was a drawbridge on the canal. It was night when I arrived, and the bridge was raised, and the monsters were asleep. I measured two feet before me and a foot behind me of the ground on which I was standing, and I sprang on the end of my spear and on my tiptoes, and reached the place where the monsters were asleep; and I drew the short spear, and I warrant you that I dealt them such a blow below the neck as did not require to be repeated. I took up the heads and hung them on one of the posts of the bridge. I then went on to the wall that surrounded the king's palace. This wall was so high that it was not easy for me to spring over it; and I set to work with the short spear, and dug a hole through it, and got in. I went to the door of the palace and knocked; and the doorkeeper called out, 'Who is there?' 'It is I,' said I. My mother and sister recognised my speech; and my mother called, 'Oh! it is my son; let him in.' I then got in, and they rose to meet me with great joy. I was supplied with food, drink, and a good bed. In the morning breakfast was set before us; and after it I said to my mother and sister that they had better make ready, and go with me. The King of the Red Shield said, 'It shall not be so. I am resolved to marry your mother, and my son is resolved to marry your sister.' 'If you wish to marry my mother, and if your son wishes to marry my sister, let both of you accompany me to my home, and you shall get them there.' The King of the Red Shield said, 'So be it.'

" We then set off, and came to where my ship was, went on board of it, and sailed home. When we were passing a place where a great battle was going on, I asked the King of the Red Shield what battle it was, and the cause of it.

' Don't you know at all ? " said the King of the Red Shield.
' I do not,' said I. The King of the Red Shield said,
' That is the battle for the daughter of the King of the Great
Universe, the most beautiful woman in the world ; and who-
ever wins her by his heroism shall get her in marriage.

Do you see yonder castle ? '   ' I do,' said I.   ' She is on
the top of that castle, and sees from it the hero that wins
her,' said the King of the Red Shield.   I requested to be
put on shore, that I might win her by my swiftness and
strength.   They put me on shore ; and I got a sight of

her on the top of the castle. Having measured two feet behind me and a foot before me, I sprang on the end of my spear and on my tiptoes, and reached the top of the castle ; and I caught the daughter of the King of the Universe in my arms and flung her over the castle. I was with her and intercepted her before she reached the ground, and I took her away on my shoulder, and set off to the shore as fast as I could, and delivered her to the King of the Red Shield to be put on board the ship. Am I not the best warrior that ever sought you ? said I. 'You can jump well' said she, 'but I have not seen any of your prowess. I turned back to meet the warriors, and attacked them with the short spear, and did not leave a head on a neck of any of them. I then returned, and called to the King of the Red Shield to come in to the shore for me. Pretending not to hear me, he set the sails in order to return home with the daughter of the King of the Great Universe, and marry her. I measured two feet behind me and a foot before me, and sprang on the end of my spear and on my tiptoes and got on board the ship. I then said to the King of the Red Shield, 'What were you going to do ? Why did you not wait for me ?' 'Oh !' said the king, 'I was only making the ship ready and setting the sails to her before going on shore for you. Do you know what I am thinking of ?' 'I do not,' said I. 'It is,' said the King, 'that I will return home with the daughter of the King of the Great Universe, and that you shall go home with your mother and sister.' 'That is not to be the way of it,' said I. 'She whom I have won by my prowess neither you nor any other shall get.'

" The king had a red shield, and if he should get it on,

no weapon could make an impression on him. He began to put on the red shield, and I struck him with the short spear in the middle of his body, and cut him in two, and threw him overboard. I then struck the son, and swept his head off, and threw him overboard.

"Stretch out your leg, Kayn, till I put a salve of herbs and healing to it. Salve and binding herb and the poultice are cooling; the worm is channering. Pressure and haste hard bind me, for I must hear Mass in the great church at Rome, and be in Norway before I sleep.

Kayn Mac Loy said:

"May it be no foot to Kayn or a foot to any one after one, or I be Kayn son of Loy, if I stretch out my foot for you to put a salve of herbs and healing on it, till you tell me whether any search was made for the daughter of the King of the Universe.

"Ah! the mischief is upon you," said the big man; "I will tell you another short tale. I came home with my mother and sister, and the daughter of the King of the Universe, and I married the daughter of the King of the Universe. The first son I had I named Machkan-na-skaya-jayrika (son of the red shield). Not long after this a hostile force came to enforce compensation for the King of the Red Shield, and a hostile force came from the King of the Universe to enforce compensation for the daughter of the King of the Universe. I took the daughter of the King of the Universe with me on the one shoulder and Machkan-na-skaya-jayrika on the other, and I went on board the ship and set the sails to her, and I placed the ensign of the King of the Great Universe on the one mast, and that of the King of the Red Shield on the other, and I blew a trumpet, and passed through the midst of them, and I said to them that here was the man, and that if they were going to enforce their claims, this was the time. All the ships that were there chased me ; and we set out on the expanse of ocean. My ship would be equalled in speed by but few. One day a thick dark mist came on, and they lost sight of me. It happened that I came to an island called The Wet Mantle. I built a hut there ; and another son was born to me, and I called him Son of the Wet Mantle.

" I was a long time in that island ; but there was enough of fruit, fish, and birds in it. My two sons had grown to be somewhat big. As I was one day out killing birds, I saw a big, big man coming towards the island, and I ran to try if I could get into the house before him. He met me, and caught me, and put me into a bog up to the armpits, and he went into the house, and took out on his shoulder the daughter of the King of the Universe, and passed close to me in order to irritate me the more. The saddest look that I ever gave or ever shall give was that I gave when I saw the daughter of the King of the Universe on the shoulder of another, and could not take her from him. The boys came out where I was ; and I bade them bring me the short spear from the house. They dragged the short spear after them, and brought it to me ; and I cut the ground around me with it till I got out.

" I was a long time in the Wet Mantle, even till my two sons grew to be big lads. They asked me one day if I had any thought of going to seek their mother. I told them that I was waiting till they were stronger, and that they

should then go with me.   They said that they were ready
to go with me at any time.   I said to them that we had
better get the ship ready, and go.   They said, ' Let each of
us have a ship to himself.'   We arranged accordingly ; and
each went his own way.

" As I happened one day to be passing close to land I
saw a great battle going on.   Being under vows never to
pass a battle without helping the weaker side, I went on
shore, and set to work with the weaker side, and I knocked
the head off every one with the short spear.   Being tired,
I lay myself down among the bodies and fell asleep.

"Stretch out your leg, Kayn, till I put a salve of herbs and
healing to it. Salve and binding herb and the poultice are
cooling; the worm is channering. Pressure and haste hard
bind me, for I must hear Mass in the great church at Rome,
and be in Norway before I sleep."

Kayn Mac Loy said :

"May it be no foot to Kayn or a foot to any one after one,
or I be Kayn son of Loy, if I stretch out my foot for you to
put a salve of herbs and healing on it, till you tell me if you
found the daughter of the King of the Universe, or if you
went home, or what happened to you."

" The mischief is upon you," said the big man ; that tale
is long to tell, but I will tell another short tale.   When I
awoke out of sleep I saw a ship making for the place where
I was lying, and a big giant with only one eye dragging it
after him : and the ocean reached no higher than his knees.
He had a big fishing-rod with a big strong line hanging
from it on which was a very big hook.   He was throwing
the line ashore, and fixing the hook in a body, and lifting

it on board, and he continued this work till the ship was loaded with bodies. He fixed the hook once in my clothes; but I was so heavy that the rod could not carry me on board. He had to go on shore himself, and carry me on board in his arms. I was then in a worse plight than I ever was in. The giant set off with the ship, which he

dragged after him, and reached a big, precipitous rock, in the face of which he had a large cave : and a damsel as beautiful as I ever saw came out, and stood in the door of the cave. He was handing the bodies to her, and she was taking hold of them and putting them into the cave. As she took hold of each body she said, ' Are you alive ? ' At last the giant took hold of me, and handed me in to her, and said, ' Keep him apart ; he is a large body, and I will have him to breakfast the first day that I go from home.'

My best time was not when I heard the giant's sentence upon me. When he had eaten enough of the bodies, his dinner and supper, he lay down to sleep. When he began to snore the damsel came to speak to me; and she told me that she was a king's daughter the giant had stolen away and that she had no way of getting away from him. 'I am now,' she said, 'seven years except two days with him, and there is a drawn sword between us. He dared not come nearer me than that till the seven years should expire.' I said to her, 'Is there no way of killing him?' 'It is not easy to kill him, but we will devise an expedient for killing him,' said she. 'Look at that pointed bar that he uses for roasting the bodies. At dead of night gather the embers of the fire together, and put the bar in the fire till it be red. Go, then, and thrust it into his eye with all your strength, and take care that he does not get hold of you, for if he does he will mince you as small as midges.' I then went and gathered the embers together, and put the bar in the fire, and made it red, and thrust it into his eye; and from the cry that he gave I thought that the rock had split. The giant sprang to his feet and chased me through the cave in order to catch me; and I picked up a stone that lay on the floor of the cave, and pitched it into the sea; and it made a plumping noise. The bar was sticking in his eye all the time. Thinking it was I that had sprung into the sea, he rushed to the mouth of the cave, and the bar struck against the door-post of the cave, and knocked off his brain-cap. The giant fell down cold and dead, and the damsel and I were seven years and seven days throwing him into the sea in pieces.

"I wedded the damsel, and a boy was born to us. After seven years I started forth again.

"I gave her a gold ring, with my name on it, for the boy, and when he was old enough he was sent out to seek me.

"I then set off to the place where I fought the battle, and found the short spear where I left it; and I was very pleased that I found it, and that the ship was safe. I sailed a day's distance from that place, and entered a pretty bay that was there, hauled my ship up above the shore, and erected a hut there, in which I slept at night. When I rose next day I saw a ship making straight for the place where I was. When it struck the ground, a big, strong champion came out of it, and hauled it up; and if it did not surpass my ship it was not a whit inferior to it; and I said to him, 'What impertinent fellow are you that has dared to haul up your ship alongside of my ship?' 'I am Machkan-na-skaya-jayrika,' said the champion, 'going to seek the daughter of the King of the Universe for Mac Connachar, son of the King of Lochlann.' I saluted and welcomed him, and said to him, 'I am your father: it is well that you have come.' We passed the night cheerily in the hut.

"When I arose on the following day I saw another ship making straight for the place where I was; and a big, strong hero came out of it, and hauled it up alongside of our ships; and if it did not surpass them it was not a whit inferior to them. 'What impertinent fellow are you that has dared to haul up your ship alongside of our ships?' said I. 'I am,' said he, 'the Son of the Wet Mantle, going to seek the daughter of the King of the Universe for Mac Connachar, son of the King of Lochlann.' 'I am your father, and this is your brother : it is well that you have come,' said I. We passed the night together in the hut, my two sons and I.

"When I rose next day I saw another ship coming, and making straight for the place where I was. A big, strong champion sprang out of it, and hauled it up alongside of our ships ; and if it was not higher than they, it was not lower. I went down where he was, and said to him, 'What impertinent fellow are you that has dared to haul up your ship alongside of our ships ?' 'I am the Son of the Wet Mantle,' said he, 'going to seek the daughter of the King of the Universe for Mac Connachar, son of the King of Lochlann. 'Have you any token in proof of that ?' said I. 'I have,' said he : 'here is a ring that my mother gave me at my father's request.' I took hold of the ring, and saw my name on it : and the matter was beyond doubt. I said to him, 'I am your father, and here are two half-brothers of yours. We are now stronger for going in quest of the daughter of the King of the Universe. Four piles are stronger than three piles.' We spent that night cheerily and comfortably together in the hut.

"On the morrow we met a soothsayer, and he spoke to us : 'You are going in quest of the daughter of the King of the Universe. I will tell you where she is : she is with the Son of the Blackbird.

"Machkan-na-skaya-jayrika then went and called for combat with a hundred fully trained heroes, or the sending out to him of the daughter of the King of the Universe. The hundred went out ; and he and they began on each other, and he killed every one of them. The Son of the Wet Mantle called for combat with another hundred, or the sending out of the daughter of the King of the Universe. He killed that hundred with the short spear.   The Son of Secret called for combat with another hundred, or the daughter of the King of the Universe.   He killed every one of these with the short spear.   I then went out to the field, and sounded a challenge on the shield, and made the town tremble.   The Son of the Blackbird had not a man to send out : he had to come out himself ; and he and I began on each other, and I drew the short spear, and swept his head off.   I then went into the castle, and took out the daughter of the King of the Universe.   It was thus that it fared with me.

"Stretch out your leg, Kayn, till I put a salve of herbs and healing to it.   Salve and binding herb and the poultice are cooling ; the worm is channering.   Pressure and haste hard bind me, for I must hear Mass in the great church at Rome, and be in Norway before I sleep."

Kayn Mac Loy stretched his leg ; and the big man applied to it leaves of herbs and healing ; and it was healed.   The big man took him ashore from the island, and allowed him to go home to the king.

Thus did O'Cronicert win and lose a wife, and thus befell the Leeching of the leg of Kayn, son of Loy.

How Fin went to the Kingdom of the Big Men.

FIN and his men were in the Harbour of the Hill of Howth on a hillock, behind the wind and in front of the sun, where they could see every person, and nobody could see them, when they saw a speck coming from the west. They thought at first it was the blackness of a shower; but when it came nearer, they saw it was a boat. It did not lower sail till it entered the harbour. There were three men in it; one for guide in the bow, one for steering in the stern, and one for the tackle in the centre. They came ashore, and drew it up seven times its own length in dry grey grass, where the scholars of the city could not make it stock for derision or ridicule.

They then went up to a lovely green spot, and the first lifted a handful of round pebbles or shingle, and commanded them to become a beautiful house, that no better could be found in Ireland; and this was done. The second one lifted a slab of slate, and commanded it to be slate on the top of the house, that there was not better in Ireland ; and this was done.   The third one caught a bunch of shavings and commanded them to be pine-wood and timber in the house, that there was not in Ireland better ; and this was done.

This caused much wonder to Fin, who went down where the men were, and made inquiries of them, and they answered him.   He asked whence they were, or whither they were going.   They said, "We are three Heroes whom the King of the Big Men has sent to ask combat of the Fians."   He then asked, "What was the reason for doing this ? "   They said they did not know, but they heard that they were strong men, and they came to ask combat of Heroes from them.   "Is Fin at Home ? "   "He is not."   (Great is a man's leaning towards his own life).   Fin then put them under crosses and under enchantments, that they were not to move from the place where they were till they saw him again.

He went away and made ready his coracle, gave its stern to land and prow to sea, hoisted the spotted towering sails against the long, tough, lance-shaped mast, cleaving the billows in the embrace of the wind in whirls, with a soft gentle breeze from the height of the sea-coast, and from the rapid tide of the red rocks, that would take willom from the hill, foliage from the tree, and heather from its stock and roots.   Fin was guide in her prow, helm in her stern, and tackle in her middle ; and stopping of head or foot he did not make till he reached the Kingdom of the Big Men.   He went ashore and drew up his coracle in grey grass.   He went up, and a Big Wayfarer met him.   Fin asked who he was.   "I am," he said, "the Red-haired Coward of the King of the Big Men ; and," said he to Fin, "you are the one I am in quest of. Great is my esteem and respect towards you ; you are the best maiden I have ever seen ; you will yourself make a dwarf for the King, and your dog (this was Bran) a lapdog. It is long since the King has been in want of a dwarf and a lapdog." He took with him Fin ; but another Big Man came, and was going to take Fin from him. The two fought ; but when they had torn each other's clothes, they left it to Fin to judge. He chose the first one. He took Fin with him to the palace of the King, whose worthies and high nobles assembled to see the little man. The king lifted him upon the palm of his hand, and went three times round the town with Fin upon one palm and Bran upon the other. He made a sleeping-place for him at the end of his own bed. Fin was waiting, watching, and observing everything that was going on about the house. He observed that the King, as soon as night came, rose and went out, and returned no more till morning. This caused him much wonder, and at last he asked the King why he went away every night and left the Queen by herself. " Why," said the King, " do you ask ? " " For satisfaction to myself," said Fin ; " for it is causing me much wonder." Now the King had a great liking for Fin ; he never saw anything that gave him more pleasure than he did ; and at last he told him. " There is," he said, " a great Monster who wants my daughter in marriage, and to have half my kingdom to himself ; and there is not another man in the kingdom who can meet him but myself ; and I must go every night to hold combat with him." " Is there," said Fin, " no man to combat with him but yourself ? " " There is not," said the King, " one who will war with him for a single night." " It is a pity,"

said Fin, " that this should be called the Kingdom of the
Big Men. Is he bigger than yourself ? " " Never you
mind," said the King. " I will mind," said Fin ; " take
your rest and sleep to-night, and I shall go to meet him."
" Is it you ? " said the King ; " you would not keep half a
stroke against him."

When night came, and all men went to rest, the King
was for going away as usual ; but Fin at last prevailed
upon him to allow himself to go. " I shall combat him,"
said he, " or else he knows a trick." " I think much,"
said the King, " of allowing you to go, seeing he gives myself enough to do." " Sleep you soundly to-night," said
Fin, " and let me go ; if he comes too violently upon me, I
shall hasten home."

Fin went and reached the place where the combat was
to be. He saw no one before him, and he began to pace
backwards and forwards. At last he saw the sea coming
in kilns of fire and as a darting serpent, till it came down
below where he was. A Huge Monster came up and looked
towards him, and from him. " What little speck do I see
there ? " he said. " It is I," said Fin. " What are you
doing here ? " " I am a messenger from the King of the
Big Men ; he is under much sorrow and distress ; the
Queen has just died, and I have come to ask if you
will be so good as to go home to-night without giving
trouble to the kingdom." " I shall do that," said he ; and
he went away with the rough humming of a song in his
mouth.

Fin went home when the time came, and lay down in his
own bed, at the foot of the King's bed. When the King
awoke, he cried out in great anxiety, " My kingdom is lost,

and my dwarf and my lapdog are killed!" "They are
not," said Fin; "I am here yet; and you have got your
sleep, a thing you were saying it was rare for you to get."
"How," said the King, "did you escape, when you are so
little, while he is enough for myself, though I am so big."

"Though you," said Fin, "are so big and strong, I am
quick and active."

Next night the King was for going; but Fin told him to
take his sleep to-night again. "I shall stand myself in your
place, or else a better hero than yonder one must come."
"He will kill you," said the King, "I shall take my
chance," said Fin.

He went, and as happened the night before, he saw no one ; and he began to pace backwards and forwards. He saw the sea coming in fiery kilns and as a darting serpent ; and that Huge Man came up. "Are you here to-night again ? " said he. "I am, and this is my errand : when the Queen was being put in the coffin, and the King heard the coffin being nailed, and the joiner's stroke, he broke his heart with pain and grief ; and the *Parliament* has sent me to ask you to go home to-night till they get the King buried." The Monster went this night also, roughly humming a song ; and Fin went home when the time came.

In the morning the King awoke in great anxiety, and called out, "My kingdom is lost, and my dwarf and my lapdog are killed ! " and he greatly rejoiced that Fin and Bran were alive, and that he himself got rest, after being so long without sleep.

Fin went the third night, and things happened as before. There was no one before him, and he took to pacing to and fro. He saw the sea coming till it came down below him : the Big Monster came up ; he saw the little black speck, and asked who was there, and what he wanted. "I have come to combat you," said Fin.

Fin and Bran began the combat. Fin was going backwards, and the Huge Man was following. Fin called to Bran, "Are you going to let him kill me ? " Bran had a venomous shoe ; and he leaped and struck the Huge Man with the venomous shoe on the breast-bone, and took the heart and lungs out of him. Fin drew his sword, Mac-a-Luin, cut off his head, put it on a hempen rope, and went with it to the Palace of the King. He took it into the *Kitchen*, and put it behind the door. In the morning the servant could not turn it, nor open the door. The King went down ; he saw the Huge Mass, caught it by the top of the head, and lifted it, and knew it was the head of the Man who was for so long a time asking combat from him, and keeping him from sleep. " How at all," said he, " has this head come here ? Surely it is not my dwarf that has done it." " Why," said Fin, " should he not ? "

Next night the King wanted to go himself to the place of combat ; " because," said he, " a bigger one than the former will come to-night, and the kingdom will be destroyed, and you yourself killed ; and I shall lose the pleasure I take in having you with me." But Fin went, and that Big Man came, asking vengeance for his son, and to have the kingdom for himself, or equal combat. He and Fin fought ; and Fin was going backwards. He spoke to Bran, " Are you going to allow him to kill me ? " Bran whined, and went and sat down on the beach. Fin was ever being driven back, and he called out again to Bran. Then Bran jumped and struck the Big Man with the venomous shoe, and took the heart and the lungs out of him. Fin cut the head off, and took it with him, and left it in front of the house. The King awoke in great terror, and cried out, " My kingdom is lost, and my dwarf and my lapdog are killed ! " Fin raised himself up and said, " They are not ; " and the King's joy was not small when he went out and saw the head that was in front of the house.

The next night a Big Hag came ashore, and the tooth in the door of her mouth would make a distaff. She sounded a challenge on her shield : " You killed," she said, " my husband and my son." " I did kill them," said Fin. They fought; and it was worse for Fin to guard himself from the tooth than from the hand of the Big Hag. When she had nearly done for him Bran struck her with the venomous shoe, and killed her as he had done to the rest. Fin took with him the head, and left it in front of the house. The King awoke in great anxiety, and called out, "My kingdom is lost, and my dwarf and my lapdog are killed!" "They are not," said Fin, answering him; and when they went out and saw the head, the King said, "I and my kingdom will have peace ever after this. The mother herself of the brood is killed; but tell me who you are. It was foretold for me that it would be Fin-mac-Coul that would give me relief, and he is only now eighteen years of age. Who are you, then, or what is your name?" "There never stood," said Fin, "on hide of cow or horse, one to whom I would deny my name. I am Fin, the Son of Coul, son of Looach, son of Trein, son of Fin, son of Art, son of the young High King of Erin; and it is time for me now to go home. It has been with much wandering out of my way that I have come to your kingdom; and this is the reason why I have come, that I might find out what injury I have done to you, or the reason why you sent the three heroes to ask combat from me, and bring destruction on my Men." "You never did any injury to me," said the King; "and I ask a thousand pardons. I did not send the heroes to you. It is not the truth they told. They were three men who were courting three fairy women, and these gave them their shirts; and when they have on their shirts, the combat of a hundred men is upon the hand of every one of them. But they must put off the shirts every night, and put them on the backs of chairs ; and if the shirts were taken from them they would be next day as weak as other people."

Fin got every honour, and all that the King could give him, and when he went away, the King and the Queen and the people went down to the shore to give him their blessing.

Fin now went away in his coracle, and was sailing close by the side of the shore, when he saw a young man running and calling out to him. Fin came in close to land with his coracle, and asked what he wanted. " I am,' said the young man, " a good servant wanting a master." " What work can you do ?" said Fin. " I am," said he, " the best soothsayer that there is." " Jump into the boat then." The soothsayer jumped in, and they went forward.

They did not go far when another youth came running. " I am," he said, " a good servant wanting a master." " What work can you do ? " said Fin. " I am as good a thief as there is." " Jump into the boat, then ; " and Fin took with him this one also. They saw then a third young man running and calling out. They came close to land. " What man are you ? " said Fin. " I am," said he, "the best climber that there is. I will take up a hundred pounds on my back in a place where a fly could not stand on a calm summer day." " Jump in ; " and this one came in also. " I have my pick of servants now," said Fin ; " it cannot be but these will suffice."

They went ; and stop of head or foot they did not make till they reached the Harbour of the Hill of Howth. He asked the soothsayer what the three Big Men were doing. "They are," he said, " after their supper, and making ready for going to bed."

He asked a second time. "They are," he said, "after going to bed ; and their shirts are spread on the back of chairs."

After a while, Fin asked him again, "What are the Big Men doing now ? " "They are," said the soothsayer, "sound asleep." "It would be a good thing if there was now a thief to go and steal the shirts." "I would do that," said the thief, "but the doors are locked, and I cannot get in." "Come," said the climber, "on my back, and I shall put you in." He took him up upon his back to the top of the chimney, and let him down, and he stole the shirts.

Fin went where the Fian band was ; and in the morning they came to the house where the three Big Men were. They sounded a challenge upon their shields, and asked them to come out to combat.

They came out. "Many a day," said they, " have we been better for combat than we are to-day," and they con-fessed to Fin everything as it was. "You were," said Fin, "impertinent, but I will forgive you " ; and he made them swear that they would be faithful to himself ever after, and ready in every enterprise he would place before them.

How Cormac Mac Art went to Faery.

ORMAC, son of Art, son of Conn of the Hundred Battles, was high King of Ireland, and held his Court at Tara. One day he saw a youth upon the green having in his hand a glittering fairy branch with nine apples of red. And whensoever the branch was shaken, wounded men and women enfeebled by illness would be lulled to sleep by the sound of the very sweet fairy music which those apples uttered, nor could any one upon earth bear in mind any want, woe, or weariness of soul when that branch was shaken for him.

"Is that branch thy own?" said Cormac.

"It is indeed mine."

"Wouldst thou sell it? and what wouldst thou require for it?"

"Will you give me what I ask?" said the youth.

The king promised, and the youth then claimed his wife, his daughter, and his son. Sorrowful of heart was the king, heaviness of heart filled his wife and children when they learned that they must part from him. But Cormac shook the branch amongst them, and when they heard the soft sweet music of the branch they forgot all care and sorrow and went forth to meet the youth, and he and they took their departure and were seen no more. Loud cries of weeping and mourning were made throughout Erin when this was known : but Cormac shook the branch so that there was no longer any grief or heaviness of heart upon any one.

After a year Cormac said : "It is a year to-day since my wife, my son, and my daughter were taken from me. I will follow them by the same path that they took."

Cormac went off, and a dark magical mist rose about him, and he chanced to come upon a wonderful marvellous plain. Many horsemen were there, busy thatching a house with the feathers of foreign birds ; when one side was thatched they would go and seek more, and when they returned not a feather was on the roof. Cormac gazed at them for a while and then went forward.

Again, he saw a youth dragging up trees to make a fire ; but before he could find a second tree the first one would be burnt, and it seemed to Cormac that his labour would never end.

Cormac journeyed onwards until he saw three immense wells on the border of the plain, and on each well was a head. From out the mouth of the first head there flowed two streams, into it there flowed one ; the second head had a stream flowing out of and another stream into its mouth, whilst three streams were flowing from the mouth of the third head. Great wonder seized Cormac, and he said: "I will stay and gaze upon these wells, for I should find no man to tell me your story." With that he set onwards till he came to a house in the middle of a field. He entered and greeted the inmates. There sat within a tall couple clad in many-hued garments, and they greeted the king, and bade him welcome for the night.

Then the wife bade her husband seek food, and he arose and returned with a huge wild boar upon his back and a log in his hand. He cast down the swine and the log upon the floor, and said: "There is meat; cook it for yourselves."

"How can I do that?" said Cormac.

"I will teach you," said the youth. "Split this great log, make four pieces of it, and make four quarters of the hog; put a log under each quarter; tell a true story, and the meat will be cooked."

"Tell the first story yourself," said Cormac.

"Seven pigs I have of the same kind as the one I brought, and I could feed the world with them. For if a pig is killed I have but to put its bones into the stye again, and it will be found alive the next morning."

The story was true, and a quarter of the pig was cooked.

Then Cormac begged the woman of the house to tell a story.

"I have seven white cows, and they fill seven cauldrons with milk every day, and I give my word that they yield as much milk as would satisfy the men of the whole world if they were out on yonder plain drinking it."

That story was true, and a second quarter of the pig was cooked.

Cormac was bidden now to tell a story for his quarter, and he told how he was upon a search for his wife, his son and his daughter that had been borne away from him a year before by a youth with a fairy branch.

" If what thou sayest be true," said the man of the house, "thou art indeed Cormac, son of Art, son of Conn of the Hundred Battles."

" Truly I am," quoth Cormac.

That story was true, and a quarter of the pig was cooked.

" Eat thy meal now," said the man of the house.

"I never ate before," said Cormac, " having only two people in my company."

" Wouldst thou eat it with three others ? "

" If they were dear to me, I would," said Cormac.

Then the door opened, and there entered the wife and children of Cormac : great was his joy and his exultation.

Then Manannan mac Lir, lord of the fairy Cavalcade, appeared before him in his own true form, and said thus :

" I it was, Cormac, who bore away these three from thee. I it was who gave thee this branch, all that I might bring thee here. Eat now and drink."

" I would do so," said Cormac, " could I learn the meaning of the wonders I saw to-day."

" Thou shalt learn them," said Manannan. " The horsemen thatching the roof with feathers are a likeness of people who go forth into the world to seek riches and fortune; when they return their houses are bare, and so they go on for ever. The young man dragging up the trees to make a fire is a likeness of those who labour for others: much trouble they have, but they never warm themselves at the fire. The three heads in the wells are three kinds of men. Some there are who give freely when they get freely; some who give freely though they get little; some who get much and give little, and they are the worst of the three, Cormac," said Manannan.

After that Cormac and his wife and his children sat down, and a table-cloth was spread before them.

"That is a very precious thing before thee," said Manannan, "there is no food however delicate that shall be asked of it but it shall be had without doubt."

"That is well," quoth Cormac.

After that Manannan thrust his hand into his girdle and brought out a goblet and set it upon his palm. "This cup has this virtue, said he, "that when a false story is told before it, it makes four pieces of it, and when a true story is related it is made whole again."

"Those are very precious things you have, Manannan," said the king.

"They shall all be thine," said Manannan, "the goblet, the branch and the tablecloth."

Then they ate their meal, and that meal was good, for they could not think of any meat but they got it upon the table-cloth, nor of any drink but they got it in the cup. Great thanks did they give to Manannan.

When they had eaten their meal a couch was prepared for them and they laid down to slumber and sweet sleep.

Where they rose on the morrow morn was in Tara of the kings, and by their side were tablecloth, cup, and branch.

Thus did Cormac fare at the Court of Manannan, and this is how he got the fairy branch.

The Ridere of Riddles.

HERE was a king once, and he married a great lady, and she departed on the birth of her first son. And a little after this the king married another wife, and she too had a son. The two lads grew up tall and strong. Then it struck the queen that it was not her son who would come into the kingdom; and she set it before her that she would poison the eldest son. And so she sent advice to the cooks that they should put poison in the drink of the heir; but as luck was in it, the youngest brother heard them, and he told his brother not to take the draught, nor to drink it at all; and so he did. But the queen wondered that the lad was not dead; and she thought that there was not enough of poison in the drink, and she asked the cook to put in more on the second night. It was thus they did: and when the cook made up the drink, she said that he would not be long alive after this draught. But his brother heard this also, and told him likewise. The eldest thought he would put the draught into a little bottle, and he said to his brother—"If I stay in

this house I have no doubt she will do for me some way or other, and the quicker I leave the house the better. I will take the world for my pillow, and there is no knowing what fortune will be on me." His brother said that he would go with him, and they took themselves off to the stable, and they put saddles on two horses and they took their soles out of that.

They had not gone very far from the house when the eldest one said—" There is no knowing if poison was in the drink at all, though we went away. Try it in the horse's ear and we shall see." The horse did not go far before he fell. " That was only a rattle-bones of a horse anyway," said the eldest one, and they got up together on the other horse, and so they went forwards. " But," said he, " I can scarce believe that there is any poison in the drink ; let's try it on this horse." That he did, and they went not far when the horse fell cold dead. They thought they'd take the hide off him, and that it would keep them warm at night which was close at hand. In the morning when they woke they saw twelve ravens come and light on the carcase of the horse, and they were not long there when they fell down dead.

They went and lifted the ravens, and they took them with them, and the first town they reached they gave the ravens to a baker, and they asked him to make a dozen pies of the ravens. They took the pies with them, and they went forward on their journey. About the mouth of night, and when they were in a great thick wood, there came four and twenty robbers who bade them to deliver up their purses ; but they said that they had no purse, but only a little food which they were carrying with them. " Good is even meat!" said the robbers, and they began to eat it, but had not eaten much when they fell hither and thither, all stone dead. When they saw that the robbers were dead they ransacked their pockets, and got much gold and silver. They went forward till they reached the Knight of Riddles.

The house of the Knight of Riddles was in the finest place in that country, and if his house was pretty, his daughter was prettier, and she had twelve maidens with her only less fair than she. Her like was not on the surface of the world, altogether so handsome was she; and no one would get her to marry but the man who could put a question to her father that he could not solve. The brothers thought that they would go and try to put a question to him; and the youngest was to stand in place of gillie to the elder brother. They reached the house of the Knight of Riddles and this was the question they put to him—"One killed two, and two killed twelve, and twelve killed four and twenty, and two got out of it;" and they were to be kept in great majesty and high honour till he should solve the riddle.

They were thus a while with the Ridere, and try as he might he could not guess the riddle. On a day of days came one of the maidens who were with the knight's daughter to the gillie, and asked him to tell her the question. He took her plaid from her and let her go, but he told her nothing. The same thing happened to the twelve maidens, day after day, and the gillie said to the last one that no creature had the answer to the riddle but his master down below. One day after this came the knight's daughter to the eldest brother, and looking her finest and handsomest, and she asked him to tell her the question. And now there was no refusing her, and he told her, but he kept her plaid. The Knight of Riddles sent for him, and he gave him the answer of the riddle. And the knight said that he had two choices: to lose his head, or to be set adrift in a crazy boat without food or drink, without oar or scoop. The elder brother spoke, and he said—"I have another riddle to put to thee before all these things happen." "Say on," said the knight. "Myself and my gillie were one day in the forest shooting. My gillie fired at a hare, and she fell, and he took her skin off, and let her go; and so he did to twelve, he took their skins off and let them go. And at last came a great fine hare, and I myself fired at her, and I took her skin off, and I let her go." "Indeed thy riddle is not hard to solve, my lad," said the knight, and he knew the lad knew he had not really guessed the riddle, but had been told the answer. So he gave him his daughter to wife, to make him hold his peace, and they made a great hearty wedding that lasted a day and a year. The youngest one went home now that his brother had got so well on his way, and the eldest brother gave him every right over the kingdom that was at home.

Now there were near the march of the kingdom of the Knight of Riddles three giants, and they were always murdering and slaying some of the knight's people, and taking spoil from them. On a day of days the Knight of Riddles said to his son-in-law, that if the spirit of a man were in him, he would go to kill the giants, as they were always bringing such losses on the country. Well, so it was, he went and he met the giants, and he came home with the three giants' heads, and he threw them at the knight's feet.

"Thou art an able lad doubtless, and thy name hereafter is the Hero of the White Shield." The name of the Hero of the White Shield went far and near.

Meanwhile the brother of the Hero of the White Shield

had wandered afar in many countries, and after long years had come to the land of the giants where the Hero of the White Shield was now dwelling, and the knight's daughter with him. His brother came and he asked to make a

covrag or fight as a bull with him. The men began at
each other, and they took to wrestling from morning till
evening. At last and at length, when they were tired, weak,
and spent, the Hero of the White Shield jumped over a
great rampart, and he asked the stranger to meet him in the
morning. This leap put the other to shame, and he said to
him, " Well may it be that thou wilt not be so supple about
this time to-morrow." The young brother now went to a
poor little bothy that was near to the house of the Hero of
the White Shield, tired and drowsy, and in the morning they
dared the fight again. And the Hero of the White Shield
began to go back, till he went backwards into a river.
" There must be some of my blood in thee before that was
done to me." " Of what blood art thou ? " said the
youngest. " 'Tis I am son of Ardan, great King of the
Albann." " 'Tis I am thy brother." It was now they knew
each other. They gave luck and welcome to each other,
and the Hero of the White Shield now took him into the
palace, and she it was that was pleased to see him—the
knight's daughter. He stayed a while with them, and after
that he thought that he would go home to his own kingdom ;
and when he was going past a great palace that was there
he saw twelve men playing at shinny over against the
palace. He thought he would go for a while and play
shinny with them ; but they were not long playing shinny
when they fell out, and the weakest of them caught him and
shook him as he would a child. He thought it was no
use for him to lift a hand amongst these twelve worthies,
and he asked them to whom they were sons. They said
they were children of the one father, the brother of the
Hero of the White Shield, who had not been heard of for

many years. "I am your father," said he ; and he asked them if their mother was alive. They said that she was. He went with them till he found the mother, and he took her home with him and the twelve sons ; and I don't know but that his seed are kings on Alba till this very day.

The Tail.

HERE was a shepherd once who went out to the hill to look after his sheep. It was misty and cold, and he had much trouble to find them. At last he had them all but one; and after much searching he found that one too in a peat hag, half drowned; so he took off his plaid, and bent down and took hold of the sheep's tail, and he pulled! The sheep was heavy with water, and he could not lift her, so he took off his coat and he *pulled!!* but it was too much for him, so he spit on his hands, and took a good hold of the tail and he PULLED!! and the tail broke! and if it had not been for that this tale would have been a great deal longer.

MAN OR WOMAN
BOY OR GIRL
THAT READS WHAT
FOLLOWS
3 TIMES
SHALL FALL ASLEEP
AN HUNDRED YEARS

JOHN D. BATTEN DREW THIS: AUG 29TH 1891 · GOOD-NIGHT.

Notes and References.

I HAVE scarcely anything to add to the general account of the collection of Celtic Fairy Tales which I gave in the predecessor to this volume, pages 237–42. Since the appearance of that volume in 1891, the publication of such tales has gone on apace. Mr. Curtin has published in the New York *Sun* no less than fifty more Irish fairy tales, one of which he has been good enough to place at my disposal for the present volume. Mr. Larminie has published with Mr. E. Stock a volume of *West Irish Fairy Tales*, of which I have also the privilege of presenting a specimen. A slight volume of Welsh Fairy Tales, published by Mr. Nutt, and a few fairy anecdotes contained in the Prize Essay on Welsh Folk-lore by the Rev. Mr. Evans, sum up Cambria's contribution to our subject during the past three years. The fifth volume of the *Waifs and Strays of Celtic Tradition*, just about to appear at the moment of writing, is the sole addition to Celtic Fairy Tales from the country of J. F. Campbell. Taken altogether, something like a hundred previously unpublished tales from Celtdom have been rendered accessible to the world since I last wrote, a by no means insignificant outcome in three years. It is at any rate clear, that the only considerable addition to our folk-lore knowledge in these isles must come from the Gaelic area. The time of harvest can be but short ; may the workers be many, willing, and capable.

XXVII. THE FATE OF THE CHILDREN OF LIR.

Sources.—Abridged from the text and translation published by the Society for the Preservation of the Irish Language in 1883. This merely follows the text and version given by Professor O'Curry in *Atlantis*, iv. He used three Dublin MSS., none of them, however, of earlier date than the eighteenth century. Dr. Joyce gives a free paraphrase in his *Old Celtic Romances*.

Parallels. — For " Jealous Stepmother," see the bibliographical references in the list of incidents at the end of my paper on the " Science of Folk-tales " in the *Transactions of the Folk-lore Congress, sub voce*. Add Miss Roalfe Cox in *Folk-lore Journal*, vii. app. 37 ; also the same list *sub voce* " Swan Maiden Transformation." In modern Irish literature Griffin has included the tale in his *Tales of the Jury-room*, and Tom Moore's " Song of Fiounala " beginning " Silent, O Moyle " is founded upon it.

Remarks.—The " Fate of the Children of Lir " is always referred to along with " The Story of Deirdre " (*cf.* the *Celtic Fairy Tales*, ix.), and the " Children of Tuireann " as one of the Three Sorrowful Tales of Erin. But there is no evidence of equal antiquity to the other two stories, of which one is as old as the eleventh century. From the interspersed verse O'Curry concluded, however, that the story was at least of considerable antiquity, and the references to the unknown Saint Mochaomhog confirm his impression. The Hill of the White Field is near Newton Hannton, in the county of Armagh. The Lake of the Red Eye is Lough Derg, in the Shannon above Killaloe.

Fingula is Fair Shoulder. The tradition that swans are inviolable is still extant in Ireland. A man named Connor Griffin killed eleven swans : he had previously been a prosperous man, and shortly afterwards his son was drowned in the Shannon, his goods were lost, and his wife died (*Children of Lir*, Dublin edit., note, p. 87). In County Mayo it is believed that the souls of pure virgins are after death enshrined in the forms of swans ; if anybody injures them, it is thought he will die within a year (Walter's *Natural History of the Birds of Ireland*, pp. 94–5). Mr. Gomme concludes from this that the swan was at one time a British totem (*Arch. Rev.*, iii. 226–7).

At first sight the tale seems little more than an argument against the Bill for Marriage with a Deceased Wife's Sister, but the plaintive lays of Fingula, the touching detail of the swans flying over the desolate hill and White Field, give a touch of Celtic glamour to the whole story. There is probably also a deep religious significance implied in the fact that the wicked Aunt Stepmother's spell is broken when the transformed Children of Lir come across the first Christian they meet.

Mr. Nutt has kindly communicated the following remarks on this tale :—

The Fate of the Children of Lir belongs formally to the so-called mythological cycle, the personages of which are the Tuatha de Danann. The Irish annalists of the 10th–11th centuries described these as members of one of the races which possessed Ireland in pre-Christian times before the coming of the Milesians. But even in the most strongly euhemerised accounts the mythic nature of these beings is apparent, and most modern scholars are agreed that they are in fact the members of a Pagan Irish Pantheon. They live on to this very day in Irish folk-belief as chiefs and rulers of the fairies.

The MS. evidence for some of the stories concerning the Tuatha de Danann is as old as that for the oldest heroic cycle (the Ultonian of Conchobar and Cuchulainn). But the Tuatha de Danann legends have retained throughout Irish literature greater plasticity and vitality than those of the Ultonian cycle, and many stories are not older in their present state than the 14th and 15th centuries. This is probably the case with the present story. The oldest known MS. only goes back to 1718, but this and the MS. of 1721, used by O'Curry for his edition, are certainly copied from much older MSS.

The interesting question for storiologists is whether the themes of the story — the swan-metamorphosis consequent upon the step-mother's jealousy, and the protecting rôle assigned to the sister—are of old native or of recent imported nature. In support of the first hypo-thesis, it may be noted that the theme of stepmotherly jealousy was current in Ireland in the 10th century at the latest, as it is woven into the saga of the Destruction of Daderga's Fort (see my article "*Folk-lore*," ii.). The final episode of the sudden aging of the miraculously long-lived swans is also genuinely Irish, but its true significance is obscured in our story in a way that sufficiently demonstrates the late and secondary character of the text. The idea is that the dwellers in Faery, whether fairy-folk or mortals penetrating thither, enjoy perpetual life, forfeited by the latter the moment they return to this earth. As children of the Tuatha de Danann, Fionngula and her brothers are deathless, and the episode as it stands in our text results from a con-tamination of the original form of the story in which the swan-meta-morphosis was annulled under certain conditions (the removal of the chains), when the original shape was resumed, and the familiar story of the mortal returning from Faery after hundreds of years, which he deems to be but a short space of time, shrinking into dust the moment he touches earth.

There is a well-known Continental folk-tale—the "Seven Swans" (or Ravens)—of which we possess several mediæval (12th to 13th century) versions, all connected with the romance of the "Swan Knight." M. Gaston Paris has studied the whole story group (*Romania*, xix. 314, &c.) with the following results : The folk-tale of the seven swans had originally nothing to do with the saga of the swan-knight. The connection apparent in the 12th century texts is artificial ; the swans owe their shape-shifting capacity to the superhuman nature of their mother ; this trait has been almost effaced even in the oldest versions. The distinguishing mark of the swans in all the versions is the possession of silver or gold chains, which are what may be called metamorphosis tokens ; it follows from this that the contamination of the two story-types (" Seven Swans " and " Swan Knight ") must be older than the oldest version of the first story, as these chains can only be derived from the one with which in the Swan Knight saga the swan draws the knight back.

In *Romania* (xxi. 62, *seq.*) M. Ferd. Lot examines the question in the light of our tale. He points out that it indicates clearly the super-human nature of the mother, and that as the silver chains figure in the story, they cannot be due in the Continental versions to con-tamination with the Swan Knight saga, as M. Gaston Paris imagines. M. Lot evidently inclines to look upon them as talismans, the aban-donment of which was the original cause of the metamorphosis, and the handling of which at the end brings about the change back to human shape. He points out that these chains form an essential part of the gear of beings appearing in bird guise (especially if they belong to Faery); thus in the 10th-century 'Sickbed of Cuchulainn' the goddesses Fand and Liban appear as two swans united by a golden chain ; in the 8th to 9th century Conception of Cuchulainn, Dechtire, the mother of the hero by the god Lug, appears with her companions in the guise of many-hued birds linked together by chains of silver (or red gold in one version). The MS. evidence for these tales reaches back to the early 11th century.

Curiously enough, M. Lot has not cited the closest parallel to our tale from old Irish literature, and one which is certainly connected with it in some measure, the fine story called the " Dream of Angus." A story of this title is cited in the epic catalogue of the Book of Leinster (which dates back to the early 11th century) as one of the introductory stories to the Tain bo Cuailgne. This assumed its present shape sub-stantially between 650 and 750. The introductory stories had origin-ally no connection with it, and were invented or re-shaped in the 8th to 10th centuries, after the Tain had taken undisputed place as the leading Irish epic. The tale may therefore be ascribed provisionally to the 9th century, if we can only be sure that the existing version, preserved in a single MS. of the 15th century, is a faithful copy of the original. There need be no doubt as to this. The text is due to a Christian scribe, and, like nearly all portions of the mythological cycle, betrays signs of Christian influence, though not of Christian remodelling. Such influence is, however, far more likely to have exerted itself in the first stage of the written existence of these tales, when the memory of organised paganism was still tenacious, than later, when the tales had become subject-matter for the play of free poetic fancy. The story, printed and translated by Dr. E. Muller, *Rev. Celt.* iv. 342, &c., is as follows : Angus (the chief wizard of the Tuatha de Danann) is visited in sleep by a maiden whose beauty throws him into love sickness. The whole of Ireland is scoured to find her ; the Dagda is appealed to in vain. At length, Bodb, fairy king of Munster, finds her at Loch bel Dracon (this is not the only trace of the impression which the story of Bel and the Dragon made upon the Irish mind). She lives there with 150 swans ; one year they are in swan shape the next in human shape. They appear as white birds with silvery chains and golden caps around their heads. Angus changes himself into a swan to be with her, and it is recorded of the music they made that " people fell asleep for three days and three nights." The soporific power of music is that which is chiefly commended in old Irish literature.

I think it is obvious that the writer of our story was familiar with this and other legends in which swan-maids encircled with gold and silver chains appear, and that we may fairly draw the following conclusions from the preceding facts : There existed an Irish folk-tale of a king with two wives, one a water or sea fairy, whose children derive from her the capacity of shape-shifting dependent upon certain talismans ; jealousy impels the human wife to tamper with these talismans, and the children are condemned to remain in their animal form. This folk-tale was, probably at some time in the 14th or 15th century, arbitrarily fitted into the *cadre* of the Tuatha de Danann cycle, and entirely re-fashioned in a spirit of pious edification by a man who was in his way a great and admirable artist. The origin and nature of the story, all the elements of which are genuinely national, assured for it wide and lasting popularity. The evolution of the Irish folk-tale is in no way dependent upon that of the Continental folk-tale of the Seven Swans, but it is possible that the Celtic presentiment of the chain-girdled swans may have influenced it as well as the Swan Knight Romance.

XXVIII. JACK THE CUNNING THIEF.

Sources.—Kennedy, *Stories of Ireland*, pp. 38–46 ; Campbell, *West Highland Tales*, i. 320 *seq.* ; " The Shifty Lad," Dasent, *Popular Tales from the Norse*, pp. 232–51, " Master Thief." Köhler has a number of variants in his notes on Campbell : *Orient und Occident*, Band ii. Mr. Clouston has a monograph on the subject in his *Popular Tales*, ii. 115–65. A separate treatise on the subject has been given by S. Prato, 1882, *La Leggenda di Rhampsinitè*. Both these writers connect the modern folk-tales with Herodotus' story of King Rampsinites. Mr. Knowles in his *Folk-tales of Kashmir*, has a number of adventures of " Sharaf the Thief." The story of " Master Thief" has been heard among the tramps in London workhouses (Mayhew, *London Labour and London Poor*, iii. 119).

Remarks.—Thievery is universally human, and at first sight it might seem that there was no connection between these various versions of the " Master Thief." But the identity of the tricks by which the popular hero-thief gains his ends renders it impossible that they should have been independently invented wherever they are found.

XXIX. POWEL, PRINCE OF DYFED.

Source.—Lady Guest's *Mabinogion*, with the names slightly anglicised, and omitting the opening incident.

Parallels.—For the incident of tearing off the hands, *cf.* Morraha ; the enchanted hill and maiden occur at the beginning of " Tuairisgeul Môr " in *Scottish Celtic Review*, i. 61, and are fully commented upon by Mr. Nutt, *l.c.* 137.

XXX. PADDY O'KELLY AND THE WEASEL.

Sources.—Hyde, *Beside the Fire*, pp. 73–91.

Parallels.—On green hills as the homes of the fairies : see note on " Childe Roland," *English Fairy Tales*, p. 241. The transformation of witches into hares is a frequent *motif* in folk-lore.

XXXI. THE BLACK HORSE.

Sources.—From J. F. Campbell's manuscript collection now deposited at the Advocates' Library in Edinburgh (MS. 53, vol. xi.). Collected in Gaelic, February 14, 1862, by Hector MacLean, from Roderick MacNeill, in the island of Menglay : MacNeill learnt the story about 1840 from a Barra man. I have omitted one visit of the Black Horse to Greece, but otherwise left the tale untouched. Mr. Nutt gave a short abstract of the story in his report on the Campbell MSS. in *Folk-lore*, i. 370.

Parallels.—Campbell gives the following parallels in his notes on the tale, which I quote verbatim. On the throwing into the well he remarks : "So this incident of 'Lady Audley's Secret' was in the mind of a Barra peasant about 1840. Part of a modern novel may be as old as Aryan mythology, which was one point to be proved." [The incident of throwing into the well almost invariably forms a part of the tales of the White Cat type.]

With regard to the Black Horse, Campbell notes that a Gaelic riddle makes a Black Horse identical with the West Wind, and adds : "It is for consideration whether this Horse throws light on the sacred Wheel in Indian Sculptures ; it is to be noted that a Black Horse is the sacrificial colour."

"The Cup is a well-known myth about winning a Fairy Cup which pervades Scandinavian England in many forms." "A silver ring, two quaint serpents' heads pointing opposite ways, is a common Scandinavian wedding-ring ; many were to be got in Barra and elsewhere in 1869, sold by emigrants bound for America."

"Those who can account for myths must settle the geography of the Snow Mountain. Avalanches and glaciers are in Iceland, in the Caucasus, and in Central Asia. There are none within sight of Menglay. Hindoo cosmogony, which makes the world consist of seven rings, separated by seas and by a wall of mountains, may account for this in some sort."

On the spikes driven into the Horse, Campbell compares the Norse story of "Dapple-grim" and the Horse sacrifice of the Mahabharata. On the building of the Magic Castle, Campbell remarks : "Twashtri was the Carpenter of the Vedic gods : can this be his work?"

On the Horse's head being struck off Campbell comments : "This was the last act in the Aryan Horse's sacrifice, and the first step in the Horse apotheosis."

Remarks.—Campbell has the following note at the end of the tale, from which it would seem that in 1870 at least he was very nearly being an *Indiamaniac*.

"So ends this horse-riding story. Taking it as it is, with the test of language added, nothing short of an Asian origin will account for it. A Gaelic riddle makes 'a black horse' mean the invisible wind, and a theorist might suppose this horse to be the air personified. As Greece is mentioned, he might be Pegasus, who had to do with wells. But he had wings, and he was white, and there is nothing in classical fable like this Atlantic myth. 'The enchanted horse' of Arabian Nights was a flying machine, and his adventures are quite different. This is not the horse of Chaucer's Squire's Tale. He is more like 'Hrimfaxi,' the horse of the Edda, who drew the car of Nött in heaven, and was ridden round the earth in twelve hours, followed by Dagr and his glittering horse Skinfaxi. The black horse who always arrives at sunrise is like the horse of night, but there is no equivalent story in the Edda. 'Dapple-grim' in Norse tales is clad in a spiked bull's hide, and is mixed up with a blazing tar-barrel, but his adventures won't fit, and he was grey.

"The story is but an imperfect skeleton. The cup was to give strength; he had to open seven gates after he got the cup, but it does nothing. The hood is to hide with; he went in and out of the palace unseen after he had got the hood, but it plays no part. The light shoes were the shoes of swiftness of course, but they never showed their paces. Baldr's horse was led to the funeral pile with all his gear; and Odin laid the gold ring Draupnir on the pile. Such rites might account for the ring in the blazing lake. Hermothr's ride northwards and downwards to the abode of Hel to seek Baldr, his leap over the grate, and his return with the ring (Edda 25), might account for one adventure.

"The many-coloured horses of the sun in the Indian mythology and solar myths may account for all these horses, astronomically or meteorologically. The old Aryan Aswa Medha or sacrifice of a black horse, and the twelve adventures of Arjuna as told in the Mahabharata, are something like this story in some general vague way. But the simplest explanation of this Menglay myth, fished out of the Atlantic, is to admit that 'the black horse' and all this mythical breed came west with men who rode from the land where horses were tamed, which is unknown."

XXXII. THE VISION OF MACCONGLINNEY.

Source.—Kindly condensed by Mr. Alfred Nutt from Prof. Meyer's edition of *The Vision* published in book form in 1892. This contains two versions, a longer one from a fourteenth century MS., *Leabhar Breac or*

Speckled Book, and a shorter one from a sixteenth century MS. in the Library of Trinity College, Dublin. A translation of the former version was given by the late W. M. Hennessy in *Fraser's Magazine*, September, 1873. Prof. Wollner, who contributed to Prof. Meyer's edition an introduction dealing with the story from the standpoint of comparative literature, considers that the later version reproduces the original common source more nearly.

Parallels.—At first sight *The Vision* seems to picture the Land of Cockayne (on which see Poeschel, *Das Mährchen vom Schlaraffenlande*, Halle, 1878), but as Prof. Wollner remarks, the Irish form is much more simple and primitive, and represents rather an agricultural conception of a past *aurea aetas*. The conception of enormous appetite being due to the presence of a voracious animal or demon within the body is widespread among the folk. Prof. Wollner gives numerous parallels, *l.c.* XLVII.–LIII. The common expression "to wolf one's food" is said to be derived from this conception. On the personification of disease, see Tylor, *Primitive Culture*, ii. 148.

I can myself remember a tale somewhat similar to *The Vision* which I heard from my nurse in Australia, I fancy as a warning against gluttony. She told me of a man, who in swallowing large pieces of food had swallowed a little hairy monster, which grew and grew and grew and caused the man to be eating all day to satisfy his visitors He was cured by being made to fast, and then a bowl of brandy was brought in front of his mouth into which the hairy thing, attracted by the fumes, jumped and was drowned.

Remarks.—We have here an interesting example of the personification of disease in the form of a demon, of which some examples occur in the Gospels. The rollicking Rabelaisian tone in which the story is told prevents us, however, from attributing any serious belief in the conception by the Irish Monk the author of the tale, who was parodying, according to Prof. Wollner, the Visions of the Saints. Still he would be scarcely likely to use the conception, even for purposes of parody, unless it were current among the folk, and it occurs among them even at the present day. (See Hyde, *Beside the Fire*, p. 183.)

XXXIII. DREAM OF OWEN O'MULREADY.

Sources.—Kindly translated by Mr. Leland L. Duncan from *Gaelic Journal*, vol. iv. p. 57 *seq.*

Parallels.—Croker's *Daniel O'Rourke* may be compared in part.

Remarks.—At first sight a mere droll, the story has its roots in the most primitive philosophy. Owen's problem is to get in the Land of Dreams. Now Dreamland, so all our students of Mythology are agreed, is the source and origin of our belief in souls and spirits. Owen's problem therefore resolves itself into this: where was he to go in order to come into closest contact with the world of spirits. Mark what he does—he clears the hearth and has his bed made in it. Now it is round the hearth that the fullest associations with the spirit life are clustered. The late M. Fustel de Coulanges in his *Cité Antique* traces back most of the Greek and Roman religions and a large number of their institutions to the worship of the ancestors localised on the hearth. The late Professor Hearn extended his line of research to the whole of the Aryans in his *Aryan Household*. It will thus be seen from this course of reasoning, that Owen was acting on the most approved primitive principles in adopting this curious method of obtaining dreams. The story is not known elsewhere than in Ireland, and we are therefore at liberty to apply the method of survivals to this case.

XXXIV. MORRAHA.

Sources.—The second story in Mr. W. Larminie's *West Irish Folk-tales*, pp. 10-30. The framework was collected from P. McGrale of Achill Island, Co. Mayo. The story itself was from Terence Davis of Rendyle, Co. Galway. There is evidently confusion in the introductory portion between Niall's mother and wife.

Parallels.—Campbell's No. 1 has a very close parallel to the opening. Mr. Larminie refers to a similar tale collected by Kennedy. Another version from West Munster has been recently published in the *Gaelic Journal*, iv. 7, 26, 35. The evasion of the promise to give up the sword at the end seems a favourite incident in Achill folk-tales; it occurs in two others of Mr. Larminie's stories. On the framework, see note on "Conal Yellow claw" (*Celtic Folk-tales*, v.). I have there suggested that the plan comes from the East, ultimately from Buddha.

XXXV. THE STORY OF THE McANDREW FAMILY.

Sources.—Supplied by Mrs. Gale, now in the United States, from the recitation of her mother who left Ireland over fifty years ago.

Parallels.—"Noodle Tales" like this are found everywhere in

Europe, and have been discussed by Mr. Clouston in a special monograph in *The Book of Noodles*, 1889. The "sell" at the end is similar
to that in the "Wise Men of Gotham." Kennedy (*Fireside Stories
of Ireland*) gives a similar set of adventures, p. 119 *seq.*

Remarks.—Mrs. Gale remarks that it was a common superstition
in Ireland, that if a raven hovered over the head of cattle, a withering
blight had been set upon the animals. As birds of carrion they were
supposed to be waiting for the carcases.

XXXVI. THE FARMER OF LIDDESDALE

Sources.—MacDougal, *Waifs and Strays*, III. ix. pp. 216–21.

Parallels.—Campbell, *West Highland Tales*, "The Master and the
Man," iii. 288–92.

Remarks.—I need scarcely suggest the identification of the Ploughman with the ——— . As usual in folk-tales, that personage does
not get the best of the bargain. The rustic Faust evades his contract
by a direct appeal to the higher powers. This is probably characteristic of Scotch piety.

XXXVII. THE GREEK PRINCESS AND THE
YOUNG GARDENER.

Sources.—Kennedy, *Fireside Stories*, pp. 47–56.

Parallels.—Campbell, *West Highland Tales*, lvi.; *Mac Iain Direach*,
ii. 344–76. He gives other variants at the end. The story is clearly
that of the Grimms' "Golden Bird," No. 57. They give various
parallels in their notes. Mrs. Hunt refers to an Eskimo version in
Rae's *White Sea Peninsula*, called "Kuobba the Giant and the Devil."
But the most curious and instructive parallel is that afforded by the
Arthurian Romance of Walewein (*i.e.*, Gawain), now only extant in
Dutch, which, as Professor W. P. Ker has pointed out in *Folk-lore*,
v. 121, exactly corresponds to the popular tale, and thus carries it back
in Celtdom to the early twelfth century at the latest.

XXXVIII. THE RUSSET DOG.

Source.—I have made up this Celtic Reynard out of several fables
given by Campbell, *West Highland Tales*, under the title "Fables,"
vol. i. pp. 275 *seq.*; and "The Keg of Butter" and the "The Fox and
the little Bonnach," vol. iii. Nos. lxv. lxvi.

Parallels.—The Fox's ruse about a truce among the animals is a well-known Æsop's Fable ; see my edition of *Caxton's Æsop*, vol. ii. p. 307, and *Parallels*, vol. i. p. 267. The trick by which the cock gets out of the fox's mouth is a part of the Reynard Cycle, and is given by Chaucer as his "Nonne Preste's Tale." How the wolf lost his tail is also part of the same cycle, the parallels of which are given by K. Krohn, *Bär (Wolf) und Fuchs* (Helsingfors, 1889), pp. 26-8. The same writer has studied the geographical distribution of the story in Finland, accompanied by a map, in *Fennia*, iv. No. 4. I have given a mediæval Hebrew version in my *Jews of Angevin England*, pp. 170-2. See also Gerber, *Great Russian Animal Tales*, pp. 48-50. The wolf was originally the bear, as we see from the conclusion of the incident, which professes to explain why the wolf is stumpy-tailed. "The Keg of Butter" combines two of the Grimm stories, 2, 189. "The Little Bonnach" occurs also in English and has been given in two variants in *English Fairy Tales*, No. xxviii. ; and *More English Fairy Tales*, No. lvii.

Remarks.—It would lead me too far afield to discuss here the sources of Reynard the Fox, with which I hope shortly to deal at length elsewhere. But I would remark that in this case, as in several others we have observed, the stories, which are certainly reproductions, have received the characteristic Celtic dress. It follows that we cannot conclude anything as to the origin of a tale from the fact that it is told idiomatically. On the other hand, the stories of "The Fox and Wrens" and "The Fox and the Todhunter," and "How the Fox gets rid of his Fleas," have no parallels elsewhere, and show the possibility of a native beast tale or cycle of tales.

XXXIX. SMALLHEAD AND THE KING'S SON.

Source.—Mr. Curtin's "Hero Tales of Ireland," contributed to the *New York Sun.*

Parallels.—Campbell's No. xvii., "Maol a Chliobain," is the same story, which is also found among the Lowlanders, and is given in my *English Fairy Tales*, No. xxii., "Molly Whuppie," where see notes for other parallels of the Hop o' My Thumb type of story. King Under the Waves occurs in Campbell, No. lxxxvi.

XL. THE LEGEND OF KNOCKGRAFTON.

Source.—Croker, *Fairy Legends of South of Ireland.*

Parallels.—Parnell's poem, *Edwin and Sir Topaz*, contains the same story. As he was born in Dublin, 1679, this traces the tale back at least 200 years in Ireland. Practically the same story, however, has been found in Japan, and translated into English under the title, "Kobutori; or, The Old Man and the Devils." In the story published by Kobunsha, Tokio, the Old Man has a lump on the side of his face. He sees the demons dancing, and getting exhilarated, joins in. Thereupon the devils are so delighted that they wish to see him again, and as a pledge of his return take away from him his lump. Another old man, who has a similar lump on the other side of his face, hearing of this, tries the same plan, but dances so badly that the devils, not wishing to see him again, and mistaking him for the other old man, give him back the lump, so that he has one on each side of his face.

I may add here that Mr. York Powell informs me that No. xvii. of the same series, entitled, "Shippietaro," contains a parallel to the "Hobyahs" of *More English Tales*.

Remarks.—Here we have a problem of diffusion presented in its widest form. There can be little doubt that "The Legend of Knockgrafton" and "Kobutori," one collected in Ireland and to be traced there for the last 200 years, and the other collected at the present day in Japan, are one and the same story, and it is impossible to imagine they were independently produced. Considering that Parnell could not have come across the Japanese version, we must conclude that "Kobutori" is a recent importation into Japan. On the other hand, as "the Hobyahs" cannot be traced in England, and was collected from a Scottish family settled in the United States, where Japanese influence has been considerable, it is possible that this tale was derived from Japan within the memory of men still living. It would be highly desirable to test these two cases, in which we seem to be able to observe the process of the diffusion of Folk Tales going on before our eyes.

XLI. ELIDORE.

Source.—Giraldus Cambrensis, *Itinerarium Cambriæ*, I. viii. I have followed the Latin text tolerably closely.

Parallels.—Mr. Hartland has a paper on "Robberies in Fairyland," in *Arch. Rev.*, iii. 39 *seq.* Davies, *Mythology of the British Druids*, p. 155, tells a story of a door in a rock near a cave in the mountains of Brecknock, which was left open for Mayday, and men used to enter, and so reach that fairy island in the middle of the lake. The visitors were treated very hospitably by their fairy hosts, but on the condition that they might eat all, but pocket none; for once, a visitor took away with him a fairy flower, and as soon as he got outside the door the flower vanished, and the door was never more opened. "The Luck of Edenhall," still in existence, is supposed to be a trophy brought back from a similar visit.

Remarks.—Mr. Hartland suggests that these legends, and the relics connected with them, are in some way connected with the heathen rites prevalent in these islands before the introduction of Christianity, which may have lingered on into historic times. The absence of sunlight in this account of the House of the Fairies, as in " Childe Rowland " (on which see note in *English Fairy Tales*), may be regarded as a point in favour of Mr. MacRitchie's theories as to the identification of the fairies with the mound-dwellers. The object of the expectoration was to prevent Elidore's seeing his way back. Thus the fairies prevent the indiscretions of the human midwives they employ.

XLII. THE LEECHING OF KAYN'S LEG.

Source.—MacInnes, *Folk-Tales from Argyleshire*, vii., combined with Campbell of Tiree's version.

Parallels.—The earliest version, from an Egerton MS. of the fifteenth century, has been printed by Mr. S. H. O'Grady in his *Silva Gadelica*, No. 20, with an English version, pp. 332–42. Mr. Campbell of Tiree has given a short Gaelic version in the *Transactions of the Gaelic Society of Inverness*, 78–100. Campbell of Islay collected the fullest version of this celebrated story, which is to be found among his manuscript remains now in Edinburgh. Mr. Nutt has given his English abstract in *Folk-lore*, i. 373–7, in its original form. The story must have contained twenty-four tales or episodes of stories, nineteen of which are preserved in J. F. Campbell's version. For parallels to the various incidents, see Mr. Nutt's notes on MacInnes, pp. 470–3. The tale is referred to in MacNicol, *Remarks on Dr. Johnson's Journey to the Hebrides*, 1779.

Remarks.—Nothing could give a more vivid idea of what might be called the organisation of the art of story-telling among the Celts than this elaborate tale. Mr. Nutt is inclined to trace it, even in its present form, back to the twelfth or thirteenth century. It occurs in an MS. of the fifteenth century in an obviously unoriginal form which shows that the story-teller did not appreciate the significance of many features in the folk-tale he was retelling, and yet it was orally collected by the great Campbell in 1871, in a version which runs to 142 folio pages.

Formally, its interest consists in large measure in the curious framework in which the subsidiary stories are imbedded. This is not of the elaborate kind introduced into Europe from the East by the Crusades, but more *naive*, resembling rather, as Mr. Nutt points out to me, the loosely-knit narratives of Charles Lever in his earlier manner.

XLIII. HOW FIN WENT TO THE KINGDOM OF THE BIG MEN.

Source.—J. G. Campbell, *The Fians* (*Waifs and Strays*, No. iv.), pp. 175–92.

Parallels.—*The Voyage to Brobdingnag* will occur to many readers, and it is by no means impossible that, as Swift was once an Irish lad, *The Voyage* may have been suggested by some such tale told him in his infancy. It is not, however, a part of the earlier recorded Ossianic cycle, though over-sea giants occur as opponents of the heroes in that as well as in the earlier Ultonian cycle.

XLIV. HOW CORMAC MAC ART WENT TO FAERY.

Source.—Kindly condensed by Mr. Alfred Nutt from an English version by Mr. S. H. O'Grady in *Ossianic Society's Publications*, vol. iii. The oldest known version has been printed from fourteenth century MSS., by Mr. Whitley Stokes, *Irische Texte*, iii. 1. The story existed in some form in the early eleventh century, as it is cited in the epic catalogue contained in the Book of Leinster.

Parallels.—Mr. Nutt in his *Studies on the Legend of the Holy Grail*, p. 193, connects this visit of Cormac to the Otherworld with the bespelled Castle incident in the Grail Legend, and gives other instances of visits to the Brug of Manannan. Manannan Mac Lir is the Celtic sea-god.

XLV. RIDERE OF RIDDLES.

Source.—Campbell, *West Highland Tales*, No. xxii. vol. ii. p. 36, *seq.* I have modified the end, which has a polygamous complexion.

Parallels.—Campbell points out that the story is in the main identical with the Grimms' "Räthsel," No. xxii. There the riddle is: "One slew none, and yet slew twelve." MacDougall has the same story in *Waifs and Strays*, iii. pp. 76 *seq*.

Remarks.—There can be no doubt that the Celtic and German Riddle Stories are related genealogically. Which is of the earlier generation is, however, more difficult to determine. In favour of the Celtic is the polygamous framework; while on the other hand, it is difficult to guess how the story could have got from the Highlands to Germany. The simpler form of the riddle in the German version might seem to argue greater antiquity.

XLVI. THE TAIL.

Source.—Campbell, No. lvii.

Parallels.—Most story-tellers have some formula of this kind to conclude their narrations. Prof. Crane gives some examples in his *Italian Popular Tales*, pp. 155–7. The English have: "I'll tell you a story of Jack a Nory," and "The Three Wise Men of Gotham" who went to Sea in a Bowl:

> "If the bowl had been stronger,
>   My song would have been longer."